Reason and Cause

Philosophy and social science assume that reason and cause are objective and universally applicable concepts. Through close readings of ancient and modern philosophy, history, and literature, Ned Lebow demonstrates that these concepts are actually specific to time and place. He traces their parallel evolution by focusing on classical Athens, the Enlightenment through Victorian England, and the early twentieth century. This important book shows how and why understandings of reason and cause have developed and evolved, in response to what kind of stimuli, and what this says about the relationship between social science and the social world in which it is conducted. Lebow argues that authors reflecting on their own social context use specific constructions of these categories to structure their central arguments about the human condition. This highly original study will make an immediate impact across a number of fields with its rigorous research and the development of an innovative historicized epistemology.

Richard Ned Lebow is author, coauthor, or editor of 40 books and more than 300 peer-reviewed articles and chapters. He has made contributions to international relations, political psychology, history, political theory, philosophy of science, and classics. He has taught at leading universities in the United States, the United Kingdom, and Europe. His books have won multiple awards.

Reason and Cause
Social Science and the Social World

Richard Ned Lebow, FBA
King's College London

CAMBRIDGE
UNIVERSITY PRESS

University Printing House, Cambridge CB2 8BS, United Kingdom

One Liberty Plaza, 20th Floor, New York, NY 10006, USA

477 Williamstown Road, Port Melbourne, VIC 3207, Australia

314–321, 3rd Floor, Plot 3, Splendor Forum, Jasola District Centre, New Delhi – 110025, India

79 Anson Road, #06–04/06, Singapore 079906

Cambridge University Press is part of the University of Cambridge.

It furthers the University's mission by disseminating knowledge in the pursuit of education, learning, and research at the highest international levels of excellence.

www.cambridge.org
Information on this title: www.cambridge.org/9781108479431
DOI: 10.1017/9781108785525

© Richard Ned Lebow 2020

This publication is in copyright. Subject to statutory exception and to the provisions of relevant collective licensing agreements, no reproduction of any part may take place without the written permission of Cambridge University Press.

First published 2020

A catalogue record for this publication is available from the British Library.

ISBN 978-1-108-47943-1 Hardback

Cambridge University Press has no responsibility for the persistence or accuracy of URLs for external or third-party internet websites referred to in this publication and does not guarantee that any content on such websites is, or will remain, accurate or appropriate.

To Naomi and Jacob

Contents

Preface		*page* ix
Acknowledgments		xi
1	Reason and Cause	1
2	Homer and Sophocles	20
3	Thucydides	68
4	David Hume	118
5	Dickens, Trollope, and Collins	154
6	Max Weber	193
7	Thomas Mann and Franz Kafka	233
8	Conclusions	268
	Bibliography	318
	Index	345

Preface

Constructing Cause in International Relations, published in 2014, made the case that cause is a creation of the human imagination, not a feature of the world. It is undeniably a useful concept for organizing social inquiry or making that research relevant to policy problems.[1] However, we can never demonstrate a causal relationship in the social world. The most we can do is make a plausible case for some causal link on the basis of a logic connecting antecedent to consequent that is consistent with the available evidence. We may rule out some causal claims on these grounds but can never validate them. On these epistemological foundations, I develop a novel approach I call "inefficient causation." It recognizes that likelihood that possible "causes" exist at multiple levels of social interaction and at varying degrees of remove from outcomes of interest. It seeks to explore their relationships and trace multiple possible pathways to outcomes, and, by doing so, provide a framework for comparison across outcomes. It rejects prediction as an unrealistic goal because of the context-dependent nature of outcomes. Rather, it seeks to use the understandings of "causes" it develops as the basis for explanatory narratives and forecasts. They in turn must constantly be updated on the basis of new information from context.

Constructing Cause in International Relations raised as many questions in my mind as it answered. Chief among these is why so many philosophers and social scientists believe that cause is real, the glue that binds together the physical and social worlds, and discovered through the application of reason. David Hume challenged these assumptions in the late eighteenth century but with little effect. Most philosophers and social scientists also treat reason as universal and relatively unproblematic concepts. Here, too, David Hume is an exception. So is Max Weber, who distinguished between the reason he thought essential to any model of the world and different ideal types of reason that might be used to study human behavior.

Western conceptions of cause and reason are characterized by a tension that is rarely discussed. There is a long tradition going back to the ancient

Greeks that treats them as universal and objective. There are also writers and philosophers, again beginning with the ancient Greeks, who regard cause as deeply problematic and conceptions of reason and cause as culturally and historically local. Not surprisingly, the first tradition is the dominant one today as reason and cause are lynchpins of social science. My sympathies lie with the second, and this book attempts in the first instance to document this tradition and foreground its principal claims. These pertain to the difficulty of establishing causes and the complex, and at times counterproductive, relationship between reason and cause. This tradition also reveals the social and labile nature of conceptions of reason and cause and identifies some of the conditions in which they are likely to evolve. I draw on these literary and philosophical works to argue that these changes have identifiable patterns to them and are largely psychological and social responses to particular kinds of changes.

Note

1. Lebow, *Constructing Cause in International Relations*.

Acknowledgments

I am indebted to Carol Bohmer, Tony Grenville, Andrew Lawrence, David Lebow, Amy Lidster, Seán Molloy, Dorothy Noyes, Daniel Tompkins, and Christian Wendt. They served as foils to my musings, suggested books and articles to read, and provided feedback on draft chapters or the entire manuscript. Thanks, too, to John Haslam, copy editor Linsey Hague, and the production staff at Cambridge University Press. I also thank Dr. Álvaro Morcillo Laiz of the Social Science Research Center Berlin (WZB) for the invitation to present a paper on Max Weber at a conference in honor of the centenary of Weber's seminal essay *Politik als Beruf* (The Vocation of Politics).

1 Reason and Cause

> It seems to each man that the ruling pattern of nature
> is in him; to this he refers all other forms as to a touchstone.
> The ways that do not square with his are counterfeit and
> artificial. What brutish stupidity!
> – Michel de Montaigne[1]

Reason and cause are central to scientific inquiry and everyday life. They are also foundational to our self-esteem. From ancient Greeks to the present, the ability to reason has been considered a defining feature of humanity and something that sets us apart from other animals. Like all concepts, reason and cause have long histories and have been used in different ways for diverse ends. The close and reinforcing relationship between them has been assumed more often than it has been interrogated. In this book, I examine both concepts and their pairing. I want to understand how and why different conceptions of reason and cause and their relationship have developed and in response to what stimuli. I use my analysis to explore the relationship between social science and the social world of which it is part.

Reason and cause are concepts as problematic as they are fundamental to scientific inquiry. Philosophers have failed to come up with a definition of cause that is logically consistent and applicable to all situations that might be considered causal. This is because cause is not an attribute of the world but a human convention. For this reason, some philosophers and scientists are dubious about its utility. Bertrand Russell rejected causation as "a relic of a bygone age, surviving like the monarchy, only because it is erroneously supposed to do no harm."[2] The scientific community nevertheless finds theories, propositions, or explanations more persuasive if they offer mechanisms or processes to account for the phenomena they purport to explain or predict. In sharp contrast to Russell, Albert Einstein insisted that "The scientist is possessed by the sense of universal causation."[3] More than a century earlier, Immanuel Kant had proclaimed the universe as lawful universe, made comprehensible through the principle of causality, the route to scientific knowledge.[4]

Social scientists frequently describe cause as the ultimate goal of inquiry. In practice, it is really only the focus of qualitative researchers who use process tracing and inter- and intra-case comparisons to construct causal narratives. Quantitative researchers hardly ever go beyond the search for regularities (i.e., correlations) that they hope to use to make predictions. Formal modelers, rational choice theorists, and students of emergence rely on "thin" understandings of cause or finesse or ignore it. Efforts to analyze the concept of cause in these diverse traditions are largely lacking.

Reason is closely connected to cause. It is a way of thinking, organizing inquiry, a vehicle for deductions and inductions, and means of defining and selecting evidence, as well as of making inferences. Max Weber observed that all attempts at explanation, and any theories on which they are based, must be rational, by which he meant logically consistent. This did not mean that people behaved rationally. He considered external rationality at best an ideal type that could be used as a template for understanding and assessing human action by determining how closely it approximated what rational people with the same goals would have done in the circumstances.[5] This is a reasonable approach if one can get inside the heads of the actors under study and reconstruct their goals or preferences, the kinds of trade-offs they must consider, their risk-taking propensity, and know what information was available to them.

These requirements are so difficult to meet in practice that researchers routinely substitute their logics, calculations, and information for those of actors they study. When this happens, reason loses any claim to being a neutral tool. It can also be a counterproductive one. In *Emma*, Jane Austen's principal character Emma Woodhouse is clever but headstrong and greatly overestimates her abilities to read other people and make matches between them. Her perceptions often lead her astray and she causes problems for others and herself. Real-world examples are offered every day by political leaders who are blind to the goals or calculations of other actors because they assume they think the same way they do.[6] Political analysts and political scientists often do the same.

Weber suggests that reason even in the best of circumstances is never a neutral tool. We use it to assess our values and the ends we seek. Ancient Greeks considered reason a fundamental human drive that generates desires of its own. Plato believed that it had the potential to lead people to understand the nature of happiness and to constrain and educate appetite and spirit to collaborate with it toward this end.[7] Aristotle thought it essential for the good life and also for *homonoia*, an undivided community (*koinonia*), whose members shared a consensus about the nature of the good life and how it might be achieved.[8] Christianity followed the Greeks in making reason central to personal and political order. For Augustine, the city of god is a culture in which human beings use their reason to control, even overcome, their passions, and act in accord with the deity's design.[9]

The Enlightenment constituted a sharp break with past thinking and practice. Its rejection of Aristotelian *telos* (the end something is intended to achieve, and how that end drives its development) helped pave the way for modernity.[10] Rejection of *telos* required a corresponding reconceptualization of reason. It was reduced from an end in itself to a mere instrumentality – "the slave of the passions" in the words of David Hume.[11] Max Weber would later coin the term "instrumental reason" to describe this transformation and explore some of its consequences. Freud incorporated it in his model of the mind; the ego embodies reason and mediates between the impulses of the Id and the external environment. Rational choice employs a similar understanding of reason; it assumes that actors rank order their preferences and engage in the kind of strategic behavior best calculated to obtain them.

The modern conceptualization of reason as instrumentality is part and parcel of the shift in focus away from the ends we should seek to the means of best satisfying our appetites. This transformation constitutes a challenge to the assumption shared by so many philosophers and social scientists that reason and cause are objective and universal concepts. Both concepts are undeniably culturally and historically specific. They are framed in ways to advance the ends we seek or are urged to seek. Karl Popper, as committed as Weber to the belief that science was distinguished by its reliance on reason, at the same time acknowledged that reason is a human invention and understandings of it are, like "all things … insecure and in a state of flux."[12]

These framings are invariably problematic but scholars and actors alike are often motivated to downplay these difficulties. I document these claims by showing how reason and cause have been conceived by representatives of Western culture in three historical eras. I argue that these framings are responses to changing political, economic, and social conditions and the psychological challenges to which they give rise.

With respect to cause, I follow David Hume in thinking it originated with peoples' practical and psychological needs. Our ancestors struggled to understand how the physical and social worlds worked to make them better able to cope with both. They wanted to make predictions that would reduce uncertainty and the anxiety it aroused.[13] The origins of cause and religion are closely connected. Max Weber argued that human beings have a strong "metaphysical need" to find order in seemingly random events to give life meaning but also to tame the world.[14] People invented deities to explain otherwise incomprehensible phenomena like storms, illnesses, and droughts. If they were the work of unseen gods who might be placated through prayers or offerings, people could assert a degree of control over threatening events.[15] All humans share this need; we still worry about natural disasters but also about recessions, wars, and climate change. To reduce anxiety, we can deny the threat or convince ourselves that we can understand how these catastrophes happen and do something to reduce their likelihood.

Elsewhere I argue that the belief in nuclear deterrence during the Cold War served this function by holding the bogey of nuclear war at bay. The national security community and many academics were accordingly unwilling to consider evidence that deterrence was more likely to provoke conflict than to prevent it.[16] In defiance of considerable evidence, economists convince themselves – and many others – that they can predict rises and falls in interest rates and other key economic trends. They succeed, I believe, not because of any demonstrable success in this regard but rather because the modern economy could not function in the absence of some degree of certainty about the future, even if it is illusory.

We cannot study the origin of causal inference because the practice emerged in human cultures long before the invention of writing and before the concepts of cause or reason were invented and named. David Hume is probably right in believing that our minds are constructed – hardwired, in today's lingo – to look for conjunctions between events and to infer causal connections on this basis. Karl Popper made a similar claim: "Biologically, we are told: you want to know – search for laws."[17] This kind of thinking may have conferred a significant survival advantage. The experimental evidence is tantalizing. Cognitive psychologists have studied the reasoning among children and there is no consensus among them about whether causal inference is innate or learned.[18]

Then next best thing we can do is to go back to the earliest texts we have that utilize, explore, or problematize cause. Origin narratives have been largely debunked as just-so stories but there is nevertheless some utility in reading the earliest sources we have that address reason and cause. My intention here is not to discover any pristine version or deep historical truth but rather to examine how reason and cause are presented and used and how central they are to these narratives. My analysis is a starting point for historical comparisons across several thousand years of what might be described as Western culture.

I begin with Homer – or the bards collectively referred to as Homer – who wrote about what call late Bronze Age Greece. Homer is foundational to Greek civilization and to Western understandings of cause and reason but also of agency, emotion, fate, and war. Homer's *Iliad* is a causal narrative that offers reasons for why people and gods behave as they do. It shows how the gods influence the actions of people, the outcomes of their actions, and how people try to influence these outcomes through appeals to gods. Those who listened to bards recite the *Iliad* and *Odyssey* in preclassical Greece were encouraged to think about how their world worked, the nature and extent of their agency, and how it was best exercised. These epics, I suggest, offer a thoughtful and problematic account of reason, cause, fate, and agency, and one, moreover, appropriate to the emergence of the polis. Homer is also of interest because he was so central to later formulations of reason and cause by fifth-century tragedians and Thucydides. The *Tanakh* or Hebrew Bible would have been another starting point, and I hope at some point to address it. Equally interesting, of course, are foundational texts of other cultures.

Tragedy is one of the most notable gifts of Greek culture. Aeschylus, Sophocles, and Euripides wrote plays that were as foundational to Western thought and literature as the epics of Homer. Space restrictions preclude treating all three playwrights so I limit myself to Sophocles. His Theban tragedies are most relevant to my exploration of reason and cause. *Oedipus Rex* (in Greek, *Oedipus Turannus*) is about fate and the effort of an intelligent and powerful actor to escape it. It encouraged fifth-century Greeks – and modern audiences and readers – to reflect on the meaning of agency, the unpredictable consequences of reason-based behavior, and, above all, the search for causes.

Sophocles offers a dual take on cause. His characters tell us what they think about it and we see how they use causal inference to make sense of the world and formulate responses to the problems and challenges. Their engagement with reason and cause generates tensions, even contradictions. It suggests that people understand reason and infer cause in self-serving and often counterproductive ways. For Sophocles and Aristotle – and for Thucydides too – tragedy is a vehicle to teach people how to live in a world in which cause is difficult to understand and the social environment unpredictable and more difficult still to control.

The shift from *oikos* to polis is mirrored much more in Sophocles and Thucydides than in Homer. It was a momentous transformation. In the *oikos*, gods and human practices were taken at face value and authority was concentrated in the hands of the king or local landowner. People's responses to others were largely predictable since they were dictated by nomos. The polis had many more people and a greater variety of statuses. Power gradually shifted from kingship to oligarchy and, in some cities like Athens, to the demos. Authority and office were based less on inheritance and physical prowess and more on rhetoric, guile, and other political and social skills.

The polis was a world of precipitous change and one in which causal inference became even more important for survival and advancement. It nevertheless became more difficult for reasons I enumerate in Chapters 2 and 3. Sophocles' Theban plays are set in a mythical past but use it to foreground and probe fifth-century preoccupations and understandings of the world. In these tragedies, events have human not divine origins, multiple rather than singular causes, and causes that are often at some remove from their effects. Causes may be hidden, and, even when discovered, generally lend themselves to different explanations. More disconcertingly, some things just happen. The search for cause, Sophocles appears to suggest, can lead us in circles and undermine rather than enhance our understanding of the world.

People could not help but search for causes in the world of the polis, an imperative that Sophocles and Thucydides recognized. Social, economic, and political life were more in flux and presented the kind of challenges that are no longer effectively addressed through either physical prowess or unyielding commitment to traditional nomos. Fifth-century Greeks, especially those in large bustling cities like Athens, were compelled to fathom causes to negotiate their lifeworlds. As noted, the tracing of cause and effect became increasingly difficult. Sophocles and Thucydides explore this dilemma.

In the writings of Sophocles and Thucydides, we encounter an early version of what Thomas Haskell calls "the recession of cause."[19] In the late nineteenth century, he argues, increasing social and economic interdependence in the United States, coupled with easier communication of goods, people, and ideas, meant that many important events could no longer be explained with reference to local causes. They had to be understood with reference to a broader, unseen set of forces and conditions. This characteristically modern concern with deep structures was anticipated in ancient Greece. Sophocles and Thucydides recognized that their world had become more complex because, among other things, high-status actors had more autonomy. They had more freedom of choice about roles and their enactment. People had to make inferences about how others would behave and used the concept of cause toward this end. They also used causal arguments to persuade others to act in ways they thought advantageous to their own interests. Thucydides explores the consequences of both kinds of behavior.

Sophocles and Thucydides had to fashion their understandings with the tools available to them. Tragedy, comedy, and history were the dominant discourses. Sophocles wrote both genres and we possess only seven of his 120 known plays. Thucydides wrote what we call history but structured it as tragedy. With the rare exception, tragedy was set in the distant past and featured mythological heroes, many of them figures out of the *Iliad* and *Odyssey*. Turning to characters from a distant past offered several advantages. They inhabited a simpler world and were motivated by heroic values. As they were mythical figures – although perhaps not to many Greeks – playwrights could take all kinds of liberties with them. Audiences familiar with Homer would pick up on these different portrayals and story lines and ponder their implications.

Philosophical discourses emerged in the late sixth century and gained prominence in the early fourth century with the writings of Plato and Aristotle. By the time of the Enlightenment, they had been an established medium for more than two millennia. They became a principal vehicle for exploring the concepts of reason and cause. Interest in these concepts intensified in the late eighteenth century and David Hume was central to this effort, although he refused to self-identify as a philosopher. Writers of fiction also interrogated reason and cause, so I follow my analysis of Hume with that of three Victorian writers: Charles Dickens, Anthony Trollope, and Wilkie Collins. There is no evidence that any of them read Hume but their understandings of reason and cause are in many ways similar.

Hume is rightly famous for his analysis of cause and concepts of "constant conjunction" and "invariant succession." He is arguably the most radical of Enlightenment philosophers. His writings were misunderstood at the time and still are today. His approach to cause is more psychological than philosophical; he is interested in how people turn to cause to help cope with the world, not in its elaboration as a concept foundational to scientific inquiry. In contrast to contemporaries who vaunt the power of reason, Hume argues for the power of imagination and emotion in forming judgments and assigning causes.

Hume urges us to give up the failed project of deductive reasoning. He excoriates philosophy for building systems on moral and logical assumptions rather than from observation of human life. He is struck by the irony that some philosophical systems claim to be descriptive and prescriptive. They insist their foundation is god-given, or at least rooted in the so-called natural dispositions of human beings, but then plead with people to act more in accord with their nature. Philosophy, Hume insists, cannot change human nature; attempts to do so are an arid exercise and waste of time. Rather, we should learn about people from experience and observation. His epistemological claim has radical normative implications, some of which he draws out. Philosophers should no longer ask what people should believe and how they should behave – for millennia the core questions of their enterprise – but investigate why they believe and act as they do. Hume insists on an equally radical methodological shift from abstract reasoning to experimentation. He wants to transform philosophy into something akin to modern cognitive and social psychology.

Jane Austen is the first English novelist to stress the dominant power of the imagination in shaping judgments. There are strong parallels in her thinking and Hume's, as there are between Hume and Dickens, Trollope, and Collins. These similarities may be independent responses to the growing importance yet enigmatic nature of civil society. In the late eighteenth century, society in Britain and the United States came to be understood as something independent of the people who composed it, even if changes in manners and customs were ultimately attributable to the behavior of individuals. For Victorians, society seemed to be governed by its own rules but was sufficiently large and diverse to work in opaque and unforeseeable ways. Society was independent of church and state, influenced by people, but not in any visible way controlled by them. This puzzle and the related unease to which it gave rise would lead social scientists later in the century to develop deep, structural explanations for the links between society and individuals, giving rise to the discipline of sociology. Their project endures despite efforts by postmodernists to discredit grand theory.[20]

Troubling too was the reversal in freedom society brought about between the upper and lower classes. Those at the top of the social hierarchy had more resources and education and should have had more freedom. In practice, they were more restricted by social rules and more ostracized when they violated them. Economic pressures on the lower orders and social pressures on the higher ones encouraged deviance at both ends of the socioeconomic spectrum. Dickens explores the underworld and those who constitute it. Trollope and Collins write about members of the elite who violate social norms or the law, how they are exposed, and how people judge them. Victorian literature diverged increasingly from contemporary social and political theories, most notably those of Bentham and Mill.

With Dickens, I focus largely, although not exclusively, on *Bleak House*. I do so as it is the most revealing text with respect to his treatment of reason and cause. Like Hume, I suggest, Dickens has little faith in the power of reason. At every level of society his characters are moved more by their emotions and also influenced by custom. They often act in irrational ways when constrained by custom or in thrall to their emotions. However, they are just as irrational – arguably more so – when liberated from custom and emotions and reliant on instrumental reason. These social truths are most dramatically illustrated by Dickens' criminals.

Trollope shares Hume's understanding of human beliefs and attributions. In *Phineas Redux* especially he offers parallel accounts of how judgments are made by society and the law courts. He challenges the conventional wisdom by showing that decisions and judgments in both domains are reached in ways that have little to do with reason and sharply at odds with the expectations of reformers and philosophers. Hume, Dickens, and Trollope developed an understanding of reason and cause based on careful observation of people that was largely stillborn. It made little headway against regularity theories, based on the belief in recurring patterns in social life. Regularity theories claim Hume as their progenitor but this involves a serious distortion of his writings. Regularity theories were given a major boost by John Stuart Mill and adopted by economics, from which it spread to the other social sciences. Their success, I argue, was in large part attributable to the Victorian quest for order and liberal belief in the power of reason. They triumphed more for psychological than intellectual reasons.

Many of the characters of Dickens, Trollope, and Collins follow Jane Austen's Emma in their inability to comprehend their own motives and appear driven more by emotion than by reason. These authors often give emotions a positive valence as they guide characters to truths they would never discover through reason alone. Collins comes across as very Humean. He wants us to recognize that so-called facts can reveal the truth or stand in the way of its discovery. They only take on meaning in context, and these contexts are by no means self-evident. Lawyers and courts, he suggests, rarely go beyond Humean-style inference. They focus on resemblance and contiguity and routinely make unwarranted inferences on the basis of them. This process leads to the simplest explanations of events and responsibility. They are the ones most likely to be believed by ordinary people, who think the same way. Lawyers and juries act alike.

Dickens, Trollope, and Collins question the rationality of people and the utility of using reason to study cause. As often as not, their characters do not seek rational ends, do not behave rationally in pursuit of their goals, do not interrogate their motives, and have only imperfect knowledge of them. All three authors suggest that rational strategies are not necessarily the most effective way of achieving desired ends. In part, this is because other people regard people who do as calculating and do not trust them. It is also attributable to the aggregation problem. People rarely act alone but do so in conjunction with others. Their interactions, as in the Jarndyce and Jarndyce lawsuit, can produce outcomes that none have anticipated or desired. Efforts to game them by instrumentally rational actors are bound to fail.

My third historical epoch is fin-de-siècle Europe. It witnessed equally radical changes in thinking about reason and cause. I pair German sociologist Max Weber with German author Thomas Mann and Austrian-Czech writer Franz Kafka. Weber was born in 1864, Mann in 1875, and Kafka in 1883. All three grew up in an era generally recognized as a high point of European culture and global influence but also of industrialization, state development, and mass politics. They experienced World War I but Weber and Kafka died not long afterwards. Mann lived until 1955 and revised his *The Magic Mountain*, set on the eve of that war, in its aftermath.

Weber was among the first to probe the cultural consequences of science and scientific thinking. The demystification of the world and the rising importance of scientific understandings of it brought about an increased emphasis on causal inference. It encouraged the belief that the physical and social worlds were organized causally and that all things could be mastered by calculation (*durch Berechen beherrschen*).[21] This imparted a rational flavor to the everyday experience of even ordinary, uneducated people. Intellectualization encouraged people to act less on the basis of habit and more in response to conscious reflection and calculation and to calculate and assess the likely consequences of their behavior for the goals they sought. Weber calls this *Zweckrationalität* (means-ends reasoning or instrumental rationality).[22] Its effect was to heighten the tension, even the contradiction, between belief in how the world was structured and the ability to grasp and manipulate this structure. The world might have meaning but its causal structure – if there was one – was ever more elusive.[23]

The paradox that cause is increasingly essential to negotiate modern life but more difficult to establish encourages diametrically opposed responses. People can devise more sophisticated means to probe causes at deeper levels of analysis. Max Weber pioneered the approach. He made important contributions to the study of cause, which explains his continuing relevance, if not centrality, to the interpretivist tradition in social science. Alternatively, people can also try to dispense with cause and find other means of coping with the complexities of modern life. The difficulty of making causal attributions, I contend, is a principal reason why regularity theories gained such prominence in the twentieth century.

Weber developed his approach to knowledge in the context of controversies between historicists and positivists and historicists and neo-Kantians. He built on these traditions while attempting to finesse what he saw as their limitations. The result was a definition of knowledge as causal inference about singular events that uses the individual as its unit of analysis, relies on ideal types, and employs counterfactual thought experiments to probe putative causes. For many reasons, his approach is no silver bullet but represents an imaginative and fruitful attempt to chart a more rewarding path toward knowledge in what Weber, following Wilhelm Dilthey, called the "cultural sciences."

Weber's approach has unresolved tensions. The most important is the contradiction between his recognition of the subjective nature of the values and interests that motivate research and his insistence on objective means by which it might be conducted. Facts and values are not so easily reconciled, and Weber ultimately recognized that they influence, if not determine, the questions we ask, the methods we choose to research them, what we consider relevant evidence, and the inferences we draw from it. Weber was unambiguous in his recognition that all research questions are subjective; we can look at reality in myriad different ways, and the ways we choose reflect our commitments, station in life, and problems that engage us. All social knowledge is inescapably cultural and local in nature.[24]

Thomas Mann and Franz Kafka went in a different direction from Weber. They recognize the importance of cause for people but are even more dubious than their Victorian predecessors about the ability to make meaningful causal inferences. Mann's characters raise numerous causal questions about medicine, biology, and the universe that are unanswerable, at least by the science of the time. Even when a cause of the disease is known, it tells us little to nothing about how to respond to it. The diagnosis and treatment of tuberculosis turn out to be hit-or-miss.

Mann emphasized impressions, emotions, and the knowledge and commitments to which they gave rise. Weber attempted to integrate intuition with causal analysis and, by doing so, transcend the limitations of both approaches. Mann largely rejects causal analysis in favor of empathy. He described his approach to knowledge as dialectical; feeling and reflection must combine to produce deeper understandings of oneself and one's society. Mann holds their failure to produce such an understanding responsible for interpersonal and interstate conflict. *The Magic Mountain* suggests that bourgeois repression, national and ethnic stereotypes, and the growing imbalance between reason and emotions are the underlying causes of World War I. They prevented the kind of learning necessary to sustain friendship and tolerance but also put intolerable stress on the psyche that found release in aggression directed against others and the self.

Kafka did not write with Weber in mind but he nevertheless produced a powerful critique of his approach to knowledge. Kafka follows Weber in believing that causal analysis depends on rational models and their fit with social reality. In *The Castle*, K. is a good rational analyst. He starts with assumptions that appear reasonable (e.g., he has been summoned for a job and will be given the information and access he needs to complete it; officials are responsible and responsive; that he can infer the motives of townspeople on the basis of his general understanding of social life and human nature). These assumptions and observation form the basis for a series of inferences that are consistently wrong. We understand why he fails, and it has, ironically, to do with his commitment to rational analysis. Given the way the castle and the world work, they make understanding difficult, and all the more so the attribution of cause. Cause is not a very helpful concept – and even costly to those who seek to apply it.

Like Mann, Kafka rejects causal narratives. He too is convinced that cause in the modern world is so complex and so layered as to be largely inaccessible. Immediate causes that derive from human motives are often just as opaque. World War I appears to have strengthened both men in this belief. It was catastrophic, made no sense, and its causes, even the most immediate ones, were unknown or, at best, gave rise to dramatically divergent interpretations. The motives of the policymakers involved were difficult to fathom as were the diverse pressures acting on them, especially the deeper cultural ones. Causal inference led to an aporia.

In Chapter 8, I review my findings about these authors and thinkers. Earlier chapters emphasize similarities and differences between or among thinkers and writers of the same era. The only real exception is my comparison of Homer and Sophocles in Chapter 2. In this chapter, I make comparisons across epochs. I offer generalizations about the conditions that encourage changes in the framing of reason and cause and identify generic strategies that have developed toward this end. I explore the changing relationship between reason and cause, the ways in which they are co-constitutive but also in other ways at odds. By placing reason and cause in comparative, historical perspective, I demonstrate the local and contextually dependent nature of contemporary understandings. This comparative analysis of reason and cause encourages a radical perspective on the social science project.

My project builds on three earlier books but does not replicate their arguments. *The Tragic Vision of Politics* (2003) sought to recapture and foreground the tradition of classical realism through a close reading of the texts of Thucydides, Carl von Clausewitz, and Hans Morgenthau. The two chapters on Thucydides address his analysis of the causes of the Archidamian War and his understanding of political order and the ways in which conflict helps to create and sustain it but also has the potential to destroy it. Chapter 3 on Thucydides in this volume revisits his analysis of the origins of the Archidamian War and Sicilian expedition but with the goal of teasing out his understanding of reason and cause.

Constructing Cause in International Relations (2014) is the immediate precursor of this book in the sense of argument. In it, I review understandings of cause in physics and philosophy. Physicists have diverse approaches to cause; some fields and subfields find it a helpful concept and others not. Those who embrace cause use quite different approaches to it (e.g., regularity theories, ideal types, Kantian) and the profession as a whole welcomes this diversity. Philosophers have struggled without success for almost a century to devise a formulation of cause that is logically defensible and universal in coverage. This is not surprising because, if causation is a cognitive construct, there is no reason to think that it should map neatly onto the physical or social worlds. In practice, causal inference is always rhetorical and must be judged on grounds of practicality.

Constructing Cause in International Relations explores the implications of this understanding of social science in general and the study of international relations in particular. I develop a new approach that I call "inefficient causation." It is constructivist in its emphasis on the reasons people have for acting as they do but turns to other approaches to understand the aggregation of their behavior. It relies on the combination of general theoretical understandings and idiosyncratic features of context. I illustrate its utility in a study of the visual revolutions of the Renaissance and nineteenth century and attempt to explain why the former, but not the latter, had profound implications for how we conceive of political units and the practice of politics.

Max Weber and International Relations (2017) is an edited volume in which my collaborators and I explore the political, epistemological, and ethical problems of modernity and the connections among them. Weber's epistemological successes and failures highlight unresolvable tensions that are just as pronounced today and from which we have much to learn. I contributed chapters on "Weber and International Relations" and "Weber's Search for Knowledge." The latter offers a reading of Weber's understanding of rationality, counterfactuals, ideal types, and ethics sharply at odds with traditional structuralist and positivist ones. I show his commitment to what is today called singular causation, his belief that our framing of research questions is largely determined by our lifeworlds, that facts and values cannot easily be separated, and that our research findings are likely to validate our prior beliefs.

My discussion of Weber in this book draws directly on this chapter. It expands on my account of Weber's understanding of cause but also explores his treatment of reason and how it relates to causal inquiry. It approaches these questions from a different perspective. I am interested in understanding Weber's epistemology as a response to the practical and psychological challenges of his era and what it shares in common with and how it differs from other efforts by contemporaries.

This book extends my critique of mainstream social science but in a different way from earlier works. It attempts to root evolving understandings of reason and cause in their historical contexts. I demonstrate the variety of ways these concepts can be framed and deployed and thereby deepen our understanding of both concepts. I show how differences in their framing can be understood as responses to particular conditions. They in turn tell us something about the ways in which people conceive of their lifeworlds and devise ways of coping with them.

There is an important parallel between causal claims and epistemological ones. Both are rhetorical in nature and accordingly lend themselves to politicization. Proponents of particular epistemologies or causal claims rely on what Aristotle called enthymemes to persuade others of their proclaimed truths. The enthymeme is a rhetorical tool, often likened to a syllogism, that tries to show that the claims in question are consistent with the convictions of the audience.[25] Different epistemologies establish different procedures and languages for doing this and judge the quality of research on the basis of how closely it adheres to them. To convince others of the validity of our methods and findings, we package them in preferred language and forms. It is hardly surprising that, in the postwar era, methods sections of dissertations, articles, and books have grown enormously in size relative to substantive sections of these texts.

Open-minded and pluralistic social scientists in the tradition of Max Weber recognize that there are no objective truths – scientific or social – but rather multiple and provisional ones. This multiplicity reflects the different interests, perspectives, and methods of researchers. Their findings must arise from the robust application of their respective methods but can ultimately be judged only on the basis of utility. Do they help us address contemporary problems? As the nature of the problems we confront changes, so do – or should – our analytical perspectives.

Less tolerant scholars rely on coercion as well as persuasion. They use their control of graduate admissions, fellowships, publication, awards, and, most importantly, jobs to reward those who buy into their approaches, adopt their research agenda, and mimic their work. They are correspondingly keen to exclude and punish those who do research in other traditions or criticize them and their approach. The same holds true for many people committed to particular causal narratives. In the 1950s and 1960s, it was difficult going on the job market for a historian who argued that the United States bore its share of responsibility for the Cold War. In Weimar and the Federal Republic, it was taboo for more than forty years to argue that Germany was responsible for World War I.[26] These attitudes changed less as a function of scholarship than of shifts in public opinion. The rise and fall of epistemologies, approaches to cause and reason, and specific causal narratives are also influenced at least as much by external developments as they are by scholarly research and writing. We know relatively little about this process and my book attempts to shed a little light on this question.

This brings us to the chicken-and-egg problem. Do conceptions of cause and reason reflect changing epistemologies or do they shape them? I argue that the arrow of influence points both ways. The appeal of new epistemologies, or even methods, encourages scholars to reevaluate the importance of cause in their research and, if important, how it should be understood and studied. Thinking about cause can also affect the appeal of epistemologies and methods. Analytical and empirical difficulties in establishing cause can push scholars toward epistemologies and methods that attempt to finesse cause. So too can the perceived need to address cause in the social world encourage development of new epistemologies and methods.

The two incentives often appear at the same time. Cause became a matter of pressing concern in fifth-century Greece and again in the Enlightenment and industrial era. In the late eighteenth and nineteenth centuries, cause was seen as more difficult to establish than in the past. Need and difficulty pushed scholars in opposite directions. Some who engaged cause formulated "thin" accounts of it, like Hume, Mill, and regularity theorists. Others devised "thick" accounts, among them Kant and Weber. Still others sought parsimonious, monocausal "thick" explanations; and some sought to develop noncausal approaches to knowledge. In the social sciences, agent-based modeling may be the most prominent exemplar. Here too, some generalizations emerge across epochs and genres that offer insight into our world time and world.

I turn to philosophical, historical, and literary writings to study reason and cause. Most analyses of most concepts focus on single genres. They usually ask questions or address controversies that are specific to those genres. I bridge genres and questions and epochs too. My research questions demand a broad-gauged approach and, although it raises its own difficulties, so too does it offer all kinds of rewards. Limiting my study to one genre – say philosophical works – would risk considerable distortion. It would ignore key treatments of cause in literature, in epics and tragedy, before the emergence of philosophical discourse. In the nineteenth and twentieth centuries, it would miss the ways in which novels built on philosophical concepts or offered critiques of them. Of equal importance it would not see how thoughtful people working in different media confronted similar problems, often in a similar manner, but just as often in ways specific to their discourse.

I do not doubt that my analysis would have benefited from an even more broad-gauged approach by including music and art. Mahler's song cycles and symphonies have much to say in music and text about reason and cause and could be read against Weber, Kafka, and Mann. Cubism, Fauvism, surrealism, and suprematism could also readily be drawn into this dialogue, as could the newer genre of film. These cross-genre comparisons must await another study.

Cross-genre comparisons entail the additional novelty of importing perspectives and research questions from one genre into another. Reason and cause are concepts found in philosophy, literature, history, social science but also in art, music, and film. They are not generally explored in literature, perhaps because they are regarded as questions more appropriate to social science. Literary critics have borrowed extensively from social science, and vice versa, but generally in the form of analytical perspectives. The two fields of study have embraced postmodernism, postcolonialism, and feminism, and they have significantly shaped their research programs. On the whole, they use these perspectives to ask questions considered pertinent to their subject matter, and these questions often differ across disciplines.

One of the few scholars to attempt to do something similar to what I am doing is the historian Stephen Kern. His *A Cultural History of Causality* attempts to trace the evolution of nineteenth- and twentieth-century understandings of cause in literature based on new understandings of them in the sciences and social sciences. He focuses on murder novels, although offers no justification for choosing this genre, in contrast to his concern for justifying the choice of male authors writing about male murderers.[27] He argues that causal understandings from the nineteenth to the twentieth century shifted in five related ways. They reveal increasing specificity, multiplicity, complexity, probability, and uncertainty.

I think Kern's findings are very much an artifact of his focus on murder mysteries. This genre requires authors to find a killer, fathom their motives, and uncover the means by which the deed was done. Murder mysteries are all about discovering causes – and usually by means of clever reasoning and investigation on the part of the detective. A noncausal murder mystery, or one in which reason failed to lead to telling clues, would be an oxymoron. This is not true of other genres of literature. For this reason and others, they are an unrepresentative sample and one must be careful about generalizing from them.

Other kinds of nineteenth-century novels, even those in which murder occurs, offer radically different takes on cause. For Dickens, cause is a problematic category for author and characters alike. Victorian novels reveal the complexity and uncertainty that Kern posits, and this is associated with their deep questioning of the utility of cause. *Phineas Redux* by Trollope and *Moonstone* by Wilkie Collins arguably qualify as murder mysteries and these novels are even more suspicious of cause and the use of reason in finding it. Society and the jury in *Phineas Redux* reach their conclusions on the basis of emotions and the vividness of associations.

Ian Hacking describes the kind of inquiry I am engaging in as historical meta epistemology. It analyzes the origins, diffusion, and subsequent history of concepts related to "knowledge, belief, opinion, objectivity, detachment, argument, reason, rationality, evidence, even facts and truths."[28] These understandings frame and enable inquiry but also, as noted, have the potential to influence our behavior by shaping our beliefs about the world and how it works. Through what Hacking calls "looping effects," they influence, even constrain, actors they are supposed to explain and enable.[29] As constructivists have long recognized, concepts not only describe the social world; they help to make it.

Max Weber was also convinced that our epistemologies and related understandings of cause and reason influence the wider society in important ways. This assumption lies at the core of his argument about Protestantism and capitalism. Weber argued that the rise of science and its broader influence on modes of knowing and arguing brought about a major shift in how values were understood. Formerly a matter of habit or belief, the latter associated with "value rationality" (*wertrationalität*), they were increasingly subjected to conceptual and empirical scrutiny. For many, they became means to ends and thus in the realm of "purposeful rationality" (*zweckrationalität*). This conceptual shift had profound practical, emotional, and even spiritual consequences.[30]

Weber worried that means would replace ends and that efficiency and order would supplant as goals the kinds of values that might lead to better and happier lives. His insight was prescient. The concept of efficiency, generally defined as cost-effectiveness, developed in economics and has been smuggled into public policy studies where it is used as a benchmark for assessing a range of public services, including education, health care, welfare, and transportation.[31] Janice Gross Stein describes "the cult of efficiency" as a means to an end has become an end in its own right. It trumps other values, suppresses their discussion, and is used to delegitimate these values if they are raised. For many advocates, it is a vehicle to critique the so-called sclerotic state because of its residual commitment to public services. For the most part, efficiency is a highly questionable end and one often destructive of the communities in whose name it is invoked. At best, it can tell us how we can allocate our resources to accomplish our goals but nothing about what those goals should be.[32]

The efficiency story highlights another far-reaching consequence of analytical concepts. As Duncan Bell notes, "the historical variability of conceptions of reason illustrate how power circulates in communities through the attribution of legitimacy, credulity and expertise – whose voice should count, according to which set of (epistemic) criteria."[33] This is another way in which the quest for knowledge becomes politicized. Knowledge claims are used to enhance the authority of a particular understanding or set of concepts and younger scholars see the career advantages of adopting them.

Engaging science and the arts at the same time encourages us to step back from the day-to-day use of social science. The juxtaposition of scientific scholarship and artistic production can be productive of insights relevant to both.[34] It may puzzle readers, or even annoy those who seek narrow, crisp arguments, but this kind of engagement has the potential to open eyes and minds. It facilitates the exploration of the relationship between social science and the social world. It demonstrates that our analytical concepts and tools are never divorced from it and the psychological conundrums to which it gives rise. It creates frames of reference, analogies, and common denominators as well as exposing tensions between and within our concepts and the different domains in which they find expression. My method might be said to represent a multiperspective form of hermeneutics. It is, I believe, the appropriate vehicle for contextualizing ideas and concepts, especially those of reason and cause.

Notes

1. Montaigne, "In Defense of Seneca and Plutarch," p. 548.
2. Russell, "On the Notion of Cause."
3. Einstein, *Ideas and Opinions*, p. 274.
4. Kant, *Critique of Pure Reason*. See also Popper, *Logic of Scientific Discovery*.
5. Lebow, "Weber's Search for Knowledge."
6. Lebow, *Between Peace and War*, chaps. 4–6 for miscalculation of this kind responsible in part for World War I, the Chinese-American component of the Korean War, and the Sino-Indian War of 1963. Lebow, "Miscalculation in the South Atlantic," for this miscalculation as a root cause of the 1982 Falklands War.
7. Plato, *Republic*, 430e6–431a2, 441d12–e2, Plato, *Symposium*, 209a–b.
8. Aristotle, *Nicomachean* Ethics, 1106b35–1107a4.
9. Augustine, *City of God*.
10. For Aristotle, this is one of four kinds of causality: efficient, material (by virtue of an object's composition), formal (the way the structure of an object gives it form), and final causality (*telos*). See *Posterior Analytics*, 71b9–11, 94a20, and *Physics*, 194b17–20, 195b21–25, *Metaph*. 1013b6–9.
11. Hume, *Treatise of Human Nature*, 2.3.3.4, *Enquiry Concerning the Principles of Morals*, Appendix 1, p. 163.
12. Popper, "Logic of the Social Sciences."

13. Hume, *Treatise of Human Nature*, 2.2.
14. Weber, "Profession and Vocation of Politics," "Social Psychology of the World's Religions" in *Economy and Society*, pp. 399–439.
15. Weber, *Economy and Society*, p. 423.
16. Lebow, *Avoiding War, Making Peace*, chap. 7.
17. For Hume, see Chapter 4 in this volume. Karl Popper, *Die bieden Grundprobleme der Erkenntnistheorie*, p. 27.
18. Griffiths et al., "Bayes and Blickets"; Sobel and Legare, "Causal Learning in Children"; van Schijndel et al., "Investigating the Development of Causal Inference by Studying Variability in 2- to 5-Year-Olds' Behavior."
19. Haskell, *Emergence of Professional Social Science*.
20. Skinner, "Introduction"; Lebow, *Cultural Theory of International Relations*, chap. 2.
21. Weber, "Über einige Kategorien verstehenden Soziologie" [On Some Categories of Sociological Analysis], p. 449.
22. Weber, *Economy and Society*, p. 24.
23. Ibid., and "Science as a Vocation."
24. Weber, *Protestant Ethic and the Spirit of Capitalism*, pp. 83, 98.
25. Aristotle, *Rhetoric*, 6.1–5.
26. Herwig, "Clio Deceived."
27. Kern, *Cultural History of Causality*, Introduction.
28. Hacking, *Emergence of Probability*, pp. 8–9.
29. Ibid., p. 22.
30. Weber, *Protestant Ethic and the Spirit of Capitalism*, "Conceptual Exposition," and "Roscher und Knies."
31. Efficiency derives from the Latin *efficere*, which meant to bring about, effect, or accomplish. It embraced or combined the notions of effectiveness, efficacy, and efficiency. In present-day use, efficiency has been narrowed and the first two meanings excluded.
32. Stein, *Cult of Efficiency*.
33. Bell, "Writing the World."
34. See the art of Iranian-Maltese artist Lida Sherafatmand for examples of how social science can stimulate artistic perspective.

2 Homer and Sophocles

Homer is the starting point for any engagement with Greek literature and philosophy. The *Iliad* and *Odyssey* are foundational to Greek civilization and to writings on, among other subjects, cause, reason, emotion, agency, and war. Plato and his contemporaries thought of Homer as a person and founder of the genre of tragic poetry.[1] With respect to the war, the *Iliad* is the first work of literature to make connections between the values of society and the causes of war and the causes of war and its conduct. Homer, or the bards that are collectively responsible for his epics, invented the immanent critique, a method of analysis that identifies contradictions in society's rules and systems and explores their disruptive consequences.[2] The *Iliad* demonstrates how the values and practices that enable and sustain honor-based warrior societies also threaten to destroy them. I unpack these claims in the pages that follow and, in the process, analyze his understanding of reason, emotion, and cause, and the relationship among them.

Greek tragedy is another highpoint of Greek culture. Aeschylus, Sophocles, and Euripides wrote tragedies that became central to Western culture. Space restrictions preclude treating all three playwrights, so I restrict myself to Sophocles. His Theban tragedies are most relevant to my exploration of reason, emotion, and cause. This choice inevitably introduces some bias but not a significant one. I believe I would end up making many of the same connections and arguments if, for example, I focused on Aeschylus and his *Oresteia*.

The bigger problem is reading of Greek texts across the gulf of time and cultures that separates us from them. Classicists have long struggled with this problem and in tandem with biblical scholars developed the hermeneutic method as a means of trying to approach the intent of authors. I employ this method in *The Tragic Vision of Politics* to theorize about how Thucydides might have wanted his contemporaries to understand his account of the Archidamian and Peloponnesian Wars and their possible lessons. I do something similar in this chapter.

I also step back from the hermeneutic method to engage in what might be called ontological gerrymandering. I approach these texts with three modern analytical categories: emotion, reason, and cause. These concepts were certainly known to the Greeks and theorized by them, most notably by Aristotle in the fourth century BCE. Aristotle's conceptualization of tragedy was already at a generation's remove from its creation and initial performance and some authorities think we should be cautious about using them to analyze tragedy.[3] We must exercise even more caution when we use modern conceptual categories to understand ancient Greek texts. It is nevertheless a defensible exercise because texts speak beyond the intentions of their authors; it is fair to ask questions about them and use analytical categories to find answers that were unknown to their authors. We routinely read the tragic playwrights this way and, later, tragedians like Shakespeare and Goethe. All these writers reflect, as well as reflect on, beliefs and practices of their society. Shakespeare does it quite deliberately with such concerns as identity, order, authority, and love.

Homer – or the bards responsible for his works – and Sophocles engaged questions of cause, emotions, and reason. I base this claim on the degree to which Homer's *Iliad* describes the actions of men and gods and provides numerous accounts of how the gods influence the actions of people and their consequences, and how people do the same through successful appeals to gods. Those who listened to bards recite Homer in preclassical Greece must have been encouraged to think about how their world worked, the extent of their agency, and how it was best exercised. Sophocles' *Oedipus Turannus* is about fate and the effort of an intelligent and powerful actor to escape it. It compels those who watch a performance or read the play – then or now – to reflect on agency, the unpredictable consequences of reasoning one's way through a challenge, and, above all, about the nature of cause in the social world. Agency for Homer and Sophocles is a product of emotion and reflection, and they interrogate both concepts.

Nietzsche observed that only concepts without any history are definable.[4] Once a concept appears it is used differently by different people, or even by the same people in varying contexts.[5] It is a mistake to think that any one framing is the right one or the most appropriate in a given context. In the modern world, there are many more diverse framings of concepts than there were in the classical age. There is accordingly a tendency to rely on those few ancient sources that discuss concepts and their meaning. Chief among these are the works of Aristotle, whose lengthy, sophisticated discussions of poetry, tragedy, fear, cause, friendship, and human emotions have significantly shaped our understanding of them and how they were understood by his contemporaries.

In this and previous books, I have relied on Aristotle's analysis of these several concepts. It is difficult to know the extent to which they are idiosyncratic representations or tap into wider cultural understandings. I suspect there is some truth to both readings and it depends in part on the concepts in question. There can be little doubt that Aristotle's discussions of cause, tragedy, ethics, friendship, and the polis influenced, even shaped, later treatments. I have been more inclined to rely on Aristotelian analysis when I could find other earlier or contemporary sources who were in general agreement. Plato and Aristotle, and Thucydides, the last implicitly, share a similar understanding of the human psyche.[6] I am also willing to take seriously Aristotle's characterization of tragedy as he wrote close to the era in which these plays were written and performed.

Cause, reason, fate, and agency are the central concepts for ancient Greeks. Fifth- and fourth-century Greeks developed the genres of philosophy and tragedy in part to problematize cause. Their approach to cause was undoubtedly influenced by a language that emphasizes the link between cause and responsibility. The word *aitiaomai* means "to blame" or "to censure."[7] In the *Iliad*, Paris' theft of Helen and her husband's prized possessions make him blameworthy and responsible for the war that follows. In *Oedipus Turannus*, the pestilence that afflicts Thebes is assumed to have a cause and the search for it reveals the link in the form of pollution (*miasma*) that Oedipus has brought down on the city.

In fifth-century Athens, *aitia* (neuter plural) were the justifications given in court and elsewhere to make one's behavior appear consistent with accepted norms. *Aitia* (feminine singular) also meant complaint or accusation, thus continuing the connection with blame and response. From the Hippocratic physicians, we get *aition*, which became the accepted word for cause.[8] By the time of Herodotus, *aitia* are closely associated with cause. Thucydides famously uses *aitia* in his account of the Archidamian War, where it can be interpreted as either "cause," "blame," "complaint," or "justification."[9] There is good reason for thinking, I ague, that Thucydides intends for his readers to read the word in multiple ways.

By the late fifth century, Greeks theorized two forms of reason. The most important to philosophers was *to logistikon*. It was the capability to distinguish good from bad, in contrast to appetite and spirit, which were guided by instrumental reasoning (*gnōmē*). Plato and Aristotle considered *to logistikon* a fundamental and universal human potential and come close to equating it with what we today might call a drive. For Socrates, *to logistikon* has desires of its own, the most important being discovery of the purposes of life and the means of fulfilling them. It possesses a corresponding "drive" to rule. Reason wants to discipline and train the appetite and the spirit to do what will promote individual happiness (*eudaimonia*) and well-being.[10] Reason would famously be described by David Hume as "the slave of the passions," which comes reasonably close to the Greek understanding of instrumental reason. Plato and Aristotle regarded it as largely destructive to individuals and society alike unless it was harnessed to forms of appetite and spirit (*thumos*) effectively constrained and educated by *to logistikon*. Such an understanding, I maintain, is implicit in Homer and Thucydides.

Fate is represented by multiple concepts and related terms that describe divine guidance, even the shaping of human desires or actions, and the reward or punishment of people for their appearance, character, or behavior. Agency superficially appears to be the antonym of fate, but Oedipus makes us aware that agency can fulfill fate. Instead of viewing them as opposites, we need to see the ways in which they are related and may even be co-constitutive.

Agency was regarded as a feature of the aristocracy in the Homeric age, and still largely so in the classical era because, as Aristotle argued, only those who lived off the labor of others had the time and resources to make meaningful choices.[11] In the fifth century, agency increasingly became associated with citizenship. It enabled participation in civic life, not only in politics but also in phratries (brotherhoods organized along kinship lines) and religious festivals. People without citizenship or a polis were thought to have lost a significant component of their humanity.[12] Agency was also associated with character traits, especially those that make people stand out and exercise leadership, or, as in the case of Medea, successfully seek revenge against those who had wronged them. Neither fate nor agency was regarded as good or bad in itself but took on meaning in context.

I utilize psychological concepts that were unknown to classical authors but can readily be applied to their texts. Sophocles knew nothing about cognitive or motivational psychology but implicitly appears to grasp and utilize some of their key findings. Freud was similarly impressed by the novels of Dostoevsky because of his intuitive understanding of dreams and their symbolic content.[13] The tragic playwrights, and philosophers like Plato and Aristotle, read Homer in the light of their times and problems and unquestionably came away with understandings that would not have occurred to audiences of the eighth and seventh centuries. Good analysis of texts requires us to try to understand them in context, but we cannot escape from – nor should we – reading them in terms of our experience, concepts, and interests.

Homer

Reading texts this way can offer unintended but nevertheless important insights into their societies. We routinely approach the Bible and

Shakespeare this way so why should Homer be any different? This strategy is also advantageous because reason, emotion, and cause were of interest to Greek writers who followed Homer. As his texts are so foundational to Greek culture, their thoughts on these matters are refracted through what they thought were his. This gives us the possibility of using later tragedies and philosophy as entry points for reading and understanding their texts and Homer's because they were closer to his culture and time than we are. We can read Homer as a starting point for understanding Sophocles and other Greek tragedians, or vice versa.

David Hume contends that cause is a concept that goes back to the early days of our species. Perhaps from the beginning, he suggests, people thought in causal terms. They looked for constant or near-constant conjunctions that enabled them to make predictions critical to their survival.[14] If we accept that people thought and functioned this way before they developed any concept of causality it is certainly reasonable to look for explicit or implicit causality in Homer. The same is true for emotions and reasons. People had feelings, would invent names for them, and emotions feature prominently in the lives of Homeric humans and divines. The *Iliad* begins with a famous account of Achilles' rage, a reaction to a slight by Agamemnon, and it is their conflict that drives the plot forward as much as the Trojan War. Classical-age Greeks would make emotions central to their poetry, histories, and philosophy. Aristotle provides a catalog and analysis of them.[15]

Reason falls somewhere between cause and emotions in the attention it receives in Homer and classical texts. In Homer's epics, characters sometimes reason aloud, but most often do so implicitly before acting. Reasoning often takes the form of causal narratives, as does the opening speech of the *Odyssey*. Telemachus shares his grief over the loss of his father and the vulture-like consumption of his inheritance by Penelope's rapacious suitors. One of them even blames Penelope for their continued presence because she kept them all at bay with her ruse of weaving a shroud during the day and undoing her labor at night.[16]

Individuals. The *Iliad* and the *Odyssey* tell the tales of individuals and their striving for *aristeia* (excellence) and *kleos* (glory, fame). *Kleos* is related to the word signifying "to hear," and implies "what others hear about you." Fame won this way carried one's name and deeds through the ages conferring figurative immortality. Homer's epics – initially sung aloud by bards – were the most important vehicle toward this end in the preclassical Greek world.[17]

Homer's characters, and those of later tragedy, differ from their modern counterparts in that they have no observable inner lives. For the most part, they are archetypes constructed from a few carefully chosen characteristics.

These attributes are often exaggerated, as courage and military skill are with Achilles, cleverness and guile with Odysseus, beauty with Helen, and age and wisdom with Nestor. Most characters are archetypes in a second sense. They are creatures of their societies and accurately reflect its values, and, by doing so, inform us of those values and related practices. Some of Homer's characters uphold these values and others violate them. Achilles, Hector, Priam, Hecuba, Andromeda, and Penelope illustrate the former, and Paris and Helen the latter. By foregrounding undesirable character traits and unacceptable behavior, the bard tells us more about what is valued is their society. There is the occasional in-between character like Odysseus, who has all the right stuff and some additional qualities, notably guile, that are not officially sanctioned but very much valued on the sly. Adam Parry makes the case for Patroclus as an independent actor and also for Achilles trying to escape from the language in which his society has entrapped him.[18]

By far the largest majority of characters we meet in both epics represent the imagined values of Bronze Age honor-based honor societies. We must exercise caution here because inferring values and practices from Homeric characters risks falling into the trap of circular reasoning, of using Homer to understand Bronze Age Greece and his portrayal of Bronze Age Greece to understand his epics. We can circumvent this methodological pitfall by comparing the *Iliad* and *Odyssey* to historical warrior-based honor societies for which there is good, independent empirical evidence. They include the Vikings, Maori, Zulu, and Native American tribes of the Great Plains like the Sioux. They reveal many striking similarities with the world of Odysseus.[19]

For our purposes, perhaps the most important feature of Homeric characters is the extent to which their behavior is socially determined. Most try to lead the life of heroes, or at least convince others that they do. Outliers – characters not in pursuit of *aristeia* and *kleos* – are a distinct minority so socialization appears robust. Hector is typical. His strategically insightful wife Andromache urges him to have the Trojans wage a defensive war behind the walls of their city until the Greeks tire of the fight and go home. Hector tells her: "Wife, what you say is surely in my mind also. But I would feel terrible shame before the men of Troy and the women of Troy with their trailing dresses, if I like a coward skulk away from the fighting ... I have learnt always to be brave and to fight in the foremost of the Trojans, winning great glory for my father and for myself."[20] Hector gives primacy to core values of his society even when they threaten its survival.

Kant was among the first to theorize the beneficial effects of socialization. The Königsberg sage observed that most people performed behavior mandated by society because they recognized that it was in their interest to be respected by others. When they routinely acted this way they made good behavior habitual. By this means, the "crooked timber" of humanity was able to sustain societies and the principles of justice on which they rested.[21] Kant recognized that proper behavior is often hypocritical. There is little of this in Homer, Helen's and Penelope's suitors aside, which makes these examples more striking. Helen alleges that Aphrodite compelled her to run off with Paris and that once her spell wore off she longed to go home, and, conveniently, well-before the Greeks arrived at Troy.[22] Eurymachus, one of the leaders of the suitors, assures Penelope that "Telemachus is his dearest friend on earth" and that she need not fear that any harm will come to him. "These encouraging words were on his lips," Homer tells us, "but death for Telemachus was in his heart."[23] There is another hint of hypocrisy in an exchange between Odysseus and Achilles.[24]

More evidence of the strength of socialization can be inferred from the striking similarity between Greeks and Trojans. This is necessary, of course, to illustrate the workings of an honor society. Greek warriors could not gain *aristeia* fighting barbarians. They must engage warriors of similar social standing who fight by the same rules, which includes the desire for fairly staged single combats. Equally striking in both camps is the extent to which warriors live up to social expectations in spite of the expected consequences. Priam honors *xenia* (guest-friendship) at the cost of inviting war with the Greeks. The Greek army camps out on the plain in front of Troy for ten years and fights a war that must have killed a higher percentage of combatants than World War I on the Western Front. There are grumblings in the ranks, but the officer class on both sides is willing to die in pursuit of honor. Hector's comments have already been cited. His nemesis Achilles chooses a young death with honor over old age without it.

The most telling proof of socialization may be the final book of the *Iliad*, where Achilles and Priam meet and Achilles returns the body of his son Hector to him. The two adversaries break bread, grieve together, and lament their fates. Their encounter is fraught with danger; Priam has to sneak through the Greek lines and camp with his cart and trust that Achilles will receive him with honor. Achilles must repress his anger, which threatens to break through and erupt in violence against Priam. Yet he is restrained by his commitment to *xenia* and respect for Priam: "Achilles marveled, beholding majestic Priam. His men marveled too, trading startled glances."[25]

Sensing his moment, Priam pours his heart out to Achilles: "Remember your own father, great godlike Achilles – as old as I am, past the threshold of deadly old age!"[26] A few lines later, he attempts to transfer some of Achilles' feelings about his father to himself: "Revere the gods, Achilles! Pity me in my own right, remember your own father!"[27] Achilles softens and Priam exclaims: "Let us put our grief to rest in our own hearts, rake them up no more, raw as we are with mourning... So, the immortals spun our lives that we, we wretched men live on to bear such torments – the gods live free of sorrows."[28] Achilles agrees to exchange Hector for the proffered ransom and instructs his retainers to wash and wrap his body for its journey back to Troy. Achilles and Priam share a meal, the symbolic end to mourning for Greeks.[29] The narrator suggests that together, but not individually, they have attained honor and wisdom.

This moving encounter does not and cannot end the war. Both men grieve for their loved ones, recognize the destructiveness, even the irrationality, of their conflict. They lack a discourse they could use to construct new identities for themselves that would allow them to terminate the war and escape their fates.[30] Priam returns to Troy, knowing that it will be destroyed and he and his family along with it. Achilles realizes that he must soon die and prepares for his final battle, proleptically brooding about his father mourning his death. The two heroes are victims of socialization and the language and habits it inculcates. The epic ends on a somber note but leaves listeners-readers with the idea that they, unlike Achilles and Priam, might be able to forge new identities and even use the text as a vehicle toward this goal.

A first cut at causation suggests that agents are constrained by their societies. Individual behavior is very predictable in Bronze Age epics because cultural norms are so robust. These are progressively less so in classical Athens and the modern West, and behavior becomes correspondingly less predictable. In the *Iliad*, actors want to achieve self-esteem and do so by favorably impressing others who matter in their society, or among its adversaries. To do this they must perform well in fighting, athletic competitions, and, when possible, display leadership. Desire for success provides the incentive to discipline themselves, not only to repress fear and face danger but also to restrain anger, envy, sexual arousal, and any other emotion that interferes with heroic actions and wise governance. Emotion is nevertheless important; it provides the incentive for this discipline and the careful exercise of instrumental reason. It contributes in another more fundamental way. Aristotle explains socialization with reference to the friends we make and the role models they offer. Friends are people we admire, feel close to, and want to please. If they are good friends and role models, that is, if they personify the positive values and practices of their society, our emotional attachment to them provides an additional incentive to act the way they do.[31]

Reason enters into the picture initially in instrumental form. It mediates between our desires and the world. It tells us not only how to achieve our goals but how to do so most effectively. There is a deeper level of reason, what Aristotle calls *phronēsis* (practical wisdom). It involves a sophisticated understanding of what goals are beneficial and realistic and what means are most appropriate for achieving them. Reflection on our actions and those of others can strengthen – or undermine – our commitment to conform to the values and practices of society.

Plato contends that when reason loses control over emotions antisocial behavior is the result.[32] This is true for Paris, Helen, Agamemnon, and the suitors in the *Odyssey*. Paris and Helen indulge in inappropriate sexual and material desires, as do the suitors. Agamemnon gives in to envy and arrogance, but, most importantly, for ancient Greeks, he transgresses his status; this latter offense is the defining condition of hubris. Like Paris, Penelope's suitors violate *xenia* (guest-friendship) in this instance by moving uninvited into Odysseus' household, consuming his food and wine, and demanding that his wife – whom they assume is a widow – wed one of them. They also plot to murder Odysseus' son Telemachus. Paris and Helen are restrained by comparison. Paris is shamed into fighting by Hector, although rescued by Athena from death at the hands of Menelaus. Helen conforms to the customs of *xenia* once Priam admits her to Troy because she has no alternative. She is also disciplined by Athena, who tells her in no uncertain terms what is otherwise likely to happen to her. Nobody reins in the suitors because Laertes and Telemachus are powerless to do so and Odysseus is still making his way home.

To some degree antisocial behavior is also explicable in terms of society's values. It is the very opposite of what society demands. We cannot predict in advance who will control their emotions and live up to social expectations and who will give in to temptations like envy and passion. However, we can readily account for the existence of these divergent patterns of behavior with reference to the dominant values of society. Rebellion is as patterned as conformity. Both kinds of behavior, as Durkheim would note, serve to teach people how to behave.

Gods. In the *Iliad* and *Odyssey*, gods act for many of the same reasons as humans.[33] They are moved by sexual passion, friendship, sympathy, rivalry, jealousy, envy, anger, and flattery. Poseidon is envious of Zeus' dominant position and thinks he and his brother should be equally honored.[34] Athena and Hera are envious of Aphrodite because Paris chose her as the most beautiful goddess. Apollo, Artemis, and Aphrodite support the Trojans, and Hera, Ares, Athena, and Poseidon, the Greeks. The gods are as bad as humans at controlling their emotions, possibly worse. They are at odds with one another and use humans as proxies in their games of one-upmanship.

Homer characterizes his heroes as "the race of men who are half gods" (*Hēmitheōn genos andrōn*).[35] They accomplish feats of strength beyond the capability of ordinary humans. Trojans and Greeks still resemble toy soldiers moved about by young boys, to be killed or protected as their fancy dictates. The third-century Roman philosopher and critic Longinus astutely observed that Homer made his men like gods and his gods like men.[36]

Humans attribute the Trojan War to the gods. Aphrodite has promised Helen, the world's most beautiful woman, to Paris in return for judging her the most beautiful goddess. King Priam tells Helen: "It is not you I blame – I blame the gods – who brought on me the misery of the war with the Achaeans."[37] Penelope expresses the conventional wisdom when she tells her husband that Aphrodite has made Helen willing to run off with Paris.[38]

Once the war begins, the gods line up on opposite sides and intervene to influence the outcome of battles and of the war.[39] In person or behind the scenes, their actions often precede human ones and appear to offer an explanation, not only for their behavior in some instances but also for its outcome. Apollo, Artemis, Ares, and Athena have Odysseus dissuade the Greeks from withdrawing and giving up the fight. Aphrodite saves Paris from Menelaus and rescues him from the battlefield, as Apollo does Aeneas. Athena persuades Pandarus to fire an arrow at Menelaus to destroy the truce between the two sides. Zeus maintains neutrality for the most part but can be cajoled into supporting one god or another in the course of the war. The war turns against the Greeks when Zeus the Thunderer orders the gods to stop interfering in the fighting. Using Aphrodite's magic girdle, Hera seduces Zeus and, while engaged in lovemaking, he forgets temporarily about the war.[40] Poseidon uses the opportunity to enter the fray and compels a Trojan retreat. Postcoital Zeus observes the rout, threatens to beat up Hera, and orders Poseidon from the field. Apollo then comes to Hector's aid, breathing vigor into him, and once again the Trojans gain the upper hand.[41] Later, Athena arranges for Priam to enter the Greek camp and for Achilles to overcome his rage and agree to the return of Hector's body to his father.[42]

The gods are less visible in the *Odyssey*. With the possible exception of the opening of book 15, they also appear in disguise. They are nevertheless implicated at every stage of Odysseus' *nostos* (return home). Penelope explains to Odysseus that all their prior unhappiness was due to the gods.[43] Zeus does his best to keep the victorious Greeks from returning home but then relents and facilitates the voyage to Ithaca of "the long-suffering" Odysseus.[44] Poseidon, the maritime counterpart to his brother Zeus, also plays a major role. He is furious with Odysseus for blinding his son Polyphemus. He does his best to prevent him from reaching Ithaca, although he knows he cannot prevail over the consensus of the gods.[45]

Athena is enamored by Odysseus and becomes his patron, perhaps because he personifies the intelligence and craftiness for which she is so admired. Odysseus is a master of deceit, disguise, deception, clever stratagem, and martial skill. Homer describes him as *polumētis* (wily) and *polutropos* (man of many turns), another way of saying ingenious. When he finally reaches Ithaca, he has a relaxed and even jocular interchange with Athena. Replete with erotic undertones, it is the most intimate encounter in Homer between a god and a mortal.[46] Athena helps Odysseus overcome challenges on his voyages. In Ithaca, she enhances his disguise as an old beggar, helps him devise his strategy vis-à-vis the suitors, and misdirects their javelins so they miss Odysseus, Telemachus, and their retainers.[47]

In contrast to the *Iliad*, Zeus does not take sides in the *Odyssey* but is invoked by humans and is supportive of human justice. This difference is signaled at the outset of the epic, where Zeus proclaims that humans invite disaster by ignoring divine warnings.[48] Zeus reappears at the end as well, where he justifies the death of the suitors and urges Ithacans to recognize once again Odysseus as their king.[49] Humans receive their just deserts. Odysseus' crew members sign their death warrants by killing and eating the sun god's cattle.[50] Aegisthus invites retribution by Orestes for ignoring divine warnings, bedding Orestes' mother, and killing his father.[51] The suitors deserve their slaughter because of their violation of Odysseus' household and attempts to murder Telemachus.[52] Those who people the *Odyssey* believe the gods to be the enforcers of retributive justice. Homer provides examples with Agamemnon, Briseis, and Mars and Helios and the oxen.[53] Zeus' punishment of Aegisthus for ignoring his admonition to steer clear of Clytemnestra is another example.[54] Antinous – which can be translated as "he who lacks all mind or insight" – is a striking exception; he has no fear of the gods, but other suitors do. They worry aloud that they prowl the earth in disguise to discover justice and injustice.[55]

The strong formulation takes Homer's gods as having meaningful agency. They push people into doing things they would not otherwise do, or restrain from doing things they would, and use them for ends they do not grasp or understand. When not restrained by gods, people possess the freedom to act but sometimes succeed or fail in their chosen ends because of divine intervention. Most often, divine intervention is behind the scenes and not evident to those being manipulated. On occasion, it is visible, as with Aphrodite's efforts to ensure that Paris swerves away when Menelaus' spear penetrates his shield, that his sword shatters on his helmet, and that the helmet strap breaks when Menelaus grabs it and tries to pull him down. Aphrodite then removes Paris from the battlefield in a thick mist she creates around him.[56]

If humans are at the mercy of the gods, they might enhance their agency by appeasing or appealing to them. In both epics, people routinely sacrifice to the gods and pray for their favorable intervention. In the first book of the *Iliad*, Chryseis pleads successfully with Apollo to secure the return of his daughter. Apollo let his arrows fly against the Greek troops for nine days until an assembly convinced Agamemnon to return his daughter.[57] In the *Odyssey*, people repeatedly make offerings at feasts to seek divine favor or avoid their wrath.

The strong formulation encourages us to see the physical and social worlds as ultimately explicable. Almost everything has a cause, even if these causes may not always be accessible to us. Exceptional people are invariably the offspring of nobles, and truly gifted ones are likely to descend from kings or gods or both. Dramatic events, like storms and favorable winds, are the work of the gods. So too is the Trojan War, the many years it takes Odysseus to reach Ithaca, and his triumph in battle against the far more numerous suitors. Prior to this engagement, Athena tells Odysseus: "I will not leave you alone for long: I am eager for the fight."[58] More ordinary events are also influenced by the gods. Those who die peacefully in old age are said to have been pierced by Artemis' arrows. Belief in the gods and their powers primes bard and listener-reader alike to look for causes to make sense of the world.

Reason and emotion enter Homer's narratives in different ways. As noted, Olympians appear to be ruled more by their emotions than by reason. As the gods are prime movers of so much of the narratives, Homer suggests that it is their emotions that set causal narratives in motion. On occasion, divine passions are directly aroused by human actions, as when Paris judges Aphrodite to be the most beautiful goddess or when Odysseus slays Polyphemus. More often, feelings of hostility, envy, sexual passion, and sympathy arise in the course of interactions among the gods themselves. Humans get drawn in as surrogates, as, for example, when gods seek to get back at other gods by thwarting or killing humans they favor and protect. This is the root cause of Odysseus' delay in reaching home. His successful *nostos* is attributable in the first instance to his craftiness, but Homer's narrative encourages us to believe that the deeper explanation is Athena's frequent intervention on his behalf.

The gods are supposed to be superior to humans, and they are in their beauty, powers, and immortality. Humans recognize these differences, and Homer has people routinely describe others who are handsome or talented as "godlike." Perhaps because they are so powerful and do not have to concern themselves with mortality, they are more unrestrained in giving rein to their passions. We observe a parallel phenomenon among people. Agamemnon is in a position to abuse his authority and does with Chryseis and then Briseis. He only relents when reined in by a higher power, Apollo, and Apollo's intervention only works because Calchas, a seer, is able to interpret the plague as punishment for Agamemnon's violation of nomos. The Greeks then pressure Agamemnon to return Chryseis to her father.

Achilles is the other most powerful human in the *Iliad* and he too lets his passions override his reason. His anger at Agamemnon prompts him to withdraw from the fighting and subsequently refuse the gifts that Agamemnon sends to appease him. His rejection is a direct parallel to Agamemnon's rejection of the ransom Chryses offered for his daughter. As a result, the Trojans get the upper hand in the fighting. Later in the epic, Achilles' passion for Patroclus leads him to run amok when the object of his affections is killed by Hector. He only regains his humanity and comes to his senses through the intervention of Athena, who arranges his meeting with Priam.

The *Odyssey* provides us with more extreme human contrasts, most notably between Odysseus and his crew and Odysseus and the suitors. Odysseus survives, and his crew does not, because he is able to restrain himself and spurn temptations. He is also a quick learner, which others are not. Earlier, in book 9, on Cyclops' island, Odysseus' men try to restrain him from exploring but he insists on it and gets some of them killed. He learns in the course of the next ten years, progressing inter alia from wiping out the Cicones in book 9 to killing no one from then on and restraining himself in other ways. Odysseus becomes increasingly focused on his long-term goal of *nostos* and is able to subordinate everything else to it. Reason also enters the picture. Odysseus is brighter than his crew and the suitors and able to calculate risk more effectively and devise strategies to reduce it.

The suitors are the most malign humans in either epic. Reason has lost control of their appetite and *thumos*, and they do not learn and exercise more restraint but rather less as the epic progresses. Odysseus' encounter with the suitors is the principal event in both epics where a god intervenes to uphold justice. Athena's support for Odysseus nevertheless appears to be motivated as much by her strong attachment to him. Emotions cut both ways in the epics for gods and humans. They can strengthen people's commitment to society and its values but also loosen them. Achilles gives evidence of both effects.

The importance of emotions and their divergent consequences heighten their causal importance but at the same time make prediction more difficult. To construct a compelling causal narrative, Homer must describe the contexts that prompt emotional arousal, just as he must introduce the gods in their context to explain events like the Trojan War, reversals in fortune of Trojan and Greek heroes, and Odysseus' travails on his journey home. Readers are left with the strong impression that everything has a cause but that they are unlikely to discover it in the absence of the "inside" knowledge of men and gods accessible only to the bard.

The weaker formulation of the gods treats them as more metaphorical than real. They are stand-ins for the reflexive self and the vagaries of fortune and nature that shape events. We have no evidence about how Homer's contemporaries understood the gods. We do know that until the classical era there was little open questioning of the gods, and it was generally done cautiously. It is reasonable to assume that most people believed in the gods and their day-to-day interventions in their affairs. This was probably also true in fifth-century Athens. It seems unlikely that Socrates would have spoken in favor of banning Homer for his unfavorable portrayal of the gods if he had thought his contemporaries did not take them seriously. Nor would the Athenian court have condemned Socrates to death for undermining belief in the gods. More evidence is offered by Protagoras, who got into trouble because he was believed to be an atheist. Many Athenians were convinced that their city would be punished by the gods if they did not punish or expel him.[59] At the same time, various accounts of Sophists and their teachings and Thucydides' account of the decline of ancient simplicity nevertheless suggest that many intellectuals and educated people no longer took seriously Mt. Olympus and its alleged denizens.[60]

There are few places in Homer where we get a glimpse of inner conflict. At best, we see heroes weighing options, bucking up their courage, and planning their next move, as Odysseus does when he struggles to better the odds in his upcoming confrontation with the suitors.[61] His indecision is not emotionally motivated; he is fully committed to killing the suitors and the maids who have consorted with them. By contrast, in book 1 of the *Iliad*, Achilles is about to act impetuously and draw his sword against Agamemnon when he is restrained by Athena. She appears at his side and promises him a reward for his constraint. In the weaker formulation, Athena is used to make listener-readers aware that Achilles is having second thoughts. He realizes that revenge is a dish best served cold and that he will gain more by acting later.

Other appearances of gods and goddesses signal internal debate about a course of action or the need for restraint. The Olympians also allow us to access reflections by actors about how others view them. Aphrodite tells Helen how others hate her and what is likely to happen if she does not behave as instructed.[62] Athena brings Priam to confront Achilles, and he evokes sympathy and empathy. Modern novelists would portray these encounters as struggles in which characters listen to and perhaps reflect on and respond to conflicting emotions. Greek literature lacks the convention of internal dialogue, so invokes gods and goddesses to achieve the same effect.

The weaker formulation still prompts us to approach the world in causal terms, but more cautiously. Without the active intervention of the gods – and before the advent of modern science – there were no known mechanisms to explain most natural phenomena. How, for example, does the sun cross the sky, as it appears to do on a daily basis, if not towed by someone's chariot? Things either just happen or have causes beyond human ken. For the most part, people feel more comfortable with the latter.

If the gods are reduced to metaphors, human agency is greatly enhanced. Individuals are responsible for their actions and must accept the consequences. They can no longer credibly explain away bad behavior as a compulsion instilled in them by a god or goddess or the result of a momentary blindness for which the gods were responsible. Human beings nevertheless require such excuses and are often sympathetic to those who invoke them. In Bavaria, a *Föhn* (a dry wind coming down a mountain slope) has long been accepted as an excuse for all kinds of unacceptable behavior, including murder.

With greater agency, social outcomes become correspondingly more difficult to explain. Decisions that lead to bad outcomes might be attributed to a lack of information or bad luck. More troubling is seemingly sensible decisions and behavior in conformity with ethical norms that produce negative, even tragic, outcomes. Without the gods, there is no longer any explanation for luck beyond the ability of clever people to position themselves to take advantage of opportunities that arise. Romans and Machiavelli would later call this *fortuna*. Fate also becomes problematic if there are no gods to ordain and enforce it. Sophocles wrestles with these problems and I return to them in the second section of this chapter where I argue that tragedy was a means of working them through.

Making the gods metaphorical solves one problem but gives rise to multiple new ones. For sophisticated people in classical Greece, the Homeric gods must have appeared increasingly incredible as they were juvenile in their behavior, unable to control their emotions, and rarely even-handed enforcers of justice. Yet dispensing with them left humans alone in a hostile world in which there was no longer any cosmic order on which norms and justice were thought to depend. This dilemma would resurface in the Enlightenment and give rise to its own set of culturally conditioned responses.

Social. The *Iliad* and he *Odyssey* are about humans and gods. Most behavior is presented as the result of individual choice, although not necessarily free choice, as people are influenced by their peers, society, and the gods. Homer's perspective is focused on individuals because he is constructing adventure narratives about heroes and villains. However, his understanding of cause is at the social level.

Homer does not explicitly account for behavior with reference to social norms and expectations. We must infer this connection. Using norms and the expectations they generate to explain behavior gives the appearance of circular reasoning, but it is only an appearance. Behavior and norms are largely self-reinforcing. By tacking back and forth between behavior and the norms that appear to motivate it, we can derive a reasonable understanding of the character and robustness of the society. Equally important in this regard is the violation of norms, its frequency, the degree to which violators are stigmatized, and its consequences for them. The more behavior reflects social norms and expectations, the fewer violations, the more stigmatized violators, and the more seriously they take their stigmatization, and thus the greater the social determinants of behavior.

Using the weaker formation, the gods can be imagined as personifications of social pressures and constraints as well as metaphoric representations for the passions that most frequently prompt their transgression. They intervene to enforce social codes and to prevent heroes from violating them but also on occasion to encourage violations. Aphrodite makes Helen receptive to Paris' overtures as promised compensation for his judging her the most beautiful goddess.[63] Athena stirs up Pandarus' hatred of the enemy to destroy the fragile Greek-Trojan truce.[64] How can the gods be the upholders of justice when they are willing to encourage its subversion – and seemingly for their own selfish ends?

This seeming contradiction makes sense if Homer is using the gods to develop an immanent critique of an honor-based warrior society. Immanent critique is a method of discussing culture that aims to locate contradictions in society's rules and systems.[65] Such a critique could try to show how the very values that sustain such a society have the potential, perhaps the likelihood, to destroy it. This is because these values are Janus-faced in their implications, as *xenia* demonstrably is. Adherence to nomos also requires control, if not repression, of powerful human impulses. They inevitably break through. If gods are stand-ins for norms and pressures to conform to them, they also provide incentives to violate them by liberating the passions these norms and social pressures attempt to hold in check.

According to Greek myth, the Trojan War was attributable to Paris' elopement with Helen, wife of King Menelaus of Sparta. This was a gross violation of Menelaus' honor and of guest-friendship (*xenia*), a convention common to most traditional societies.[66] In Greece, the obligation to receive guests was considered so important that hospitality was made one of the suffixes of the father of the gods: Zeus Xenios.[67] In return, guests must not abuse their hosts' hospitality or overstay their welcome. *Xenia* creates bonds across households that created and sustained the Greek community. In the *Iliad*, it is responsible for numerous connections among people that enable both coalitions to form. It ends mortal combat between Diomedes and Glaucus when they discover they are guest-friends. In the *Odyssey*, whenever Telemachus and Odysseus arrive in some foreign land, they expect to be welcomed because of existing guest-friendships or *xenia* that will establish new ones. The succoring, even honoring, of guests, makes possible Odysseus' successful return home, just as its violation prolongs it.

In the *Iliad*, Menelaus defends his honor by attempting to punish Paris and regain Helen. He asks Zeus to grant him revenge "so that any man born hereafter may shrink from wronging a host who has shown him friendship."[68] The Greek conception of honor required those connected to Menelaus by ties of obligation, family, or guest-friendship to come to his aid.[69] On the Trojan side, guest-friendship moves King Priam to offer refuge to his son Paris and the woman he has run off with, even though he and most Trojans thoroughly disapprove of the pair and recognize that their presence is certain to provoke war with the Greeks. Like every convention, *xenia* has the potential to sustain or undermine society.

Paris, Helen, and Agamemnon are the most extreme violators of *nomos* in the *Iliad*. Paris grossly abuses *xenia* by running off with his host's wife and treasure. Helen commits adultery and theft. Agamemnon in turn abuses his authority. If Paris and Helen are responsible for the Trojan War, Agamemnon's violation of nomos is responsible for the war between himself and Achilles. The two conflicts are reinforcing and threaten the survival of honor society and its values.

Warfare is the principal activity of Greek and Trojan society. It justified their existence and hierarchies and allowed heroes to gain honor through success in battle. Toward this end, warriors must engage others with similar values who are equally committed to fair engagements, even to allowing the other side to strike first. Homer's world requires men to face death with equanimity. Emotional involvements threaten to undermine the commitment to fight and sacrifice oneself, as do extended dalliances that keep men away from the battlefield. Paris is the perfect antihero.

While not a coward, he takes no pleasure in fighting and absents himself from battle to frolic in the sack with Helen. In their values and behavior, they are mirror opposites of Hector, Paris' brother, and Andromache, his sister-in-law. Their violations problematize the values of warrior-based honor societies by showing how difficult they are to sustain in the face of human nature.

Agamemnon is our third negative role model. All honor societies have rule packages and they become thicker as one ascends the status ladder. Those at the top receive honor and office (*timē*) and, in return, must exercise self-restraint and provide security and material advantages to those who honor them.[70] Agamemnon, leader of the Greek expeditionary force, is unable to control his emotions and abuses his power by making unreasonable claims on others. He refuses to return Chryseis to her father after being offered ransom, triggering a deadly plague among his forces. He is then compelled to release Chryseis to her father but insists on taking Briseis from Achilles as compensation, triggering a feud that removes Achilles and his Myrmidons from the fighting.

Agamemnon's behavior is in part a reflection of his personality and inability to constrain his envy. Today, we would describe him as immature and insecure and would not be surprised if he tapped out nasty tweets about Achilles on a daily basis. His behavior, and that of Achilles, is also a response to a structural situation. Multiple hierarchies are a source of conflict when they compete for primacy. In warrior-based honor societies the king or chief is also expected to be the best fighter and military leader. In the *Iliad*, Agamemnon is a king and at the top of the Greek achieved status hierarchy. Achilles, repeatedly described by Homer as "the best of the Achaeans," is at the apex of the achieved hierarchy. If and when these hierarchies diverge, because there are different people at their apex, conflict is inevitable.[71]

Achilles can also be considered a negative role model. He is "the best of the Achaeans" because of his military prowess but is as sensitive about his status as Agamemnon. Nestor warns Achilles: "If you are the stronger, since a goddess mother bore you, Yet he is more powerful, since he rules over more."[72] Achilles has been awarded Briseis for his bravery in the raid in which she was captured. She is more than a sex object. She is a *geras*, a symbol of his status in the Greek community and one he believes he loses by giving her up to Agamemnon. He withdraws from the fighting, refuses recompense from Agamemnon, and puts the Greek army at risk.[73]

Achilles' rage flares once again after the death of Patroclus. He forbade him to go into battle; but Patroclus, feeling he would be shamed for avoiding combat, takes Achilles' helmet and body armor and enters the fray. Hector mistakes him for Achilles, seeks him out, and kills him.

Achilles is beside himself at his loss and becomes a warrior unrestrained by any honor code. He displays what Italians call *terribilità*, literally awesomeness, but with overtones of temper, pride, vehemence, grandeur, and arrogance. He captures and sacrifices a dozen Trojan boys. He slays Hector and defiles his body.[74] Warfare is violent and destructive and generates grief and anger that lead warriors to violate the code that makes honor possible. The quest for honor (*timē*) in Homer's Bronze Age world is a double-edged sword.[75]

Marx and Freud would later develop immanent critiques about capitalism and modernity respectively.[76] Homer was arguably the first person to make such a critique. He shows us how the very values and practices responsible for the success of the honor-based warrior societies are also fundamental causes of its decline. This critique also provides an underlying explanation for the behavior responsible for the Trojan War and that between Agamemnon and Achilles.

Sophocles

Sophocles wrote at the height of Athenian power and self-confidence. His Theban trilogy explores some of the principal tensions generated by the transition from *oikos* to polis and develops conceptions of reason and cause appropriate to them.

The Theban trilogy is not a trilogy in the strict sense of the term. The plays were written over a period of many years: *Antigone* in 442, *Oedipus Turannus* was first performed in 429, and *Oedipus at Colonus* was written in 406, near the end of Sophocles' life. Each play is independent of the others. The middle play is the first chronologically, the last the second in order of creation, and the first the third. They fit together as a whole but not without some inconsistencies.[77] I will analyze them individually but also collectively. The play of most interest to me is *Oedipus Turannus* because it explores agency versus fate, reason versus emotion, and problematizes cause.

Sophocles' treatment of these issues differs in important ways from Homer's. The gods are central figures in the *Iliad* and *Odyssey*. They interact with one another and with humans and intervene, openly or behind the scenes, to influence human outcomes. None of this happens in Sophocles. In the Theban trilogy, fate is sometimes related to the gods, but they are in the background, remote and inaccessible. Sophoclean characters believe in the gods, attempt to appease them, appeal to them for support or courage, and invoke them to explain outcomes. Yet the gods exist in their minds as they make no utterances or appearances in their own right. Sophocles also differs from Aeschylus in this respect. In his *Eumenides*, the Erinyes and Athena intervene directly in the course of human events.

The closest we come in Sophocles to a direct godly encounter is Apollo's advice to Oedipus at Delphi; but the god's words come secondhand from the priestess and are ambiguous in their meaning. Moreover, fifth-century Greeks knew that Pythia and others at the shrine were open to bribery. In the *Iliad*, people were often stand-ins for gods in the sense of being their agents, and conflicts between them were sometimes personifications of conflicts between gods. In Sophocles' plays, the gods are invoked as stand-ins for human laws and nomos, their defense, and also punishment for their violation. In *Antigone*, the older gods, the Erinys, defend families, women, and customary law. The newer gods, Zeus, his brothers, their consorts and progeny, are associated with men, the polis, its legislation, and judicial decisions. This same generational divide is evident in Aeschylus' *Oresteia*. It encourages us to understand the conflicts in these trilogies as something more than interpersonal squabbles and representative of change and, in particular, of the emergence and consolidation of the polis.

If there are behind-the-scene movers and shakers in Sophocles, they take the form of prophecies. They perform two distinct but related functions: They guide the immediate, and sometimes longer-term, behavior of actors and provide explanations for outcomes. Readers of the *Iliad* know that Calchas foretells that Agamemnon must sacrifice Iphigeneia to get a divine wind for the Greek fleet and, after arriving at Troy, must return Chryseis to her father to end the plague afflicting the Greek expeditionary force. Poseidon later assumes Calchas' form to prod the Greeks into battle at a favorable moment because Zeus, who supports the Trojans, has momentarily directed his attention elsewhere. By impersonating Calchas and speaking through him, Poseidon lends additional credibility to Calchas' prophecies by making him a spokesman for the gods. Sophocles also uses Calchas for this end; in his *Ajax*, Calchas tells Teucer that he will die if he leaves his tent before the sun sets.

Oedipus Turannus follows *Antigone* in the Theban trilogy but its events, as do those of *Oedipus at Colonus*, come before it, just as Oedipus precedes Creon as king of Thebes. This reversal gives prophecy an importance it would not otherwise have. Teiresias twice foresees exile for Oedipus, and Oedipus asks for exile when he discovers the truth about his parents.[78] He in turn offers a prophecy when he is led away from town.[79] *Oedipus in Colonus* opens with his pronouncement that his arrival at a sacred grove fulfills Apollo's prophecy that in such a sanctuary he would finally find rest.[80]

Oedipus curses his two sons and prophesizes their demise at one another's hands. This comes to pass in the battle that forms the background to *Antigone*.[81] The death of Antigone completes the destruction of his family, which we are encouraged to believe is attributable to the curse Oedipus has brought down upon it. Curse and prophecy are the threads binding the individual plays into a whole and provide an alternate explanation for Polyneices' rebellion against his brother, Creon's ban on his burial, and Antigone's suicidal violation of his decree. Her intended marriage to Haemon is forestalled by their joint death, which prevents the curse of Oedipus from being carried forward into another generation.

Prophecy drives the plot of *Oedipus Turannus* even more directly. As Oedipus grows to manhood with his adoptive family in Corinth, he hears gossip that he is not the son of Polybus and his wife, Merope. He asks the Delphic oracle about the identity of his parents but the oracle seems to ignore this question. He is told that he is destined to "mate with [his] own mother and shed with [his] own hands the blood of [his] own sire."[82] Oedipus still believes that Polybus and Merope are his true parents and, desperate to avoid this terrible prophecy, he leaves Corinth.

Oedipus is responding to a human rumor about his parentage, one the Delphic oracle refuses to confirm. As the tragedy proceeds and the prophecy is confirmed, we never learn whether it is divine or human in origin. Its validation tells us little because some of the other prophecies that come true originate with people, as does the curse Oedipus lays on his sons. Sophocles compels us to work out for ourselves the role of fate, why it exercises its hold on humans, and the extent to which it is a divine or human phenomenon.

There is another sharp difference between Sophocles and Homer. The Trojan War, as all Greeks knew, arose from Paris' abduction of Helen, and this was made possible by his earlier judgment that Aphrodite was the most beautiful of gods. So too is Achilles' death foretold and made known to him by his mother, an immortal nereid. Homer's prophecies involve the gods, as do so many human outcomes. Homer's listeners and readers are encouraged to think of fate and the gods as closely bound. People have agency but it is constrained by fate, and that appears to be a web woven by the gods.[83] Sophocles does not offer this easy way out for people who seek a refuge from agency. By leaving the origins of prophecies unclear, he encourages us to think about not only their causes but cause more generally. This is most evident in the case of Oedipus, where human calculation and agency, not merely anger, are necessary to fulfill the prophecy.

Chance is implicated in a way that it is not in Homer. Consider the unplanned encounter of Oedipus and Laius at the crossroads, the latter's road rage and death at the hands of Oedipus. In *Antigone*, the chorus tells Creon to release Antigone and then bury Eteocles.[84] He does as they suggest, but in reverse order. Antigone therefore has time to kill herself, and her death prompts Haimon to take his life. These outcomes require willful agency to achieve their desired effects. Laius had to provoke Oedipus, and he had to respond. Creon had to decide to act in a different order than instructed.

Laius' and Creon's actions were "in character," so we might consider fulfillment of the prophecies as contingent but hardly random. Laius was arrogant and aggressive, so likely to strike out at someone whom he thought should step aside. Creon consistently values his own opinion over that of others and insists on his total freedom of action. He equates law and authority with his own will. In *Oedipus Turannus*, the chorus proclaims that "arrogance and insatiable pride breed the tyrant."[85] Antigone characterizes Creon as a tyrant.[86] His fear of being seen as weak and his overconfidence in his judgment blinds him to the likely consequences of his actions. It was likely, perhaps predictable, that he would reverse the order of tasks when responding to the pleadings of the chorus.

Prophecy and fate are linked to nomos because so often they are realized by adherence to or violation of nomos. The Trojan War was the combined product of the abuse of *xenia* by Paris and Helen and the honoring of it by Priam. Violation of nomos is also an underlying cause of the tragedies of Thebes and Oedipus. As a youth, King Laius was the guest of Pelops, the king of Elis, and became the tutor of Chrysippus, the king's youngest son. Laius abused Pelops' friendship by either seducing or abducting Chrysippus, who, according to some accounts, killed himself in shame. Pelops laid a curse on Laius and his descendants.[87]

Nomos is more directly implicated in *Antigone*, where conflict, as in the *Iliad*, is the result of its violation and honoring. Yet there is a difference. People were expected to honor dead family members with proper burial rites. Creon was in his rights when he ordered the traitor Polyneices' body be placed outside the walls of the city, thereby protecting its citizens from pollution. His refusal to allow Polyneices subsequent burial was nevertheless extreme by fifth-century standards. In keeping with convention, Aeschylus has Polyneices buried outside the walls in *Seven Against Thebes* and *Phoenician Women*. This outcome avoids pollution but honors family. Creon was deeply invested in the matter and dwells at length on Polyneices "the traitor."[88] He also worries about the consequences of his will being flouted. "There is no greater evil," he insists, "than lack of rules. This is what brings cities to ruin."[89]

Violence is a central feature of these epics and plays. In the *Iliad*, the named dead number more than 100 and the unnamed dead are more numerous still. There is death in almost every episode of the *Odyssey*, culminating in the destruction of the suitors and disloyal serving girls. Death in Homer is more expected as the *Iliad* describes a war. Death is inflicted by adversaries, in battle or ambush. In the *Odyssey*, death is more random and the killers are not for the most part human beings until the final confrontation in Ithaca.

In the Theban trilogy, death is personalized in a way it is not in Homer. *Antigone* revolves around what to do with the corpse of one of the rebels and casualties on both sides set the stage for the play. The deaths that occur at the dénouement – those of Antigone, Haemon, and Eurydice – are all connected and more tragic because they are self-inflicted and responses to the actions of other family members. The same is true for Jocasta in *Oedipus Turannus*. Creon survives but may wish he had not. His wife Eurydice dies with a curse on her lips, calling Creon "killer of sons" – in effect, equating him with Oedipus.[90] Oedipus lives but blinds himself. Both men outlive their plays but as crushed and pitiable human beings. Their two houses come to resemble each another. Creon has gained the city of Oedipus only to suffer the fate of the house of Oedipus. Like Oedipus, Creon survives but without self-confidence or authority and with the recognition that he has been responsible for a tragedy. Antigone is the thread connecting the two skeins; Sophocles consistently used the metaphor of weaving in both tales.[91]

In Homer, violence is a means of gaining honor, and warriors are willing to risk death for this end. We feel sorrow for those who die but only a few deaths affect us emotionally. The most significant is Hector's because he leaves a family behind and we know his death is the prelude to the destruction of his father, wife, son, and city. We do not witness the deaths of Achilles or Agamemnon but know their fates. Achilles has no more right to live than Hector or anyone else he has killed and is reconciled to his death; he has chosen it over a long and boring life. Nobody will shed tears for the unappetizing Agamemnon when he gets his comeuppance for sacrificing his daughter. Deaths are the end product of causal chains, but also their initiator, a connection to which I will return.

For Homer, many deaths settle scores. For Sophocles, many deaths are self-willed and self-inflicted; those who take their lives would find it more painful to continue living. In *Oedipus*, Jocasta hangs herself because of the pollution her coupling has brought on her and her family. Oedipus survives but blinds himself, resigns the kingship, and becomes a beggar. His new role requires meekness and compliance in sharp contrast to his former assertiveness as king. He is now dependent on his daughter, who must act with wit and skill to keep them alive.

Antigone resembles Homer's Penelope but is far more independent. Like Penelope, she displays steely determination in the face of threat and, in doing so, acts like a male hero. She rejects Creon's authority and decides for herself what is more important. She acknowledges that she has buried her brother and faces up to the consequences unflinchingly, just as Sophocles' Ajax does. She nevertheless takes her own life in a woman's way after being shut up, by hanging herself as opposed to falling on a sword. Yet, like everything else in Sophocles, there is an ironic twist. Antigone's suicide is not an act of desperation but a final effort to thwart Creon. By taking her own life, rather than dying of starvation in her walled-up tomb, she pollutes the city.[92] She initiates a cycle of deaths: her own, Haimon's, and his mother's, Creon's wife. These events lead Creon to exclaim: "Ah, harbor of Hades, never to be purified! Why do you destroy me?"[93] Creon tried to avoid pollution for the city only to bring it on his own house. His assertion that he is being punished by the gods is best understood as a rationalization to escape responsibility for the consequences of his own freely chosen actions.

Antigone is violating a gender stereotype, and this might be considered a source of tragedy for her and her family; but then so is Creon. He is hypermasculine and unconstrained by any norms. He reveals his true character in *Oedipus at Colonus*, where he attempts to kidnap Antigone and Ismene to compel Oedipus to agree to be buried just beyond the borders of Thebes. In an assertion of brazen power and equation of justice with rightful possession, he proclaims: "I take what is mine."[94]

Creon encourages Antigone's gender violation by treating her as a man. His exchanges with her, and then with Haimon, degenerate into *stichomythia*: sharp, short exchanges, reminiscent of sword thrusts. Creon refuses to treat either interlocutor as anything other than a challenge. His anger overrides his reason, and he offers sharp rebukes rather than making serious arguments. Creon and Antigone's escalations are mutually reinforcing and lead to the triumph of passion over reason. Creon insists that "while I am alive, a woman will not rule!"[95] Yet he acts to make his fear self-fulfilling. Antigone has gained strength from looking after her father all these years. She is "masculine" in her commitment and exercise of power. Creon, in turn, becomes "womanlike" in his loss of power and submission. There is a double *peripeteia* in both plays. Aristotle defines *peripeteia* as *eis to enantion tōn prattomenōn metabolē*. This phrase has a certain ambiguity and can mean a complete reversal or a change into the opposite.[96] Both take place for Creon and Antigone.

Another significant parallel between Homer and Sophocles concerns *nostos*. In the *Odyssey*, Odysseus struggles to return home to Ithaca and must overcome the hurdles put in his way by Poseidon and his agents. He succeeds by virtue of his skill and Athena's help. *Oedipus* and *Oedipus at*

Colonus might be read as Oedipus' attempt to reach home. Odysseus is aware of his goal from the outset and increasingly focused on it. It is the underlying cause of all of his actions. Unlike many other Homeric characters, his commitment to his goal is unyielding and everything he does is subordinate to it. Oedipus by contrast begins committed to a goal and that commitment becomes the cause of tragedy. This divergence is also signaled by the direction of travel: For Odysseus, it is trying to return home, while Oedipus is leaving home and trying to get far away. Unwittingly he returns to his original home of Thebes, and his belated and unwanted recognition of *nostos* is the *peripeteia* and catalyst for his mother-wife's suicide, his blinding, and the curse on his family. Oedipus then leaves home on a journey with no destination; it is the voyage and not the end point that matters. There is an element of this in the *Odyssey*, a theme emphasized by the modern Greek poet C. P. Cavafy in his "Ithaka."[97]

The journeys of these heroes differ in fundamental ways. Odysseus knows all along where his home is. Oedipus has three successive homes, each of which supplants the other. He discovers what he comes to recognize as his real home only when he arrives at the sacred grove in the vicinity of Athens. His wanderings prior to his arrival there have been random. So too were those of Odysseus, but not by choice. We know everything about Odysseus' wanderings and nothing about those of Oedipus. Odysseus does not change during his long voyage. His intelligence, craftiness, physical prowess, and commitment to reach Ithaca are constants and serve him well. Oedipus undergoes a major transformation. He is metaphorically blind when he is able to see but only really begins to "see" when he loses his eyes at the climax of *Oedipus Turannus*. We assume that his change in status from king to beggar and the suffering and reflection it prompts are the catalysts for his change in character. By not allowing us to observe his transformation, it is more dramatic in its impact. By having Oedipus change in fundamental ways – something that never happens to Homeric characters – we are again invited to think about cause in novel ways.

Cause. All of Sophocles' plays interrogate cause. *Oedipus Turannus* offers the most explicit investigation in Oedipus' search for the cause of the Theban plague and what can be done to end it. Cause is more in the background in *Antigone*. However, theatergoers and readers are encouraged to figure out why Creon and Antigone act as they do and the extent to which their behavior and its consequences is a product of the curses of Laius and Oedipus. Both plays contrast agency with fate and raise questions about the relative responsibility of gods and humans for shaping fate and bringing it to fruition. The two plays approach these questions in somewhat different ways.

Both have multiple levels of causation. The first, and most evident, level is agency. All of the principal characters appear to have choices, and many make the wrong ones. Creon decrees the death penalty for anyone who buries Polyneices, Antigone buries her brother in violation of his orders, Oedipus flees Corinth, Laius succumbs to road rage, and Oedipus seeks refuge in Thebes and accepts the challenge of the Sphinx and then the kingship. Later, Oedipus sends Creon to Delphi, Teiresias tells Oedipus about his parentage, Jocasta hangs herself, Oedipus blinds himself, Antigone goes into exile with her father, and her two brothers have nothing further to do with him.

Are these actions meaningful evidence of choice? Sophocles offers something of a controlled comparison in the case of Antigone's burial of her bother. Her sister Ismene is horrified by her decision and urges her to obey Creon. Two women from the same generation of the same family make opposite choices. This would point to individual character, not context, as determinate. We can make the same argument about Creon, who spurns the advice of the chorus and the plea of his son and insists on the death penalty for anyone who buries Polyneices. His behavior violates convention and the norms of kingship.

Teiresias is more problematic. He tries to keep the truth about Oedipus' parentage a secret but blurts it out when summoned by Oedipus to appear before him. He is not intimidated by Oedipus – quite the reverse – so his behavior is all the more inexplicable. It might be understood as the seesawing of an old, frail, and blind man. Alternatively, it reflects intense internal conflict between his commitment to his city and its royal family. The latter explanation would have us interpret his choice as more situational than personal.

Oedipus is the most enigmatic character when it comes to agency, and deliberately so. As everyone knows, he desperately tries to avoid making a prophecy come true and in doing so fulfills it. Oedipus the detective solves a major homicide and saves the city; but he turns out to be the regicide and the necessary scapegoat. Agency succeeds but with unexpected consequences. One reading, perhaps dominant in the era the play was produced, is that, try as you might, you cannot escape your fate – and all the more so when it is decreed by the gods. A more agent-oriented account, focuses attention on Oedipus' free will. Nobody forced him to make the choices he did, nor were they determined by the situation.

Good arguments can be made for either reading but neither is sufficiently compelling to rule out the other. An emphasis on fate requires us to ask what it is and how prophecy functions as its mechanism? Perhaps complexities, twists and turns, and unlikely coincidences are the work of the gods – Zeus and Apollo – who read the future or arranged for it to happen. The argument is not circular because the prophecy is made before the outcome, but this ordering is, of course, an artifact of the plays. Its credibility relies on the same kind of belief in deities and their powers expected of Homer's listeners. In Homer, divine intervention does not do away with agency or free will; gods often have to intervene to get people to act in ways they would otherwise not and to forestall or reverse the consequences of their freely chosen behavior.

Sophocles' gods are invisible. As noted, his characters believe they manipulate events behind the scenes, but Sophocles gives us no evidence in support of this. Paradoxically, the power of the gods might appear all the stronger to some because of their invisibility. There is no human action that can unambiguously be established as freely willed. An alternative reading is that, by keeping the gods out of the action, but very much in people's minds, Sophocles makes the strongest case for fate.

Meaningful agency requires that people's lives are not predetermined at the macro or micro levels. They make their own choices, and some of them must be free choices. To read Sophocles as supportive of this kind of agency, we need to consider the motives behind young Oedipus' initial and most momentous decision to flee Corinth. Its genesis is an unsubstantiated rumor from a drunken companion that his father and mother are not really his parents.[98] The man calls him a bastard (*plastos*), a word that also means formed, molded, constructed, or fabricated in the sense of being contrived.[99] This second set of meanings raises the prospect that it is a false allegation or that Oedipus' response, and his very identity, is something constructed by him rather than being predetermined.

What really seems to trouble Oedipus is the thought that he might be a bastard and the shame he associates with it. "That stung me," he admits. "I was shocked. I could barely control my anger. I lay awake all night. The next day I went to see my father and mother. I questioned them about the man and what he said. They were furious with him, outraged by his insult, and I was reassured. But I kept hearing the word 'bastard' 'bastard' – I couldn't get it out of my head."[100] Oedipus' reaction suggests that he fled more to escape the onus of illegitimacy than the fear that he would somehow murder his father and have sex with his mother.

Oedipus has the gift of great intelligence. Yet he gives no evidence of having thought through his problem, in the way that, say, Odysseus certainly would almost have. He makes speedy decisions, often without much reflection. Creon warns him that "those who are quick [*hoi tacheis*] to think things out are not infallible."[101] Oedipus' flight, which sets all in motion, is less a product of reflection than of anger. Freud – who thought long and hard about this play – could readily diagnose it as an act of denial. If there is any truth to the rumor about Oedipus' parentage, staying put in Corinth would have been the most likely means of defeating the prophecy. There is no reason to think Oedipus would act toward them as the prophecy suggests, deliberately or accidentally. If Oedipus turns out to be adopted, this is all the more reason to stay in Corinth where he is safe and sheltered from the outside world. Once on the road, he has no way of knowing whom he will encounter or what kind of relationship these people might have to him.

Oedipus is again moved more by emotion than reason at the crossroads where he kills Laius. As he tells the story:

> The man was riding in a chariot
> And his driver tried to push me off the road
> And when he shoved me I hit him. I hit him.
> The old man stood quiet in the chariot until I passed
>   under him,
> The he leaned out and caught me on the head with an ugly
>   goad –
> its two teeth wounded me – and with this hand of mine,
>   this hand clenched around my staff,
> I struck him back even harder – so hard, so quick he couldn't
>   dodge it,
> and he toppled out of the chariot and hit the ground, face
>   up.
> I killed them, every one of them. I still see them.[102]

Oedipus' behavior is understandable because he has been attacked. He still might have left Laius alive on the ground after striking him down. Instead, he kills all of his attendants and, we can infer, gives Laius a coup de grace. Already smarting from one totally unexpected insult – being called a bastard – he is primed to respond with force to the next one: a nasty sucker punch from a man with a cudgel. Once he associates shame with his past – and, given the curse, his future as well – this sensitive young man, whose behavior may be over the top, is nevertheless acting in character.

Oedipus' intellect only comes to the fore once he arrives in Thebes. He solves the riddle of the Sphinx and later attempts to discover the cause of the plague. He arrogantly proclaims: "I will begin the search again, I will reveal the truth, expose everything."[103] He sends Creon to consult the oracle at Delphi, who tells him that Apollo insists that they must discover Laius' murderer and drive him from the city and rid it of pollution. Oedipus' inquiry resembles a legal proceeding; he summons and interrogates witnesses to bring the truth to light. He asks more questions than are posed in any other tragedy.[104]

Metaphors about hunting, tracking, discovery, revelation, and conjecture now predominate. They underline Oedipus' belief that the world can be understood by evidence, reasons, and inference. He looks for signs (*semeia*, *symbola*) that will lead him to the murderer. They will bring to light what is now hidden. Oedipus pursues the task with intelligence and diligence but initially and understandably avoids any inferences that would incriminate him. In the end, he succeeds brilliantly and with tragic consequences for himself and his family.

The inquiry sheds light on Oedipus' character, not only on his intellect. He resembles his father and brother-in-law in important ways. He is intelligent, swift in thought and reaction, but arrogant and deeply suspicious. Like his father, he is quick to take offense and to lash out. Like Creon, he is prone to sniff out a plot against him when there is none, suggesting more than a touch of paranoia. Also like Creon, he wants to do well by his city. He is more open to advice, although, again like Creon, hostile to it at first. Creon and Oedipus refuse to heed Teiresias or the chorus, and herein lies the proximate cause of their tragedies. However, Oedipus, at the urging of Jocasta, takes no action against either Creon or Teiresias.

What can we conclude about agency? Oedipus believes that he is an undeserving victim of fate, but then most people responsible for their predicaments convince themselves that they could not have acted otherwise. Oedipus complains to the chorus: "Apollo, Apollo. It was Apollo, always Apollo, who brought each of my agonies to birth. No one's hand struck me but I, wretched I." It is interesting that the word *outis* (no one) is the same word Odysseus uses to Cyclops: "no man put your eye out."[105] Fate for Oedipus is a convenient rationalization.

Oedipus believes he is motivated by reason and takes pride in his intelligence. His unrelenting pursuit of the truth through interrogation and inference leads to the discovery of his origins and the related causes of the Theban plague. In truth, Oedipus is moved at least as much by his passions. In Corinth, he is driven by shock and outrage and, in Thebes, by insecurity; he wants to prove himself an able king – to himself as much as to the citizenry; and perhaps to Jocasta too, an experienced older woman who is now his wife. He is also motivated to solve the riddles of the Sphinx and plague because they are challenges he cannot pass up without losing his self-esteem. For these reasons, he remains obtuse to all hints from Teiresias and pleas from Jocasta that his inquiry is likely to reveal some very unpleasant truths.

Like Creon, Oedipus' efforts to preserve his authority undermine it. Both men are victims of their hubris, and that in turn is an expression of passions unchecked by reason. In the first stasimon of *Antigone* – the Ode to Man – the chorus proudly enumerates human accomplishments.[106] They famously describe humans as *deina*, which means wonderful but also fearful, strange, uncanny, and terrible. The play explores the double meaning of *deina* through the character of Oedipus, where the wonderful – intelligence, skill, commitment – are transformed into the terrible. The chorus, which has the final word, blames the tragedy on the lack of "good sense."[107]

A first cut at cause – at the individual level – prompts caution about what actors think and say. When Oedipus does well, as, for example, when he overcomes the challenge of the Sphinx, he claims full credit and attributes his success to intelligence and courage. When he is responsible for tragedy, he also accepts responsibility and gouges out his eyes. Creon and Antigone consistently minimize their agency and exaggerate the constraints they face while at the same time minimizing those affecting others. They attribute their behavior to the constraints they face but interpret that of adversaries as indicative of their character. Creon and Antigone succumb to what psychologists call the fundamental attribution error.[108] The truth of the matter is that much of what Oedipus, Creon, and Antigone do is a matter of choice and reflects *their* character. They are moved by their passions and show lack of judgment.

There are several competing explanations for the fundamental attribution error. The most interesting for our purposes may be Lerner and Miller's concept of the "just-world phenomenon."[109] This is the belief that people get what they deserve and deserve what they get. Attributing others' bad luck or failures to dispositional rather than situational causes satisfies our need to believe the world is fair. We are motivated to see the world this way because it reduces perceived threats and gives us a greater sense of security, so long as we consider ourselves to be virtuous.[110] The just-world hypothesis may be responsible for the tendency of people to blame and disparage victims of accidents, rape, domestic abuse, and other mishaps.[111] They may also look for faults in a victim's prior behavior to explain and justify what has subsequently befallen them.[112] By doing so, they increase their confidence that such events will not happen to them.

The just-world phenomenon predicts how others are likely to respond to Oedipus after he blinds himself; and this is indeed how Creon's and Oedipus' sons respond. Sophocles has an intuitive understanding of psychological phenomena that would not be theorized and documented for another 2,500 years. His play is psychologically realistic in a double sense: The actions of its protagonists reflect now well-documented responses to insecurity and stress and the reactions of others to them appear to be rooted in either the fundamental attribution error or the just-world phenomenon.

Given the self-serving nature of Sophoclean characters' beliefs about agency and fate, we should not be misled and convince ourselves that they represent those of the playwright's. Contrary to their claims, Sophocles characters give ample evidence of agency and free choice. Those who come to tragic ends have made relatively free choices and are in some way responsible for their fates. This is true even of Jocasta. She handed the newborn Oedipus over to Laius. Either she or Laius pierced and pinned the infant's ankles together. Laius then instructed his chief shepherd to expose the infant on Mount Cithaeron. Like Oedipus, Jocasta and Laius acted to forestall a prophecy but unwittingly helped to realize it. They could be considered more responsible than Oedipus because their intended killing was of a child and fully volitional, and they had ample time to reflect on what they were doing. The most innocent character who comes to a bad end is Haimon, who loves Antigone and his father and tries unsuccessfully to intercede on her behalf; but then, all of the unnamed citizens who die from the plague in Thebes are also innocent victims.

The strongest case for agency made by Sophocles is through Oedipus after tragedy strikes. He blames his fate on Apollo but insists that he alone is responsible for blinding himself: "I, nobody else, I raised these two hands of mine, raised them above my head, and plunged them down, I stabbed out these eyes."[113] Until this point in the play, he believes his life and destiny to have been *dysdaimon* (arranged by an evil spirit), presumably by Apollo. Ironically, he expects, or at least hopes, to become more independent when blind, even though he is superficially more dependent on others. For him, sight is no longer "the sweetest thing on earth."[114]

Aided by his daughters, Oedipus walks from polis to polis as a beggar. In the course of his wanderings, he develops insights into himself and life that almost certainly would never have developed if he had remained a successful king. Oedipus no longer commands but submits. He opens his ears to what others say. At the outset of *Oedipus in Colonus*, he explains: "Place me here and make me sit, so that we can learn Where we are: for we have come in order to learn As strangers from the locals, and to accomplish whatever we here."[115] Ironically, by humbling himself before others, he achieves meaningful agency.

In Athens, Oedipus displays sensitivities to the customs and needs of others. They reflect his better appreciation of life and the human conditions; he has reached an accommodation with life that ancient Greeks described as *sōphrosunē*. In his opening speech in *Oedipus in Colonus*, Oedipus expresses his contentment with his bare-bones existence. He is one "who asks little and gets less, though even less than little is enough."[116] He has learned to be "easy with whatever happens."[117] This is in contrast to his opening speech in *Oedipus Turannus*, where he proclaims: "Everybody, everywhere knows who I am I am king: Oedipus the King."[118] In the same speech, he asserts his intention to solve the riddle of the plague. "As king, I had to know. Know for myself, know for me."[119]

At the outset of *Oedipus Turannus*, the priest describes Oedipus as "more like a god than any man alive."[120] Oedipus comes to believe this himself; he pays lip service to the gods but is supremely confident about his ability and worth in comparison to other men and perhaps the gods. This is one reason why the rumor about his birth stings so deeply. The priest's observation turns out to be ironic, as do the many references by Oedipus and others to seeing what lies in front of them. In *Oedipus in Colonus*, the eyeless Oedipus sees better than other humans. Like the blind Teiresias of the *Iliad* and the Theban Teiresias, he has the gift of prophecy. Rather than searching for the truth he is now in a position to enlighten others: "Words. When I speak they will see everything," he tells the stranger he encounters at Colonus.[121] He has also become godlike in his ability to curse and bless. He curses his two sons, and they will die as he foresees.[122] He blesses Theseus and Athens and hopes that his burial site will become "a defense mightier than a multitude of shields."[123] Sophocles' Athenian contemporaries could only hope that Oedipus' blessings proved as successful and powerful as his curses.

The grove where Oedipus has sought refuge and where he will soon end his life is sacred to the "all-seeing" Eumenides, or well-wishers. Formerly the Erinyes, ancient gods who defend family and custom, they pursued Orestes for killing his mother but were transformed into the well-wishers after his trial in Athens. So too has Oedipus been transformed, in his case from a pariah into well-wisher. This transformation is signaled by the many parallels and ironies between *Oedipus in Colonus* and *Oedipus Turannus*.

First in appearance and importance is Oedipus' initial encounter with the chorus, who has come from Athens to warn him to stand back and not pollute the sacred grove. It can be likened, at least superficially, to his encounter with Laius at the crossroads. The chorus shouts "Move! Stand off! Step away from where you are!"[124] Oedipus does not become enraged, as he did when Laius ordered him to turn aside, but asks Antigone for her advice. "Be as careful, father, as those who live here," she warns, "we should yield to what's needed: we should listen."[125] Oedipus meekly replies: "take hold of me, so."[126] Instead of lashing out at lightning speed – to, admittedly, a double assault – Oedipus moves at a snail's pace from the grove to a rock ledge.

The chorus then asks Oedipus some pointed questions. Who is he? Where is he from? What is the cause of his pain? These are the very questions Oedipus asked himself in *Oedipus Turannus*. His unremitting pursuit of answers was the catalyst for tragedy but also necessary to save his city. Now, in a rare triple repetition, he pleads with the chorus to stifle its curiosity. "Do not! Do not! Do not! Ask who I am."[127] By *not* posing questions and seeking the truth, Oedipus gains meaningful agency. He has not escaped fate but become reconciled to it. He implores Antigone: "Let us not struggle against necessity."[128] This outlook is most evident in his acceptance of death, forecast by Apollo, which he tells his daughter will take place "in a shelter for strangers, a sanctuary of the Holy Ones."[129] Oedipus not only accepts this prophecy, he wills it. He pleads with the Eumenides: "Now grant me, Goddesses ... some limit, some end to my life's journey."[130]

Oedipus largely escapes his social identity in the final play. He has not become an autonomous individual in the modern sense but rather someone who has in part transcended himself by establishing a more general appreciation of humanity and his place in the world. He is able to contrast the laws of society with his understanding of himself. He is no longer the sum of the roles that he plays or what others think of him. In Greek eyes, he is closer to a "thing" than a man. Creon calls him "this cursed, naked holy thing, hide him from the earth and the sacred rain and the light."[131] He has become *agos*, both cursed and sacred.

Oedipus has developed a sense of himself independent of his role and of how others categorize, treat, or think of him. It is this understanding that provides the insight and authority he aspired to but never achieved as king. It may also explain the otherwise profound irony that a despised outcast, who violated the most fundamental family norm, now finds sanctuary in a grove sacred to its defenders.[132] There is a second equally remarkable irony here. Greeks considered people who had no polis, or were not citizens of the one in which they resided, as not capable of living up to their human potential because they were denied identities and the possibility of developing and expressing uniquely human qualities through civic participation. Oedipus has become such a person but at the same time he appears to have achieved a higher form of humanity. Suffering and learning enabled this transformation.

The agency Sophocles has granted Oedipus is to accept what fate has in store with him. It is a defining attribute of *sōphrosunē*. Reason and emotion have combined to raise Oedipus to this enlightened and happier state, just as they were responsible for his tragedy. The difference is in the nature of the emotions (empathy and feeling for others versus *thumos* and anger) and reason (instrumental versus deeper forms of reflection). In modern psychological parlance, we might say that Oedipus has overcome his ego and the barriers it erects to understanding and happiness and by this means has opened himself up to the feelings, needs, and opinions of others.

Sophocles' understanding of agency finds a modern resonance in Nietzsche's *Amor Fati* (love of fate).[133] It involves freely willing what is necessary. For Nietzsche, you must do this an infinite number of times. It reflects and reaffirms contentment with one's life, or at least acceptance of it, and a willingness to live the same life over and over for eternity. By this means, it reconciles free will with necessity. The mechanism involved is reversing past and future, by willing the past that has already happened. The will is, of course, a Christian invention; and Nietzsche is trying to escape from the aporia to which he believes Christianity and metaphysics have led. This troubled sense of alienation, rebellion, and pessimism is missing in Sophocles. He had a deep attachment to Athens and its culture, lived during the high-water mark of its cultural and political achievements, and was optimistic about its future. Unlike Nietzsche, he was reconciled to his life and would happily have lived it again.

It is not far-fetched to read an element of autobiography into *Oedipus at Colonus*. The play was written in the last years of Sophocles life – he died in 406 BCE – and produced posthumously. Like Oedipus, Sophocles is looking back on his life and bidding farewell to it and perhaps using Oedipus to confer his own blessing on his beloved city. It is an interesting blessing: he wishes that the "all-seeing Helios" will confer on Theseus and his kin "a life like the life I've led in old age."[134] Sophocles presents its ruler Theseus as a thoughtful and sensitive man and Athens a deserving polis because of its leader's honor of *xenia*. Oedipus' encounter with Theseus stands in sharp contrast to that with his son Polyneices. The choice of Colonus for the setting of the last play in the trilogy is also significant because it connects playwright and subject. Oedipus comes to die in the town of Sophocles' birth.

From agency I turn to prophecy, the next level of cause. It is closely related to fate because it is the vehicle by which fate makes itself known. In *Antigone* and *Oedipus Turannus*, fate is in the hands of the gods. In *Oedipus Turannus*, the chorus says humans are not good prophets.[135] By contrast, "the gods grasp everything." They are *xunetoi* (intelligent and far-seeing).[136] In *Oedipus Colonus*, I suggest, the distinction between gods and humans is at least partially bridged as Oedipus displays some ability to foresee the future and has attained the gift of prophecy.

Four related prophecies drive the action of the trilogy. The ur-prophecy is the curse on Laius for his abuse of *xenia* in his treatment of King Pelops' son. It promotes celibacy between Laius and Jocasta and the laming and attempted killing through exposure of the baby who is the product of their one sexual congress. Next is the prophecy that Oedipus will kill his father and bed his mother. In *Oedipus in Colonus*, Oedipus tells us that Apollo has told him that he would meet his end in a sacred grove. Finally, there is Oedipus' prophecy that his two sons will kill each another.[137] *Antigone* takes place after Oedipus' death. Sophocles' characters take all these prophecies seriously and believe they originate with the gods. The exceptions are Polyneices and Eteocles. They are almost entirely in the background and about whom we receive only secondhand information aside from the former's short encounter with his father in *Oedipus Turannus*.

Sophocles gives us no evidence that prophecies originate with gods. The curse on Laius is an ancient myth of uncertain origin and was most likely laid on him by King Pelops. When Oedipus is born, Laius consults an oracle and learns that he is doomed to perish at the hands of his son. Oedipus later hears a variant of this prophecy, which he tries unsuccessfully to ascertain the truth of by going to Delphi.[138] The Pythia may be speaking for Apollo but perhaps only for herself. The third prophecy is said to originate with Apollo, but we only have Oedipus' word for it, and the fourth prophecy is unambiguously human in origin. We are free to attribute these prophecies to gods or men.

Can agency be reconciled with prophecy? I provided a partial answer to this question in discussing Oedipus' transformation. A second, more general response can be formulated by considering the relationship between fate and character. Homeric heroes seek *arēte* (excellence), which is achieved through action, usually, but not always, on the battlefield. *Arēte* is a quality of character. It is revealed, not created, through action. In Sophocles' plays, tragic outcomes reveal the destiny or *daimon* of heroes. The hero struggles to become who he is, as Antigone and Oedipus certainly do.[139] Considerable agency goes into making heroes and making their destinies manifest. Put another way, Oedipus does not so much fulfill a prophecy as come to the realization that it has been fulfilled by virtue of who he is. Apollo, moreover, never predicted that Oedipus would discover the pollution for which he is responsible or that he would gouge out his eyes and choose the life of a homeless beggar.[140]

Heraclitus expressed this relationship when he described character as "destiny" (*ethos anthropoi daimon*).[141] The relationship between character and fate is akin to an equation; we can treat either term as causal. I think Sophocles chose to emphasize fate because it seems more appropriate to what he and his contemporaries regarded as the "pre-modern" era in which tragedies are for the most part set. Fate is also a vehicle interrogating justice, an issue very much in the forefront of Athenian thought and politics. Prophecies that come true can be understood by his audience as the unfolding of justice. Believers can attribute them to the gods and come away from the theater more committed to time-honored norms.

Skeptics, of whom there were certainly some among the wealthy, educated citizenry, could conjure up more complex readings.

There is a striking and revealing intergenerational parallel between Oedipus and his parents. They do what they can to escape the prophecies hanging over their lives and, in the process, realize them. This is not at all the case with Polyneices and Eteocles, who ignore the curse laid on them by their father and make it come to pass by virtue of their stubbornness, lack of reflection, incaution, and single-minded pursuit of power. They nevertheless share in common with the young Oedipus an exaggerated concern for honor and the need to assuage their anger through decisive action when challenged or thwarted. Creon also displays these characteristics and, to some extent, Antigone does too, although honor in her case is that of her brother and her family. These similarities across characters that are ultimately responsible for their tragedies prompt us to consider a third and deeper level of analysis.

People differ in natural gifts and character. The former is channeled by society and the latter shaped by it. The anger that drives the protagonists of the Theban trilogy – and of Homer's epics – is very much a product of the honor-based warrior society in which they live. It emphasizes standing achieved through prowess on the battlefield but also wisdom used for the common good. *Thumos* trumps appetite. People compete for standing and feel good about themselves to the degree they are respected by others. Failure to be recognized provokes fury, as it does for Homer's Achilles and Sophocles' Ajax. For the latter, it prompts suicide as the only means of regaining honor.

According to Aristotle, anger is accompanied by pain and pleasure; the former because a slight that arouses anger diminishes one's dignity and the latter from the anticipation of revenge. Aristotle defines anger as something that is "properly felt when anyone gets what is not appropriate for him, though he may be a good enough man. It may also be aroused when anyone sets himself up against his superior."[142] Aristotle quotes Homer to the effect that revenge is "Sweeter ... by far than the honeycomb dripping with sweetness."[143] Anger is the dominant emotion of a *thumos*-oriented society, just as envy is in appetite-based ones. It leads to the kinds of ill-considered and intemperate behavior responsible for Sophoclean tragedy. The character of the society inhabited by Laius, Oedipus, Creon, Eteocles, and Polyneices is the root cause of tragedy. It motivates them to act in predictable, if destructive, ways, and tragedy is compounded by how others are primed to respond to their provocations.

Aristotle tells us that people suffer pain when they cannot gain revenge for challenges, slights, and humiliations.[144] Anger is accordingly not an appropriate response to affronts from people who are more powerful than we are because it is unlikely that we can gain revenge. We can, Aristotle suggests, experience this pleasure vicariously when these offenders receive their comeuppance by other means.[145] Many, perhaps the majority of, Athenian citizens attending the festivals at which tragedies were performed were in such a position. They were relatively powerless in their society, subject to a variety of humiliations, and accordingly forced to quell any anger that rose up within. By watching tragedies, seeing the powerful yet self-centered receive their comeuppance must have been very satisfying. Dispensing justice not only underlined the value of norms but it also helped to win votes for playwrights in competitions.

Finally, we must consider the role of chance and luck (*tuchē*). Social science considers luck something outside of its theories and, ever since Hume, has thought to minimize its importance.[146] Ancient Greeks viewed chance and luck as an expression of the divine order, not a negation of it. Oedipus just happens to drink with a loose-mouthed and thoughtless companion and to meet his father at a crossroads where one of them must give way. His journey brings him to Thebes as opposed to any number of other poleis where he might have sought refuge and made a new live for himself. Earlier, his survival as a baby depended on his chance discovery by a shepherd or, in some accounts, being given to the shepherd by the servant sent to expose him on the mountain.

At least some seemingly chance events might be accounted for with reference to the character of the people involved. It is predictable that Creon, when following the advice of the chorus, would deal with Polyneices first and Antigone second but not that this choice would mean that Antigone dies and that Haemon kills himself before an effort is made to liberate her.[147] Other absolutely critical events, most notably the meeting at the crossroads, appear truly random. The chorus admits as much, describing Laius as the victim of bad luck.[148] The last chorus of *Oedipus in Colonus* extols luck as the source of happiness (*eudaimonia*).[149] Similarly, in *Oedipus Turannus*, Jocasta exclaims: "Luck is everything. Things happen. The future is darkness. No human mind can know it."[150] However, she says this to distract her husband from prophecy and to encourage him to live for the day – as indeed he would do in *Oedipus in Colonus*.

Sophocles' plays are the product of careful design that involve interwoven narratives, connected by language and plot, with hints from the chorus at the outset, and often later, about what is to follow. They are a masterful blend of reason, design, and purpose that set in motion – most notably in *Antigone* and *Oedipus Turannus* – multiple, largely independent chains of causation that produce tragic outcomes when they come into confluence. The plotlines and the reality they purport to describe are thus overdetermined at their core but depend on agency and contingency for their effects.

At a still deeper level, *Oedipus* could be read as a play with a predetermined outcome. Oedipus insists on knowledge and clarity about everything that happens to him and every problem he confronts. He wants a rational foundation for his existence and will accept neither mysteries nor half-measures. Such a person is almost certain to act in self-defeating ways, and all the more after initial success further convinces him of his godlike abilities. If indeed Sophocles intended Oedipus to be read as a stand-in for Athens, and perhaps even for Pericles, as Bernard Knox suspects, then he is offering a critique of the hyper-rationalism of late fifth-century Athens.[151] It will lead to tragedy for Athens just as it does for Oedipus. Oedipus is a misfit in Bronze Age Thebes but Pericles is certainly an expression of fifth-century Athens. Oedipus is unique but Pericles is very much a product of his society. Sophocles' play offers no structural account of Oedipus and his fate but the play might be said to provide one for Athens and its fate. It has to do with a society's overvaluation of reason and the overconfidence to which success leads.

Sophocles compels us to use reason to understand his plays but they also caution us about reliance on this faculty. Oedipus resembles the attentive playgoer or critic who searches for clues to make inferences about the design and meaning of the work. Oedipus ultimately discovers the truth about himself and life more generally: There is no purpose to it and no explanation for it. Sophocles contrasts the search and discovery in his plays with what is found and thus plays reason off against the irrational and catastrophic outcomes to which it can lead. The servant who discovers Jocasta dead and Oedipus blind rushes onto the stage crying out: "wailing, madness, shame, death, every evil men have given a name."[152]

Conclusion

Homer offers a layered take on cause with three different levels – agents, society, and gods – and these levels are generally reinforcing. The principal uncertainty concerns the gods: To what extent are they fully independent actors or stand-ins for the inner self? Are they responsible for contingency, good and bad luck, and otherwise inexplicable outcomes? Understandably, Homer is not interested in cause as a concept in its own right but rather as a vehicle for exposing the tensions of warrior-based honor societies. It helps to demonstrate how the values on which they are based also threaten to destroy them. This happens because people act in terms of them, as do Menelaus, Priam, and Hector, or because they feel unduly constrained by them, rebel, and cut themselves free from ethical restraints, as do Paris, Helen, and Achilles.

People have choices. The most meaningful concern the degree to which they conform to their rule packages and live up to social expectations. Paris, Helen, and Agamemnon do not and their behavior fuels personal and international conflicts. Agamemnon does what is expected of him when he sacrifices his daughter Iphigenia to gain the wind necessary for the Greek fleet to depart for Troy. It is the catalyst for his wife to take a consort and murder him on his return. Homer does not describe these events but they would have been well-known to those who listened to bards reciting his epics. It is yet another example of conformity to nomos being as destructive as its violation.

Homer's epics prompt us to think less about the nature of cause and more about its agents. To the extent he addresses cause, it is in the reasons he provides for agents to act as they do. For gods and humans alike, these almost invariably concern their sense of honor, loves, jealousies, envies, and competition for standing. What the gods can do, and humans cannot, accounts for natural phenomena like storms and thunderclaps and chance, which are so important in shaping human outcomes of all kinds.

Regardless of whether we conceive of the gods literally or metaphorically, they function in both epics to drive home the extent to which we are not the masters of our fates. Our lives are affected by beings or things out of sight, unknown, and often implacable. It is the rare human like Odysseus who is able to finesse or surmount life-threatening challenges. He only does so with the direct help of a god and he is still subjected to multiple, unpleasant, and life-threatening situations. Homer's epics teach us that self-restraint is the best, but by no means necessarily effective, means of minimizing personal tragedy.

Homer's gods are active agents. Sophocles' gods are remote. To the extent they intervene in human affairs, it is through prophecies, but we never know if these prophecies are of divine or human origin. Jocasta is deliberately vague; she speaks of voices that "gave shape" (*diorisan*) to a future in which Laius would be killed by his son.[153] Other Sophoclean characters treat the gods as distant but knowing observers. The chorus in *Oedipus Turannus* tells us: "Zeus and Apollo know, they understand, only to see, the dark threads crossing beneath our life."[154] It may be that those invocations of divine intervention in Sophocles – and in Euripides too – are intended to make us consider why people really act as they do.

The shift from *oikos* to polis reduced the importance of the gods and also led to them being presented more unambiguously as defenders of justice. Where there is conflict among the gods, it is no longer personal and attributable to envy but to different understandings of justice. In Aeschylus'

Oresteia, the Furies are primal defenders of the family, its reproduction, and survival. They pursue Orestes for killing his mother. Apollo has urged him to kill his father's murderers, and, at his trial on the Areopagus, Athena votes to acquit him. The Furies – now the Eumenides – are very much present in the background of *Oedipus in Colonus*. They have not changed. Oedipus calls them "the daughters of the fears, of the dark!"[155]

Sophocles is fascinated by cause but has no interest in developing a single, logically consistent formulation that can be used to make sense of the world. Nor does he seem to care whether cause is a feature of the world or human artifice, a question that has attracted considerable attention since the time of David Hume. Rather, he is interested in what people think about cause and the purposes it serves for them. He accordingly offers us an analysis of cause at two levels: what people believe and what a more detached inquiry might suggest.

Cause for Sophocles remains elusive, as does almost everything else in his corpus. There is perhaps an intended parallel between his plays and life: The more we think we understand key features of either, the more we succumb to dangerous illusions. However, we cannot do without cause because, to get on in the physical and social worlds, we need some beliefs about how they work. For Sophocles, these beliefs are always of questionably validity. We accordingly confront a quandary. Disillusionment about gods and causes can incapacitate us, while unquestioning belief in them will almost certainly mislead us. For Sophocles, the most sensible approach to life appears to be one that hovers uneasily between belief and skepticism, clarity and obscurity, self-confidence and doubt, search for causes and answers, and acceptance of what has happened. This kind of understanding is far removed from that of modern social science but arguably has real benefits in confronting the world.

In Homer, social causes supplement and generally reinforce individual and family-based ones. In the *Iliad*, social solidarity and conflict are both attributable to the core values of a warrior-based honor society. These values are presented as immutable and as having divine backing. Heroes, their women, and lesser folk, like Thersites, must learn to live with socially defined constraints. Ordinary people have few choices, their fate being determined by nature and the actions of others. Elites are not much better off because rule packages are thicker and more constraining the higher one ascends the social ladder. Consider Agamemnon having to come to his brother's aid to regain Helen and punish Troy and having to sacrifice his daughter for the sake of the expedition. Or Achilles, Ajax, and Odysseus, dragged away from home to fight a far-off foe against whom, Achilles repeatedly reminds anyone who will listen, he has no quarrel.

For the most part, Homeric heroes subordinate their private interests to social ones. Socialization is sufficiently strong that private interests are largely socially determined. This is true of Menelaus' desire to regain Helen and punish Troy for giving her and Paris refuge, Achilles' preference for a short life in which he achieves great fame over a long one in which he does not, and Hector's decision to fight Achilles even though it is likely he will be killed and Troy defeated. Achilles' withdrawal from the fighting and Agamemnon's taking of Briseis are notable exceptions.

In Sophocles, causal relations across levels of analysis are more complex. This is because self-interest is stronger. In *Antigone* and *Oedipus Turannus*, Creon's and Laius' desire to retain power and enjoy its privileges overrides all other considerations and leads them to act in ultimately destructive ways. The same is true of the Oedipus in pursuit of his origins and those of the plague. The differences with Homer are subtle but important. Socialization is still dominant in the sense that it determines the goals actors seek. The difference has to do with means. The competition for honor has increasingly given way to one for standing. The rules governing competition and the exercise of power are more frequently violated. What counts is power, not how it is achieved or maintained.

There is a corresponding rise in hypocrisy. Sophoclean characters, in contrast to most of their Homeric counterparts, convince themselves that they are acting in the communal interest. Creon's decision not to allow the burial of Polyneices is motivated by anger, but he defends it on the self-serving grounds that it is necessary to preserve authority and civil order. Oedipus has never been honest with himself or others about his motives. Even at the end of his life in Colonus, he is still trying to convince himself that he was innocent of murdering his father and bedding his mother because he did not know who they were at the time.[156] In *Ajax*, Sophocles presents a more hypocritical Agamemnon and Menelaus than Homer does, and they are called to task for it.[157]

These differences may have to do with the different societies of Homer and Sophocles. Homer's world is more that of the *oikos* and Sophocles that of the polis.[158] Aeschylus' *Oresteia* symbolizes the emergence of the latter and the corresponding shift in responsibilities, but the overlap between family and city is still very evident in *Antigone* and *Oedipus*. The world in which gods and values were taken at face value, if not always followed, has given way to the more problematic world of the polis. Values differ and compete within and across poleis. In many cities, the basis of power has shifted away from kingship to oligarchy and, in some, to democracy. Authority and office are based less on inheritance and physical prowess and more on political skills, rhetoric, and guile.

Sophocles' plays are set in Bronze Age Greece, and some of his characters (e.g., Ajax, Agamemnon, and Odysseus) are from the *Iliad*. He offers a different take on them and one more fitting with the world of the polis. The contrast between his Ajax and Odysseus and those of Homer are revealing. Homer's Ajax is a shield, "the bulwark of the Achaeans," who stands firm, cannot be moved, and defends a position with all his might. In *Ajax*, Sophocles depicts its eponymous hero as obstinate and old-fashioned and whose hubris in the form of overconfidence in his military prowess is responsible for his tragedy.

Homer's Odysseus succeeds because of his consummate practical intelligence and social skills. He is strong but strategic, wily, at times duplicitous, willing to retreat when it is advisable, always focused on his goal but open to different means of attaining it. If Ajax is a hedgehog, Odysseus is a fox. In the Rumble in the Jungle, Ajax would be George Foreman and Odysseus Muhammad Ali. For all these reasons, Pindar loathed Odysseus and thought the age of heroes died with the suicide of Ajax.[159]

Sophocles portrays Odysseus more sympathetically than he does Ajax. Unlike Creon, Odysseus pities his fallen enemy and intervenes to convince Menelaus to allow him a proper burial. He empathizes with Ajax: "the poor wretch, though he's my enemy. He's yoked to an evil delusion, but the same fate could be mine."[160] Agamemnon accuses Odysseus of acting out of self-interest: "It's all one then, and each man works for himself."[161] Odysseus admits as much: "There is reason in that. Who else should I work for?"[162] He is nevertheless moved by empathy as well and respect for tradition. He warns Agamemnon that denying Ajax his burial would be "against the laws of god."[163]

This kind of exchange is unimaginable in Homer. With Sophocles, we are in a different world in which intelligence, political nous, and rhetorical skill count as much as brute force. For all these reasons, Odysseus is better adapted to the age of the polis. Oedipus, who formerly aspired to the role of bulwark of Thebes, has reached the conclusion late in life that efforts at permanence of any kind in a world of uncertainty are doomed. Nowhere is the truth more applicable than in Athens. The city's survival in the face of two Persian invasions was the result of Odysseus-like skills. The Athenians chose to fight at Marathon because marshes and mountainous terrain prevented the Persian cavalry from supporting their army. Miltiades, the Athenian general, ordered a general attack against the Persian infantry-bowmen. He reinforced his flanks, luring the Persians' best fighters into his center. The inward wheeling flanks enveloped the Persians, routing them. The Persian army broke in panic toward their ships, and large numbers were slaughtered. At Salamis, Themistocles tricked the Persians into a sea battle and at the precise hour when the tides would play havoc with their formation.

Belief in a world of precipitous change is one that required a new understanding of cause, to which Sophocles makes an important contribution. He offers a more complex and nuanced understanding. Events are likely to have multiple rather than singular origins, and these causes usually operate at multiple levels of analysis. Outcomes depend more on chance. Causes may be hidden – as the plague in Thebes was at first – and, even when they are seemingly unearthed, they still lend themselves to competing interpretations. More disconcertingly, some things just happen, as Jocasta suggests. Searching for their causes can lead us in circles and threaten to make us more confused and uncertain about ourselves and our social environment.

We cannot help but search for causes in the world of the polis. Social, economic, and political life are more in flux and present the kind of challenges that are no longer best addressed through physical prowess and unyielding commitment to people, positions, or traditional values. Odysseus is the new role model, and his tactical skills – in battle, politics, and social relations – depend very much on reading the motives and behavior of others and, more fundamentally, on a deeper understanding of other actors and the world they populate. Fifth-century Greeks have accordingly become more reliant on fathoming causes to negotiate their world but paradoxically in an era when this is much more difficult to do.

In Sophocles works, we see an early version of what Thomas Haskell calls "the recession of cause." In the late nineteenth century, increasing social interdependence coupled with increasing geographic scope meant that events could no longer be explained with reference to local causes. Rather, they had to be understood with reference to a broader, unseen set of forces and conditions.[164] Something similar is going on in fifth-century Athens, and with similar cognitive consequences that Sophocles helps to negotiate.

Notes

1. Plato, *Republic*, 10.607a2, *Theaetetus*, 152e4–6.
2. Immanent critique has its roots in the dialectic of Georg Wilhelm Friedrich Hegel and the criticisms by Karl Marx. Today it is strongly associated with the critical theorists such as Theodor Adorno.
3. Reviewer A of this manuscript, in particular.
4. Nietzsche, *Genealogy of Morals*, p. 80.
5. Wittgenstein, *Tractatus*.
6. Lebow, *Cultural Theory of International Relations*, chaps. 2–3.
7. Williams, *Shame and Necessity*, pp. 57–58.

8. Rawlings, *Semantic Study of Prophasis*.
9. Thucydides, *History*, 1.23.5–6. Tompkins, "Aitia in Thucydides," notes forty-four uses of the term in Thucydides.
10. Plato, Republic, 441c1–2, 441e4, 442c5–6, 580d7–8, 8505d11–e1; Aristotle, *Nicomachean Ethics*, 1098a4, 1102b13–31, 1147b25–28 and b31–35, 1148a8–9, 1247b18–19, 1378a20–22, and *Rhetoric*, 1369b16–19, 1370a18–1370b4.
11. Aristotle, *Nicomachean Ethics*, 1338a1.
12. Ibid., 1334a20 and *Economics*, 1345a16.
13. Freud, "Dostoevsky on Parricide."
14. See Chapter 4 in this volume on Hume for elaboration.
15. Konstan, *Pity Transformed*; Konstan, *Emotions of the Ancient Greeks*; Konstan and Rutter, *Envy, Spite and Jealousy*.
16. Homer, *Odyssey*, 2.40–430.
17. Ibid., 1.338, 1.338, 17.418.
18. Parry, "Language of Achilles."
19. Lebow, *Cultural Theory of International Relations*, chap. 4 for these comparisons.
20. *Iliad*, 6.640–666.
21. Kant, "Perpetual Peace," and *Anthropology from a Pragmatic Point of View*; Schneewind, "Good out of Evil"; Molloy, *Kant's International Relations*, pp. 94–96, 100–111.
22. Homer, *Odyssey*, 1.338, 4.259–264, 17.418.
23. Ibid., 16.435–451.
24. Ibid., 9.158–161. Agamemnon tells Odysseus to speak to Achilles:
All these things I might grant him if he leaves off his wrath.
Let him yield: Hades is, I say, implacable and relentless,
For this reason the most hateful of gods to men:
And let him surrender to me, since I am the more kingly
And inasmuch as I claim to be to be his senior.
In 9.225–320, Odysseus repeats a large part of Agamemnon's speech to Achilles but knows not to recite its condescending conclusion. Achilles spots the hypocrisy and responds, "I hate like the gates of Hell the man who thinks one thing and says another" (lines 323–324).
25. Ibid., 24.567–568.
26. Ibid., 24.567–573.
27. Ibid., 24.588–589.
28. Ibid., 24.610–614.
29. Ibid., 24.740–745.
30. Parry, "Language of Achilles" argues that Homer does not make a language of his own but draws from a common store of poetic diction. It is a product of bards and a reflection of society. Neither Homer in his role as narrator nor the characters he dramatizes can speak any language other than the one that reflects the assumptions of heroic society – assumptions beautifully and serenely enunciated by Sarpedon in book 12. Achilles has no language with which to express his inner thoughts and disillusionment. He does this by misusing the language he has at his disposal. He asks questions that cannot be answered and demands that cannot be met. He uses conventional expressions

31. Aristotle, *Nicomachean Ethics*, books 8–9.
32. Plato, *Republic*, 439d1–2, 553d4–7, 571c8–9, 579d9–10.
33. Kearns, "Gods in Homeric Epics."
34. *Iliad*, 15.185–195.
35. Ibid., 12.23.
36. Longinus, *Sublime*. 9.7.
37. *Iliad*, 3.168–172.
38. *Odyssey*, 23.219–224.
39. *Iliad*, 7.16–83, for example.
40. Ibid., 14.154–360.
41. Ibid., 14.361–522.
42. Ibid., book 24.
43. *Odyssey*, 23.210.
44. Ibid., 116–179, 5.27–43.
45. Ibid., 1.68–79.
46. Ibid., 13.221–452. In 3.221–225, Nestor tells Telemachus that he has never seen a god display such open affection as Pallas Athena has toward Odysseus.
47. Ibid., book 22.
48. Ibid., 1.7–9, 1.32–43.
49. Ibid., 24.477–509.
50. Ibid., 1.7–9.
51. Ibid., 1.32–43.
52. Ibid., 22.35–41, 23.63–67.
53. *Iliad*, 1.1–40 and *Odyssey*, 12.262, 348, 363.
54. *Odyssey*, 1.25–30.
55. Ibid., 17.484–486.
56. *Iliad*, 3.340–382.
57. Ibid., 1.33–168, 1.444–467.
58. *Odyssey*, 16.170–171.
59. Diogenes, *Lives of Eminent Philosophers*, 9.51.
60. Thucydides, *History of the Peloponnesian War*, 3.83.
61. *Odyssey*, 20.1–26. Also, Tydeus in the *Iliad*, 8.188–192.
62. *Iliad*, 3.3111–3115.
63. Or so Helen alleges, *Odyssey*, 4.259–264.
64. *Iliad*, 4.84–478.
65. Immanent critique has its roots in the dialectic of Georg Wilhelm Friedrich Hegel and the criticisms by Karl Marx. It is also associated with the critical theorists such as Theodor Adorno.
66. Kant, "Perpetual Peace," pp. 105–108, describes *xenia* as probably the most universal form of conduct.
67. Finley, *World of Odysseus*, pp. 99–101, on guest-friendship in the Homeric world; Homer, *Iliad*, 3.351–354.
68. *Iliad*, 23.199–201.

69. Seaford, *Reciprocity and Ritual*, pp. 13–25, on gift-exchange in the *Iliad*. Taplin, *Homeric Soundings*, pp. 56–58, on the problematic nature of these obligations.
70. Lebow, *Cultural Theory of International Relations*, chaps. 2–3.
71. Linton, *Study of Man*, p. 115, on achieved and ascribed status.
72. *Iliad*, 1.280–281.
73. Ibid., 9.155–524.
74. Ibid., 22.394–503, 23.17–24.
75. Ibid., There is an additional, cruel irony in Patroclus' death. Achilles is upset about his loss of honor in book 1. Zeus promises to provide this in his exchange with Athena at 1.505–510. However, at 15.60–77 he adds that this recompense will come at the cost of Patroclus' life. Scholars have noted that both "honor" and "punishment" are words describing payment, and the Greek words *poinē* and *timē* go back to the same Indo-European root, k^wey, meaning "payment." Achilles does get his payout.
76. On Freud, see his *Civilization and Its Discontents*.
77. Burian and Shapiro, "Foreword," vol. 1, p. viii.
78. *Oedipus*, 1451–1454.
79. Ibid., 1455–1457.
80. *Oedipus at Colonus*, 96–128.
81. Ibid., 1770–1772.
82. *Oedipus*, 707–725 for Jocasta's account of the prophecy.
83. Dodds, *Greeks and the Irrational*, chap. 1, on the extent of Homeric agency.
84. *Antigone*, 1175–1176.
85. *Oedipus*, 1115.
86. *Antigone*, 556–558.
87. Many scholars regard Laius' transgressions against Chrysippus a late addition to the myth.
88. *Antigone*, 408–414, 203–206.
89. Ibid., 722–734.
90. Ibid., 1391–1392.
91. Ibid., 450–470.
92. Loraux, *Tragic Ways of Killing a Woman*; Segal, "Introduction."
93. *Antigone*, 1284–1285.
94. *Oedipus at Colonus*, 903.
95. Ibid., 587. Also, 722–734.
96. Aristotle, *Poetics*, 1452a.11; Knox, *Heroic Temper*, pp. 30–31.
97. C. P. Cavafy, "Ithaka," www.cavafy.com/poems/content.asp?id=74 (accessed December 1, 2017).
98. Ibid., 780.
99. *Oedipus*, 1023.
100. Ibid., 799–807.
101. Ibid., 617.
102. Ibid., 801–815.
103. Ibid., 132.
104. Berg and Clay, "Introduction."
105. *Oedipus*, 1731–1733.

106. Ibid., 377–416. Parodos is the entrance song of the chorus. The first, second, and third stasimon refer to the strophic choral odes.
107. *Oedipus*, 1348–1353.
108. Ross, "Intuitive Psychologist and His Shortcomings"; Jones and Harris, "Attribution of Attitudes."
109. Lerner and Miller, "Just World Research and the Attribution Process."
110. Burger, "Motivational biases in the Attribution of Responsibility for an Accident"; Walster, "Assignment of Responsibility for an Accident."
111. Gilbert and Malone, "Correspondence Bias"; Abrams et al., "Perceptions of Stranger and Acquaintance Rape"; Bell, Kuriloff, and Lottes, "Understanding Attributions of Blame in Stranger-Rape and Date-Rape Situations."
112. Summers and Feldman, "Blaming the Victim versus Blaming the Perpetrator."
113. *Oedipus*, 1734–1738.
114. Ibid., 1375.
115. *Oedipus in Colonus*, 13–15.
116. Ibid., 5–6.
117. Ibid., 9.
118. *Oedipus*, 11.
119. Ibid., 10–11.
120. Ibid., 67. Also, the leader of the Chorus, 409.
121. Ibid., 84–85.
122. Ibid., 1482–1544.
123. Ibid., 1673–1721.
124. Ibid., 171.
125. Ibid., 178–179.
126. Ibid., 180.
127. Ibid., 214–221.
128. Ibid., 201.
129. Ibid., 100–104.
130. Ibid., 116–119.
131. Ibid., 1852–1853.
132. Noted by Grennan and Kitzinger, "Introduction."
133. Nietzsche, *Gay Science*, section 276.
134. *Oedipus at Colonus*, 950–954. He has nevertheless not risen above desires for revenge. In lines 864–870, Oedipus appears to be addressing Creon and wishing him a stressful old age like his own!
135. *Oedipus*, 498–507.
136. Ibid., 901–902.
137. *Oedipus at Colonus*, 458–499, 1515–1520.
138. *Oedipus*, 1110–1138.
139. Golden and Pevear, "Introduction."
140. On this last point, Knox, *Oedipus at Thebes*, pp. 7–8.
141. Heraclitus, Fragment 119.
142. Aristotle, *Rhetoric*, 1387a31–33, *Nicomachean Ethics*, 1117a5–15.
143. Aristotle, *Rhetoric*, 1370b11–12; Homer, *Iliad*, 18.109.
144. Aristotle, *Rhetoric*, 1370b30–32.
145. Ibid., 1379b17–19.

146. Lebow, "Nuclear Luck."
147. *Antigone*, 1175–1176.
148. *Oedipus*, 359.
149. Ibid., 1518–1519.
150. Ibid., 1235–1236.
151. Knox, *Oedipus at Thebes*, pp. 47–49, 168–169.
152. *Oedipus*, 1657–1658.
153. Ibid., 723.
154. Ibid., 675–678.
155. *Oedipus at Colonus*, 47–48.
156. Ibid., 280–293.
157. *Ajax*, 1170–1250.
158. We must be careful about making too sharp a binary here because Troy is a polis of sorts but without the kind of decision-making we see in Athens. The Greeks become more of a polis after their debates in book 1 and building a wall in book 8. The shield in book 17 depicts polis-like judicial processes in cities.
159. Pindar, *Nemean*, 8.23–34.
160. *Ajax*, 148–150.
161. Ibid., 1548–1549.
162. Ibid., 1552–1553.
163. Ibid., 1500–1518.
164. Haskell, *Emergence of Professional Social Science*, pp. 301–306.

3   Thucydides

Thucydides (ca. 460–400 BCE) was a contemporary of Sophocles whose life also coincided with the high point of Athenian political influence and culture. His account of the Peloponnesian War purports to describe actual events and speeches but is nevertheless structured as a tragedy. The Athenian alliance with Corcyra is the *hamartia* (missing of the mark, error of judgment) that sets the tragedy in motion. The Sicilian expedition is presented as a second, related *hamartia* that leads more directly to tragedy. Athens is portrayed as culpable and *polutlas* (long-suffering) in the eight years between the failure of the Sicilian expedition and its final defeat and then endures a civil war.[1]

Thucydides probes many of the same questions as Sophocles. He too is interested in why and how people act in self-destructive ways, the extent to which they are masters of their fates, and the role of reason and emotion in their decisions. Neither playwright nor historian theorizes the concept of cause, but it is central to their analysis of social and political behavior. Tragedy and cause may superficially appear to be strange bedfellows. Tragedy may have causes but unfolds in mysterious ways with its causal mechanisms often hidden from sight. Causal analysis by its characters, as Oedipus demonstrates, can be one of its contributing causes. Tragedy is nevertheless a causal narrative and is certainly structured this way by Thucydides. His tragic framework facilitates his analysis of reason, emotion, and cause, just as his understanding of them provides insight into tragedy.

Thucydides makes little mention of the gods; his account relates the actions of men. He focuses on individuals and their choices, how they are embedded in and shaped by context, and how their consequences are often the opposite of what they intended. Like Sophocles, he is writing at a time in which traditional values and norms were being challenged and evolving, when reason as a source of knowledge was increasingly valued over faith, and when wealth and political power were changing not only the way in which the polis functioned but the goals its citizens sought, and how they pursued them.

Epistemology

My analysis of Thucydides builds on my earlier work on his accounts of the origins of the Archidamian and Peloponnesian Wars and their possible lessons for international relations.[2] My focus was on international relations theory and realism in particular because realists claim Thucydides as their founding father. I developed a hermeneutic reading of his text to challenge their readings of Thucydides. I approached his text in light of ongoing philosophical debates – especially those between Sophists and their opponents – and read it against the writings of Herodotus and the tragic playwrights. I argued that Thucydides opposed sophism but emulated their method of argumentation. Rather than telling people what they should think, Sophists sought to lead people to these beliefs through the structure of their text, whether oral or written. They build tensions into their texts in the form of seeming contradictions that prompt alert readers to find ways of reconciling them at a deeper level of analysis. These tensions include those between the immediate and underlying causes of war and among different underlying causes.

Realists mistake the superficial for the profound in Thucydides' text and read his authorial statements and speeches out of historical and literary context.[3] They describe the Archidamian War as inevitable and the first account of war attributable to power transition. They interpret the Athenian claim in the Melian Dialogue that "the powerful do what they can while the weak endure what they must" as a universal truth about relations among states when Thucydides, I believe, presents it as a pathology and one, moreover, that makes the Athenians appear the linear descendants of the hated Persians. I offer what I believe to be a more nuanced and defensible reading of Thucydides and his understanding of the causes of war.

The focus of this chapter is epistemological. I am interested in the extent to which Thucydides frames his inquiry as causal, how he understands cause, and the implications of his analysis for political order. I contend that reason and cause are important to him because he recognizes that they have increasingly replaced tradition and habit as the basis for behavior. Like Sophoclean characters, the historical figures Thucydides describes most often misjudge the likely consequences of their actions. This is attributable to emotions that cloud their judgments but also to their overreliance on reason. They construct elaborate scenarios that are premised on their ability to influence and predict the behavior of others. Pericles bears a strong resemblance to Oedipus in this regard, and one prominent classicist contends that Sophocles intended him to represent Pericles.[4] Miscalculations and their unintended consequences are features of both Sophocles' play and Thucydides' history.

Thucydides is more explicit about the relationship between reason and cause. Like Sophocles, he is interested in how reason is understood and used by political actors to formulate their goals and choose means appropriate to achieving them but also in how they rely on reason to predict others' responses. These expectations influence, sometimes determine, the choices of political actors and are a major source of their miscalculations. So too are what today we call emergent properties. These are outcomes, invariably at a higher level of social aggregation, that are the unintended product of the interaction of multiple actors. Adam Smith, one of the first to view cause this way, describes economic development as the unanticipated consequences of the desire by multiple agents, motivated by need and greed, to make money.[5]

Like Sophocles – and unlike most contemporary social scientists – Thucydides relativizes reasons and emotions. He nevertheless identifies causal pathways that are rooted in human nature and give rise to behavior that can be expected to reoccur in different settings. He conceives of human nature (*anthrōpeia phusis*) as universal but indeterminate as its expressions are context-specific.[6] Sparta and Athens are both Greek city-states but behave quite differently in similar circumstances, although in other ways they converge in response to similar pressures. Much of Thucydides' narrative is devoted to describing these contexts, how they change, and how they influence behavior. Thucydides mentions human nature only five times in his text and rarely invokes it as a cause.[7] In other passages, other terms are used to suggest human nature but, again, only the most general kinds of inferences are drawn from it.[8] He nevertheless implies that all behavior is ultimately its expression.

Social scientists have long assumed the freer agents are from foreign and domestic constraints, the more rational and predictable they will behave. Thucydides offers a more complex understanding of agency and context. His narrative indicates that actors may grossly under- or overestimate the constraints they and other actors face. He further suggests – in sharp contrast to today's conventional wisdom – that actors who feel unconstrained will give freer rein to drives for status, wealth, and power, making their behavior more irrational and less predictable by others. Thucydides appears to believe that there are patterns of irrationality and that they are amenable to rational analysis. Thucydides, like Sophocles – but again unlike social scientists – gives emotions equal billing when it comes to human motives, decision, and policymaking.

To the extent that law makes any appearance in Homer, it is that of the gods. For Thucydides, human laws are front and center, both time-honored practices and norms and more recent legislation. Assemblies and courts are features of the polis, not the *oikos*, and increasingly important in political life and in the writings of fifth-century Athenians. The gods nevertheless are alive and well in the minds of key actors. Many Athenians believe that Apollo has caused the plague in their city to help Sparta.[9] Spartans conclude that some religious infraction is responsible for their bad fortune in the Archidamian War.[10] Thucydides prefers what we call scientific accounts of natural phenomena and attributes social outcomes entirely to human behavior.

Thucydides is interested as much in what people say as what they do. He emphasizes the parallels between law courts and political assemblies; rhetoric is central to both and significantly influences how jurors and those attending the *ekklesia* framed problems and make attributions. Courts and assemblies are also important because people must offer reasons for their behavior in both venues and often they bear little relationship to their actual motives. Citizens serving as jurors or members of the assembly expect this kind of hypocrisy and are supposed to see behind it. Rationalist accounts assume that political actors can distinguish between what they did or want and the explanations or justifications they offer in support. Part of Thucydides' novelty is his recognition that they often cannot do this; that they fail to recognize their own hypocrisy or its likely consequences. He gives ample evidence of rhetorical blowback: Frames of reference people devise and the language they use to convince others come to shape their own belief and thoughts, and not infrequently with results opposite of those they sought.

I begin with a discussion of the origins of the Archidamian War, the first phase of what we now call the Peloponnesian War. I argue that, in keeping with Thucydides' sophistic mode of presentation, he creates a sharp tension between the authorial statement in book 1 (1.23.6) and the narrative that follows. The former attributes the war to Athens' rise in power and the fear this inspired in Sparta, but the narrative that follows reveals that Spartans who favored war had no fear of Athens and wanted to fight for other reasons. These had to do, I argue, with the self-esteem of its warrior citizens. Book 1 accordingly offers two different underlying causes of war: security and identity. They are seemingly at odds but, I believe, are self-reinforcing at a deeper level of analysis. The key to their reconciliation is a better understanding of what Thucydides means by power.

Thucydides devotes more space to the immediate causes of war than he does to the underlying ones. In the former, agency is paramount. People in multiple poleis made decisions they hoped or believed would enhance their security, power, or standing. In every instance, they have the opposite effect.

While the consequences of their actions were not directly foreseeable, the policies that led to them should have been recognized – and sometimes were – as extremely risky. The willingness of leaders and citizens in Corinth, Corcyra, Athens, and Sparta to risk war was an important cause of war. To explain this willingness, we must turn to the deeper causes of war.

Risk acceptance is equally evident in the decisions leading up to the Sicilian expedition. In the second part of the chapter, I analyze its cause and the similarities between the origins of the Archidamian War and those of the Sicilian expedition. This pairing is not arbitrary because Thucydides links the two wars through his placement of speeches, discussion of key actors, and, above all, their coequal status as *hamartia* responsive for the Athenian tragedy.[11] Following a consensus among classicists, I treat the speeches as written by Thucydides, possibly reporting what actors said, and, at least as often, what he thinks they could or should have said. This uncertainty creates no epistemological problem as my goal is not to recreate an accurate account of the events in question but rather Thucydides' analysis of them, with a particular focus on his understanding of reason and cause.

Thucydides' narrative of the origins of the Archidamian War is often described as the first account of war that distinguishes underlying causes from immediate ones. I doubt that Thucydides had such a binary in mind but he certainly did frame his causal narratives in layers. There are superficial causes, deeper causes, and more fundamental ones still. His analysis is more complex than modern counterparts that address war at only two levels of cause.

Modern-day structural accounts of war, especially realist ones, privilege underlying causes, although they do not necessarily agree on what they are. Structural accounts assume that, if the relevant underlying causes are present, war will occur; some provocation will come along to trigger it. The assassinations in Sarajevo in June 1914 are a famous case in point. Until recently, many historians, and certainly international relations scholars, subscribed to the idea that Europe was "like dry kindling waiting for a spark to set it aflame." More recently, prominent historians have come around to the understanding that the outbreak of war in 1914 was by no means inevitable.[12] I make the most forceful cases for its contingency.[13] I contend that Sarajevo was an independent cause in its own right because of the way it allowed Austrian and German leaders to set in motion what would become a continental war while convincing themselves that Austria would likely start only a short localized war against Serbia. It is difficult to imagine another event, or set of events, that could have triggered a general European war in the second decade of the twentieth century.

Realists invariably cite Thucydides on the inevitability of the Archidamian War. They treat the proximate causes as epiphenomena. Thucydides, I think, would be likely to adopt a middle position on this question. He believes in agency, contingency, confluence, and good and back luck, all of which feature prominently in his account. However, he would accept that many, if not most, of the developments that make outcomes contingent are not entirely independent of deeper causes that moved actors to behave as they did. This is also true of luck. He seems to suggest – as would Machiavelli – that capable leaders can sometimes create their own good fortune. Yet clever leaders, he makes very clear, are just as likely to be responsible for their bad luck.

Pace Sophocles, Thucydides' "characters" offer their own assessments of cause. We should not give them any particular credence as their accounts are invariably self-serving and for many of the same reasons as those of key characters in *Antigone* and *Oedipus Turannus*. These explanations are nevertheless important because they tell us something about why people acted as they did and convinced others to support them. Like Sophocles, Thucydides is especially interested in distinguishing between the rhetoric of justification on the one hand and the dispassionate analytical explanation on the other.

In this connection, we must make a related distinction: between what may be the "truest cause" (*alēthestatē prophasis*) of war and what people think it is. The attribution of cause by political actors is superficial because it invariably focuses on the most proximate causes and with the purpose of blaming others for it. Thucydides addresses deeper causes but without dismissing the importance of proximate ones. His more detached analysis offers a contrast with the court of public opinion; but it too is relevant because what people believe affects how they behave.

Finally, we come to the role of reason and emotion. They are both implicated in Thucydides' analysis of cause, which is in many ways similar to that of Sophocles. For both tragedians, instrumental reason has divergent consequences depending on the extent to which actors pursue ends and use means sanctioned by social norms. Instrumental reason is likely to be most counterproductive when it is yoked to narrow self-interest. Thucydides offers a powerful critique of the autonomous individual and self-interest and does so, I believe, because early variants of them had emerged in his society. He suggests, as does Sophocles, that people who act instrumentally and solely on the basis of narrow self-interest are a danger to themselves and everyone around them.

As for the emotions, their range is more restricted in Thucydides than in Sophocles because he is describing the polis, not the *oikos*. Anger features prominently and so too does friendship. Both influence behavior, the former almost invariably in a negative way and the latter more positively. Aristotle tells us that many emotions are mediated by reflection, as anger is in comparison to fright.[14] Fright is an instant, reflex reaction to something threatening, say a loud noise in our vicinity. Fear is induced by imagining a future situation that could produce fright or great loss. Emotions are cultural and therefore subject to political manipulation.[15] Thucydides' narrative hints at the recursive relationship between our imagination and emotions, emotions and political behavior, and the fears, hopes, and emotions imagined consequences arouse.

Reading Thucydides

Thucydides' text is like a great musical score. Just as Toscanini and Klemperer working with the same score might decide on different emphases and tempi but produce equally worthy results, scholars will read Thucydides in different ways. I do not pretend that my interpretation is the correct one – only one of the universe of defensible possibilities. It is among the more difficult Greek texts to understand and analyze. It is long, unfinished, and full of neologisms and *hapax legomena* (words that appear in only one text). The writing is often dense and overloaded with dependent clauses but is by no means random in its complexity. Thucydides' words and phrases sometimes reference Homer, Herodotus, or Sophocles and, by doing so, hint at interpretative frames of reference. So do his use of homonyms, like *prophasis* (crisis stage of a disease and rationalization offered in a law court), choice of tenses, and the stretching and compression of sentences.[16] Ancient Greek makes frequent use of *men/de* (either/or) constructions, and Thucydides takes them to a new level, using these oppositions not only in sentences but in paragraphs and entire books. Paragraphs and books are, of course, later introductions, first made by Hellenic scholars working at the library in Alexandria.

Thucydides provides our principal account of the Peloponnesian War but not the only evidence for it. Scholars have used other writings and, increasingly, epigraphic evidence to assess, among other things, his depictions of Sparta, Pericles, Cleon, and the Athenian alliance. There are also questions about the accuracy of Thucydides' accounts and especially the speeches he reports. Like all historians, Thucydides had to make do with incomplete information and weigh and assess differing accounts, and he brought his own prejudices and goals to this task. Historians are understandably interested in finding independent validation – or disconfirmation – for key aspects of his narrative.[17]

I ignore these questions and the controversies surrounding them because they are orthogonal to my project. My analysis of Thucydides is entirely internal. I am interested in *his* understandings of reason, emotion, and cause. I infer these by means of a two-step process. I begin with his depiction of actors, their motives and goals, the means they use to achieve them, their estimates of the constraints and opportunities they confront, and the likely consequences of their behavior. I then look at Thucydides' take on these questions and his attempt to present and interpret them in a larger framework. My inquiry involves asking why Thucydides emphasizes the actors and events that he does, and the frameworks – most notably tragedy – that he uses to organize his narrative and coordinate it with his speeches.

The first level of analysis is by far the most straightforward, although it is clearly subjective and open to multiple readings. The second is more problematic because it involves inferences about Thucydides' goals in writing his account of the Archidamian and Peloponnesian Wars and, largely, although certainly not entirely, from the perspective of Athens. It involves judgments about why he emphasizes some events and ignores or downplays others. These judgments are not internal to the text alone but reflect the kind of questions we ask about it. Different perspectives are equally applicable and lead to different conclusions. Max Weber rightly maintains that our choice of questions and framework reflects our interests, position in society, and the broader Zeitgeist. There is no way of separating fact from value.[18] The best interpreters can do is be explicit about their questions and perspectives and the reasons for choosing them. They must also rely on accepted, or otherwise defensible, methods and protocols of analysis.

I will, of course, make references to relevant secondary literature. The corpus on Thucydides and the Greece of his era is sizeable. It is germane to both my levels of analysis but also inadequate for my purposes. There is little said in the secondary literature about reason and less about the tensions between emotions and reason and their consequences for cause. These are nevertheless important relationships to explore because they were of interest to Thucydides and his near-contemporaries Plato and Aristotle, who theorized about them.

David Hume maintained that history is distinguished from chronicles by emplotment.[19] Plots tell stories, and stories are linked together by temporal progression. They have beginnings, development, and endings that are connected by causes. Causation is the glue that holds a story together and imparts plausibility to it. Cause is what gives stories legs, making them of interest and relevant to other audiences, situations, and times. Thucydides is clearly interested in understanding why the Archidamian and Peloponnesian Wars came about, how they were fought, and what was responsible for their origins and outcomes.

76   Reason and Cause

Given Thucydides' interest in cause, and the interest of scholars in the causes they surmise he advances, it is surprising that there is no discussion of the more general meanings of cause in the ancient and classical literature. The concept – in contrast to its application – is more or less taken for granted. Like contemporary social scientists, at least some classicists give the impression of assuming that reason and cause have objective and universal meanings. This is indeed surprising for a field that is so committed to reading meanings in context. I make Thucydides' understanding of cause the central question of this chapter. It is interesting in its own right and a key for understanding his text.

Archidamian War

There are many ways of interpreting Thucydides' account of this war. The most obvious – and most questionable – is to take at face value his authorial statement in book 1 (1.23.6) that "the growth of the power of Athens, and the alarm which this inspired in Sparta, made war inevitable."[20] A close reading of book 1 indicates that Thucydides did not describe the Archidamian War as inevitable and considered shifts in relative capabilities at best an indirect cause of war and not because these shifts made Spartans more concerned about their security.[21] The debates in Sparta indicate that there was some concern for security; Sparta's position in Greece would seriously erode if its alliance system disintegrated. However, the ephor Sthenelaïdas and those who voted with him for war did not fear Athens; they were confident of their ability to wage a brief and victorious campaign. King Archidamus sought an accommodation with Athens in large part because of his more accurate assessment of its military strength and fear that any war they started would last for decades.

Sparta's initial refusal to back Corinth in its dispute with Athens, its unsuccessful pressure on Corinth to agree to mediate that dispute, its vote for war under pressure from its allies, and its subsequent efforts to reach an accommodation with Athens at Corinth's expense reveal little concern for Athenian military power or belief that war was inevitable. Thucydides' account suggests that Spartans went to war to preserve their honor and standing in Greece, which was threatened by the political, economic, and cultural changes spearheaded by Athens. Spartan identity, not power, was the fundamental concern for both sides in prewar debate.

How do we account for the seeming contradiction between Thucydides' explicit statement about the cause of war earlier in book 1 (1.23.6) and the more nuanced and implicit arguments he develops in the rest of book 1? It is in part an artifact of translation. Contextual understanding of key words and phrases in book 1 (1.23.5–6) – *dunamis, anagkē*, and *alēthestatē prophasis* – goes some way toward reconciling these arguments. They suggest that Thucydides is answering two different questions: Who was responsible for war and what caused it? In *The Tragic Vision of Politics*, I argue that a real tension nevertheless exists between this description (1.23.5–6) and the narrative that follows, one that is deliberate and intended to lead thoughtful readers to deeper levels of analysis and understanding.[22] I use my analysis to argue that Thucydides offers an account of war that stresses identity and is more consistent with constructivist understandings of international relations.

In this chapter, I exploit the tension between authorial voice and narrative as an entrée into Thucydides' understanding of cause. It alerts us to the existence of causes of war at different levels of analysis, from individual to systemic, and encourages us to ask if these causes were independent or somehow connected? This is the approach I used in the previous chapter to explore Sophocles' understanding of cause. Sophocles recognized tensions but also reinforcing connections between agency and fate, with prophecy as the mechanism linking them. He does not give pride of place to either fate or agency. He leads us to a more profound understanding of contingency and determination without giving primacy to either. Thucydides does something similar with individuals, poleis, and interpolis relations and the question of whether war was inevitable or might have been averted.

Thucydides finds causes for war at several levels of analysis. They are generally, but not always, reinforcing, and sometimes causes at one level can be read as an expression of those at another. In contrast to conventional approaches to cause in comparative politics and international relations, there is no single, dominant explanation or preferred level of analysis. What emerges from Thucydides' narrative is a multifaceted account, more circular than linear, in which beliefs and perceptions share equal billing with contextual constraints and opportunities. It suggests that cause is a necessary concept for making sense of the political world but also a deeply problematic one.

Self-Esteem. I begin my analysis of the war with the critical assembly in Sparta that succumbed to allied pressures. The most rabid warmonger was Corinth, who desperately sought Spartan military backing to compensate for Athenian naval support of Corcyra. Megara and Aegina also had grievances against Athens. Corinth readily enlisted them in its campaign to goad Sparta into war and sent envoys to other allies to drum up fear of Athens and complain about the lack of Spartan support.[23]

In August 432, the Spartan ephors convened an assembly at which the Corinthians, other allies, and friendly states were invited to voice their grievances. Despite an eminently sensible plea for caution by King Archidamus, the Spartan assembly voted that the treaty had been broken and war must be declared. The order of speeches was carefully orchestrated by the ephors to achieve the maximum political effect. In addition to Sparta's allies, the ephors invited "others who might have complaints to make about Athenian aggression." They allowed the Corinthians to speak last, after the other envoys had worked the crowd to inflame anti-Athenian sentiment.[24]

The Corinthians made a masterful appeal.[25] Analyses of it usually emphasize the Corinthian portrayal of Athenians as daring (*tolmētai*) beyond their capability, running risks beyond reason (*gnōmēn*), and ever hopeful (*euelpides*) amid dangers.[26] The Athenians are described as restless, ambitious, and intent on subjugating all of Hellas. The Corinthians, who by now had an "intense hatred" of Athens, insist that Athens must be stopped while it is still possible to do so, which seems consistent with Thucydides' claim that Sparta went to war because it feared the growing power of Athens.[27] However, the context of the speech indicates that this argument was a rationalization for a war Corinthians and their Spartan backers sought for other reasons.

The Corinthian motive for war was entirely selfish. An oligarchy located on the isthmus connecting the Peloponnesus with the rest of Greece, Corinth was a wealthy commercial metropolis and transit route for east–west trade. By offloading goods, transporting them across the narrow isthmus in either direction, and reloading them at the other side, shippers could avoid the long, perilous sea route around the Peloponnesus. Corcyra was an obstacle to Corinth's ambition to establish a sphere of influence in the northwest corner of Greece. Unwilling to submit its dispute with Corcyra to arbitration or renounce its ambitions to regain great power status by means of colonial expansion, Corinth sought to use Spartan power to humble Corcyra, and Athens too, for supporting Corcyra.

The Corinthian speech was a frontal assault on accommodation. The effort to which the ephors went to orchestrate a series of appeals to the assembly culminating in the Corinthian presentation indicates that, even after Megara and Potidaea, many Spartans must still have favored peace with Athens. The Corinthians tell the assembly that the Thirty Years Peace has been exploited by Athens to become powerful enough to threaten the peace and security of Greece. They warn that

Athens will become too strong to oppose if it extends its dominion over Sparta's allies. The Corinthians recognize their argument was unlikely to persuade because they follow it with a threat: If the Spartans allow Athens to humble Megara and subjugate Potidaea, they will "sacrifice friends and kindred to their bitterest enemies and drive the rest of us in despair to some other alliance."[28]

Modern authorities have generally treated this threat as a significant cause for alarm in Sparta.[29] Corinth was Sparta's wealthiest ally and the third naval power of Greece and its defection from the Lacedaemonian Confederacy would have dealt a severe blow to Spartan power and influence. Even if the Corinthians were bluffing – and there is reason to believe they were – Sparta's rejection of Corinth's plea for support would have seriously weakened the alliance and might have been interpreted as a sign of weakness by Athens.[30]

The Corinthian threat was a cleverly calculated appeal to the self-images of the audience. Spartans prided themselves on their virtue, honor, and military prowess. The Corinthians sought to shame Spartans for their failure to come to the aid of Potidaea and Megara, defenseless in the face of Athenian aggression. The Corinthians warned that Sparta's policy of nonintervention would lead to the "sacrifice of friends and kindred to their bitterest enemies." Sparta's standing in Greece would "degenerate from the prestige that it enjoyed under that of your ancestors."[31]

The Spartan assembly was full of impressionable young men with little knowledge of the wider world and no experience of prolonged warfare or prior exposure to this kind of emotional pressure.[32] There can be little doubt that they had already been made to feel uncomfortable by the speeches of the allies and the friendly states who had harangued them about Athenian high-handedness and pilloried them for their passivity. By the time the Corinthians rose to speak, the Spartan audience had been suitably softened up. The Corinthian speech had its intended effect; Spartan anger and shame were intensified and, together with the jealousy many Spartans had long harbored toward Athens, prompted a vote for war. The Athenian attempt to explain and defend their policy was dismissed with a short, derisive speech by one of the ephors, who simply asserted that "we have good allies whom we must not give up to Athens."[33] Emotion triumphed over reason.

Perceptions of Athenian Power. After the Athenian speech and before the vote for war, the Spartans dismissed all foreigners and consulted among themselves. In another pair of revealing speeches, supporters and opponents of war offer divergent predictions of what such a conflict would be like.

King Archidamus, spokesman for those who favored caution, addressed the assembly first. He implored his fellow Spartans, especially the young men who had never experienced a military campaign, not to romanticize war or minimize the sacrifice it would entail. Athens' wealth, navy, large population, and many tribute-paying allies made its power unrivaled in the Greek world. Sparta's greatest asset, its heavy infantry, could devastate Attica but could not prevent Athens from importing everything it needed by sea. To bring Athens to its knees, it would be necessary to defeat its navy or destroy its empire to deny the navy the revenues on which it depended for ships, sailors, and food. This would be a long and hazardous undertaking, Archidamus warned, one "that we may leave it as a legacy to our children; so improbable is it that the Athenian spirit will be the slave of their land, or Athenian experience be cowed by war."[34] His strategic estimate mirrors that of Pericles.[35]

Thucydides describes Archidamus as intelligent (*xunetos*).[36] He certainly makes a reasoned argument in contrast to those who favored war. His appeal nevertheless fell on deaf ears. Those in favor of war had no understanding of naval power and nothing but contempt for Athenian infantry. The ephor Sthenelaïdas proclaimed that the Athenians were in the wrong and deserved punishment. Athenian power also got short shrift. "Others have much money and ships and horses," he acknowledged, "but we have good allies." At his urging, the Lacedaemonians voted that the treaty had been broken and that war must be declared.[37] In this passage, Thucydides says Spartans voted for war because they feared Athens, "seeing most of Hellas already subjected to them."[38] Here too we must be careful in reading this as a statement about security. Most of Hellas was decidedly not subject to Athens, but Greeks almost everywhere increasingly looked up to it for its cultural and other accomplishments. This is what Spartans feared.

The several years of unsuccessful military campaigning that followed demonstrate the extent to which Sthenelaïdas and his followers misjudged Athenian resolve and power. They seriously underestimated Athenian military capability and the ease with which the Athenian economy could sustain that capability in a long war. They apparently expected to invade Attica, overwhelm the Athenians in a single pitched battle, dictate the terms of settlement, and return home to bask in the glory of their victory.[39] As Archidamus predicted, the Athenians refused to give battle and used their fleet to harass the Peloponnese and attack Spartan allies in other theaters of war. Lack of respect for Athenian power, not fear of it, was a principal precondition and incentive for war. King Archidamus had a far more accurate grasp of military and economic realities, and this assessment made him and his supporters cautious of war and anxious to reach an accommodation with Athens.

Was War Inevitable? Corinthian, Spartan, and Athenian illusions about the likely consequences of their policies suggest that the Peloponnesian War was the result of an improbable series of remarkably bad judgments made by the leaders of the several powers involved. The most critical decisions, from the Corcyraean rejection of Epidamnus' appeal for assistance to Pericles' stubborn rejection of Sparta's final peace overtures, were contrary to polis interests and based on inaccurate understandings of military and political realities. Most of these decisions seem to have been a response to narrow situational consideration, not deeper strategic realities. These considerations have more to do with honor than with self-preservation.

The first link in this chain was Corcyra's decision to turn a deaf ear to appeals from the Epidamnian envoys for help in defending their city against local tribesmen in league with their exiled nobles.[40] Thucydides does not tell us why the Corcyraeans spurned these pleas, so scholars have ventured their own opinions.[41] The most persuasive hypothesis is that Epidamnus, a colony of Corcyra, had become powerful in its own right and the Corcyraeans welcomed the prospect of having it reduced to relative impotence by civil strife.

Corcyra's dismissal of the Epidamnian ambassadors encouraged them to turn to Corinth for assistance. The Corinthians responded with alacrity, Thucydides tells us they did this because of their hatred of Corcyraeans who failed to show them the respect and honor due a founding city.[42] What happened next is well known. Corinth sent a large force to Epidamnus. The Corcyraeans, outraged by Corinthian intervention, promptly laid siege to Epidamnus. Corinth readied a fleet to come to the aid of the city. Fearful of war with Corinth and its allies, Corcyra proposed negotiations and then arbitration. Corinth refused and sent its fleet toward Epidamnus, where it was defeated by Corcyra at Leucimme. Corinth now prepared for war in earnest, and Corcyra appealed to Athens for support.

The Corcyraeans had not foreseen any of these developments when they refused aid to Epidamnus.[43] That Epidamnus would turn to Corinth for support should have come as no surprise. The city had been a Corcyraean colony. Following custom, Corcyra chose a founder from its Corinthian metropole, and this provided the basis for its appeal. Further, despite strenuous past efforts to preserve its independence, Epidamnus was now desperate enough to seek support in any quarter. Corinth was motivated to intervene by practical as well as emotional reasons. For some years, it had been building a sphere of influence in northwest Greece at the expense of Corcyra. By 435, Corinth had gained control of all the mixed Corinthian-Corcyraean colonies in the region except for Epidamnus.[44] The Epidamnian appeal for assistance was seen by many in Corinth as a gods-sent opportunity to consolidate their influence in the region.

The Corinthians made a double miscalculation: They did not realize their expedition to Epidamnus would provoke war with Corcyra, and, when this came to pass, they were overconfident of victory. They might have behaved more cautiously if they had had a better appreciation of Corcyraean resolve and naval prowess. Following their defeat at Leucimme, the Corinthians thought only of revenge and their judgment became more clouded by emotion. They spurned Corcyraean and Spartan pleas for negotiation or mediation, although it was likely that they would have emerged with considerable gains from either process. Instead, they spent two years preparing for a renewed round of fighting.

The second Corinthian expedition was a failure. With Athenian assistance, the Corcyraeans beat back the Corinthian attack. Once again, the Corinthians miscalculated; they failed to consider that Corcyra would turn to Athens for assistance and be rewarded with a defensive alliance. After the Corcyraean-Athenian alliance, Corinth still persevered with its plans for war. Corinthian emotions ran so high that leaders and people alike were unwilling to recognize the foolishness of risking war against both Athens and Corcyra.

The decisive step in this tragic chain of events was the Athenian decision to ally with Corcyra. Thucydides wanted readers to believe that the alliance was a foregone conclusion and a wise strategic decision because the Corcyraean fleet might otherwise have been captured by Corinth. Yet his narrative indicates that the alliance was extremely controversial. After listening to the speeches of the Corcyraeans and Corinthians, the Athenian assembly rejected the Corcyraean plea for support.[45] Thucydides offers no explanation for this decision but it seems likely that a majority of those present worried that the proposed alliance would lead to war with Corinth and Sparta. Athenians, moreover, had no affection for the Dorian Corcyraeans.[46] We can surmise that Pericles was busy drumming up support behind the scenes and reconvened the assembly when he had enough votes for the alliance.[47] Pericles probably addressed the second assembly; Plutarch says that he persuaded the people to send aid to Corcyra.[48]

Thucydides tells us nothing about the Athenian volte-face, although he acknowledges that it was the point of no return on the road to war. Reproducing speeches for and against the alliance would have drawn attention to the division of Athenian opinion and the fact that a majority of the first assembly opposed the alliance with Corcyra. It would have revealed that the alliance that was ultimately approved was a strictly defensive one, a restriction intended to keep Athens from violating the Thirty Years Peace. Concern to avoid war may also explain why Pericles sent only ten ships to Corcyra. If his objective was to deter Corinth, a force of 50 or 100 ships would have been much more effective.[49] The inescapable conclusion is that the alliance was a near thing. It took all of Pericles' considerable political and rhetorical skills to convince a pacifically inclined citizenry to vote for it. Without his intervention, the Corcyraean appeal would have been rejected. This is not a novel judgment; it was conventional wisdom in ancient Greece.[50]

The next step toward war was the Spartan assembly's vote on the grounds that Athens had broken the Thirty Years Peace. A more accurate appraisal of Athenian power would have dictated caution, as King Archidamus urged. The final step toward war was Athens' refusal to respond favorably to the second and third Spartan embassies. These proposals offered a reasonable basis for negotiation and accommodation. They evoked a positive response from many Athenians. Once again, Pericles felt the need to speak out. He opposed repeal of the Megarian Decree and succeeded in deflecting Athenian opinion away from peace.[51]

In 433, there was every reason to believe that Sparta would continue to uphold the peace if unprovoked by Athens. For Pericles to jettison his decades-old policy for a naval alliance with Corcyra seems odd indeed. The most likely explanation is that Pericles perceived the Corinthian-Corcyraean conflict as a low-cost opportunity to enhance Athenian power. In politics as well as business, Athenians were famous for making the most of an opportunity (*kairos*), and Pericles may have calculated that Athenian support of Corcyra would be sufficient to deter Corinth from attacking. If so, Athens would gain a valuable ally and at the same time impede Corinthian plans for expansion in the northwest.[52]

Pericles had a fallback position. If war came, he planned to fight the most limited campaign against Sparta. He would not contest the expected Spartan invasion of Attica but would conduct a low-key campaign of naval harassment in and around the Peloponnese. Pericles expected Spartans to become increasingly frustrated by their inability to engage Athens, tire of war, and return those more inclined to peace to power. Pericles and Archidamus between them would then conclude a more enduring peace. Again, Pericles miscalculated. This strategy and the assumptions on which it was based bear an uncanny similarity to German calculations in 1914, all of which were equally flawed. German leaders supported Austria's démarche with Serbia in the expectation that it would deter Russia from intervening. If Russia refused to stand aside and allow Serbia to be subjugated, they were unreasonably confident that France would not come to the aid of its Russian ally. If both countries defied German expectations and went to war, Britain was expected to remain neutral. In the unlikely event that it did not, Germany counted on defeating both of its continental adversaries in a short campaign before British sea power could have any effect on the war.

In 1914, the short war illusion was attributable in part to the general failure to understand the ways in which modern technology had transformed warfare.[53] Yet its deeper cause was political: European statesmen ignored Clausewitz's prescient warning that war between peoples is extraordinarily difficult to control. When people's passions become engaged, Clausewitz wrote, "a reciprocal action is begun" that tends to carry war to its most extreme expression regardless of any intention of leaders to keep it in check. Once this spiral begins, war is most likely to end in the exhaustion of one or both sides.[54] This was true of the Peloponnesian War and World War I. In 431, and in 1914, there were individuals like King Archidamus and Edward Grey who foresaw what lay ahead. Had there been more of them, war might have been averted.

Thucydides' account indicates that leaders had considerable freedom of choice. This is most clearly demonstrated by the success of key individuals to shift the direction of state policy in the face of considerable opposition. The ephors and the allied representatives did this in Sparta, and Pericles' intervention convinced his compatriots to reverse their stance and ally with Corcyra. Without Pericles, Athens would not have concluded its fateful alliance. An offensive realist might argue that Pericles' success in swaying the Athenian assembly is the ultimate confirmation of relative gains and the balance of power. Pericles assumed that war with Sparta was unavoidable in the long term and therefore worth risking in the short term for the sake of an alliance that would significantly enhance Athenian military capability. His belief in the inevitability of war made those additional capabilities more important. The fact that Pericles could impose his policy on a pacifically inclined citizenry who at first rejected alliance with Corcyra could be said to demonstrate the determining influence of deeper strategic realities.

This argument verges on the tautological. It assumes that war was inevitable because of Athens' rise to power and the fear that this inspired in Sparta and offers the Peloponnesian War as proof of the thesis. It makes Pericles appears prescient and his policy a triumph of strategic reason, even if it led to a long and disastrous war. Yet, if a more restrained Athenian foreign policy could have kept the peace, as seems likely, Pericles' actions must be judged the product of a flawed vision that led to a war from which Athens, and Greece more generally, never recovered. Pericles' war policy also represents a contradiction of classical balance of power theory as the balance was changing in Athens' favor. The longer peace prevailed, the more powerful Athens was likely to become relative to Sparta.

Levels of Analysis. Like most tensions in Thucydides, that between agency and structure exists at multiple levels. Political actors in Thucydides resemble characters in Greek tragedies in being an amalgam of traits. Sthenelaïdas and Pericles represent defining qualities of their respective polities. Pericles personifies almost perfectly the description the Corinthians offer of Athenians.[55] He is restless and aggressive, quick to act, risk-accepting, clever, and very ambitious. Sthenelaïdas and Archidamus represent two distinctive aspects of Spartan culture. Sthenelaïdas embodies the stereotype of Spartans as emphasizing brawn over brains and action on the basis of simple time-honored principles. Archidamus represents the inherent caution of his countrymen, their preference for inaction over action but also their ability to calculate carefully their self-interest. One cannot imagine either man making a speech that the Athenian assembly would find persuasive. Sthenelaïdas offers not one argument but succeeds by arousing the anger and shame of his audience. Of course, this may be a deliberate choice. June Allison suggests that Sthenelaïdas is cannier and more calculating and for this reason more successful at seizing control of the discourse.[56]

The preferences of Pericles, Archidamus, and Sthenelaïdas – as depicted by Thucydides – are as much the expressions of their political cultures as they are individual choices. So too are the reactions of the Athenian and Spartan assemblies to them. To the degree that actors express the imperatives of these cultures, and assemblies validate them, Athenian and Spartan miscalculations have general as opposed to idiosyncratic causes.

The peculiar character of Sparta was also responsible for the assembly's vote for war. Because of Sparta's self-imposed isolation, its citizens had little experience of the wider world and little appreciation for the power of their adversary, based as it was on entirely different political and economic foundations. Socialized from childhood into believing in their invincibility and that manliness (*andreia*) was established by pugnacious bravery, Spartans were ill-prepared, intellectually and emotionally, to make the kind of considered judgments the situation required.

Greeks were fed Homer with their mother's milk, and nowhere was the diet so rich as in Sparta where respect for the past and its values was actively fostered by the state. Spartan customs, as the Corinthians hastened to point out, were old-fashioned and unchanging. Spartans rejected a money economy and material goods, and its citizens were prohibited from engaging in commerce or becoming artisans. They were full-time soldiers and judged on the basis of their bravery, courage, honor, and other personal attributes like wisdom and self-control.[57] For centuries, Spartans had been driven by a fierce ambition to achieve and then maintain hegemony in Hellas. They lived to serve their *polis* and internalized its goals. Their self-esteem was inextricably connected with their city's honor and standing, which in turn derived from the bravery and accomplishments of its hoplites. As Archidamus put it: "We are both warlike and wise, and it is our sense of order that makes us so. We are warlike, because self-control contains honor as a chief constituent, and honor bravery."[58] This argument appears not to have gone down well with those Spartans who were deeply angered by the power and confidence of Athens and shamed by their inaction and complaints from their allies that they had left them to fend for themselves. Sparta's decision for war had less to do with security that it did with Spartan values and identity.

Archidamus and Sthenelaïdas recognized that Athens posed a serious threat to their self-esteem and way of life. Unwilling to transform their society as the Corinthians urged them to, they advocated diametrically opposed, but equally unrealistic, strategies to cope with this threat. Sthenelaïdas and his followers wanted to assert Sparta's military superiority, overwhelm Athens' army, and deflate the appeal of Athenian style commercial democracy. Archidamus and his supporters sought an accommodation with Athens that would allow Sparta to pursue its conservative, agrarian lifestyle in relative isolation, protected in part by Athenian power. Peace would have preserved Sparta's standing and way of life in the short term but accelerated the transformation of Greece in the longer term. A quick victory would only have slowed the pace of changes associated with the growth of commerce and accumulation of surplus wealth.

There is good reason to suspect motivated bias in Sparta's decision-making. Motivated bias is triggered by threats that are not easily addressed or those that involve difficult trade-offs in values.[59] It prompts people to interpret reality in a manner consistent with their needs. Motivated bias is well documented in politics and international relations, where it often blinds leaders to the interests and signals of other actors and leads to self-serving intelligence estimates and denial of information that suggests their preferred course of action is likely to lead to disaster.[60]

In Sparta, there were those who desperately wanted to uphold Sparta's honor and international standing but who were equally committed to its isolation and unique way of life. These contradictory goals could only be advanced by a quick, victorious war against Athens that could be fought with existing forces, would not make Sparta dependent on Corinth, and would avoid prolonged contact with foreigners – hence Sthenelaïdas' unrealistic expectation that Athens could be defeated in a single season of campaigning. Those favoring peace eschewed war because they were more sensitive to the threat it posed to Sparta's institutions and way of life. They were motivated to see Athens as a placable foe and one, moreover, whose power might be used to guarantee Spartan isolation and security. Thucydides' juxtaposition of the speeches of Archidamus and Sthenelaïdas brings out the bias, wishful thinking, and denial of both men. Sthenelaïdas fails to respond in any substantive way to the arguments of Archidamus or to propose a military strategy for coping with Athenian naval supremacy and economic self-sufficiency. Archidamus gives no real reason for thinking the Athenians are keen to remain at peace as defenders of the status quo.

Archaic Sparta is a good foil for thoroughly modern Athens. Here too, honor played an important role. In their speech to the Spartan assembly, the visiting Athenians explain that "the nature of the case first compelled us (*katēnankasthēmen*) to advance our empire to its present height; fear being our principal motive, though honor and interests afterwards came in."[61] Later, Pericles tells Athenians: "It is right for you to stand up for the honor the city receives from ruling an empire, honor that glorifies you all."[62]

The Athenian ambassadors also emphasize fear. "And at last," they assert, "when almost all hated us, when some had already revolted and had been subdued, when you had ceased to be the friends that you once were, and had become objects of suspicion and dislike, it appeared no longer safe to give up our empire, especially as all who left us would fall to you."[63]

Thucydides tells a different story: analysis in lieu of self-justificatory rhetoric. The Athenian assembly ultimately backed Pericles' appeal for an alliance with Corcyra because

> it began now to be felt that the coming of the Peloponnesian War was only a question of time, and no one was willing to see a naval power of such magnitude as Corcyra sacrificed to Corinth; though if they could let them weaken each other by mutual conflict, it would be no bad preparation for the struggle which Athens might one day have to wage with Corinth and the other naval powers. At the same time the island seemed to lie conveniently on the coasting passage to Italy and Sicily.[64]

There was certainly an element of fear in the background, but, if we credit Thucydides' analysis, Athenians were moved by the kind of complex calculations we associate with strategic and economic interests.

Daniel Tompkins suggests that Thucydides uses fear in two different ways. In the run-up to the war, the Athenians speak of *deos*, or "apprehension," the kind of fear that is likely to arise when people confront risky decisions that may encourage thoughtful and even rational assessments.[65] Sparta, by contrast, is motivated by *phōbos* or "panic fear," far less rational and deliberate.[66] Tompkins argues that the Athenians are prodding the Spartans here, nagging them about points on which they are insecure, very likely hoping to get them angry enough to declare war, which they do. Thucydides (at 1.23) says Sparta panicked and again (at 1.88) after the Athenians have made their case. If the Spartans were ontologically insecure, the Athenians recognized and exacerbated it.

Athenian and Spartan policies were also influenced by the wider political environment and the perceived opportunities and constraints it generated. Both cities had dissatisfied middle-rank powers for allies or would-be allies. Conflicts between these middle-rank powers, or between them and smaller powers, set in motion the chain of events that led to war. The Epidamnus-Corcyra conflict escalated into a confrontation between Corcyra and Corinth, which then dragged in Corinth and Athens. Thebes' long-standing conflict with Platea also pitted the two hegemons on opposing sides.

Athens and Sparta were vulnerable to third-party pleas for assistance. Militarily, the Athenian and Spartan alliances were roughly equal but had different force structures. The Spartan army was the most powerful ground force in Greece, and Athens had the most powerful navy. The Spartan hoplites, with their purple cloaks, crested helmets, and polished shields, advanced slowly in perfect order to the sound of the flute. Their skill in lance and sword, and commitment to return home victorious or carried on their shields, struck fear into the hearts of their adversaries, some of whom fled at the prospect of engagement.[67] There was a relatively small number of Spartans, maybe 4,000 in all at the outbreak of war. Sparta had to rely on Corinth for naval forces and the money to finance a long campaign. Athens was largely self-sufficient; it was wealthier than Corinth and, with approximately 50,000 men of military age, could muster an impressive contingent of hoplite and lighter infantry and rowers for its fleet.[68] Its land and naval forces were augmented by those of the empire and independent allies.

The rough military balance between the two alliances was a source of stability but that stability was fragile. It could be undermined by addition or defection of one or more middle-rank powers. Both considerations came into play with the Athenian alliance with Corcyra. "Can you conceive of a stroke of good fortune more rare in itself, or more disheartening to your enemies?" the Corcyraeans ask the Athenian assembly.[69] Some

Athenians undoubtedly relished the prospect of the Corcyraean navy added to their own; but Thucydides reports that the Athenians were moved more by fear that the Corcyraean fleet would end up in Sparta's service through a Corinthian victory, and "no one was willing to see a naval power of such magnitude as Corcyra sacrificed to Corinth."[70]

Unlike the Athenian empire, in which Athenian will was law, Sparta was *primus inter pares* in a much looser confederacy. It could dictate policy to weaker, nearby cites, like Phlius and Orchomenus, but had to woo more powerful allies like Corinth and Thebes.[71] Often, these allies succeeded in mobilizing Spartan arms in support of their parochial ends.[72] This happened in 431 and again in 421, when Corinth and Thebes succeeded in sabotaging the Peace of Nicias and rekindling war between Athens and Sparta.

International relations theorists have long debated the relative stability of multipolar versus bipolar international systems.[73] Greek politics on the eve of the Peloponnesian War contained important elements of both. There were two hegemons, each dominating a major alliance system, which gave the system its bipolar characteristics. Yet second-rank powers like Corinth, Thebes, Corcyra, and Argos, the last two unaffiliated with either alliance, were powerful enough to play important, independent roles on the stage of Greek politics. Other, powerful units on the periphery of the system, most notably Persia and Syracuse, also affected the balance. This distribution of power and a certain fluidity in alliances – the decisive political events were Athens' alliance with Corcyra, which gave rise to the war, and Sparta's much later alliance with Persia, which made its ultimate victory possible – imparted multipolar characteristics to the system.

Greek city-states were for the most part oligarchies or democracies, and the two great alliance systems reflected this ideological and interest-based division.[74] In some poleis (e.g., Epidamnus, Plataea, Mytilene), the balance of power between the elite of rich and influential men and the masses of citizens was uncertain, and coups or revolutions, or fear of them, encouraged factions to seek support from outside powers sympathetic to their cause. Civil war in Epidamnus led to war between Corcyra and Corinth when they were drawn in on opposite sides and in turn led to war between Athens and Sparta when they came to the aid of their respective allies. Thucydides' narrative prompts the conclusion that allies were also a principal cause of the renewal of war in 414. Given the reinforcing cleavages between domestic and international politics, and the tight links between the two realms, internal cleavages in any strategically located polis were highly destabilizing to the system as a whole.

Had the Greek world been unambiguously bi- or multipolar, some of these problems might have been avoided. In a bipolar system, the capabilities of the hegemons vis-à-vis other states would have been significantly greater. The hegemons would not have been so much at the mercy of their allies and important third parties as the support or defection of these powers would have mattered less. A multipolar system would have offered different advantages. With more independent players possessing a greater variety of capabilities, the support or defection of any one of them would have been less important because of the possibility of compensating for this change from the pool of uncommitted states. Nor is it likely that any single alliance system would have developed the capabilities to challenge the rest of the system.

The mixed system of fifth-century Greece combined the worst features of bi- and multipolarity. The addition or defection of a middle-rank power could have profound strategic implications; it made Athens willing to risk war for the sake of Corcyra, and Sparta in turn for Corinth; and there were enough independent and quasi-independent powers around to make it likely that such changes would occur from time to time.

Truest Cause. Let us revisit the seeming contradiction between Thucydides' authorial statement (at 1.23.6) and the narrative of book 1. My analysis suggests that we err in our reading of *dunamis* (power). Most interpreters, influenced by Hobbes and twentieth-century realist approaches to international relations, have a narrow and cramped understanding. They think of power as military and economic capability. Thucydides' coupling of fear and power (at 1.23.6) appears to encourage this understanding because realists think of fear in physical terms. There is little support for such fear on the Athenian side until late in the Peloponnesian War. The Athenian ambassadors tell the Spartans before the war that they fear for the survival of their empire. This is most likely a rhetorical claim offered to justify otherwise unacceptable behavior. In half a century of empire building, imperial Athens never, in Thucydides' narrative, experiences fear.[75] In the same speech, Athenians assert that honor also moves them to maintain and extend their empire. Before the war, honor and appetite, which find expression as the search for wealth, are the dominant motives. By the time of the Melian Dialogue, fear enters the picture.

I believe that Thucydides is sensitive to what today we call "soft power." I further suggest that he has a more sophisticated understanding of it than contemporary international relations scholars. Joseph Nye Jr., who coined the term, maintains that American culture and its way of life are widely emulated or envied by people around the world. Consumption of Coca-Cola, the sporting of blue jeans, and interest in American TV and movies – in entirely unspecified ways – make foreign publics more receptive and supportive of US foreign policy goals.[76]

Soft power is soft in its conceptualization and weak in its empirics. It is by no means evident why the appeal of American material or cultural products should make foreigners more supportive of American foreign policy. Surely, the appeal of Japanese electronics, Chinese manufactures, and Cuban cigars does not make Americans any more pro-Japanese, pro-Chinese, or pro-Cuban – quite the reverse in the case of Chinese products. The same is true for certain American exports; McDonald's and fast-food chains more generally have done much to arouse anti-American feeling in Europe. Most consumers seem capable of distinguishing between a country's products and its policies. Every anti-American demonstration in Europe and Asia features protesters clad in jeans. Jeans and many other popular American exports are neither supportive nor hostile to American foreign policy. Those few that are distinctly hostile, like the widely acclaimed and popular *South Park* and *Daily Show*, are extremely popular. They may build respect for American democracy and toleration of dissent but certainly not for its foreign policy.

Thucydides understands soft power but, in contrast to Nye, gives no indication of believing that cultural or constitutional respect translates into foreign policy support. He suggests that it is more likely to result in emulation. Other people also desire wealth and want to use it to beautify themselves and their cities and gain renown for their cultural achievements. This shift in values and preferences made Athens more of a role model than Sparta, gave it a higher standing in the Greek world, and threatened to marginalize Sparta. The rise of Athens inspired more fundamental fears than security among Spartans. They imagined a world in which their status was greatly diminished, and, with it, their self-esteem and identity.

The seeming contradiction in book 1 (at 1.23.5–6) is needlessly sharpened in many English translations, including those of Richard Crawley and Rex Warner. They use the word "inevitable" for the Greek *anangkē*.[77] In Greek tragedy, *anangkē* conveys a constraint or external pressure but still leaves an agent with choice. It implies compulsion but not determinacy.[78] Additional support for this understanding comes in the same passage where Thucydides distinguishes grounds for complaints from accusations and underlying causes. He uses *alēthestatē prophasis* to describe underlying causes, a phrase that can be rendered as "the truest cause" or "the truest precondition" of war. The superlative *alēthestatē* implies multiple causality and nothing more than the primacy of one among several causes.[79]

Prophasis entered the Greek lexicon with Herodotus who used it to signify that a statement of self-justification, not necessarily of true intention, is about to follow.[80] A *prophasis* (rationalization) is essential to mask unacceptable motives. Herodotus reports that Miltiades sailed against Paros with a fleet of seventy ships because of a grievance he had against the Parians. Miltiades is careful to offer a *prophasis*: the Parians provided one ship to reinforce the Persians at Marathon. This ridiculous justification is necessary because Greeks did not level cities to settle personal scores.[81]

Hunter Rawlings III makes a compelling case against the traditional view of *prophasis* as one word that took on two meanings (polysemy) in favor of two words with different origins and meanings but the same phonological form (homonymy).[82] *Prophasis* appears to have undergone a parallel development with the Hippocratics, students of medicine who emerged in south Italy and Ionia in the fifth century, and coined new words to fill in gaps in medical terminology. In the *Hippocratic* corpus, a collection of medical treatises attributed to Hippocrates of Cos, and written between 430 and 420, *Prophasis* is used repeatedly to describe a "precondition" or "something that appears before a disease."[83] The term in this context implies association but not causation.[84] Thucydides appears to have been aware of this distinction and used the two meanings systematically to distinguish between Spartan and Athenian propaganda and the conditions that led to both stages of the Peloponnesian War.

Viewed in this light, Thucydides' statement in book 1 (1.23.6) about the growth of Athenian power and Sparta's concomitant fears should be read as neither pretext nor motive but as a *precondition* for war. There was no Greek word to express the difference between precipitant and precondition, so Thucydides borrowed *prophasis* from the Hippocratics. To mark the different use of the word in this context, he used the superlative form of the adjective *alēthestatē*.[85] Like a physician, Thucydides was making a clinical observation, in this case about the political symptoms that preceded the onset of crisis. This passage is accordingly best translated as "I consider the most verifiable precondition, though obscure when spoken of [perhaps], was that the Athenians becoming great and terrifying the Spartans, compelled them to fight."

This double meaning of *prophasis* and its specific use in book 1 (at 1.23.6 and 1.146) has important implications for my broader argument. It indicates that Thucydides is not suggesting that Athens' rise to power was the truest cause of war, only that it was the most important precondition. To the extent that Thucydides was interested in causation in our sense of the concept, his take on the causes of war must be inferred from the text, especially its detailed examination of the multiple preconditions, the *prophaseis* offered by the two sides, and the interaction among preconditions and *prophaseis*.

Fifth-century Greeks, and Sophists in particular, wrote in a different tradition.[86] They considered themselves teachers and intended their works as courses of study. They introduced the idea that every argument had a contrary thesis and that all ideas were open to criticism. Their works started with simple arguments or statements of a problem and went on to develop increasingly complex and sophisticated arguments. Their deeper-level arguments were generally left implicit in the expectation that readers whose intellects and emotions became engaged would draw these conclusions for themselves.[87]

There are sound historical and textual reasons for reading Thucydides this way. Sophists dominated Athenian philosophy during the second half of the fifth century and had considerable political influence. Pericles chose one of them, Protagoras, to write the laws for the colony of Thurii, founded in 444; hired another, Hippodamus of Miletus, to lay out the streets of Piraeus in a grid pattern; and is reported to have spent an entire day debating Protagoras.[88] Thucydides appears to have accepted the sophist antithesis between nature and convention and explains human behavior with reference to both. He was greatly attracted to the sophistic style of argument, which he adopted for his own, quite different purposes.[89]

Sophistic rhetoric was considered a more effective way of teaching. Sophists recognized, and modern psychology confirms, that people everywhere are more convinced by lessons embedded in stories than by mere arguments, and by conclusions they reach themselves in contrast to those laid out before them.[90] Thomas Hobbes was among the first to recognize this feature of Thucydides.[91] W. Robert Connor builds his highly regarded postmodernist reading of Thucydides around this insight. He suggests that Thucydides uses his narrative to draw readers into the war and, in the process, broadens and deepens their assessments and understandings. We should be prepared to consider the text itself as a progression, that is, the first part of the work may reflect attitudes, assumptions, and ideas that are eventually modified, restated, subverted, or totally controverted.[92] I build on this insight in detail in a reading of Thucydides that identifies and unpacks four levels of tensions and related meanings.[93]

Thucydides' account of the origins of the war can best be understood as an adaptation of sophistic rhetorical strategy. He opens his history with a discussion of responsibility for the war. He explores the accusations Athens and Sparta made against each other and their justifications for drawing the sword. He engages the question of the war's origins at the most superficial level, but so did ordinary citizens, consumed, as were Europeans in the aftermath of World War I, by the *Kriegsschuldfrage* – the war guilt question. Thucydides signals to more sophisticated readers that charge and countercharge were little more than propaganda and obscured the real causes of the war. The subsequent narrative and paired speeches investigate these preconditions in more detail and use them to address the more interesting question of causation.

My interpretation of the origins of the Archidamian War is a useful entry point into Thucydides' understanding of cause, not only in this instance but more generally. I will elaborate this understanding at the end of the chapter. For now, I want to turn to a second case within Thucydides, the Sicilian expedition, as it provides more evidence for the argument I will make.

Sicilian Expedition

At the very outset of book 1, Thucydides distinguishes the Archidamian and Peloponnesian Wars from conflicts that preceded them by offering the judgment that they would become "the greatest disturbance in the history of the Hellenes ... and, I might almost say, the whole of mankind."[94] Book 6 describes the decision to invade Sicily. It is presented as an equally momentous decision. Thucydides reports that the Athenians "did not realize that they were taking on a war of almost the same magnitude as their war against the Peloponnesians."[95] This is because "they aimed at conquering the whole of it, though they wanted at the same time to make it look as though they were sending help to their own kinsmen, and to their newly acquired allies there."[96]

Thucydides is recounting two great wars. They begin independently of each other but soon become entwined. Thucydides introduces additional parallels in his account of these wars. He structures the Archidamian-Peloponnesian War as a tragedy. It is triggered by a *hamartia* (miscalculation) that was the result of hubris and ultimately leads to catastrophe for Athens. The *hamartia* was the alliance with Corcyra, and the catastrophe, the defeat of Athens. He imposes the same structure on the war with Syracuse. The *hamartia* is the decision to send an expedition to Sicily, and the catastrophe, the defeat and destruction of the expeditionary force. The tragedies are reinforcing because Athens' defeat in Sicily is the catalyst for its defeat in the war with Sparta.

Aristotle described *peripeteia* (reversal) as the defining feature of tragedy.[97] In the previous chapter, we observed how Oedipus went from being "equal to the gods" to being "equal to nothingness."[98] Athens undergoes a similar transformation. The city was at the height of its power in 431 but, by 412, has lost its empire and depends on others for its survival. It resembles Oedipus after he loses his kingship. Thucydides builds in further irony by giving the Syracusans the same characteristics that previously made the Athenians great.[99] The Athenian defeat, moreover, is the result of a battle that mirrors – outcome aside –

their earlier success at Pylos against the Spartans. In both contests, the besiegers become the besieged.

I address the origins of these wars and do so to probe Thucydides' understanding of cause. His principal vehicle toward this end in the Archidamian War were speeches: those of Corcyra and Corinth before the Athenian assembly, that of Pericles before the same body, and, in Sparta, the speeches of Corinth, Archidamus, and Sthenelaïdas. The decision to ally with Corcyra was the subject of two debates in the Athenian assembly.[100] Pericles makes the case for a defensive alliance and ultimately convinces his countrymen of its wisdom. The Sicilian expedition is also debated twice in the assembly, and this time Thucydides presents speeches for and against.

These decisions are fundamentally different in that the vote for alliance with Corcyra was not a vote for war, although the alliance triggered a chain of events that led to war. The vote for the Sicilian expedition was unambiguously a vote for war. There is an important irony here. Thucydides justifies his decision to recount these wars because they were among the greatest disturbances in the history of the Hellenes, but, in neither case, did Athenians have any real understanding of the magnitude of the wars they were setting in motion. Pericles and Alcibiades make light of them. They paint an entirely false picture, deliberately misleading the assembly. Pericles, moreover, sells the alliance as more likely to prevent a war than to provoke it.

The decisions for war were similar in that their catalysts were fortuitous appeals by third parties keen for Athenian support. Corcyra and Corinth were at war and the former was desperate for Athenian naval intervention. As noted, the Corcyraeans held the prospect of their fleet – the third largest in Greece after Athens and Corinth – acting in unison with that of Athens against their joint enemies. "The general belief," Thucydides reports, "was, whatever happened, war with the Peloponnese was bound to come. Athens had no wish to see the strong navy of Corcyra pass into the hands of Corinth."[101] There was also an expectation of gain. Athenians were "not averse from letting the two powers weaken each other by fighting together; since, in this way, if war did come, Athens herself would be stronger in relation to Corinth and to the other naval powers." The alliance would deter Sparta and Corinth from going to war or, if not, lead to the certain defeat of the latter. A closer connection with Corinth was also appealing because it was an important way station on the sailing route to Italy.[102]

The debate over Sicily was also prompted, and seemingly decided, by the fortuitous plea of a third party. The Sicilian Egestaeans, at war with their neighbors, the Selinuntines, "begged" Athens to send their fleet in their support. They promised the Athenians enough silver to defray the cost of their expedition.[103] Like the Corcyraeans before them, the Egestaeans held out a carrot and stick before the Athenian donkey. They would provide a base for Athenian military operations in Sicily. Failure to come to their aid would allow Syracuse to "drive out the people of Leontini ... and to go on destroying the remaining allies of Athens, until she acquired complete control of Sicily."[104] The Egestaeans did not stop there but invoked further dominos to magnify the threat: "the danger would then have to be faced that at some time or other the Syracusans, who were Dorians themselves, would come with a large force to the aid of the Dorian kinsmen and would join the Peloponnesians, who had originally sent them out as colonists, in the work of utterly destroying the power of Athens."[105]

The following spring, the Egestaeans brought thirty talents of silver, a month's pay for the sixty ships they asked the Athenians to send to their aid. The Athenian assembly voted to send the sixty ships and appoint as commanders with full powers Alcibiades, Nicias, and Lamachus.[106] Nicias opposed the expedition and did not want to command it. Thucydides tells us that "his view was that the city was making a mistake, and on a slight pretext which looked reasonable, was in fact aiming at conquering the whole of Sicily – a very considerable undertaking indeed."[107] He came forward to speak at a second assembly, hoping to make the Athenians change their mind.

Nicias argues against what he describes as a far-reaching and risky adventure when Athens still faced powerful enemies closer to home. He questions the Egestaean assertion that Syracuse will conquer Sicily and denies that its success in doing so would constitute any danger to Athens. It is unlikely the Syracusans would come to the aid of the Peloponnesians. If our goal is to intimidate them, Nicias suggests, "The best way to make ourselves feared by the Hellenes in Sicily is not to go there at all; and the next best thing is to make a demonstration of our power and then, after a short time, go away again."[108] He describes the Athenian desire to conquer Sicily as "a hopeless passion." "Success," he advises, "comes from foresight and not much is ever gained simply by wishing for it."[109]

Alcibiades is Pericles on steroids. He too is restless, aggressive, quick to act, risk-accepting, clever, and ambitious but lacks any of Pericles' caution, self-restraint, and, above all, commitment to his city. He is "the most ardent supporter of the expedition" and claims that conquest will be easy because the Sicilians are a polyglot lot of peoples unwilling and unable to unite.[110] The subtext of his speech is that there is great profit to be made at little cost. Useful allies helped to win our empire and now we have the opportunity to expand it.

And it is not possible for us to calculate, like housekeepers, exactly how much empire we want to have. The fact is that we have reached a stage where we are forced [*ananke*] to plan new conquests and forced to hold on to what we have got, because there is a danger that we ourselves may fall under the power of others unless others are in our power.

Remaining passive, which is what Nicias advises, would be dangerous because "the city, like everything else, will wear out of its own accord if it remains at rest, and its skill in everything will grow out of date; but in conflict it will constantly be gaining new experience and growing more used to defend itself, not by speeches, but in action."[111]

Nicias rose to make a rejoinder. He sought to deflate enthusiasm for the expedition by making an "exaggerated estimate of the forces required."[112] His appeal had the opposite effect. It encouraged people to believe that with more effort and expenditure they could make success a sure thing.

There was a passion for the enterprise that affected everyone alike. The older men thought that they would either conquer the places against which they were sailing or, in any case, with such a large force, could come to no harm; the young had a longing for sights and experiences of distant places and were confident that they would return safely; the general masses and the average soldier saw the prospect of getting pay for the time being and of adding to the empire so as to secure permanent paid employment in the future.[113]

Neither ally delivers on its promises. The Corcyraeans keep their fleet at home, or use it for their own ends, and never come to the aid of Athens. The Egestaeans lie about the wealth in their temples.[114] They deliver only thirty talents, leaving Athens to bear the brunt of the cost of the expedition. Both decisions of the Athenian assembly were based on false expectations aroused by allies intent on entrapping Athens and using her navy to advance their parochial goals. Allied success was made possible by Athenian naiveté, as was, of course, the Spartan decision for war in 431. This naiveté was played on not only by Corcyra and Egesta but by their supporters in Athens and, in Sparta, by the ephors who invited Corinth and other allies to present their grievances about the Athenians to the Apelia. Athenian and Spartan citizens were manipulated by allies but also by their own leaders.

There are nevertheless important differences. Pericles, Archidamus, and Sthenelaïdas had the best interests of their poleis in mind; and Pericles, in contrast to Alcibiades, found it difficult at the outset to sell the Corcyraean alliance to the Athenian people. Alcibiades – Nicias and Thucydides tell us – is motivated by his quest for lucre and glory. He later defected to Sparta when he was recalled home by the assembly to face criminal charges.[115]

Agents can be influential but only in appropriate contexts. This is why Nicias makes no headway with his sensible arguments that juxtapose *pronoia* (foresight) with *epithumia* (desire).[116] Their wartime experiences should have taught Athenians to be more cautious, but they do the reverse. They throw caution to the winds in search of material gain. Nicias is nicely paired with Archidamus, whose reasoned appeal for restraint also had little effect. The similarities between their approaches and their failure not only connect to two wars but connect Sparta with Athens, and this despite their different values, ways of life, and constitutions.

Readers approach Thucydides' text with the same degree of foreknowledge they do Homer and Sophocles. There is a fatal inevitability to *Antigone* and *Oedipus*, and it greatly heightens the irony of many of the pronouncements of key figures in these plays. What these characters intend to convey to one another or the audience is undercut by our knowledge that things will work out very differently. Foreknowledge encourages us to put a different interpretation on their words. Thucydides makes considerable use of this technique; numerous figures confidently make predictions when we know the reverse will come to pass.[117]

Thucydides hints at greater contingency than Sophocles. This may be because the outcomes he describes are not the result of personal interactions but those among political units. They are the product of war, one of the most uncertain of human ventures. These outcomes have deeper causes but are also very much affected by weather, timing, and chance – what Clausewitz would later call "the fog of war." In 431, on the eve of the Archidamian War, Thucydides has the Athenian visitors in Sparta warn the Spartan assembly of the incalculable nature (*ho paralogos*) of war. They urge the Spartans to "think in advance about how unpredictable war can be before you find yourselves involved in one."[118] They fail to heed their warning. Thucydides' actors, like those of Sophocles, consistently exaggerate their ability to predict the future and control the events that lead to it.

Hans-Peter Stahl identifies a series of "crisis points" or "hinges of history" where military outcomes could have gone either way.[119] Most notable is the near completion by the Athenians of their wall around Syracuse when the Corinthian commander Gongylus arrives just in time to stiffen the spine of the Syracusans and dissuade them from withdrawing.[120] He is reinforced by the latter arrival of Gylippus, who had been delayed by a storm.[121] Thucydides says that Gylippus "arrived in the nick of time. The Athenians had already completed a double wall of nearly a mile down to the great harbour, except for a small section by the sea ... Syracuse had thus been in very great danger indeed."[122]

According to Thucydides, Syracuse "was not so much a mistake of judgment about the enemy they were attacking as a failure on the part of those sending the men abroad to follow up this decision with further support for them."[123] He seems to suggest that more forces would have given the Athenians enough of an edge to have triumphed over Syracuse despite the interventions of Gongylus and Gylippus. This counterfactual is at odds with his treatment of the expedition in book 6. On the eve of the Sicilian expedition, Thucydides has Nicias advise the assembly that Athens would be "running the greatest risk in its history."[124] Echoing the Corinthians he uses the word *tolma* (reckless daring) to describe Athenian behavior. Thucydides' account suggests that the expedition is foolish, should never have been attempted by rational actors, and is doomed to failure.

Here too, perhaps, this seeming contradiction can be reconciled. Let us suppose that more forces and support at home might have enabled the Athenians to conquer Syracuse, and perhaps much, if not all of Sicily. Success would only have whetted Athenian appetite for further conquests. Thucydides tells us that Alcibiades, who abhorred accepting the status quo and favored expansion whenever possible, intended to challenge the Carthaginians next. Success in Sicily would have strengthened his hand, made Athenians more aggressive, and promoted an even more ambitious adventure. So, here too, disaster would only have been postponed.

Revisiting Cause

Thucydides claims to be interested in "the truest cause" (*alēthestatē prophasis*) of the Archidamian War and the Sicilian expedition.[125] The truest cause he identifies – the rise to power of Athens and the fear it inspired in Sparta – has been narrowly read by realists and some classicists to mean the growth of Athenian military power and the threat it posed to Spartan security. *Dunamis* has a wide lexical field and can refer to different kinds of power and, more particularly, their exercise. *Phōbos* can describe fears arising from diverse causes. I contend that most Spartans did not feel physically threatened. Those in favor of war were overconfident in their ability to thrash the Athenians – not unlike the hotheads in southern states ready to draw their swords in 1861 and "whup" the Yankees in a short and glorious war. Spartans were threatened because of Athenian economic and cultural power that made it increasingly respected in Hellas, a source of envy and emulation by others. Sparta, and its way of life, was increasingly seen as anachronistic and respected only for its military power. Prestige and identity were the principal concerns of Spartans in favor of war and also of those who hoped for an accommodation with Athens.

Thumos was perhaps the most important underlying cause of war, making Thucydides' account "a possession for all time" because the drive for recognition, honor, and standing is so fundamental to human beings. Those advocating military action in Sparta did not regard it as a war of defense but of revenge. They were getting back at Athens for its increasingly dominant role in Hellas, thereby stealing their thunder and threatening to marginalize them and their culture. Anger (*orgē*), not calculation, motivated them and it pervades the speeches of both Sthenelaïdas and Sparta's allies. Pericles and those who supported him were no more willing to accept the status quo. The Corinthian depiction of Athens, while perhaps an exaggeration, captures elemental features of its political culture. Pericles' successors were less thoughtful and less inclined to tread carefully. It was no accident that Alcibiades, not Nicias, won the support of the assembly.

Thumos may have been the deepest cause of the war but there were many enabling causes. By examining the origins of the Archidamian War and the Sicilian expedition at several levels of analysis, I have been able to identify these causes. They include dissatisfied lesser powers, the ability of allied tails to wag hegemonic dogs in both alliances, the distinct political cultures of Athens and Sparta, changes in Athenian cultures due to the pressure of war, the goals and political skills of leaders, and good and bad fortune. We could stop here but a laundry list of causes is not a very satisfying conclusion. We need to ask the extent to which these enabling causes, and perhaps, good and bad fortune as well, were dependent or independent of fundamental underlying causes.

Structural approaches of international relations, which include realist, power transition, and Marxist theories, emphasize underlying causes. They assume that immediate causes are mere pretexts and unproblematic. This assumption is sometimes warranted. In February 1965, in the aftermath of a Vietcong attack on the American advisors' barracks at Pleiku, National Security Advisor McGeorge Bundy wrote a memorandum to President Lyndon Johnson urging the sustained bombing of North Vietnam. Secretary of State Dean Rusk advised him that incidents like Pleiku were like "streetcars." He could count on repeated Vietcong attacks against South Vietnamese forces or their American advisors to provide him with the pretext he needed at the opportune moment to sell escalation to the president.[126]

Pretexts do not always resemble streetcars. They may be infrequent, inappropriate, or fail to materialize and, without a catalyst, the expected behavior may not occur. In a matter of months, or years, underlying conditions can evolve to make war less likely even if an otherwise appropriate catalyst ultimately comes along. The window of opportunity for war – or peace – may be temporally narrow or broad depending on the nature and rate of changes in the underlying conditions. Either may require a conjunction of underlying pressures and appropriate catalysts.[127]

Catalysts are often complex causes in their own right, as Sarajevo was in 1914. The twin assassinations caused the Austrian leadership to reframe the problem of Serbia. Risks that had been unacceptable in the past now became tolerable, even welcome. The independent role of catalysts creates another problem for theories and attempts to evaluate them.[128] All the relevant underlying causes for a war or accommodation may be present, but, absent a catalyst, it will not occur. The uncertain and evolving relationship between underlying and immediate causes not only makes point prediction impossible; it renders problematic more general statements about the causes of war and system transformations – and many other international phenomena – because we have no way of knowing which of these events would have taken place in the presence of appropriate catalysts, and we cannot assume that their presence or absence can be treated as random.[129]

In *Forbidden Fruit: Counterfactuals and International Relations*, I identify four classes of catalysts or immediate causes. Type I catalysts are common occurrences linked to the underlying causes of the event we are trying to explain. Border incidents might also fit into this category. They are generally outgrowths of deeper conflicts between countries and historically have served to trigger wars. They have sometimes been arranged with this end in mind.

Type II catalysts are events with independent causes but that nevertheless occur frequently and can serve as catalysts when the appropriate conditions are present. Rainfall is independent of traffic but a regular event in temperate climates. It will almost certainly bring about an increase in fender benders on heavily trafficked and slick streets and more so still in aggressive driving cultures or in countries like India where one does need a license to purchase or drive a car.

Type III catalysts consist of events that are not only independent of underlying causes but infrequent. Staying with our illustration of road accidents, this might include fatalities caused by a bridge collapse, as happened in August 2007 on Interstate 35 where it crosses the Mississippi River in Minneapolis. The collapse occurred during the rush hour and at dusk, a time of poor visibility, which increased the number of fatalities, but the timing was unconnected to the causes of the collapse. Bridge failures are relatively infrequent events and their distribution is entirely independent of the underlying causes of the events in which we are primarily interested.

Type IV catalysts are also independent of underlying causes. Like viruses that require a specific surface architecture to penetrate a target cell, they must meet a set of additional requirements to serve as catalysts. Sarajevo is the quintessential example. The assassinations were the outgrowth of an internal struggle for power in Serbia and their timing was entirely independent of the confluences that made leaders in Vienna, Berlin, and Petersburg more risk-prone. As noted, Sarajevo created or helped to bring about four critical conditions without which Austria would not have declared war on Serbia. This is one important reason why World War I was so contingent.

What about the proximate causes of the Archidamian and Peloponnesian Wars and the Sicilian expedition? They strike me as a combination of Type I and Type II catalysts. Events were set in motion by rivalries among lesser powers. In 431, the major offenders were Corinth and Corcyra. In 418, it was Argos, and, in 415, Egesta. Conflicts and wars were endemic among Greek poleis and largely independent of the tensions between Athens and Sparta. They are like Dean Rusk's streetcars. Not every polis looked to Athens or Sparta for support against their rivals. These appeals were independent but less frequent and therefore a Type II catalyst. What is interesting is that the three times such streetcars stopped at the Pnyx, Athenians clambered aboard.

This behavior suggests that willingness to support third parties at the risk of triggering wider wars was perfectly acceptable to a majority of Athenians and that on all three occasions at least some of them were looking for pretexts for war. Certainly, this is true of Alcibiades and his supporters. With Pericles, it is not self-evident. Did he think a defensive alliance with Corcyra would lead to war with Sparta? He recognized the possibility it could because he justified the alliance on the grounds that war with Sparta was all but inevitable. He also seems to suggest that the alliance might deter Sparta, making war less likely. Whatever he believed, he must have recognized that the alliance could make war more likely in the near future.

The relevant comparison may be to the German chancellor Theobald Bethmann-Hollweg in 1914. He and Kaiser Wilhelm believed that war was inevitable and better fought now than later but neither had the political courage or psychological sangfroid to commit themselves directly to war in the July crisis. The chancellor also faced a domestic political problem. To go to war, he needed the support of the Social Democratic Party (SPD), the largest party in the Reichstag, and they would not vote funds for what they regarded as an aggressive war. By giving their so-called blank check to Austria, the Kaiser and the chancellor set in motion a chain of events whereby Austria sent a draconian ultimatum to Serbia, Serbia rejected it, and Austria declared war on Serbia and mobilized, provoking Russian mobilization in return. The Russians could not mobilize against Austria-Hungary alone but had to do so against Germany as well. This triggered German mobilization and, with it, the invasion of Belgium and France, as stipulated by the Schlieffen

Plan. Bethmann-Hollweg was able to portray Russian mobilization as an act of aggression against Germany. The socialists viewed autocratic Russia with loathing and rallied to the government's support.[130]

Pericles had to overcome considerable opposition to get support in the assembly for alliance with Corcyra. There is no way he could have convinced Athenians to vote outright for war. The best he could do was, like Bethmann-Hollweg, set events in motion in the expectation or hope that they would either humble Corinth or lead to war in a way that made it look defensive. He succeeded in the latter objective. Bethmann-Hollweg and Kaiser Wilhelm were incapable of starting a war. They had to convince themselves that they were only supporting their ally Austria and that, if war came about, others would bear responsibility for it.[131] As Pericles was more stable psychologically than either German leader, he may well have had war in mind but his scenario still resembled theirs, and had to because of his domestic problem.

We can make a similar case with respect to leadership, which I will do momentarily. If Athens produced the kind of leaders it did because of the character of its citizenry, their policy preferences cannot be considered random. Leaders offer more evidence that underlying and immediate causes of the Archidamian and Peloponnesian Wars and the Sicilian expedition were tightly coupled. Underlying causes did not determine events but influenced the beliefs, expectations, fears, and thus the actions of leaders and peoples that made some outcomes considerably more likely than others.

Cause is a central concept for Thucydides. He uses it to order and make sense of events and knows his readers will do the same. To the extent that he suggests or attributes causes, they are social in origin, something like the plague aside. As noted at the outset of this chapter, the demos and some political leaders look to the gods for explanations of events but Thucydides does not. His account of the plague, in contrast to Sophocles in *Oedipus Turannus*, focuses on its etiology and physical and consequences.[132]

Because Thucydides is interested in what we call underlying and immediate causes and their relationship, he creates or suggests what we call causal sequences. The most elaborate of these is his account of the causes of the Archidamian War. The first causal chain describes the escalating conflict between oligarchs and democrats in Epidamnus and how it leads to stasis. A second chain describes the origins of the conflict between Corcyra and Corinth, which quickly intersects with the first in ways that bring to the two cites into conflict. A third causal chain provides an account of the conflict between Athens and Sparta, and this intersects with the second chain. In each instance, the mechanism that brings about confluence between causal chains is a disadvantaged party in one conflict looking for outside support against its adversary. There is an increase in scale at each step of escalation. An international conflict in a small city at the periphery of Hellas is transformed into one between two sizeable naval powers and this in turn into a larger conflict still between two alliance systems. Once the war begins, other cities are ineluctably drawn in.

The Archidamian War is the precursor to the Peloponnesian War, and here too we confront a similar pattern of interlocking causal chains. In this follow-on war, the search for support carries the war further afield, notably to Sicily, and involves additional actors, including Persia. The mechanism of escalation is the same: weaker units seek the support of stronger ones. The Persian intervention, which in many ways proves decisive, is sought by Sparta to offset Athenian wealth and naval superiority.

In both wars, escalation is the product of confluences among multiple chains of causation. One way of determining the contingency of outcomes is to evaluate the independence of these chains of causation and the reasons why they came into confluence. Thucydides makes no effort to do this but gives us enough information to attempt the task. The chains of causation appear independent but their confluences less so. The Corcyraeans jump at the chance to support the democrats from Epidamnus, and the Corinthians at the opportunity to support their opponents. As we have seen, the Athenians repeatedly succumb to such requests, and for multiple reasons. So too do further involvement and escalations seem highly likely given the nature of these alliances and the duration of the wars between them.

Again, we can make a comparison to World War I. Elsewhere I have described a confluence in 1914 among three independent chains of causation that made leaders in Vienna, Berlin, and St. Petersburg significantly more risk-prone than they had been even six months earlier.[133] These chains only came into confluence for a relatively short period of time: three years at most. By 1916 or 1917, developments in each of these countries would have made policymakers increasingly risk-averse. Sarajevo was an independent and unlikely proximate cause, and it is difficult to imagine an alternative catalyst that would have served the same purposes or any other European great powers starting a war. For all these reasons, World War I was highly contingent in both its underlying and its immediate causes. This is not true of the Archidamian and Peloponnesian Wars or of the Sicilian expedition. They have degrees of contingency but not nearly as much as World War I.

Speeches. Like Homer and Sophocles, Thucydides presents two different understandings on cause: his own and that of participants. Like Sophocles, he encourages us to compare and contrast the two perspectives.

Thucydides' take must be inferred from the occasional authorial statement, what political actors say and do, the structure of his narrative, the overall sequence of events, what is included and omitted, the pairings of events, and parallels between them.

The speeches that figure so prominently have long been recognized by scholars as critical to any reading of Thucydides' text.[134] They purport to tell us something about the perspectives of individual actors, although we must be careful to not take their words at face value. They also speak beyond themselves when we make comparisons between speakers, across sets of paired speeches, the issues they address, the stage of the conflict at which they occur, and the cities they represent. I have used actor and analytical perspectives to explore cause and contingency. The speeches illuminate an as yet unexplored aspect of cause: the way in which speakers invoke it rhetorically to advance their ends. This is interesting in its own right but also has causal implications. Rhetoric and action are connected because *logoi* (words) are not distinct from *erga* (deeds) but are another form of them. Indeed, the speeches emphasize the power of words to construct different worlds for their audiences. Speakers do this through arguments but, more importantly, through priming. By arousing, intensifying, and focusing emotions, most notably fear (*phōbos*), *orgē* (anger, passion), *erōs* (desire), and *elpis* (hope), they get listeners to reframe what is at stake and how their city should respond.

Speakers almost always offer reasons of state for the policies they advocate, and most of these pertain to warding off threats or exploiting opportunities. Successful speakers like Pericles and Alcibiades arouse emotions to reinforce their arguments and undercut those of their opponents. Reactions to speeches by Athenians and Spartans suggest that emotions are more persuasive than arguments and that rhetorical skill is a more important political asset than *gnome* (rational intelligence). Sthenelaïdas offers the strongest support for this assertion, and his successful speech in favor of war offers not one argument but succeeds with his audience by arousing their anger and sense of shame. The Mytilenean debate, that pits Cleon against Diodotus, reveals that a change in heart among Athenians was largely responsible for their policy reversal.[135] In the Sicilian debate, Alcibiades' arguments are so far-fetched they border on the farcical. His audience is clearly swayed by his ability to arouse fear and hope in ways that make these emotions reinforcing.

Modern-day realists invoke underlying causes to explain international events, especially wars. Constructivists also recognize the importance of underlying causes but do not treat them as objective, as many realists do. Rather, they look to the subjective understandings actors have of events and perceived opportunities and constraints and which they think most important. Thucydides seems akin to constructivists because his speeches indicate that so-called underlying causes are never features of the environment but creations of actors. As a sophisticated student of politics, he recognizes that actors often exaggerate the constraints and opportunities they perceive. They even invoke or invent them to mobilize support for policies they desire for other reasons. Perceived opportunities and constraints are rarely determinant. Consider the Spartan fear of becoming marginalized in Hellas due to the rising power and influence of Athens. As we saw, this widely shared fear promoted diametrically opposed strategies of coping.

The search for underlying causes brings us back to agents. Why do they emphasize certain environmental constraints or pressures? One answer is that they do it to justify and arouse support for policies that will advance their political or personal interests. This is evidently true of Alcibiades in the Sicilian debate.[136] Today's equivalent are politicians who warn of being overrun by immigrants merely to gain an audience and a political base. Nicias, by contrast, plays the same game as Alcibiades, albeit in a much-attenuated form; he exaggerates what he believes to be the impediments to success in Sicily in an attempt to forestall the expedition, a goal he honestly believes is in his city's best interest.

Some political actors are honestly moved by their understandings of their domestic and foreign environment. Thucydides encourages us take Archidamus and Sthenelaïdas at face value. They call it as they see it, although they do not necessarily see it correctly. Sthenelaïdas is most certainly wrong in his expectation of a quick, easy victory, and Archidamus may be overly optimistic about the possibility of living in peace with Athens. His premise remains an untested counterfactual, although one I suspect was unlikely given Athenian restlessness.

Pericles is a more ambiguous case. He insists that war with Sparta is inevitable and therefore urges alliance with Corcyra. If this leads to war, Athens will fight it at a significant advantage; and, if not, Corinth will be humbled, Sparta isolated, and Athens strengthened. He plays on the emotions of the demos but in a manner that Thucydides would have us believe is the opposite of what Alcibiades does. Victoria Wohl suggests that Thucydides sees the demos is "congenitally passionate," and "without Pericles' wise guidance it veers naturally between hubristic overconfidence and irrational despair."[137] Thucydides attributes Pericles' skill and commitment to the higher interest of polis to his character. Yet he still exercised bad judgment. Donald Kagan suggests that Pericles hoped to avoid war but seriously miscalculated, an argument with which I am sympathetic.[138] If so, Pericles made his expectation of war self-fulfilling, giving truth to Bismarck's wry observation that "preventive war is like committing suicide for fear of death."[139] An alternative, and equally compelling, reading is that Pericles wanted war and deliberately provoked Sparta to bring it about. If so, the difference between him and his successors was one of degree not of kind.

Key actors invoke cause as a rhetorical device. They depict dire scenarios that will come to pass unless their advice is followed. Pericles and Archidamus offer such scenarios as justifications for their preferred courses of action. To understand the causes of the Archidamian and Peloponnesian Wars, or of the Sicilian expedition, we must start with the recognition that cause is not only something we deploy to understand the world but something used by political actors to shape it. They describe pathways to positive or negative outcomes to frame and sell policies. Some actors have the best interest of their society in mind and believe in their causal narratives. Others sell snake oil. They frighten or titillate their audiences to advance their own ends. The Bush administration's full-court press to convince the American people to support an invasion of Iraq is a modern example. Americans were told that Saddam Hussein was on the verge of acquiring weapons of mass destruction and had to be stopped before he succeeded. None of these allegations were true and key players in the Bush administration knew it at the time. They wanted to invade Iraq and overthrow Saddam for very reasons different than those they offered.[140] Like Alcibiades, they followed Groucho Marx's advice to "always be sincere whether you mean it or not."[141]

Both kinds of political agents have considerable freedom to construct and sell their scenarios because the future is largely opaque. We are never sure how others will behave or respond to our initiatives, nor do we know what the knock-on effects of these interactions will have. All too often, they have consequences not at all like those predicted. This was true of Iraq. The Anglo-American invasion destabilized not only Iraq but much of the Middle East, diminished American influence, probably accelerated North Korea's efforts to become a nuclear power, increased Iran's influence, and helped to create the political vacuum and intensified anti-Western feelings that propelled ISIS into prominence.[142] Like Oedipus, the Athenians and the Bush administration made their worst fears self-fulling.

Thucydides follows Sophocles in using what might be called a reverse form of irony: Actors sometimes make forecasts that turn out to be more accurate than they realize. Creon, Antigone, and Oedipus all do this, as do the Athenians in the Melian Dialogue where they deride the Melians for precisely the kind of folly they will soon commit.[143] Both kinds of irony rest on the contrast, even contradiction, between the knowledge actors think they have and the knowledge that their audience or readers actually possess. Sophocles and Thucydides are telling us that politics involves commitment and that actors commit themselves in ignorance of the consequences of their actions. Human nature requires them to believe they are making good judgments so they convince themselves of this and do so by means of causal narratives.

These narratives often stress necessity because it is another means of reducing anxiety. "I had no choice but to do what I did" is an excuse we tell others after our behavior or policies produced unfortunate results.[144] Of equal importance, necessity is something we convince ourselves of before we act. We reduce anxiety by reducing choice and make possible commitment to a risky action. The Athenians present in Sparta insist that they were "forced" (*katēnankasthēmen*) to establish their empire, "first by fear, then by honor, and finally by advantage (*ōphelias*)."[145] We also convince ourselves, as I noted in the previous chapter, that others are freer to act because they do not face the same constraints. This is an important underlying cause of miscalculation and one reason, among many, why scenarios like that of Pericles often prove illusory.

Necessity – or its imputed absence in the actions of others – is another cognitive tool like cause and closely related to it.[146] Both are responses to emotional needs. When we take risks we are often motivated by fear, anger, ambition, hope, or envy. Invocations of necessity make it easier to commit to this kind of behavior by reducing the anxiety associated with it. For the same reason, we are driven to construct rosy forecasts to advance and justify our actions, to others certainly but, of equal importance, to ourselves. This tendency is powerful enough to affect even selfless actors who want to act with the best interests of their political unit in mind. They may behave little differently from those who are patently committed to their own self-interests.

Tragedy. Sophocles' and Thucydides' tales are populated by individual people, although their actions may have wider consequences. It is generally accepted that tragic heroes make bad choices because of their natures (*phusis*) but that these choices are free ones because they have the power to act otherwise.[147] Charles Segal describes Oedipus as "both free and determined, both able to choose and helpless in the face of choices that he has made in the past or circumstances (like those of his birth) over which he had no power of choice."[148] Philip Vellacott suggests that Oedipus reveals choice and predetermination to be "a box of mirrors."[149] The same can be said about the Athens and Sparta of Thucydides.

Cause and the Polis

In this chapter and Chapter 2, I have tried to unpack this box of mirrors and explore the relationships between actions and their consequences at different levels of analysis. Sophocles and Thucydides feature people and poleis whose actions have unintended consequences. They suggest two fundamental explanations for this phenomenon. First is wishful thinking. People are overly confident about their forecasts even though they often entail complex scenarios that require multiple actors to behave in prescribed ways. Second is chance, which can take the form of accidental encounters, events with unexpected outcomes, and confluences. Wishful thinking is often a product of arrogance. Political actors make forecasts consistent with and supportive of their goals and expect to succeed because they have in the past. They deny, distort, and ignore information to the contrary and the possibility that chance will interfere with the scenarios and outcomes they envisage. The two causes are, of course, reinforcing because the more complex a scenario, the more open it is to chance. Powerful actors are the most likely people to be arrogant, succumb to hubris, and pursue risky policies and practice denial.[150]

Sophocles and Thucydides suggest that tragedy also occurs in the absence of hubris. People are driven by their appetites and *thumos*, and their efforts to gain wealth and status bring them into conflict with one another. *Thumos* is the bigger offender of the two drives because honor, unlike appetite, is a relational quality. It drives Creon, the young Oedipus, and his sons, and most of the key figures in Athens and Sparta. The resulting competition among them is intense and violent, as it is in the *Iliad*, and for much the same reason. The search for security, but even more for honor, has the potential to make everyone less secure and less respected. The ultimate source of tragedy is human nature. Liddell and Scott show that appetite (*epithumia*) and *thumos* derive from the same root and are largely inseparable in Homer.[151] By the time of Plato, they are conceptualized as distinct and even competing drives.[152] Thucydides is arguably closer to Plato in this regard.

Sophocles and Thucydides differ from Homer in that they are writing in the era of the polis. They reflect a shifting emphasis on what people seek and why they violate norms. For Homer's characters, human and divine, the motive is most often the quest for honor. This is most evident in the *Iliad* but is a theme that also runs through the *Odyssey*. Honor, and the drive for revenge when heroes feel slighted, is the root cause of the conflicts between Hellas and Troy and Achilles and Agamemnon. Honor is won by excelling in rule-based competitions. Violation of these rules provokes anger, as when Paris is whisked away by Aphrodite and Menelaus is wounded by the Trojan archer Pandarus.[153]

Honor degenerates into a struggle for standing when competitors disregard the rules governing this competition. Agamemnon does this when he appropriates Briseus and so do Penelope's suitors when, like locusts, they descend on Odysseus' estate and consume its resources. This behavior justifies Achilles' rage and Odysseus' slaughter of the suitors and hanging of the maids who became their bed partners. Heroes are distinguished from villains by their adherence to the rules. Achilles loses status when he violates them, initially in his response to Agamemnon and more so after the death of Patroclus. He regains his honor – and with it his humanity – in the final book of the *Iliad*, when he hosts Priam and returns Hector's body to him. Sophocles and Thucydides tell stories about people who are initially honorable but then ignore rules in their quest for power. Creon attempts to kidnap Antigone and later refuses Polyneices a proper burial. Athens and Sparta begin the Archidamian War as honorable actors but soon seek victory by any means. The Spartan killing of the prisoners they take at Platea and the Athenian slaughter of the Melians represent paired turning points in this process. The Peloponnesian War degenerates into a struggle for standing, achieved by any means.

In the *Iliad*, Paris and Helen stand out because they are driven by their appetites. So too are Penelope's suitors in the *Odyssey*. Appetite becomes more pronounced in Sophocles and dominant in Thucydides. Creon claims to be committed to civil order and the honor associated with kingship. Sophocles makes clear that he has a lust for power that leads him to act in ways that undermine order and his authority. Polyneices is his mirror image. Athenians claim to be motivated by fear, interest, and honor, but interest becomes paramount as the war progresses and it is visions of wealth that move the Athenian assembly to vote in favor of the Sicilian expedition. This is presaged by the debate at the outset over the Corcyraean alliance. The Corinthians appeal to the Athenians to remain neutral and use the language of justice throughout, admittedly in a two-faced way. The Corcyraeans use the new language of money and economic exchange, in an equally underhanded way, but prove persuasive.

The world of the polis is more complex than that of the *oikos*. The polis contains more people, has more elaborate bottom-up and top-down orders, and has a civil hierarchy distinct from familial ones.[154] The polis has assumed responsibilities that were once private, most notably the dispensing of justice. Cause has become more problematic. This is attributable in the first instance to the more complex and multilayered nature of Greek societies. It makes cause more difficult to track when outcomes are the product of interactions among many agents, some of them collective agents like the courts and assembly.

Cause is also more complex because it has become a means to an end. It is not something for the aloof analyst to ponder but central to the everyday lives of people. They think more in causal terms more than their predecessors because they are acting less habitually – that is, less in response to their knowledge of the right way to behave and more in pursuit of their perceived interests. They must "game" situations and make forecasts of how others will respond to their initiatives, and vice versa. Their forecasts are invariably causal in nature.

Cause is also more important and more difficult to fathom in a world characterized by pervasive and ceaseless change. The Homeric *oikos* faced challenges but they were known ones, as were the repertoire of ways of responding to them. In the late fifth-century polis, especially democratic cites, the nature of challenges evolved as did responses thought appropriate to them. Individuals and political leaders had to be alert to these changes and the reasons why one response might be preferable to another. Both kinds of inquiry are causal in nature.

Cause also became an important political tool. People offer explanatory narratives to others to justify their behavior, something Athenians witnessed every day in the law courts. In the assembly, they heard forward-looking narratives about what would or would not happen if a particular policy was or was not adopted. Causal narratives had become an art form used for self-aggrandizement and were accepted as such. Failure to offer them to support one's policy or justify one's behavior was considered inappropriate in personal relations and in the courts. The most egregious violation of this norm in Thucydides is in the Melian Dialogue, where the Athenian generals make no references to justice, only to the right of the powerful to do what they want. The omission of hypocrisy is intended as a pathology and suggests a certain similarity with how the Persians treated the Athenians.

Responsibility and cause are closely linked in Homer. The plague at the outset of the *Iliad* is a direct result of Agamemnon's violation of nomos and refusal to return Chryseis to her father. Homer provides the mechanism linking cause and effect: Chryses prays successfully to Apollo. In *Oedipus Turannus*, the plague that strikes Thebes is the result of Oedipus' pollution of the city. We learn about the causal connection from Tiresias the seer, who has a connection to the gods. The Athenian plague, by contrast, just happens. Perhaps some Athenians interpreted it as a punishment for the actions that led to war with Sparta, but Thucydides never suggests anything of the kind. In his narrative, other significant outcomes are more difficult for actors to understand.

Sophocles differs from Homer in that he compels his audience to make their own causal inferences. They might conclude, without ever being told so by Sophocles, that tragic outcomes are the work of the gods. Alternatively, they might reason that they are due to chance. Sophocles' characters voice both explanations, often in self-serving ways. Causes and their mechanisms are hidden and problematized in Sophocles in a way they are not in Homer. This seems more in keeping with the experience, and perhaps the expectations, of his fifth-century audience.

Thucydides takes this uncertainty to another level. There are known unknowns but many more unknown unknowns. The fact that something has happened one way in the past does not mean it will happen the same way again. The mechanisms that mediate between action and consequences are rarely evident and we are never offered divine intervention as an easy way out. We are left with the impression that it is not so difficult to understand why people act as they do or why they can persuade others to follow them. Yet the relationship between action or policies and their outcomes remains largely opaque. Depending on the circumstances, the same actions can have diametrically opposed results. This happens because the chain of events they set in motion are affected by other decisions and events, which may be independent and unforeseeable. The Athenian success at Pylos offers a striking example.

In Homer, responsibility and cause are more closely connected than they are for his successors. There is less of a gap in time between cause and effect, greater transparency of causal mechanisms, and a closer connection between violations of nomos and bad outcomes. In Sophocles and Thucydides, adherence to nomos is no protection against tragic outcomes, and blatant violation of nomos can sometimes lead to success. The fifth-century polis is a world in which ethical anchors are harder to defend and in which their absence makes cause and effect more important but correspondingly more difficult to understand.

Notes

1. Fisher and Hoekstra, "Thucydides and the Politics of Necessity."
2. Lebow, *Tragic Vision of Politics*, chaps. 3–4.
3. For example, Gilpin, *War and Politics*; Organski and Kugler, *War Ledger*; Waltz, *Theory of International Politics*; Mearsheimer, *Tragedy of the Great Powers*. For critiques of the realist literature, see Garst, "Thucydides and Neorealism"; Forde, *Ambition to Rule*; Lebow, "Thucydides the Constructivist."
4. Ehrenberg, *Sophocles and Pericles*, pp. 95–98, 145–149.
5. Smith, *Wealth of Nations*, 4.2.9., *Theory of Moral Sentiments*, 4.1.10.
6. Thucydides, 1.22.4, 2.50.1, 3.84.2, 1.22.4, 3.82.2, and 5.68.2 on human nature.
7. Ibid., 1.76, 2.50, 3.39, 3.45, 4.61, 6.78.
8. Ibid., 1.70, 1.121, 2.35, 2.64, 3.39, 3.40, 4.3, 4.19, 4.60, 4.61, 5.103, 6.16, 6.17, 6.79, 7.14.
9. Ibid., 2.54.4.
10. Ibid., 1.78.4, 140.2, 141.1, 144.2, 145, 7.18.2.
11. Rawlings, "Writing History."

12. Remak, "1914"; Lebow, *Forbidden Fruit*, chap. 3. More recently, Clark, *Sleepwalkers*, pp. 361–366; MacMillan, *War That Ended Peace*, p. xxviii; Strachan, *First World War*; Mulligan, *Origins of the First World War*; Otte, *July Crisis*. Especially, Afflerbach and Stevenson, *An Improbable War*.
13. Lebow, *Forbidden Fruit*, chap. 3; Thompson, "A Streetcar Named Sarajevo"; Lebow, "A Data Set Named Desire."
14. Aristotle, *Rhetoric*, 1382a20–1383b10.
15. Konstan, *Emotions of the Ancient Greeks*, pp. 3–40.
16. Rawlings, *Structure of Thucydides*; Connor, "Scale Matters"; Rusten, "Tree, Funnel, and Diptych."
17. Forsdyke, "Thucydides' Historical Method"; van Wees, "Thucydides on Early Greek History"; Kallet, "Pentecontaetia"; Low, "Thucydides on the Athenian Empire and Interstate Relations."
18. Weber, "Objektivität," pp. 170–172; Lebow, "Weber's Search for Knowledge."
19. Hume, "Of the Association of Ideas," section 3, and "On the Study of History." For a modern discussion, White, *Content of the Form;* Danto, *Narration and Knowledge*.
20. Thucydides, 1.23.
21. Technically, "Spartans" is the proper representation, or Lacedaemonians. Spartans is now widely used.
22. Lebow, *Tragic Vision of Politics*, chap. 3.
23. Thucydides, 1.67, 119.
24. Ibid., 1.66–88.
25. Ibid., 1.119–125.
26. Ibid., 1.70.3.
27. Ibid., 1.103–104 on the Corinthian hatred.
28. Ibid., 1.71.
29. Ste. Croix, *Origins of the Peloponnesian War*, p. 60, and a personal communication to the author, contends that Corinth might have cut a deal with Athens. Sordi, "Scontro di Blocchi e Azione di Terze Forze nello Scoppio della Guerra del Peloponneso," also finds the Corinthian threat convincing. Kagan, *Outbreak of the Peloponnesian War*, pp. 292–293, argues against the seriousness of the Corinthian threat, as does Brunt, "Spartan Policy and Strategy in the Archidamian War." Crane, *Thucydides and the Athenian Simplicity*, p. 215, concludes that it is impossible to know if Corinth was bluffing but thinks that Sparta's position would have been considerably weakened if Corinth and other allies had left the alliance.
30. Forrest, *A History of Sparta*, p. 108, "The choice appeared to lie between a technically unjustified war and a serious risk of seeing the alliance disintegrate, a nasty dilemma." Brunt, "Spartan Policy and Strategy in the Archidamian War," pp. 256–257, argues that rejection of Corinth might have had "incalculable results on the cohesion of the Peloponnesian League."
31. Thucydides, 1.71.
32. Diodorus, *Historical Library*, 11.50, cited in Ste. Croix, *Origins of the Peloponnesian War*, p. 170.
33. Thucydides, 1.86.
34. Ibid., 1.80–85.

35. Ibid., 1.144 for Pericles, and 2.65 for Thucydides.
36. Ibid., 1.79.2.
37. Ibid., 1.86–88; Tompkins, "Dialogue, Diplomacy, and the Crisis of Spartan Identity in Thucydides."
38. Thucydides, 1.88.1.
39. Ibid., Brunt, "Spartan Policy and Strategy in the Archidamian War," pp. 255–280.
40. Thucydides, 1.24.
41. Kagan, *Outbreak of the Peloponnesian War*, pp. 208–209.
42. Herodotus, 3.49.1; Thucydides, 1.13.4, 1.25.3; Graham, *Colony and Mother City in Ancient Greece*, pp. 4–8.
43. Crane, *Thucydides and the Ancient Simplicity*, pp. 95–100.
44. Kagan, *Outbreak of the Peloponnesian War*, p. 218.
45. Thucydides, 1.44.
46. Ibid., 1.37–38, pp. 23–24.
47. Plutarch, *Pericles*, 29.
48. Ibid., 29.1.
49. Kagan, *Outbreak of the Peloponnesian War*, pp. 242–245.
50. Plutarch, *Pericles*, 29, p. 196; Connor, *Thucydides*, p. 39.
51. Thucydides, 1.139–145.
52. Kagan, *Outbreak of the Peloponnesian War*, pp. 222–250.
53. Farrar, *Short-War Illusion*; Fischer, *War of Illusions*; Snyder, *Ideology of the Offensive*.
54. Clausewitz, *On War*, pp. 119–121.
55. Thucydides, 1.70.1–9.
56. Allison, "Sthenelaïdes' Speech," supports her claim by analyzing parodic elements, sentence structure, and repetition; Tompkins, "Dialogue, Diplomacy, and the Crisis of Spartan Identity in Thucydides."
57. Ibid., 1:119–125, pp. 65–69; Crane, *Thucydides and the Ancient Simplicity*, chap. 8.
58. Thucydides, 1.84.3.
59. Janis and Mann, *Decision Making*.
60. Lebow, *Between Peace and War*, chaps. 4–6; Jervis, Lebow, and Stein, *Psychology and Deterrence*; Lebow and Stein, *We All Lost the Cold War*; Lebow, *Avoiding War, Making Peace*.
61. Thucydides, 1.75.2–3.
62. Ibid., 2.61.1. See also Pericles' statements in 1.140.2, 1.141.1, 2.63.1.
63. Ibid., 1.75.3–4.
64. Ibid., 1.44.2–3.
65. Ibid., 1.75–76. Tompkins, "Dialogue, Diplomacy, and the Crisis of Spartan Identity in Thucydides."
66. Thucydides, 1.23, 1.88.
67. Herodotus, 9.53.2, 55.2.
68. Meiggs, *Athenian Empire*, p. 196.
69. Thucydides, *The Peloponnesian War*, 1.33.
70. Ibid., 1.44.

71. On the Peloponnesian League and Sparta's position in it, see Ste. Croix, *Origins of the Peloponnesian War*, chap. 4.
72. Kagan, *Outbreak of the Peloponnesian War*, pp. 22–25, offers several examples.
73. Deutsch and Singer, "Multipolar Power Systems and International Stability"; Singer, Bremer, and Stuckey, "Capability Distribution, Uncertainty and Major Power War, 1820–1965"; Waltz, "Stability of a Bipolar World."
74. Thucydides, 1.19, observes that the Spartans made sure that their allies were governed by oligarchies.
75. Ibid., 1.89–118.
76. Joseph Nye, Jr. is the person most associated with the soft power position on continued US power. For an example of his more recent statement see "The Future of American Power." For a liberal institutional variant, Ikenberry, *Liberal Order and Imperial Ambition*, pp. 1–18.
77. Thucydides, *The Peloponnesian War*, Crawley Translation.
78. de Ste. Croix, *Origins of the Peloponnesian War*, pp. 60–63; Dover, appendix 2, p. 419; Schneider, *Information und Absicht bei Thukydides*, pp. 101–110; Gomme, *Greek Attitude to Poetry and History*, pp. 156–158; Rawlings, *Semantic Study of Prophasis*, pp. 92–95; Rosenmeyer, *Art of Aeschylus*, p. 302; Connor, *Thucydides*, p. 32.
79. Crane, *Thucydides and the Ancient Simplicity*, p. 37.
80. Browning, "Greek Abstract Nouns in -*sis*, -*tis*"; Rawlings, *Semantic Study of Prophasis*, pp. 22–24.
81. Herodotus, 6, 133.
82. Rawlings, *Semantic Study of Prophasis*.
83. Lloyd, *Hippocratic Writings*; Philipps, *Greek Medicine*.
84. Browning, "Greek Abstract Nouns in -*sis*, -*tis*"; Rawlings, *Semantic Study of Prophasis*.
85. Rawlings, *Semantic Study of Prophasis*; Kerferd, *Sophistic Movement*.
86. White, *Acts of Hope*, p. 6.
87. Untersteiner, *Sophists*; Guthrie, *Sophists*; Kerferd, *Sophistic Movement*; de Romilly, *Les grands sophistes dans l'Athènes de Périclès*; Cassin, *L'effet Sophistique*; Détienne, *Masters of Truth in Archaic Greece*.
88. Plutarch, *Life of Pericles*, 5.
89. Heinemann, *Nomos und Physis*, chap. 3, section 1–2; Untersteiner, *Sophists*, p. 3; Kerferd, *Sophistic Movement*, p. 18; Saxonhouse, "Nature & Convention in Thucydides' History."
90. Neisser, "John Dean's Memory"; Spence, *Narrative Truth and Historical Truth*; Bruner, "Life as Narrative"; White, "Recall of Autobiographical Events"; Polkinghorne, "Narrative and Self-Concept"; Neisser, *Perceived Self*; Neisser and Fivush, *Remembering Self*; Nelson, *Language in Cognitive Development*; Eakin, *How Our Lives Become Stories*.
91. Grene, "To the Readers."
92. Connor, *Thucydides*, pp. 15–19, 236; Iser, *Implied Reader*, p. 58; Euben, "Creatures of a Day."
93. Lebow, *Tragic Vision of Politics*, chaps. 3–4.
94. Thucydides, 1.1.10–12.

95. Ibid., 6.1.5–7.
96. Ibid., 6.6.
97. Aristotle, *Poetics*, 1452a.
98. Vernant, "Ambiguity and Reversal," pp. 123–124, offers Oedipus as the *locus classicus* of Peripeteia.
99. Thucydides, 7.12.3, 14.1.
100. Ibid., 1.44.1–3.
101. Ibid., 1.1.44.
102. Ibid.
103. Ibid., 6.6.
104. Ibid.
105. Ibid.
106. Ibid., 6.8.
107. Ibid.
108. Ibid., 6.11.
109. Ibid., 6.13.
110. Ibid., 6.46.
111. Ibid., 6.18.
112. Ibid., 6.19, 6.24, 1–4.
113. Ibid., 6.24.
114. Ibid., 6.8.
115. Ibid., 6.12.2, 6.15; Martin, *Pericles*, pp. 139–180.
116. Thucydides, 6.9.1.
117. Joho, "Thucydides, Epic, and Tragedy."
118. Thucydides, 1.78.1–2.
119. Stahl, *Thucydides*, pp. 189–223.
120. Thucydides, 7.21.
121. Ibid., 7.2.4.
122. Ibid.
123. Ibid., 2.65.11; Rood, *Thucydides*, pp. 160–161; Stahl, *Thucydides*, pp. 89–222; Greenwood, "Thucydides and the Sicilian Expedition."
124. Thucydides, 6.23.1.
125. Ibid., 1.23.6, 6.6.1.
126. *Pentagon Papers*, vol. 3, pp. 687–691; Hoopes, *Limits of Intervention*, p. 30.
127. Lebow, *Forbidden Fruit*, chaps. 1, 3–4.
128. Ibid., chap. 3.
129. For a debate, Lebow, "Contingency, Catalysts and International System Change"; Thompson, "Streetcar Named Sarajevo"; Lebow, "Data Set Named Desire."
130. Strachan, *First World War*; Otte, *July Crisis*; MacMillan, *War That Ended Peace*; Clark, *Sleepwalkers*; Mombauer, *Helmuth von Moltke and the Origins of the First World War* and "Of War Plans and War Guilt"; Afflerbach, *Falkenhayn*; Herwig, *First World War*; Sondhaus, *Franz Conrad von Hötzendorf*; Wawro, *A Mad Catastrophe*.
131. Lebow, *Between Peace and War*, chap. 4.

132. Hornblower, "Religious Dimension to the Peloponnesian War," accuses Thucydides of deliberately downplaying the importance of the gods for Greeks of his era.
133. Lebow, *Forbidden Fruit*, chap. 3.
134. Tompkins, "Stylistic Characteristics in Thucydides: Nicias and Alcibiades"; Scardino, "Indirect Discourse in Herodotus and Thucydides"; Morrison, "Interaction of Speech and Narrative in Thucydides"; Tsakmakis, "Speeches."
135. Thucydides, 3.36–50.
136. Ibid., 6.88–93, for the latter.
137. Wohl, "Thucydides on the Political Passions."
138. Kagan, *Outbreak of the Peloponnesian War*.
139. Otto von Bismarck, "Speech of 9 February 1876."
140. Cockburn, *Occupation*; Galbraith, *End of Iraq*; Fallows, *Blind into Baghdad*.
141. Groucho Marx, *Night at the Opera* [film], 1935.
142. A US Army War College study commissioned by the then Army chief-of-staff concluded that Iran was the big winner from the war. Mary Louise Kelly (host), "U.S. Army War College Says 'Iran Was The Only Winner' In Study Of Iraq War," National Public Radio, *All Things Considered*, January 22, 2019, www.npr.org/2019/01/22/687527749/u-s-army-war-college-says-iran-was-the-only-winner-in-study-of-iraq-war?t=1548434493334 (accessed January 25, 2019).
143. Joho, "Thucydides, Epic, and Tragedy."
144. Aristophanes parodies this kind of excuse in *Clouds*, 1075–1082.
145. Thucydides, 175.2–3.
146. Ostwald, *Anangkē in Thucydides*, pp. 17–19; Fisher and Hoekstra, "Thucydides and the Politics of Necessity."
147. Knox, "Introduction," *Oedipus at Thebes*, pp. 3–14, and *Heroic Temper*; Williams, *Shame and Necessity*, pp. 21–49.
148. Segal, "Introduction."
149. Vellacott, *Sophocles and Oedipus*, p. 108.
150. Janis and Mann, *Decision Making*.
151. Liddell and Scott, *Greek-English Lexicon*, http://stephanus.tlg.uci.edu/lsj/#cid=1 (accessed September 7, 2019).
152. Plato, *Republic*, 440c–441c.
153. *Iliad*, books 3–4.
154. On bottom-up and top-down orders, Lebow, *Rise and Fall of Political Orders*, chaps. 1 and 9.

4   David Hume

> Such a philosophy [based on self-interest] is more like a satire than a true delineation or description of human nature; and may be a good foundation for paradoxical wit and raillery; but is a very bad one for any serious argument or reasoning.
>
> – David Hume[1]

David Hume was born in Edinburgh on April 26, 1711. He died there in 1776, age fifty-five, on the eve of the American and French revolutions. He spent his early years in Edinburgh and Ninewells, the family's country house at Chirnside, not far from the English border. His father died when he was two and his mother raised him and his two brothers. Hume appears to have begun his studies at the College of Edinburgh in 1721, two years younger than most other students. In university, he read law but quickly switched to philosophy where he engaged many of the questions he would later address in his *Treatise on Human Nature*. He felt stymied in his investigation and took off for France, where he remained three years. During this time, he produced a draft of the *Treatise*. In 1737, he relocated to London, revised the *Treatise*, and arranged for the first two volumes to be published in January 1739. The third and final volume appeared in October 1740 and his two-volume *Essays, Moral and Political* in 1741 and 1742.

The *Treatise on Human Nature* was a consuming passion for Hume, who believed that he had authored a revolutionary study of human nature and hoped that it would be recognized as a seminal contribution. He wrote the *Treatise* in near total isolation and suffered a psychological breakdown. His recovery was not helped by the general lack of interest in his imagined magnum opus, which proved too long and theoretical for even the educated reading public.

In the 1750s, Hume took part in an acrimonious and public debate with the Scottish church. Clerics accused him of heresy. His friends defended him, among them Henry Home, later Lord Kames. He was close to other members of the Scottish Enlightenment, most notably Adam Smith with whom he had an extensive correspondence. Short of funds, Hume took up a series of positions over the next fifteen years. He was a companion to a deranged nobleman, aide-de-camp and then secretary to a British general, and, subsequently, Keeper of the Advocates Library in Edinburgh. His publications ultimately made him financially independent but he accepted two further appointments. He served as secretary and then chargé d'affaires at the British embassy in Paris and later worked in London as undersecretary of state for northern affairs.

Hume is arguably the most radical of Enlightenment philosophers. His understanding of reason, cause, and philosophy more generally differ dramatically from that of his peers. His writings were not surprisingly controversial and often misunderstood. He was read as endorsing the skepticism of Hobbes and Malebranche and Mandeville's claim that appetite was a source of order, not disorder. Kant made him his philosophical "other" and sought to counteract skepticism by providing a logical basis for moral foundations. Hume's radicalism is still resisted. The so-called New Hume literature attempts to transform him into a realist because the philosophers involved in this project are unprepared to accept his contention that cause is an artifact of our imagination, not a feature of the world.

Hume is a powerful *avant la lettre* critic of rationalist approaches to the study of human behavior. It is ironic that positivists and regularity theorists have enshrined Hume in their pantheon. Hume would be extremely critical of their efforts to explain political, economic, and social behavior in terms of the so-called Humean causation.

Hume has original ideas about reason, cause, history, modernity, and the nature of social and political order that are worth revisiting. Ideas arise in context, and it is appropriate and interesting to ask why Hume was attracted to these questions in the late eighteenth century and found the answers he did. It is equally interesting to inquire why modern social science took what it did from Hume, seriously misrepresenting him in the process.

Skepticism lies at the heart of Hume's approach to learning. He opens his *Treatise of Human Nature* with the observation that philosophy is in ill repute. Even the "rabble" recognize that "The most trivial question escapes not our controversy, and in the most momentous we are not able to give any certain decisions."[2] Reason, the currency of philosophy, is unable to provide knowledge of this kind, let alone provide the foundations for morality. Every deductive approach is in one way or another flawed and, even if not, would never meet with anything but controversy among philosophers. For this reason, he maintains "any hypothesis, that pretends to discover the ultimate original qualities of human nature, ought at first to be rejected as presumptuous and chimerical."[3] The conclusion to *An Enquiry Concerning Human Understanding* throws down the gauntlet more dramatically. "We should commit to the flames any book or divinity or school metaphysics that contains neither *any abstract reasoning concerning quantity or number*" nor "*any experimental reasoning concerning matter of fact and existence.*"[4] Rather, we must rely on experience.

Hume also seeks to disassociate himself from Hobbes and Mandeville, regarded in his day as the key spokesmen for skepticism. Hume is undeniably a skeptic but at odds with both thinkers. He is more radical in his understanding of reason and truth than Hobbes and more nuanced in his take on appetite than Mandeville. His critiques of these and other thinkers led him down a pathway that few of his contemporaries were willing to follow. In contrast to Hobbes and Enlightenment thinkers, he minimizes the benefits of reason. Like Mandeville, he emphasizes the benign consequences of the passions but denies that egoism is the principal, much less the only, human motive. He rejects the state of nature and social contracts as useless fictions and offers a historical account of the emergence of society and government that emphasizes the role of the passions, notably sexual attraction. His approach to order is an absolute provocation to Enlightenment peers and churchmen, who regarded the passions, especially erotic ones, as a principal threat to order. Hume's construction of human nature, which I unpack in this chapter, generates a powerful and original approach to social science and the problem of political order.

Hume addresses the practical rather than the philosophical consequences of skepticism. The impossibility of making truth claims requires people to live in worlds of their own making or delude themselves into believing that there are social and religious truths. Ordinary people do the latter, Hume observes, and so do many educated people. Only intellectuals are troubled by the absence of demonstrations and few of them are prepared to accept the consequences of uncertainty. Hume sounds much like Nietzsche but there are important differences. Nietzsche was contemptuous of the masses, whom he derided for having succumbed to a slave morality. He wrote for the minority of the elite who were psychologically courageous and prepared to break free, live by their own rules, and become *Übermenschen*. Hume is sympathetic to the demos and to elites who fervently believe in what can never be demonstrated. He understands that indefensible beliefs enable people to get on with their lives; they are functional and should be judged by their consequences, not by their logic or supporting evidence. He reserves his contempt for practices that dampen and interfere with ordinary pleasures of life, like fasting, scourging, and other forms of abstinence and self-abuse dictated by religion.

Hume urges us to give up the failed project of deductive reasoning. He excoriates philosophy for building systems on logic or moral assumptions rather than on observation of human life. He foregrounds the irony that some of these systems claim to be descriptive and prescriptive. They allege to build on the god-given or natural dispositions of human beings and then urge people to act this way. Philosophy, Hume insists, cannot change human nature; it is an arid exercise and waste of time. Instead, we should learn about people from experience and observation. This epistemological claim has radical normative implications, which Hume draws out. Philosophers should no longer ask what people should believe and how they should behave – for millennia the core questions of their enterprise – but investigate *why* they believe and act as they do. How do people come to believe in the importance, indeed the necessity, of such things as cause and justice? What kinds of beliefs and behavior are universal and which are specific to particular cultures? In method too Hume insists on a radical reorientation, from abstract reasoning to experimentation. In effect, he hopes to transform philosophy into something akin to cognitive psychology.

Like present-day psychologists, Hume is committed to the experimental method and using research findings to construct "the science of human nature." He claims to be following in the footsteps of Newton, whom he asserts – incorrectly – built a science of the physical world on experiments. Hume's understanding of experimentation bears no relationship to the procedures of modern psychology. It takes the form of "a cautious observation of human life." Hume studies his own mental activities and "men's behaviour in company, in affairs, and in their pleasures."[5] His method is not as radical as he would have us believe because many of his predecessors who wrote about human nature claimed an understanding of human nature based on observation. Hume is trying to differentiate himself from philosophers who reasoned deductively and, in particular, from those who assume a deity that created people for specific ends.

Hume was careful to avoid public rejection of god and religion but in private conversations and in a posthumous essay did not drawback from the normative implications of his arguments. David Fate Norton rightly observes that Hume is better described as a "postskeptical philosopher" than an empiricist. He recognized that earlier skeptics – notably, Nicolas Malebranche, Pierre Bayle, John Locke, and George Berkeley – had made a persuasive case for skeptical metaphysics and epistemology. The task he set himself was to show how we could manage our personal and intellectual lives without any foundational knowledge. Here too, experience was a guide because, he maintained, people had been doing precisely this for many millennia.

Hume's appeal for recasting philosophy fell on deaf ears. Psychology did not develop as a discipline until the second half of the nineteenth century. It emerged in Germany and then the United States, not in England or Scotland. It addressed a very different set of questions than Hume envisaged, and developed experimentation along novel lines. Few psychologists claim Hume as a founding father as economists do his contemporary and friend Adam Smith. Ironically, utilitarians would unreasonably claim Hume as one of their own. Tom Beauchamp rightly observes that Hume offers a utility-based account of useful and agreeable qualities that people possess but never develops a normative theory founded on the greatest good for individuals or societies.[6]

Hume's influence was of a different kind. Many of his contemporaries and immediate successors regarded him as the dark prince of skepticism, the opponent of religion, and propagandist of the passions. So-called Humean skepticism inspired Kant's monumental efforts to find an alternative foundation for morality. Kant's innovative search for moral and philosophical warrants was foundational to German idealism and historicism. These movements and their offshoots took modern philosophy and epistemology in very different directions. It is worth considering the counterfactual of what might have happened if Hume had been better understood and appreciated and his pioneering endeavor built on by his contemporaries. It is conceivable that we might have avoided the sharply divergent paths of social science and philosophy that led to the impoverishment of both in the second half of the twentieth century. Social science denigrated and detached itself from the larger, enduring questions of philosophy and philosophy never took up Hume's engagement with empiricism. It is only in recent decades that some international relations theorists have sought to bridge this gap. Unfortunately, the movement remains unidirectional as there is little inclination among philosophers to become more empirical.

Humean Nature

The traditional view of human nature, going back to the Platonists, described people as hybrids between gods and animals. They had an immortal and rational part – the soul – and an animal part – the body with its senses. The soul was closer to god, and reason accordingly more valuable than the senses. Philosophers assumed that reason had the ability to guide people to god, morality, and social responsibility. God made man in his image and thus endowed him with the ability to see the world as he intended. Because the universe has been constructed in an intelligent and accessible manner, we can use our reason to understand it. Descartes gave this doctrine a boost and a modern twist in his Third Meditation. Only an infinite being, he insisted, could endow us with the imagination to infer the existence of an infinite being. Kant would be the last great exponent of this position but by no means the last philosopher or social scientist to use reasoning to make substantive and metaphysical claims about knowledge, morality, and the world.[7]

In his *Treatise* and *Enquiry*, Hume rejects the dual nature of man and the associated "Image of God" doctrine. More shocking still to his contemporaries, he upgrades the body and its senses over the mind and reason. He does his best to strip away the aura surrounding reason, arguing that people and animals reach conclusions in a similar manner.[8] By contrast, "the systems philosophers have employ'd to account for the actions of the mind ... suppose such a subtility and refinement of thought, as not only exceeds the capacity of mere animals, but even of children and the common people in our own species."[9] To add insult to injury, Hume denies the existence of the soul and, with it, any link to a creator and support for the uniqueness and continuity of individuals.

Hume offers a thin account of human nature. It differs significantly from the depiction of Descartes and others, who describe an internal struggle between reason and the passions, but also from Locke, who considers the mind a *tabula rasa*. Hume follows Locke in his interest in sensory experience but differs in his effort to reconstruct in a detailed way how the mind responds to information. He contends that it is constructed – "hardwired" in information age terminology – to respond in certain ways. Book 1 of the *Treatise* is devoted to these mental processes.

Schemas. Hume follows Descartes and Locke in believing that all sensory experience is indirect. We experience the world by means of mental phenomena, notably impressions and language. "Nothing is ever really present with the mind," he insists, "but its perceptions or impressions and ideas, and ... external objects become known to us only by those perceptions they occasion."[10] They produce something akin to what cognitive psychologists call schemas. This is Hume's core epistemological claim and he repeats it in each book of the *Treatise*, in the *Abstract*, and in *An Enquiry Concerning Human Understanding*. He is interested in how we come to believe that these impressions represent an external world.

Hume refers to sensory input of all kinds as "impressions." They consist of "our sensations, passions and emotions." Some enter the mind more forcefully and vividly than others, encouraging Hume to distinguish between strong and "faint images" or impressions. The difference between them is temporal; strong impressions are immediate ones and faint ones are those called up from memory. However, some of these latter impressions can be very vivid. The more important difference, it appears, is that faint impressions are the product of initial, vivid ones.[11] All ideas are accordingly faint impressions as they are derivative of strong impressions and based on reflections about them.

Vividness is the most important characteristic of an impression and makes us more attentive to it. Impressions have greater vivacity than ideas, which, as noted, are derivative of them.[12] Sensory impressions, not rational reflection, for the most part determine our beliefs. Hume's argument finds ample resonance in cognitive psychology, where experiments indicate that vividness increases credibility, especially when it comes to counterfactual scenarios.[13] Hume's conception differs from cognitive schemas in his insistence – mistakenly – "that it's utterly impossible to conceive any quantity or quality, without forming a precise notion of its degrees."[14]

The *Treatise* offers a lengthy account of beliefs. Impressions can give rise to secondary impressions, or ideas. Ideas can generate their own, or tertiary, impressions in the form of beliefs. If I run my finger across a knife blade, cut myself, and bleed, I experience pain and mental anguish. These primary impressions can give rise to secondary impressions – a commitment not to run my finger over a knife-edge again – and perhaps to the tertiary impression, or belief, that anything sharp is dangerous.[15]

For Hume, ideas are "causally dependent copies of impressions." "An idea assented to feels *different* from a fictitious idea, that the fancy alone presents to us: And this different feeling I endeavor to explain by calling it a superior *force*, or *vivacity*, or *solidity*, or *firmness*, or *steadfastness*."[16] Put another way, a belief is a "particular manner of forming an idea."[17] It is so forceful that it feels different from other ideas or mere expectations. For an idea to become a belief, Hume stipulates, it must have great force through its vividness. Enlivened ideas feel like primary impressions and are practically indistinguishable from them.[18] Vividness not only determines our ideas but the connections we make among them: *"when any impression becomes present to us, it not only transports the mind to such ideas as are related to it, but likewise communicates to them a share of its force and vivacity."*[19] Vividness also determines our preference for one idea over another. "When I give the preference to one set of arguments above another, I do nothing but decide from my feeling concerning the superiority of their influence."[20]

Reason. Reflection plays an important role in the creation of secondary and tertiary impressions.[21] Hume nevertheless means something different by reasoning than do most philosophers. It has nothing to do with the formal processes of deduction and induction characteristic of Aristotle and the Scholastics or modern analytical philosophy. Hume recognizes the ability of people to reason this way; his own arguments are never deductive but certainly involve very sophisticated forms of reasoning that determine what counts as evidence and how to make inferences from it. He is interested above all in discovering what people believe and why they believe it. Sophisticated reason, he contends, plays little to no part in determining beliefs. The majority of people rely instead on the limited reflective capacity necessary to create and compare ideas. Even here, the primary mechanisms at work are custom, experience, and imagination; they are the source of ideas and generally responsible for moving us from one idea to another. In the *Enquiry*, he creates more distance between reason and ideas by suggesting that ideas also arise from dreams and inaccurate memories.

For Hume, the kind of cognitive capacity people display in their everyday lives is no different from that of many beasts.[22] Dogs learn to obey their masters because they associate rewards with following their commands and punishment with disobeying them. All kinds of domesticated animals recognize feeding times and show up on schedule at their dishes or troughs. Through habit and imagination, they recognize a constant conjunction between a certain time of day and the appearance of food. Humans do the same when they infer cause. Hume insists that he wants "to make the reader sensible of the truth of my hypothesis, *that all our reasonings concerning causes and effects are deriv'd from nothing but custom, and that belief is more properly an act of the sensitive, than of the cogitative part of our natures.*"[23]

Hume denies that reason is a distinct faculty with the power to make us moral and explain the world. It is merely another cognitive faculty not in any way superior to others. In contrast to Plato and Aristotle, for whom reason was a drive in its own right that sought to discover what makes for a happy life, and to Christian philosophers, who described its putative ability to lead us to god and morality, Hume recognizes only instrumental reason. He describes two kinds of instrumental reasoning: demonstrable and probable. They come into play at the prospect of pain or pleasure and help us avoid the former or achieve the latter. He is adamant that "Reason is, and ought only to be, the slave of the passions, and can never pretend to any other office than to serve and obey them."[24] By this he means "Reason, being cool and disengaged, is no motive for action, and directs only the impulse received from appetite of inclination, by showing us the means of attaining happiness or avoiding misery."[25] He admits that people may moderate their passions, or become averse to an otherwise desired outcome, if instrumental reason convinces them that their current course of action will be more costly than advantageous.[26]

Passions. Humans are moved by their passions. *Contra* Locke, these passions are not the product of experience but inherent in us. Hume is adamant that "our stronger perceptions or impressions are innate, and that natural affection, love of virtue, resentment, and all the other passions, arise immediately from nature."[27] Like Mandeville, Hume was impressed by the wide range of things and experiences that gave people pleasure. *Pace* Rousseau, he noted that possessions were increasingly desired not for their utility or beauty but for the status they conferred. This led him to a very social understanding of passions and values. People are sensitive to and respond to cues from others because they want to be respected and admired by them.

Sensitivity to others, Hume argues, is due in the first instance to our sense of pride. It is "inner directed," to use the language of *The Lonely Crowd*.[28] We feel pride and self-satisfaction when we behave virtuously.[29] Pride is also "other directed" because it arises from the esteem of others and the praise we receive from them. It is our strong desire for pride that makes us receptive and responsive to social cues. Pride works in the same manner as other feelings; it arises from impressions that habit and imagination connect to ideas and have the potential to make them as vivid as impressions. If we feel good, we communicate this sentiment to others in our facial expressions and body movements. Friends especially respond to these signals and may experience our satisfaction vicariously. Hume attributes pride and humility alike to the ability of human beings to communicate and empathize. "The minds of men," Hume tells us, "are mirrors to one another."[30]

Sympathy for Hume is closer to our understanding of empathy; it is the ability of people to know and experience the feelings of others.[31] It plays an important part in our moral lives.[32] When we see people grieving or celebrating, Hume argues, their emotions invoke a mirror but lesser emotion in us.[33] Misery can evoke pity or contempt depending on the circumstances.[34] It also "gives us a more lively idea of our happiness."[35] Hume opposes sympathy and selfishness. Sympathy can prompt a forgetting of the self by close association with the feelings, thoughts, and needs of others so much so that the sufferings of others become one's own.[36]

Book 2 of the *Treatise* seeks to rescue the passions from the unrelievedly negative assessment of them by Plato, the Stoics, and their Christian successors. Blaise Pascal (1623–1662) wrote about "the internal war of reason against the passions" and Pierre Bayle (1647–1706) described something similar.[37] Francis Hutcheson (1694–1746) contended that god gave us an internal moral sense. This deeply entrenched philosophical tradition calls for reason to constrain and educate the passions and attributes disorder to its loss of control over them. Hume denies any internal struggle between reason and the passions. This is impossible because reason is largely instrumental. It serves the passions by mediating between them and the external environment.[38]

Hume turned to observation and introspection to see if reason could control the passions. He concluded that it was another myth. Imagination was the source of our beliefs, religion, metaphysics, moral, and identities. He insisted that "a vigourous and strong imagination is of all talents the most proper to procure belief and authority."[39] The more man turns to reason, the more befuddled he becomes. He wrote, perhaps, with his own breakdown in mind:

> The *intense* view of these manifold contradictions and imperfections in human reason has so wrought upon me, and heated my brain, that I am ready to reject all belief and reasoning, and can look upon no opinion even as more likely or probable than another. Where am I, or what? ... Most fortunately as it happens, since reason is incapable of dispelling these clouds, nature herself suffices to that purpose, and cures me of this philosophical melancholy and delirium, either by relaxing this bent of mind, or by some avocation, and lively impression of my senses, which obliterate all these chimeras.[40]

Self-Interest, Reason, and Order

Hume deploys his analysis of the mind to address key philosophical, moral, epistemological, and political questions. Central to all these claims is his critique of Hobbes and Mandeville, who assert that human beings are motivated by self-interest. Modern economics, rational choice, and all rationalist models of politics are based on this premise. Hume does not dispute the importance of self-interest but accuses Hobbes and Mandeville of defining it too narrowly. He is the author, *avant la lettre*, of one of the most powerful critiques of this approach to the study of social behavior.

Rationalist approaches wed reason to self-interest. Hume has already argued that people are guided more by habit and emotions than by reason. He goes on to challenge the belief that self-interest is the dominant, if not the exclusive, human motive. People are egoistic but also moved by benevolence.[41] He insists that concern for others – especially people we know and love or like – leads us to restrain or reformulate self-interest. This is a universal phenomenon:

> While the human heart is compounded of the same elements as at present, it will never be wholly indifferent to public good, nor entirely unaffected with the tendency of characters and manners. And though this affection for humanity may not generally be esteemed so strong as vanity or ambition, yet, being common to all men it alone can be the foundation of morals, or of any general system of blame or praise. One man's ambition is not another man's ambition; nor will the same event or object satisfy both: But the humanity of one man is the humanity of everyone; and the same object touches the passion in all human creatures.[42]

Self-interest is accordingly only one of several human motivations. People are moved by "such dispositions as benevolence and generosity ... [and] affections as love, friendship, compassion gratitude."[43] These motives cannot be reduced to self-interest.

> This principle that all *benevolence* is mere hypocrisy, friendship a cheat, public spirit a farce, fidelity a snare to procure trust and confidence; and that, while all of us, at bottom, pursue others off their guard, and expose them the more to our wiles and machinations. What heart one must be possessed of who professes such principles, and who feels no internal sentiment that belies so pernicious theory, it is easy to imagine.[44]

Restricting our focus to egoism, Hume argues, is bad psychology. Those who do this are "Superficial reasoners" and perhaps people with "no very strong restraint in their own disposition."[45] Reductionism of this kind does injustice to the complexity of the human mind and motives.[46] This diversity means that not everyone will respond the same way in the same circumstances.[47]

Self-interest is further checked by human sociability. Man is the "creature of the universe, who has the most ardent desire of society, and is fitted for it by most advantages." As evidence, Hume offers the observation that isolation is the worst punishment imaginable.[48] In effect, people tame their egoism to retain the benefits of association and intimacy with others. In his last work on the subject, Hume insists:

> We must renounce the theory, which accounts for every moral sentiment by the principle of self love. We must adopt a more public affection, and allow, that the interests of society are not, eve on their own account, entirely indifferent to us ... If usefulness, therefore, be a source of moral sentiment, and if this usefulness be not always considered with a reference to self; it follows, that every thing, which contributes to the happiness of society, recommends itself directly to our approbation and good-will. Here is a principle, which accounts, in great part, for the origin of morality.[49]

If people are not guided by reason, and if reason is unable to control the passions, how does order arise and what sustains it? Hume draws on his analysis of the emotions for an answer. He distinguishes calm from violent passions. Among the former are the sense of beauty and deformity of actions, human creations, and nature, benevolence, and sympathy. "To the most careless observer, there appear to be such dispositions as benevolence and generosity; such affections as love, friendship, compassion, gratitude. These sentiments have their causes, effects, objects, and operations, marked by a common language and observation, and plainly distinguished from those of the selfish passions."[50]

The violent passions encompass other "natural" impulses or instincts and include "the desire of punishment to our enemies, hunger, lust, and a few other bodily appetites." Passions are also divided into categories of direct and indirect. Aversion, grief, joy, hope, fear, despair, security, and among the latter, pride, humility, ambition, vanity, love, hatred, envy, pity, malice, and generosity are all direct passions because they are triggered directly by immediate impressions. The indirect passions arise from the interaction of impressions with ideas.

Hume uses this typology of the emotions to offer a radical take on individual and social order. They have little to do with reason and rather are the product of the emotions. Order prevails when there is "the prevalence of the calm passions over the violent."[51] Anger, hate, and envy are the violent passions the most in need of controlling. This is accomplished by the calm passions, especially benevolence and sympathy. Reason, by contrast, can easily lead us astray and into violent conflicts based on ideological differences. It follows that society and government should do what they can to encourage the calm passions, a strategy Hume elaborates in his political essays and *History of England*.

Hume next turns to virtues and distinguishes natural from artificial ones. Generosity, sympathy, humaneness, and all other forms of benevolence are among the natural virtues.[52] They generally make people feel good who exercise them and secure for them the approval of others.

The signs of sorrow and mourning, although arbitrary, affect us with melancholy; but the natural symptoms, tears and cries and groans, never fail to infuse compassion and uneasiness. And if the effects of misery touch us in so lively a manner; can we be supposed altogether insensible or indifferent towards its causes; when a malicious or treacherous character and behavior are presented to us?[53]

In contrast to ancient Greek philosophers, who stress the social benefits of virtuous behavior, Hume is equally sensitive to what he believes is the positive feeling that it arouses even if unobserved or unknown to others.

The artificial virtues develop over the course of time, in response to problems people encounter as their societies become larger and more complex.[54] Justice is the most important artificial virtue. It differs from and is not an extension of natural justice. Natural justice is a form of love of oneself and one's friends. Following Plato, Hume argues that we extend our love of self to love of others through the natural virtue of sympathy. It allows us to fathom and experience the feelings of others.[55] This ability does not usually extend to people we do not know or think resemble us. Sympathy "is much fainter than our concerns for ourselves, and sympathy with persons remote from us, much fainter that that with persons near and contiguous."[56] Artificial justice is a set of conventions intended to reduce conflict – largely by protecting property – in conditions of scarcity. It is a convention but one, Hume thinks, that is nearly universal although it finds local expression.

Hume's account of the development of justice and government is a historical one that dispenses with the fictions of the state of nature and the social contract.[57] At the outset, he contends, people everywhere lived in small kinship groups and natural virtues – self-love, benevolence, sympathy, and the natural justice they encourage – maintained order.[58] Life was nevertheless difficult because humans have few natural advantages vis-à-vis their predators and environment. They need to live in groups and these groups form naturally because people are drawn to one another because of their sexual appetites and security needs. "Love between the sexes begets a complacency and good-will, very distinct from the gratification of an appetite."[59] It encourages kindness and support of partners and offspring.

As the size of communities increases, so too do disputes over possessions, including women. This provides the incentive to develop conventions to manage these conflicts. There is no contract but the gradual development of norms by means of trial and error. These experiments usually take the form of one-on-one interpersonal agreements and, if successful, prompt imitation. By this means, local conventions become more general.[60] When society reaches a certain size, a crisis develops. People have more anonymity and more leeway to flaunt some conventions without being observed or punished. Violations generate the need for some enforcement mechanism, and this is the incentive for government.[61]

Justice cannot develop until conditions are ripe, and these conditions are cognitive, not just contextual. In our "wild uncultivated state," artificial conventions are inconceivable. Hume offers the amusing but compelling thought experiment of the difficulty he or any of his contemporaries would have trying to explain the concept of justice to Adam and Eve. Justice must be internalized to work, a process beyond the ken of the inhabitants of the Garden of Eden, Hume believed, or of any small group of hunter-gatherers. People will only restrain themselves when they believe that others will as well: "'tis only in the expectation of this, that our moderation and abstinence are founded."[62] Moderation ultimately rests on the desire to protect our property, another concept that took millennia to develop. The expectation of reciprocity in self-restraint requires that some authority enforces rules and makes society and justice dependent on government.

The *Treatise on Human Nature* is an undeniable tour de force. Hume offers a novel, if complicated, account of the mind and builds on it to offer what he considers a more accurate and useful account of how society develops. It is relatively parsimonious and links together seemingly different cognitive processes like imagination and reason. He begins with process, what we would call today a model of information processing, that emphasizes the primary importance of cognition in shaping our beliefs. From a simple ordering of the relative importance of imagination, habit, reason, and beliefs, and analysis of how each is primed or formed, he is able to construct a subtle account of the mind that purports to capture the ways in which people respond to each other and the world around them.

Hume then introduces substantive elements, and, here too, he dispenses with the kind of false parsimony endemic to rationalist accounts. He rejects Locke's claim of the blank slate but also the assertions of "image of god" theorists that a deity provided our species with sufficient ratiocinative capacity to recognize "his" role in creation and will regarding them. Hume's substantive account of the mind is largely a catalog of the passions, some of them more conducive to harmony and order and others inimical to them, but all in some way beneficial to individuals. He does not attribute these passions to a creator but offers an evolutionary account of their development, which was quite a novelty at the time. The natural passions are inherent in humans and provide the basis for families, clans, and societies. The artificial passions are the product of societies. Collectively, they abet individual and group survival as well as possessions and, by extension, prosperity. Rousseau, whom Hume knew well, also develops an evolutionary argument, but of human decline.

Hume extends his observations about procedure and substance to account for seemingly complex beliefs like that of causation. He focuses on causation for two reasons. It is central to how we think about the world and assumed by other accounts to be an exemplary product of human reason. Causation is, in effect, the "hard case" for a theory of the mind that downplays the role of reason. Hume attempts to show how we can reach conclusions about cause without it – and most tellingly – in a manner no different from animals. Hume does not deny the existence of complex forms of reasoning; he is a close reader of the ancient philosophers and praises Newton for his calculus and discoveries about the physical world. Hume, however, is interested in ordinary people and how they think and act.

Reason is more important to Hume's model of the mind than he acknowledges. His account of justice is rationalist. It arises from individual agreements whose success relies on reciprocity and success in turn leads the community to follow suit. The mechanisms at each step are reason and imagination. People are struck by the novelty of these agreements, observe their positive benefits, and conclude that they would be better off in a society that embraced, and subsequently enforced, similar arrangements.[63]

Epistemology

Malebranche, Locke, and Bayle made the case for skepticism with regard to metaphysics and epistemology. A leading Cartesian, Malebranche insisted that that there were no true causes in nature and that our inquiries are even incapable of demonstrating the existence of the world. Locke challenged conventional demonstrations of the existence of substances. Bayle demonstrated that contemporary theories of space and time were incoherent. Hobbes and Mandeville denied morality, or at least existing defenses of it. Hume follows these several philosophers in their skepticism but distances himself from them in important ways.

Locke insisted that we build knowledge about the world on the basis of experience and reason. Reason "perceives the necessity, and indubitable connexion of all the ideas or proofs one to another, in each step of any demonstration that produces knowledge."[64] Hume agrees that all concepts and beliefs are learned but, as we have seen, minimizes the role of reason in this process. He rejects Locke's argument that some of our impressions are accurate representations of mind-independent objects and processes, indicating at least a partial correspondence between our mind and the world. Hume finds no evidence for this claim. He insists "that nothing is ever really present with the mind but its perceptions or impressions and ideas, and that external objects become known to us only by those perceptions they occasion."[65] He repeats this claim in each book of the *Treatise*, in the Abstract to it, and in *An Enquiry Concerning Human Understanding*.

Hume would have rejected Kant's epistemology for the same reason. The Königsberg sage posited a homology between our minds and the world; this is a secular version of the "image of god" thesis. Our mind was designed to lead us naturally to concepts that describe essential features of the world. Kant offered Euclidean geometry as his most compelling example – a century later, Einstein's general theory of relativity would demonstrate that it does not map well onto the universe. Hume repeatedly rejects the idea that we can know what the world is like or anything about the powers that might be responsible for what we observe. Such powers, if they exist, remain hidden from view and unknowable. As Weber and the American Pragmatists would argue a century later, Hume believes that concepts, beliefs, and practices are best assessed on the basis of how they advance our well-being and that of our society.

Hume is not interested in the validity of beliefs about space, time, or anything else that philosophers since Aristotle have considered essential categories of understanding.[66] Rather, he wants to know what categories people invent and why they come to be regarded as natural. He distinguishes between two kinds of relation: natural and philosophical. The three natural relations are resemblance, contiguity, and causation.[67] When we see something we recognize it by comparing it to other things we have seen and know. When things touch or connect or follow closely on one another we think of them as contiguous. When one event regularly follows another, we infer a causal connection. Natural relations prompt the imagination to make "union or cohesion" among sensory impressions and create categories in which to organize them. Philosophical relations build on these categories and the concepts we use to make comparisons. They include resemblance, proportion in quantity or number, degree in any quality, and contrariety.[68] A causal connection is a natural relation but causation the concept is a form of philosophical reasoning that goes "beyond the evidence of our memory and senses."[69]

By contrast, identity and contiguity are self-evident "natural" impressions. They do not require "exercise of thought, or any action, properly speaking."[70] Known as "the copy principle," this categorization allows Hume to downgrade the importance of reason. "But though our thought seems to possess this unbounded liberty," he writes, "we shall find, upon nearer examination, that it is really confined to within very narrow limits, and that all this creative power of the mind amounts to no more than the faculty of compounding, transposing, augmenting, or diminishing the materials afforded to us by the senses and experience."[71] Put another way: "All kinds of reasoning consist in nothing but a *comparison*, and a discovery of those relations, either constant or inconstant, which two or more objects bear to each other."[72] Thinking consists of a finite set of simple manipulations and takes the form of weak impressions. The more abstract these impressions, the "more faint and obscure" they become.[73] "In short," Hume insists, "all the materials of thinking are derived either from our outward or inward sentiment: The mixture and composition of these belongs alone to the mind and will. Or, to express myself in philosophical language, all our ideas or more feeble perceptions are copies of our impressions or more lively ones."[74]

Our thoughts are mental constructs derived from external reality but can make no claim to capture that reality. We nevertheless believe that our ideas of space, time, external existences, and cause are accurate representations of the world. Hume sets himself the task not of explaining the world but of explaining why and how we come to hold beliefs about the world. Like all beliefs, they are the product of feelings and impressions, and we convince ourselves, incorrectly, that they are natural. Hume comes close to being a phenomenologist.

Cause. Hume's famous definition is a simple one. "We may define a cause as 'An object precedent and contiguous to another, and where all the objects resembling the former are plac'd in like relations of precedents and contiguity to those objects, that resemble the latter.'"[75] Hume refers to events that occur in "a regular order of contiguity and succession" as a "constant conjunction."[76] People infer a causal relationship when "A" precedes "B" and "B" always occurs in the aftermath of "A," then the former can be considered the cause of the latter. Hume's definition includes the caveat that "B" must not only precede but also closely follow upon "A," although he does not specify what he means by "contiguous." Philosophers might consider this sloppy thinking but Hume is not attempting to define cause in any objective or scientific way. Rather, he is describing how people come to see something as a product of something else and develop, in contrast to other animals, the concept of cause.[77]

Cause is a philosophical relation that builds on a natural one. It involves more than direct observation, or primary impressions. We make inferences from primary impressions to the existence of an unobserved cause or effect. It "produces such a Connexion, as to give us assurance from the existence or action of one object, that 'twas follow'd or preceded by any other existence or action."[78] Causation is the product of vivid secondary and tertiary impressions. The responsible mechanisms are custom and imagination. "For after a frequent repetition, I find, that upon the appearance of one of the objects, the mind is *determin'd* by custom to consider its usual attendant, and to consider it in a stronger light upon account of its relation to the first object. 'Tis the impression, then, or *determination*, which affords me the idea of necessity."[79] When a belief is established, it creates expectations about the world. This is attributable in the first instance to the belief itself but, secondarily, to the ability of a belief to make alternatives less easy to imagine. "When a demonstration convinces me of any proposition, but also makes me sensible, that 'tis impossible to conceive any thing contrary."[80] Hume is proposing an early version of cognitive consistency.

Our belief in cause leads our imagination to other beliefs. First and most important is the expectation that the future will resemble the past. "For whenever the repetition of any particular act or operation produces a propensity to renew the same act or operation, without being compelled by any reasoning or process of the understanding, we always say, that this propensity is the effect of *Custom*."[81] This may be the source of our propensity for linear projection and the general expectation that the future will be like the past. Second is the belief that everything has a cause. When we make repeated connections between putative causes and effects, it becomes a habit and we look for other examples and come to organize the world in terms of causation. We come to believe that nothing can exist without a cause.

Hume also contends that we are predisposed to view the world in causal terms because of the survival advantage this confers. Without causal reasoning, he insists, "all human life must perish ... All discourse, all action would immediately cease; and men remain in total lethargy, till the necessities of nature, unsatisfied, put an end to their miserable existence."[82] It is "the most instructive [form of reasoning] since it is by this knowledge alone, we are enabled to control events, and govern futurity."[83] Cause makes the physical and social worlds more predictable and thereby enhances our ability to satisfy our passions.[84] Hume is thinking like a modern-day cognitive psychologist; he understands cause as an important and useful heuristic. Our minds rely on heuristics and they develop within each of us as a result of experience, imagination, and sympathy. Hume goes further and suggests that causal inference is not only a cognitive bias but also a motivated one.

Survival has always depended on prediction. For our ancestors, knowledge of when cereals and other plants would bloom or herds of animals migrate was essential. In the modern world, we rely on the prediction of everything from traffic patterns to interest rates. Traffic patterns are highly predictable – although less so traffic jams. Interest rates are unpredictable but usually do not vary that much in the short term. We need to convince ourselves that interest rates are predictable in the longer term because, without the false confidence this allows, we could not have or sustain a modern economy. Hume lived at the beginning of the industrial age in the most commercial country of his era. He wrote essays on economic questions and was very sensitive to our need at the micro and macro level to see the world as ordered and predictable.

For Hume, what we call cognitive and motivational biases combine to convince us that cause is a feature of the world and that everything that begins to exist must have a cause.[85] He describes causation as "the most violent" of all beliefs.[86]

As nature has taught us the use of our limbs, without giving us the knowledge of the muscles and nerves, by which they are actuated; so has she implanted in us an instinct, which carries forward the thought in a correspondent course to that which she has established among external objects; though we are ignorant of these powers and forces, on which this regular course and succession of objects totally depends.[87]

Hume explains this phenomenon with reference to his prior account of belief. Some events create vivid primary impressions that we store in our memory. Dark clouds followed by rain are such impressions and lead to the idea of necessary connection. Repeated experience of what appear to be causal connections encourage the belief in cause. "When a demonstration convinces me of any proposition, but also makes me sensible, that 'tis impossible to conceive any thing contrary."[88] This belief encourages us to generalize and impute causes to all "effects" we observe. He is very clear that that causal attribution is never the product of a priori reasoning but "arises entirely from experience."[89]

Hume makes frequent references to "secret powers" and an "inviolable connexion" between perceived causes and effects.[90] He nevertheless contends that we can never know anything about such forces let alone demonstrate their existence. He adheres to a thin account of cause – avoiding any discussion of possible mechanisms – because they are unobservable and he is committed to a metaphysics-free psychology. Consider his example of a billiard ball that collides with another ball at rest. The second ball moves after being hit, assuming it is not resting against a cushion and hit head-on.

> We cannot penetrate into the reason of this conjunction. We only observe the thing itself, and always find that from the constant conjunction the objects acquire an union in the imagination. When the impression of one becomes present to us, we immediately form an idea of its usual attendant; and consequently we may establish this as one part of the definition of an opinion or belief *that 'tis an idea related to or associated with a present impression.*[91]

Try as we like to find some hidden explanation, "In no one instance can I go any further, nor is it possible for me to discover any third relations betwixt these objects."[92] Cause, like other beliefs, may or may not be real. Hume is agnostic.[93]

Hume tries hard to limit his analysis of cause to the mental world. It is not really possible to do this. For a start, all cognitive processes in Hume's model of the mind are initially based on impressions from our body or the external world. In their absence, we could not have the secondary and tertiary impressions that led to concepts and beliefs. Hume further assumes that constant conjunctions occur often enough in the world for people to recognize them and form a concept of causation. People accordingly believe in cause not only because of their mental processes but because it is an extremely useful concept. If so, there must be some degree of homology between cognition and the physical world.

Hume never admits this relationship, and, as noted, is keen to distinguish himself from Locke, who insists on it. In contrast to Locke and other predecessors, Hume argues that what people believe bears no relationship to the external world. The "difference between *fiction* and *belief*," he contends, "lies in some sentiment or feeling, which annexed to the latter, not to the former, and which depends not on the will, nor can be commanded at pleasure."[94] Belief is not a function of proof but of vividness. Yet vividness is not an entirely internal outcome. It is very much influenced by the external nature of the information we process. Here too, there is an unacknowledged relationship to the world.

There are few constant conjunctions in the real world but many regularities. It does not rain every time dark clouds appear and the wind picks up, but it does so often enough for us to make a connection between the two phenomena. If we assume, as I think Hume does, that we exaggerate the instances where something like this happens and minimize those where it does not, constant conjunction is more a product of the mind than it is of the world.[95] We impose a degree of order that is unwarranted, transforming inconstant conjunctions into constant ones. This bias serves a useful purpose. Cognitive psychologists argue that heuristics and biases became widespread among humans because they conferred important survival advantages. They nevertheless recognize that crude decision rules of this kind are likely to be misleading and even counterproductive in the performance of complex cognitive tasks. I believe that Hume has a similar understanding of cause; it is useful in daily life but not as the foundation for scientific inquiry.

Not everyone is happy with the limitations Hume imposes on his enterprise. Ken Winkler and, more recently, Galen Strawson and others try to read him as a realist concerning causal powers.[96] Their argument builds on Hume's frequent use of the terms "secret powers" and "inviolable connexion."[97] They contend that Hume believes the world exists, that causation is the cement that holds it together, but that we can never know how and why it works. This is, of course, a secularized version of religious explanations that claim god made the world and us and in a way that we could know the world and him. Realists make unwarranted empirical assumptions to resolve logical problems.[98] Worse still, they make Hume into the very kind of philosopher he denounced.

Hume indeed asserts that resemblance, contiguity, and causation are "the only links that bind the parts of the universe together, or connect us with any person or object exterior to ourselves ... They are the cement of the universe, and all the operations of the mind must, in a great measure, depend on them."[99] He is not suggesting, as Strawson and other philosophical realists assert, that resemblance, continuity, and cause structure the universe together in a literal sense. Hume is largely agnostic about the world and to the extent to which it can be described in causal terms. "Necessity," Hume insists "is nothing but an internal impression of the mind."[100] Cause and necessary power are mental constructs that do not necessarily map onto the world. They are "founded on imagination."[101]

He observes that they are often applied inappropriately, that is, in unwarranted or counterproductive ways.[102]

Stephen Turner describes the desire to make inferences – Humean and any other kind – as "a metaphysical itch that seems not to want to go away."[103] Hume would consider present-day regularity theories and philosophical realism emblematic of how humans think, which may be why they have so much appeal. In practice, Hume observed, people intuitively made causal connections and made predictions based on them.[104] In recent decades, psychologists have identified a number of cognitive biases and heuristics that appear to serve similar functions to causal inference; they help people make rapid decisions about what information to pay attention to and how to interpret it. These biases are ubiquitous and sharply at odds with rational procedures for estimating probabilities or making attributions.[105] Psychologists distinguish the former from the latter and political scientists and philosophers should do the same when thinking about causation.

Humean association captures folk practice. It is an unwarranted leap of faith to make it the foundation for scientific inquiry. It is not entirely irrelevant. Causal inference of the Humean kind might help to explain why many people are reluctant to accept global warning. Contiguity and precedence are its psychological triggers and the human causes of carbon dioxide buildup in the atmosphere are far removed in time from their putative effects. It might also help account for the prevalence of conspiracy theories. In a complex world, events, trends, and tragedies are often the unintended, unforeseen, and even unwanted result of nonlinear interactions across diverse domains of human endeavor. People accustomed to thinking in causal terms are receptive to seemingly simple explanations that attribute explanations for otherwise complex and seemingly inexplicable events to the behind-the-scenes machinations of small coteries of actors.

In Homer and Sophocles, as we have seen, the gods perform this role and might be regarded as the precursor of conspiracy theories. Reviewing the anthropological literature of his day, Claude Lévi-Strauss, citing Evans-Pritchard, attributed belief in witchcraft to the need people have to find causes for events that affect them. He described magical thinking as invariably deterministic and making the epistemological error of not allowing for contingency.[106] Umberto Eco makes a similar point.[107]

Hume's novel way of thinking about cause was enabled by developments in other fields. Ian Hacking contends that the idea of singular predictions was made possible by a series of events connected with the concept of the sign.[108] This may be true but it is tangential to Hume's fundamental claim that people from time immemorial made predictions on the basis of the conjunctions they observed. At most, the concept of the sign was useful. More germane may be Mary Poovey's argument the modern "fact" began with double-entry bookkeeping. She defines facts as tidbits of information, down-to-earth, definable, and at times countable. She suggests, rightly I think, that Hume thought in terms of facts when he formulated his problem of induction in 1739. Central to his more general argument about how we learn is his claim that all we do is process bits of information from the outside world. Poovey contends Hume as so fascinated by this realization that he left philosophy and looked at other kinds of knowledge production.[109]

Experimental Method. Hume tells us at the outset of the *Treatise*, and repeatedly in the text and other writings, that he adopts the scientific method as the best means of gaining what passes for knowledge.

> We must therefore glean up our experiments in this science from a cautious observation of human life, and take them as they appear in the common course of the world, by men's behavior in company, in affairs, and in their pleasures. Where experiments of this kind are judiciously collected and compar'd, we may hope to establish on them a science, which will not be inferior in certainty, and will be much superior in utility to any other of human comprehension.[110]

Is Hume really an experimentalist? He conducted no empirical tests, ran no controlled experiments, and certainly did not use statistics to evaluate his findings. Yet neither did he deduce his model of the mind from a few arbitrary assumptions. He claims to have built his account on observations of himself and others in the first instance and, secondarily, on his knowledge of other epochs and cultures. We should credit his claim that his model of the mind is based on informal observations of himself and others. The account Hume builds is parsimonious but messy as its components – impressions, vivacity, ideas, and beliefs – are rather loosely and imprecisely defined and related. It would have to be reformulated to make it amenable to empirical evaluation as we understand it today. Hume nevertheless lays the foundations for a rigorously empirical research program. That such a project did not develop until the late twentieth century, and quite independently of him, is hardly his fault. We should also recognize that he wrote at the cusp of a historical shift in the meaning of the term experiment. In Hume's day, it was largely equated with experience and only later came to be understood as a controlled procedure.[111]

Hume should be credited for recognizing some of the problems of the experimental method. He contends that laboratory experiments will not work in the social world because, unlike their counterparts in the physical sciences, they will interfere with and influence whatever is being studied. Rather, he insists, we must be passive observers and watch human life. His concern is legitimate but satisfactorily addressed for the most part by the use of controls in contemporary experiments. Hume is optimistic about what we can learn from experiments. "Experience can teach us much about people," he writes, "but the most fundamental aspects of our nature will always remain inaccessible; we observe only their manifestations."[112] He nevertheless warns that any theory or approach that claims to have discovered "the ultimate original qualities of human nature, ought at first to be rejected as presumptuous and chimerical."[113]

Hume's attempt to construct a science of the mind on the basis of observation encountered what we call the problem of induction. According to Mary Poovey,

> the problem of induction is the gap between one's ability to observe discrete qualities by discrete perceptions and the impossibility of explaining why we believe that qualities to the same object or perceptions belong to the same person. Without universals based on mathematical principles, we cannot know if our observations are general or particular, and whether the subjective observations or perceptions of an observer are idiosyncratic or have some epistemological significance. We cannot generalize from the or make predictions on the basis of them.[114]

The expectation of future repetitions based on observation of past events requires some prior conception of connection. They are repetitions, Karl Popper insisted, "only from a certain point of view."[115] Hume is aware of the problem and struggles unsuccessfully to find ways around it. He tries to wiggle out on the grounds that the study of human politics is in its infancy. He suggests – really hopes – that with more data and experience we will be able to gain knowledge. In a 1741 essay on civil liberty, he argued the study of man was still a young science: "We have not as yet had experience of three thousand years, so that not only the art of reasoning is still imperfect in this science, as in all others, but we even want sufficient materials upon which we can reason."[116]

An Interpretivist?

I think a persuasive case can be made that Hume is a qualified constructivist in his epistemology and analysis of politics and of human affairs more generally. His model of the mind starts with sensory experience and theorizes how we make sense of it. He follows Descartes and Locke in recognizing that we experience indirectly through language and mental phenomena. He emphasizes the importance of language in a way that resonates with constructivism; it encodes concepts that make possible mutual intelligibility and predictability. He argues for the universality of fundamental emotions and, accordingly, the need of speakers to frame their words in a way that taps into them.

> When a man dominates another his *enemy*, his *rival*, his *antagonist*, his *adversary*, he is understood ... to express sentiments, peculiar to himself, and arising from his particular circumstances and situation. But when he bestows on any man the epithets of *vicious* or *odious* or *depraved*, he then speaks another language, and expresses sentiments, in which, he expects, all his audience are to concur with him. He must here, therefore, depart from his private and particular situation, and must choose a point of view, common to him with others. He must move some universal principle of the human frame, and touch string, to which all mankind have an accord and sympathy ... The humanity of one man is the humanity of every one, and the same object touches this passion in all human creatures.

Hume recognizes that language is not a neutral medium. It teaches specific values and practices that are central to a social order. More fundamentality, language helps to make us ourselves. We are not born with interests and identities but develop them through socialization and interactions with others. "We can form no wish," Hume maintains, "which has not a reference to society."[117] Here, Hume recapitulates Hobbes, whose state of nature is intended to show that, deprived of the roles and relationships society enables, people are little more than a bundle of raw appetites and instrumental reason.

Culture. Hume read and corresponded with Montesquieu. He agreed with him that economic considerations were increasingly dominant in politics but did not accept his argument about the superiority of mixed constitutions.[118] He also rejected Montesquieu's argument about the determining effects of climate and terrain on culture.[119] Hume nevertheless shared his fascination with the diversity of human political life and constitutions and their respective causes. His reading of Montesquieu and the ancients, and his firsthand observation of political and social life in Scotland, England, and France, led him to conclude that there could never be universal morality or practices, only those specific to cultures and epochs. The principles of human nature are universal, but not their application.[120] His fellow Scots – Lord Kames (Henry Home), Adam Smith, Adam Ferguson, and John Millar – shared this perspective.

Hume was interested in national political cultures and how they changed. His *History of England* attributes the civil war to religious fervor and the intolerance and inability to compromise that it encouraged. The Protestants would not suffer royal imposition of Catholicism, and Charles I did not understand the need to reach a modus vivendi with his opponents. Both sides turned to history to justify their extremist positions; the Protestants appealed to supposed ancient liberties and the monarch to the divine right of kings.[121] Passions had since cooled but contemporary political cleavages in Britain coincided with religious ones, making politics, in Hume's view, highly charged and unstable. He worried – quite incorrectly as it turned out – that Britain was vulnerable to revolution, unlike France, which he thought relatively immune due to upheaval because of its powerful monarchy.

Hume wanted to modify Britain's political culture.[122] He modeled his political essays and *History of England* as conversations with readers in the style of the essays of Addison and Steele in *The Spectator*. Like his role models, he aspired to civilize political debate in the hope that polite exchanges could transcend the prejudices on which these differences were based, moderate positions on all sides, and encourage mutual respect and compromise. Hume's enterprise was based on the belief that the arts encouraged politeness and that it could be imported into politics.[123]

Narratives for Hume were vehicles for constructing, defending, and changing political culture. History and literature were the critical narratives for British political culture, and Hume was interested in both. His *History of England* is a history of the constitution and the role played by the crown, parliament, church, and, less often, the people. It is a tale of unremitting greed, corruption, unchecked emotions, and bad judgment. Hume details the efforts of corrupt rulers to expand or preserve their power in the face of challenges from equally corrupt individuals and institutions. The church is implicated in corruption and double-dealing at every stage of history. Neither monarchs nor parliament exercised power prudently. Contemporaries who praised the British system admired its checks and balances, which they described as critical to preserving the liberties of the people. Hume shows that the separation of powers was more myth than truth, and, when it functioned, its effect was often to intensify conflict. As for public opinion, it was frequently motivated by ignorance, superstition, and zealotry. Party competition and the inability of ordinary people to rise above their prejudices were injurious to stability.

Hume sought to expose baseless portrayals of the past that fueled partisan conflict. Not only Tories and Whigs but also country and court faction as well as different Scottish political groups looked to history for legitimization. He argued that references to Magna Carta as the origins of a balance of power between an autocratic monarch and rapacious nobles had no basis in fact because that document was merely a temporary compromise in their ongoing struggle. The British constitution was not – as Burke would shortly allege – a product of slow, organic evolution, built on the accumulated wisdom of the elite – but a recent and conscious creation. It dated back to the so-called Glorious Revolution of 1688 and its beneficial consequences were largely unintended. The mutual dependence of the king and commons, and the resulting constraints on both, worked to the country's advantage but rested on a fragile compromise. Conversely, the centralization of authority that critics of the Walpole government lamented and condemned as a novel break with the past had a long history. Royal power had begun to increase during the reign of Henry VIII, if not earlier, and was part of a general trend mirrored elsewhere in western and central Europe. Kings James I and Charles I built on the Tudor tradition of centralization. The only novelty was a standing army.

Agency vs. Structure. Hume followed Montesquieu in directing his attention away from individual actors to the institutions and other general conditions that shaped their destiny. Both men emphasized the importance of constitutions but also of religion, manners, and commerce. Hume's *History of England* differed from its predecessors in stressing general factors over personalities, although never denying the role of the latter. Like Montesquieu, he believed that the growing importance of commerce in France and Britain was creating a political culture distinct from anything in the ancient world. Hume thought that philosophy and the arts were also products of their culture and that the writings of the Greeks and Romans, brilliant as they were, had little relevance to the present.

Hume was committed to discovering general laws of human nature but was dubious about their utility for explanation and prediction. He believed that people everywhere were the same and behaved in more or less the same way. As evidence, he pointed to universal emergence of society, religion, property, marriage, and gender roles, although he acknowledged considerable variation in their practice. He recognized that people are fickle by nature, making change, not stability, the norm. These beliefs led him to conclude that "all general maxims in politics ought to be established with great caution; and that irregular and extraordinary appearances are frequently discovered in the moral, as well as in the physical world."[124]

Hume was particularly interested in conventions governing property and female behavior because of their centrality to all societies. He attributed these conventions to their utility and variation among them to differences in moral viewpoints.[125] These differences in turn reflected local traditions, access to different information, and a lack of impartiality. The last explanation implied that a better understanding of utility would encourage convergence and the jettisoning of practices that were of no benefit to the society. Ever ready to take on what he considered the absurdities of religion, Hume pointed to Christian fasting and scourging as cases in point.

Variety in practices led Hume to ponder the role of chance in human affairs. He was keen to downplay it because of its consequences for explanation and prediction.

Nothing requires greater nicety, in our enquiries concerning human affairs, than to distinguish exactly what is owning to *chance*, and what proceeds from *causes*; nor is there any subject, in which an author is more liable to deceive himself by false subtleties and refinements. To say, that any event is derived from chance, cuts short all farther enquiry concerning it, and leaves the writer in the same state of ignorance with the rest of mankind.

Hume nevertheless recognized that chance had a powerful effect in everyday life. The history of England would have been different under different rulers, and so too would his own life if he had been born in another time or place or raised in different circumstances. His solution to this problem was to distinguish micro from macro level phenomena. "Those principles or causes, which are fitted to operate on a multitude, are always of a grosser and more stubborn nature, less subject to accidents, and less influenced by whim and private fancy, than those which operate on a few only."[126] The former includes gradual revolutions of state, depression of lords, rise of the commons, increase of trade "more easily accounted for by general principles."[127]

Hume's efforts to circumscribe chance appear at odds with his agnosticism about cause. Perhaps he was unwilling to accept the radical conclusion that I believe follows ineluctably from his argument. If cause is a human artifact and not a feature of the world, there are no epistemological grounds for denying contingency, chance, and seemingly inexplicable outcomes. We should study, not dismiss or minimize, them as Hume tries to do.

Hume's analysis of the mind indicates that human behavior is unpredictable because of the multiple motives – passions, in his language – that move individuals and the inability of reason to govern or constrain them. He was adamant that self-interest was of only limited use in explaining human behavior for both reasons. People are governed more by their emotions and imagination, making their behavior, while not idiosyncratic, much more difficult to explain or predict. This is equally true of political opinions and policies. Imagination does double duty for Hume. It makes connections between and among our primary and secondary impressions, generating concepts, beliefs, and expectations. Flights of fancy also motivate action because they arouse expectations of pleasure or fears of loss. These expectations may be realistic or greatly exaggerated and the latter, he believed, were relatively immune to factual arguments.

As noted, Aristotle distinguished fright from fear. The former is an emotion aroused in response to an immediate threat, like the sudden appearance of a predator. Fear is a product of the imagination and associated with the visualization of a future threat. Hume adheres to a similar understanding. Imagined and inflated threats drive political actors, making compromise more difficult, if not impossible, between them. This is equally true in foreign affairs, where Hume considers British hatred of France to be far out of proportion to the threat it poses. Fear leads to war, further arouses the emotions, and makes defeat of France our primary goal: "we are such true combatants, that, when once engaged, we lose all concern for ourselves and our posterity, and consider only how we may best annoy the enemy." Half our wars with France and our public debts, Hume argues, "are owing to our own imprudent vehemence, [rather] than to the ambition of our neighbours."

Hume recognizes and approves of the fact that Britain "has stood in the foremost" in opposing ambitious continental powers. The British people have not shirked their responsibility. "On the contrary, if we may judge by the past, their passionate ardor seems rather to require some moderation; and they have oftener erred for a laudable excess than from a blameable deficiency." His antidote is the balance of power. It "is founded so much on common sense and obvious reasoning" that it was known to and practiced by the ancients as well as contemporary Europeans.[128] Hume hopes that the balance of power will serve as a justification for restraint and, perhaps more importantly, as a mechanism for fear reduction. The naval and financial strength of Britain can provide security if and when it is shown as equal to the task of besting France in any military conflict. Such knowledge should restrain leaders on both sides. It should also create a common frame of reference, and it is not too much to hope that it might promote a polite discourse that has the potential to build trust and encourage compromise.

Hume might be considered a realist in the international relations theory use of the term, given his emphasis on the balance of power. However, the costs and benefits he attributes to this mechanism are not those of most modern realists.[129] He argues that, for British Whigs, the balance of power was a discourse used not to constrain a defeated France but to justify further aggression against it in the pursuit of a commercial empire. He respected the concept of the balance of power and, used properly, he thought it might engender self-restraint by directing the imagination down a different pathway and, by doing so, increase hope and diminish fear. His approach to the balance of power is constructivist in the sense that it is unrelated to any objective assessments of power but rather stresses its rhetorical ends and the ways in which it has the potential to create beneficial intersubjective understandings.

The constructivist approach to behavior is bottom-up rather than top-down. Constructivists are interested in the reasons people have for acting as they do, although they recognize that these reasons are often shaped by the broader culture and the roles actors perform. Hume clearly adopts this approach. He attempts to explain human behavior in a bottom-up manner, but in full recognition that the passions and imagination that move people are responsive to cultural cues. More than many constructivists, Hume downplays the role of human reason. The "reasons" people have for acting are largely emotional; they are expressions of their passions guided in part – and only in part – by instrumental reason.

Hume's account of the mind is also in tune with constructivism in the sharp distinction it makes between the physical and the social worlds. The latter is heavily context-dependent. Hume is adamant that people vary in their imagination, egoism, and benevolence and, of equal importance, that accident significantly influences our secondary impressions – the ideas we come up with through the links we make among primary impressions.[130]

Hume goes beyond many constructivists in his belief that there is more to the social world than individual behavior. He is interested in long-term developments, like the emergence of societies, the development and internalization of justice as a control mechanism, the centralization of power, and the role of discourses in affecting imagination and behavior. He is not a precursor of Nietzsche, Gramsci, critical theory, or evolutionary psychology but deserves credit for directing his attention to many of the questions that would become central to these thinkers and approaches.

Identity. For many constructivists, identity is the master variable, the way power is for realists. They believe that identity confers those interests that are responsible for human behavior. Elsewhere I have critiqued this approach and its use by constructivists to explain foreign policy. I argue that there is no such thing as identity, although people very much believe they have one. We are rather a collection of labile identifications, based primarily on affiliations, roles, relationships to our bodies, and understandings of our past that rise and fall in importance as a function of context and priming. Identities neither define interests nor serve as a foundation for ethics because different identifications give rise to different interests and ethical imperatives.[131] I build my argument on the findings of modern psychology but also on the insights of philosophers, most notably Hume.

John Locke invented the concept of person and made the case for the continuity of living things without invoking the soul. He held that a tree was still a tree even though its parts had changed and it had grown or wilted. So too was a person, with the important difference that a person is a "thinking, intelligent Being" who can reflect and reason. Locke describes reflexive self-consciousness and memory as the sources of personhood and continuity.[132] Condillac, Diderot, and Rousseau follow Locke in making memory the locus of selfhood.[133]

Hume dismisses soul and self as comforting "fictions." He rejects the idea of a persisting, self-identical object, distinct from our punctuated, imperfect impressions of it, and the corollary that time could pass without "the self" changing in important ways.[134] The mind, he argues, is best conceived of as "a bundle or collection of different perceptions which succeed one another with an inconceivable rapidity and are in perpetual flux and motion."[135] It follows that "there is no impression constant and invariable" and no continuous self.[136] To posit such a creature would require us to deny its existence during all the hours when we sleep and are insensible of ourselves.[137]

Hume acknowledges that we have a feeling of selfhood but rejects it "as something simple and identical through time." He asks why we harbor this mistaken belief and finds the answer in the imagination. "Our reason neither does, nor is it possible it ever shou'd, upon any supposition, give us an assurance of the continu'd and distinct existence of a body. That opinion must be entirely owning to the IMAGINATION."[138] Identity is a trick our mind plays on us. Our succession of objects and selves are distinct, but, because they are filtered through our minds, they take on a unity that is not present in reality. We imagine – "feign" – "some new and unintelligible principle" – a self, soul, substance – something "unknown and mysterious" – that somehow holds acts, perceptions, and self together.[139]

The proper question for constructivists is not discovering the identities of individuals or states but rather understanding why people believe they have identities and what consequences that has. As for states, they differ from people in having no reflexive selves. They are passive recipients of identities that actors attempt to foist on them because they are perceived as supportive of their political or psychological needs. As Hume understood, once such discourses are established, they help to shape the passions and imagination of citizens.

Hume and Modernity

Hume straddles the traditional and modern eras. He is old-fashioned in his political beliefs that monarchy is more stable than democracy or mixed constitutions and that a free press is a great danger to public order. However, he welcomes commercial development and its ability to raise living standards, and his political writings are intended to demonstrate that there is no such thing as a correct belief or constitution. His philosophical texts extend the argument to knowledge more generally. He is a religious skeptic who challenged the belief that an ordered universe is proof of a benign supreme being. He is a committed relativist who recognizes that all beliefs, practices, and constitutions are local to cultures, peoples, and epochs. He has no interest in establishing what is true or appropriate but a great fascination with what people come to believe is right and beneficial.

Hume is generally considered a political liberal, and subsequent liberal philosophers claimed him as one of their own. This is a defensible acquisition in light of his support of civilized discourse, commerce, the free circulation of ideas, and individual self-fashioning. The liberal commitment to free speech and tolerance of those with different religious, political, or social beliefs benefited from and was justified by a decline in the belief in a cosmic order. In the absence of given truths, Hume was convinced, as John Stuart Mill would elegantly argue, that there is no justification for enforcing conformity and much to gain by its absence. Skepticism provided the foundations for liberalism, and Hume is a key figure in its development and acceptance.

Thucydides, Hobbes, and Rousseau were misappropriated by international relations realists, and Kant by liberals. Philosophical realists are attempting to do the same with Hume by alleging that he believed in a universe ordered by secret powers. I am not alone in challenging their unwarranted appropriation of him. Until quite recently, philosophers were relatively insensitive to his desire to transform their discipline into an experimental one, bringing it closer to today's field of psychology. In contrast to moral philosophy, Hume never sought to discover what people should believe or how they should behave but why they believed and acted as they did. His goal was a quintessentially modern one because it assumed the absence of a justifiable foundation for any moral order.

A century before Nietzsche, Weber, and Durkheim, Hume was grappling with modernity and its consequences. Like them, he believes that increased personal choice in a wealthier, more educated, and demystified world makes his era different from everything that went before it. His contemporaries – at least those with some wealth and education – had more freedom but also more difficulty in deciding what to do with it. Conservatives worried, as they always have, that freedom will lead to license. Liberals and radicals welcomed it as the essential condition of self-construction and fulfillment. With Rousseau, a third perspective arose that derides liberal freedom as illusory and considers modernity a more thorough form of enslavement.

For Hume, the modern world is dangerous in novel ways. Individual freedom has the potential to lead to anarchy, especially as even the educated population was vulnerable to emotional arousal. He regarded Britain's accidental and mixed constitution as precarious. Wars with France had greatly increased the public debt, which he considered the greatest danger to the country. Like Smith, he thought colonialism corrupting but welcomed foreign trade. Hume's history gropes toward the answer of how we live politically in the absence of certain truths. We must accept the arbitrary and conventional nature of governments and the need to moderate our beliefs and attitudes because none of them are in the end defensible. Hume's conclusion is strikingly similar to Thucydides, who adopted this position for more or less the same reasons.[140]

There are delightful ironies here. Hume offers the same strategy as Thucydides for addressing the political dilemma of modernity after having rejected the writings of the ancients as irrelevant to the contemporary age. This strategy involves deception for the benefit of the community at large. It demands reason to constrain the emotions, a task Thucydides thought extremely difficult and dependent on skillful political leadership, and Hume, all but impossible. It requires the kind of leadership that Thucydides attributed to the early Pericles and Hermocrates but found nowhere else in Hellas. Hume's account of England should have made him more pessimistic about elite self-restraint. Yet both men wrote their books with this pedagogical purpose in mind. Thucydides intended his account of the Peloponnesian War as "a gift for all time." Hume hoped his *History of England* would "open the eyes of the Public." Did both thinkers believe that elites would respond appropriately? Or was this the only solution they could envisage, as unrealistic as it was?

It seems fitting to allow Hume to have the last word. In his *History of England*, he offered an encomium to Newton. It misrepresents Newton's approach to physics, making it more like what Hume thought he was doing in philosophy. Having made no secret about his desire to achieve fame, initially in literature and, later, in philosophy, the paragraph suggests that Hume is describing how he would like to be regarded by posterity:

In Newton this island may boast of having produced the greatest and rarest genius that ever arose for the ornament and instruction of the species. Cautious in admitting to no principle but such as were founded on experiment; but resolution to adopt every such principle, however new or unusual; From modesty, ignorant of his superiority above the rest of mankind; and thence, less careful to accommodate his reasonings to common apprehension: More anxious to merit than acquire fame; He was from these causes long unknown to the world; but his reputation at last broke out with a lustre, which scarcely any writer, during his own lifetime, had every before attained. While Newton seemed to draw off the veil from some of the mysteries of nature, he shewed at the same time the imperfections of the mechanical philosophy; and *thereby* restored her ultimate secrets to that obscurity, which they ever did and ever will remain.[141]

Notes

1. Hume, *Enquiry Concerning the Principles of Morals*, Appendix 2.13.
2. Hume, *Treatise of Human Nature*, Introduction, 2.
3. Ibid., 7–8.
4. Hume, *Enquiry Concerning Human Understanding*, 12.34. Also 1.3.
5. Hume, *Treatise*, Introduction, 30.
6. Beauchamp, "Editor's Introduction."
7. Beebee, *Hume on Causation*, pp. 2–3, on this point.
8. Fudge, *Brutal Reasoning* on the extent to which the English since the Middle Ages had distinguished humans from animals on the basis of the reasoning capability of the former.
9. Hume, *Treatise of Human Nature*, 1.3.16.3. Also 2.3.16 and *Enquiry Concerning Human Understanding*, 9.2–3.
10. *Treatise* on Human Nature, 1.2.6.7.
11. Ibid., 1.1.1.1, 1.1.2.11, 1.4.3 and 6–7.
12. Ibid., 1.1.3.1, 1.3.7.5, 1.4.7.3.
13. Ross et al., "Social Explanation and Social Expectation"; Tversky and Kahneman, "Extensional versus Intuitive Reason"; Tetlock and Lebow, "Poking Counterfactual Holes in Covering Laws"; Lebow, *Forbidden Fruit*, chap. 6.
14. *Hume, Treatise on Human Nature*, 1.1.7.2.
15. Ibid., 1.1.9.
16. Ibid., 1.3.7.7.
17. Ibid., 1.3.6–7, Appendix 3, 1.3.7.5.
18. Ibid., 1.3.8.12.
19. Ibid., 1.3.8.2, italics in original.
20. Ibid., 1.3.8.12. Also, *Enquiry Concerning Human Understanding*, 2.3.
21. Owen, *Hume's Reason*, and Garrett, "Reason, Normativity, and Hume's 'Title Principle'," for thoughtful accounts.
22. Hume, *Treatise*, 1.76–77.
23. Ibid., 1.4.1.8.
24. Ibid., 2.3.3.4.
25. Hume, *Enquiry Concerning the Principles of Morals*, Appendix 1.21.
26. Ibid.
27. Hume, *Abstract of the Treatise*, 6; *Treatise*, 1.1.1.12; *Enquiry*, 2.9 n.1.
28. Riesman, Denney, and Glazer, *Lonely Crowd*.
29. Hume, *Treatise*, 2.1.
30. Ibid., 2.2.5.
31. Ibid., 2.3.6.8; Vitz, "Nature and Functions of Sympathy in Hume's Philosophy," for a general discussion.
32. Hume, *Treatise*, 2.11.2, 2.2.5.15–16, 2.2.9.13–14, 2.3.6.8.
33. Ibid., 3.3.1.7. Aristotle, *Poetics*, 1450a–b, 1452a1–10, 1453b1–2 make a similar argument about tragedy producing *catharsis*.

34. Hume, *Treatise*, 2.2.9.16.
35. Ibid., 2.2.8.
36. Ibid., 2.1.2.
37. Pascal, *Pensées*, p. 410; Bayle, *Dictionary*; Malebranche, *Search after Truth*, 6.2.
38. Hume, *Treatise*, 2.3.3.
39. Ibid., 1.3.10.8.
40. Ibid., 1.4.8.
41. Hume, *Enquiry Concerning the Principles of Morals*, section 2.
42. Ibid., 9.6.
43. Hume, *Enquiry Concerning Human Understanding*, Appendix, 2.6.
44. Ibid.; Hume, *Enquiry Concerning the Principles of Morals*, 5.2.17, and Appendix 2.
45. Ibid., Appendix 1.
46. Ibid., Appendix 2.
47. Ibid., 9.7.
48. Hume, *Treatise*, 2.2.5.
49. Hume, *Enquiry Concerning the Principles of Morals*, 5.2.17.
50. Ibid., Appendix 6.
51. Ibid.; *Treatise*, 2.3.3.
52. Hume, *Treatise*, 3.3.
53. Hume, *Enquiry Concerning the Principles of Morals*, 5.2.18.
54. Hume, Treatise, 3.2.2.4.
55. Ibid., 2.3.6.8; *Enquiry Concerning the Principles of Morals*, section 3, Appendix 3.
56. Hume, *Enquiry Concerning the Principles of Morals*, 5.2.42.
57. Hume, *Treatise*, 3.2.2.15, on the state of nature.
58. Ibid., 3.2.1–2, for an account of the emergence of justice. Also, *Enquiry Concerning the Principles of Morals*, section 3, Appendix 3.
59. Hume, *Enquiry Concerning the Principles of Morals*, Appendix 2.9, 3.40.
60. Hume, *Treatise*, 3.2.2.1–22.
61. Ibid., 3.2.7, 3.3.1.10; *Enquiry Concerning the Principles of Morals*, section 4.
62. Hume, *Treatise*, 3.2.2.10.
63. Hume, *Enquiry Concerning the Principles of Morals*, section 3; Appendix 3.
64. Locke, *Essay Concerning Human Understanding*, 4.7.2; Harris, *Hume*, 95–114.
65. Hume, *Treatise*, 1.2.6.7.
66. Baxter, "Hume's Theory of Space and Time in Its Skeptical Content"; "Hume on Space and Time"; and Dicker, "Hume on the External World," for good accounts.
67. Hume, *Treatise of Human Nature*, 1.1.4.1, 1.1.5, 1.3.1.1–2, 1.3.8.5, 1.3.15.2; *Enquiry Concerning Human Understanding*, 1.3.2.
68. Hume, *Treatise*, 1.3.11.
69. Hume, *Enquiry Concerning Human Understanding*, 4.4.
70. Hume, *Treatise*, 1.3.2.2.
71. Hume, *Enquiry Concerning Human Understanding*, 1.2.6–7.
72. Hume, *Treatise*, 1.3.2.2.
73. Hume, *Enquiry Concerning Human Understanding*, 2.9.
74. Ibid., 2.5.
75. Ibid., 11.3.14.31. See also 2.3.1.18, 3.2.6–11.

76. Ibid., 1.3.6.2. 1.3.2.11.
77. Beebee, "Hume and the Problem of Causation," pp. 228–247, for controversies among philosophers concerning Hume's understanding of cause.
78. Hume, *Treatise*, 1.3.2.2.
79. Ibid., 1.3.14.1.
80. Ibid., *Abstract*, 18.
81. *Enquiry Concerning Human Understanding*, 5.6.
82. Ibid., 12.23.
83. Ibid., 3.9.
84. Hume, *Treatise, Abstract*, 4.
85. Ibid., 1.3.3.
86. Ibid., 1.3.14.24, 26.
87. Hume, *Enquiry Concerning Human Understanding*, 5.22.
88. Hume, *Treatise, Abstract*, 18.
89. Hume, *Enquiry Concerning Human Understanding*, 4.6, 4.15, 5.4–5.
90. Hume, *Treatise*, 1.3.12.5, 1.3.14.24; *Enquiry Concerning Human Understanding*, 4.14, 4.21.
91. Hume, *Treatise*, 1.3.7.14. Also, 1.3.14.1, 2.3.1.4., *Abstract*, 9.
92. Ibid., 1.3.14.1.
93. Ibid., 1.3.16.
94. Hume, *Enquiry Concerning Human Understanding*, 5.11.
95. Hume, *Treatise*, 1.3.12.6–8.
96. Wright, *Skeptical Realism of David Hume*; Strawson, *Secret Connexion*; Read and Richman, *New Hume Debate*.
97. Ibid.
98. Beebee, *Hume on Causation*, pp. 48–61.
99. Hume, *Treatise*, 1.1.4.6.
100. Ibid., *Abstract*, 35.
101. Ibid., 1.4.7.3.
102. Ibid., 1.3.14.24–25.
103. Turner, *Social Theory of Practices*, p. 9.
104. Hume, *Enquiry Concerning Human Understanding*, 3.2, 8.1.5.
105. Kahneman, Slovic, and Tversky, *Judgment Under Uncertainty*.
106. Lévi-Strauss, *Savage Mind*, p. 7.
107. Eco, *Interpretation and Overinterpretation*.
108. Hacking, *Emergence of Probability*, pp. ix–xiv.
109. Poovey, *History of the Modern Fact*.
110. Hume, *Treatise*, Introduction, 10, *Enquiry Concerning the Principles of Morals*, 1.10.
111. I am grateful to Dorothy Noyes for this insight.
112. *Treatise*, Introduction, 8.
113. Ibid.
114. Poovey, *History of the Modern Fact*, pp. 202–203.
115. Popper, *Conjections and Refutations*, pp. 44–45.
116. Hume "Of Civil Liberty."
117. Ibid., 2.2.5.15.
118. Burton, *Life and Correspondence of Hume*, vol. 1, pp. 456–458.

119. Montesquieu, *Spirit of the Laws*, book 11, chap. 5.
120. Hume, *Enquiry Concerning the Principles of Morals*, 3.47, 5.43.
121. Hume, *History of England*, vol. 2.
122. McArthur, "Hume's Political Philosophy," for a good overview.
123. Siebert, "Hume's History of England."
124. Hume, "Of Some Remarkable Customs," pp. 179–185.
125. His view of women is very traditional. He defends female chastity but not its male counterpart. Hume, *Enquiry Concerning the Principles of Morals*, 6.1.14.
126. Hume, "Of the Rise and Progress of the Arts and Sciences."
127. Ibid.
128. Hume, "Of the Balance of Power"; Molloy, "Cautious Politics."
129. Hans J. Morgenthau is the exception. In early editions of *Politics Among Nations*, he describes the Cold War has having become a Manichean struggle between good and evil in which compromise is regarded as a deal with the devil. Morgenthau hoped that reframing the Cold War as a power struggle that could be managed by a combination of deterrence and diplomacy could restrain American leaders in the short term and possibly wind down the Cold War in the long term.
130. *Enquiry Concerning Human Understanding*, Appendix, 4.
131. Lebow, *Politics and Ethics of Identity* and *National Identifications and International Relations*.
132. Locke, *Essay Concerning Human Understanding*, book 2, chap. 27.
133. Ibid.
134. Hume, "On the Immortality of the Soul."
135. Hume, *Treatise*, 1.4.6.4–5.
136. Ibid., 1.3.9.13, 1.4.2.6, 1.4.6.5; *Enquiry Concerning Human Understanding*, 2 and 3.
137. Bundle theory finds its most radical exponent in Daniel Dennett, *Consciousness Explained*, who dismisses our sense of continuity as an illusion that we impose on our perceptions.
138. Hume, *Treatise*, 1.4.1.8.
139. Ibid., 1.4.6.6–7.
140. Thucydides, *The Peloponnesian War*; Strassler, *Landmark Thucydides*; Lebow, *Tragic Vision of Politics*, pp. 257–309.
141. Hume, *History of England*, vol. 6, p. 542.

5 Dickens, Trollope, and Collins

> The Lord Chancellor then threw down a bundle of papers from his desk to the gentleman below him, and somebody shouted, "JARNDYCE AND JARNDYCE." Upon this there was a buzz, and a laugh, and a general withdrawal of the by-standers, and a bringing in of great heaps, and piles, and bags, and bags-full of papers.
>
> – Charles Dickens[1]

The Victorian age experienced an extraordinary economic transformation. Friedrich Engels thought the England of 1800 "a country like every other, with small towns, few and simple industries, and a thin but proportionately large agricultural population." By the early 1840s, due to industrialization, England had become "a country like no other."[2] John Stuart Mill predicted that "the nineteenth century will be known to posterity as the era of one of the greatest revolutions of which history has preserved the remembrance, in the human mind, and in the whole constitution of human society."[3]

Economic development encouraged and was facilitated by political, social, and cultural change. This transformation encouraged, perhaps necessitated, reexamination of core concepts used to make sense of the world. Reason and cause were chief among them and were extensively analyzed in Victorian England by philosophers and legal theorists. The debate in philosophy pitted John Stuart Mill against T. H. Green. Mill was attracted to Hume's parsimonious understanding of cause and sought to reformulate it in a way that could be used to study the physical and social worlds. Modern social science builds on Mill's assumptions that cause is a feature of the world and many of its practitioners contend that it is best explained by regularity theories. Green, by contrast, thought the fit between human concepts and the world more problematic because all concepts were human constructions, a function of language, and ultimately subjective. At the end of the nineteenth century, Bertrand Russell rejected the concept of cause altogether, describing it as about as useful as the British monarchy.[4] These three positions continue to resonate in contemporary philosophy and social science.

Legal thinkers engaged the concepts of reason and cause but in the narrower context of torts and crime and the need to establish responsibility. The common law system was thought by most practitioners to enshrine the collective wisdom of the ages and to represent a vast improvement over the determination of guilt by torture or trial by ordeal. Legal authorities nevertheless recognized that discovery of cause and responsibility was difficult to establish in practice. A sharp controversy emerged between those who supported the existing adversarial system as the best method of establishing responsibility or guilt and those who condemned it as not only inadequate but counterproductive.

Judicial decisions allowed accommodation with social and intellectual change, and common law sought to maintain its legitimacy over time through inclusion, mediation, and reconciliation of competing perspectives. Beginning in the late eighteenth century, the "commonality" of the common law was challenged by radicals who contended it excluded much of the population. The common law was put on the defensive. To further muddy the waters, seeming efforts to uphold existing law and practices often served as a vehicle for their change, even transformation.[5]

Jeremy Bentham's *The Rationale of Judicial Evidence*, published in 1825, offered a critique of direct testimony and argued that all so-called real evidence was never more than circumstantial. Benthamites sought to develop the "science of proof." They also made a big push to replace common law with a Napoleonic-style legal code in the expectation that it would make the law more scientific and deprive judges of much of their discretion. They were opposed by Henry Maine, the greatest legal scholar of his generation. He argued that, along with equity and legislation, case law and the judicial discretion it enabled, were the means by which "Law is brought into harmony with society." The legal fiction of precedent encourages and conceals gradual change, keeping the letter of the law the same but allowing its operation to be modified over time and used to sustain a different set of practices or values.[6] Victorian jurist and legal theorist A. V. Dicey offered the example of the evolving judicial interpretation of equity; it secured for all married women the rights that the Court of Chancery had recognized initially only for the daughters of the rich with property settlements.[7]

Victorian novelists took sides in this controversy, usually against the adversarial system of justice. They were fascinated by the legal system and its procedures and what insights it offered into reason and cause. They explored the similarities and differences in how the legal system and society made judgments. In Trollope's *Orley Farm*, the exchange between the opposing attorneys Furnival and Chaffanbrass documents the shift from law as representative of community values to law based on impartiality. Furnival wants Lady Mason to be judged by her character and social status. Chaffanbrass demands that judge and jury judge her solely on the basis of the evidence. This encounter dramatizes the conflict between natural and positive law.

Charles Dickens (1812–1870), Anthony Trollope (1815–1882), and Wilkie Collins (1824–1889) were very much interested in reason and cause. They considered both concepts increasingly problematic in a complex world in which almost every aspect of people's lives was affected by forces they did not understand and over which they had little control. They pioneered a perspective on reason and cause at odds with more optimistic thinkers of their time like Jeremy Bentham and John Stuart Mill. All three authors came to an understanding closer to that of David Hume (1711–1776). As we saw in the previous chapter, Hume downplayed the role of reason in making inferences, arguing that people, like farm animals, are more influenced by resemblance and contiguity. When a belief is established, it creates expectations about the world and has a tendency to be self-confirming. This is attributable in the first instance to the belief itself but also to the ability of a belief that has taken hold to make alternatives more difficult to imagine.

There is no evidence that Dickens, Trollope, or Collins read Hume. The many parallels in their thinking might best be explained as responses to the growing importance and enigmatic nature of civil society. In the late eighteenth century, society began to assume an autonomous existence in people's minds. In Britain and the United States, it came to be understood as something distinct from the people who composed it, even if changes in manners and practices originated in the behavior of individuals.[8] For Victorians, society seemed to function on the basis of its own rules, whatever they were. It appeared to function in opaque and often unforeseeable ways.

Interest in society led authors to grapple with its power and character. It was considered powerful because political, economic, and social advancement were achieved through society. This was in sharp contrast to continental practices where sponsorship or employment by court, government, or patrons was the principal means of economic and social mobility. British society was independent of church and state, influenced by people but not in any visible way controlled by them. English writers increasingly saw the arrow of influence pointing in the other direction. As early as Jane Austen, characters in novels attempt to understand and exploit society for their benefit, often in pursuit of marriage partners but also of material well-being and social recognition. In nineteenth-century English novels, characters often find themselves enmeshed in society but increasingly alienated from it. In contrast to eighteenth-century heroines, who stretched the limits of freedom, their Victorian successors are more concerned with maintaining the social order and direct their energies toward containment and self-management.[9]

Strangest of all was the seeming disconnect between the social rules people had to follow and the way in which these rules came into being. Social rules were clear to all who observed society and were very much class-based. Yet class was increasingly a function of following rules and acting with social confidence. The blurring of class boundaries, while undoubtedly appealing to many upwardly mobile members of the so-called middling classes, was threatening to much of the nobility. Regardless of what position people took on the porosity of class boundaries, this controversy heightened interest in how society functioned and how its rules evolved, were enforced, and were exploited by individuals to advance their own ends.

Puzzling too was the seeming reversal in freedom society brought about between the upper and lower classes. Those at the top of the social hierarchy had more resources and education and should have had more freedom. In practice, they were more restricted by the rules of society and more ostracized when they violated them. Economic pressures on the lower orders and social pressures on the higher ones encouraged deviance at both ends of the socioeconomic spectrum. Dickens, Trollope, and Collins are fascinated by social deviance. Dickens explores the underworld and those who constitute it. Trollope and Collins write about members of the elite who violate social norms or the law, how they are exposed, and how people judge them.

As Durkheim would make clear at the end of the century, labeling an actor a deviant represents an effort to define what behavior is acceptable and thereby to uphold particular values, norms, and practices.[10] So-called deviance can also be a conscious attempt to challenge them. Contestations of this kind can promote shifts in thinking about what constitutes acceptable behavior and deviance. Shifts in thinking and behavior are tightly coupled because what actors think influences how they behave, and how other actors behave influences what we think is normal and appropriate.

Victorian novelists were sensitive to these relationships. Beginning in the 1830s, the so-called Newgate novel focused on transgressions of diverse kinds. Complex representations of deviants prompted critics to accuse Edward Bulwer-Lytton, William Harrison Ainsworth, Charles Dickens, and William Makepeace Thackeray of being sympathetic to criminal misconduct in such novels as *Eugene Aram* (1832), *Jack Sheppard* (1839–1840), *Oliver Twist* (1836–1837), and *Catherine* (1839). Wilkie Collins and other authors of "sensation" novels, which came into vogue in the 1860s and 1870s, carried on this tradition. They explore the connections between law and society, and stigma and acceptance, and what they say about changing values and practices.

The law and courts were also an appealing subject to these writers for artistic reasons. Bakhtin described the romance novel as "the adventure novel or order."[11] Its heroes undergo repeated trials to test their courage, loyalty, nobility, and other qualities. Resolution often depends on some kind of judicial intervention. Elsewhere, I have described Mozart's *Magic Flute* as the quintessential example of this genre.[12] Jan-Melissa Schramm notes that many a Victorian novel takes the form of an exculpatory tale.[13] From Henry Fielding's *Tom Jones* to Thomas Hardy's *Tess*, its characters are arraigned, judged, and usually acquitted, bringing about a reversal in their circumstances. Ian Watt draws our attention to this process in novels and in the courts.[14] Readers and jurors want to know the particulars of the case, receive firsthand accounts from witnesses, weigh evidence, and reach a verdict.

This connection was particularly evident to Victorian authors with legal training or law-related employment. Among their number were Charles Reade, Charles Dickens, William Makepeace Thackeray, Anthony Trollope, and Wilkie Collins. Trollope had been trained in legal modes of presentation and argument and depicts trials in several of his works. He deploys legal terms with precision.[15] Wilkie Collins makes the law–novel link explicit to his readers in *The Woman in White*, telling readers that "as the Judge on the bench might have heard it once, the reader will hear it now."[16] The interest in crime, courts, and their judgments was interesting in its own right and certainly so to the reading public. For Dickens, Trollope, and Collins, it was also a vehicle to explore how courts and society made attributions, which in turn shed light on the role of reason and the nature and utility of cause.

Readers

My interpretation of the novels I analyze differs in important ways from those of contemporary readers. In part, this is because I ask different questions about these texts. I also approach these questions with knowledge and sensitivities that were all but impossible at the time. I will return to these differences in the conclusion to this chapter because they offer us interesting insights into Victorian Britain.

In the course of the nineteenth century, the novel became the predominant genre for middle-class readers of all ages. John Sutherland estimated that 50,000 novels were published during Victoria's long reign.[17] By the second half of the century, encounters with novels became part and parcel of everyday life for all classes. Books were sold everywhere and circulated through an expanding network of libraries. Many public libraries and Mechanics' Institutes libraries made books available to working-class readers.[18] Between 65 and 90 percent of the books that circulated were fiction.[19] In 1870, Trollope noted that "We have become a novel reading people ... We have [novels] in our library, our drawing-rooms, our bedrooms, our kitchens – and our nurseries."[20] "Our memories are laden with the stories which we read, with the plots which are unraveled for us, and with the characters which are drawn for us."[21] They became "almost imperceptibly ingrained in the subjectivities and material lives of their readers."[22] George Eliot observed that "Art is the nearest thing to life; it is a mode of amplifying and extending our contact with our fellow men beyond the bounds of our personal lot."[23]

How did readers understand novels? This question is frequently posed by literary critics who acknowledge just how elusive it is to describe the subjective experience of readers, historical or contemporary."[24] Ian Duncan suggests that "a novel belongs to the market and the reading public convened there" and thus "lays itself open to imaginative appropriation by different communities and interests and for divergent intentions."[25] Readers moved in their imaginations from novels to real life and back again, so their readings depended very much on their lives and what they thought about them.

Margaret Oliphant imagined this "perfect liberty of reading" as a distinct part of English life.[26] Most authors were not so sanguine. Many were uncomfortable with the freedom with which readers could pick and choose and browse what attracted their attention. This "deep-seated English prejudice against random reading" began in the late sixteenth century, intensified under the Puritans, and was fanned by utilitarians.[27] Victorian authors expressed anxiety about facing such a large, unknowable readership, many of whom were newly literate.[28] They attempted to influence, if not control, how their books were read. Many addressed readers in the authorial voice, or had their characters do so, to advise them how to respond to what they would read or to urge acceptance of what they knew were unconventional ideas or behavior.[29] Charlotte Brontë, Eliot, Trollope, and Dickens addressed their readers in prefaces or the text itself, instructing or urging them how to connect with their lifeworlds what they read in an imaginative, constructive, and compassionate way. Perhaps as a form of encouragement, George Eliot, in her *Middlemarch*, published in 1872, has Mr. Brooke exclaim: "I have always been in favor of a little theory."[30]

There is no way of knowing if these efforts paid off. Victorians were equally puzzled by the press and the extent to which it shaped public opinion or reflected it.[31] There is, however, a consensus among scholars that reviewers for the newspapers and influential quarterlies, like the *Edinburgh Review* and the *Quarterly*, became "a popular source of authority" and significantly influenced moral, aesthetic, and intellectual responses and tastes.[32] Dickens and Trollope appealed to reviewers for their realism. This was less true for Wilkie Collins and other authors of the so-called sensation novels that made their appearance in the 1860s. Thomas Hardy characterized the typical sensation novel "as a long and intricately inwrought chain of circumstance" that generally involved "murder, blackmail, illegitimacy, impersonation, eavesdropping, multiple secrets, a suggestion of bigamy, amateur and professional detectives."[33] Nineteenth-century British critics saw the publication of such novels as motivated by commercial considerations and thought they had a deleterious effect on their readers. Critics praised them for the complicated plots and ability to engage readers but thought they were unlikely to be read a second time.[34] Conservative critics joined the Victorian "discourse of moralization," aimed at resisting the kind of character-eroding effects they attributed to these novels.[35]

Uncertainty about readers and the press brings us back to civil society. It was a novel phenomenon, appearing first in Britain in the Georgian era and then elsewhere in western Europe. It was welcomed by the likes of Boswell, Hume, and Mill, who were all committed to individualism and its liberating potential.[36] Mill considered people's "likings and dislikings" to be "full of the most important inferences as to every point of their character."[37] For Mill, as for many of his contemporaries, good character was encouraged by the ability to step outside oneself and take on, at least temporarily, another's perspective as one's own. The "whole truth" is approximated "by combining the points of view of all the fractional truths, not, therefore, until it has been fully seen what each fractional truth can do itself."[38] This kind of role-playing horrified conservatives, who saw it as threatening to hierarchy and the social order.

Dickens

Charles Dickens, Anthony Trollope, and Wilkie Collins produced a vast corpus of works, and, of necessity, I limit myself to certain works and questions about them. This is especially true with respect to the highly prolific Dickens. I focus largely, although not exclusively, on *Bleak House*. I do so to elicit his understandings of reason and cause. Like Hume, Dickens has little faith in the power of reason. At every level of society, his characters are moved more by their emotions and are deeply influenced by custom. They often act in irrational ways when guided by custom. However, they are just as irrational – arguably more so – when liberated from custom, as are Dickens' criminals.

In the 1830s and 1840s, Dickens sided with reformers and welcomed the end of public hangings, gibbetings, and dissections of hanged bodies and the improvement in prison conditions. In the 1850s and 1860s, his opinions were more conventional and lagged behind those of more advanced opinion.[39] Dickens offers some friendly public remarks about judges but no good judges feature in his novels. They are more often bungling characters and figures of parody. His growing conservatism reflected his belief that Victorian society was decaying and dangerously close to disorder.

Hume's analysis of cause was intended to describe how ordinary people functioned. Resemblance and contiguity arguably enable people to make inferences that helped them negotiate everyday life. Dickens' characters act like good Humeans but this often does not get them very far, given the way the Victorian world works. By showing the ways in which the micro and macro levels of society interact, Dickens raises doubts about the utility of cause as an analytical concept for people and social observers and might be said to offer one of the earliest critiques of it.

Hume used introspection and observations of others as his source of evidence. Dickens looked to his characters for the same end. The contrast between the two men is not so great because all of Dickens' characters are figments of his imagination but based on his observations of real people. Modern psychology differs from Hume and Dickens in its method of validation: carefully specified propositions, experiments that attempt to limit the number of possible causal factors, the use of representative samples, control and experimental groups, and statistics to assess the internal and external validity of any correlations. Dickens sought, and achieved, validation through his readers. They bought and read his novels in large numbers, making him the bestselling author of the nineteenth century. They read his works in large part because of his "realism": the close fit between his characters and people they observed in the real world – as did the critics who coined the term. Who is to say which form of validation is more reliable?

Dickens' critique of reason and cause at the micro and macro levels goes hand in hand with his interest in criminal deviance and the law. Most of his novels involve crimes against property or persons. His offenders invariably face human or divine justice in the form of disgrace, prison, hanging, or death from natural causes. In the early works, his criminals are outsiders, generally from the lower orders (e.g., Sikes, Fagin, Quilp, Chuzzlewit). The murderers in his last two novels – *Our Mutual Friend* and *The Mystery of Edwin Drood* – are middle class: a school master and a church organist. In effect, Dickens shows that neither criminals – considered by society the most extreme deviants – nor judges – the highly respected enforcers of the law – act rationally. They are often blinded by dishonesty, hypocrisy, and self-deception. Sir Leicester Dedlock, Baronet, of Chesney Wold is proud of his heritage and his haunted home, polite in his dealings with those he considers his equals, and magnificent in his condescension to everyone else. He is "an honourable, obstinate, truthful, high-spirited, intensely prejudiced, perfectly unreasonable man."[40] Like many other characters, he behaves in ways strikingly at odds with our assessments of his best interests.

Fathoming the motives of *Bleak House* characters is not easy because neither narrator really takes us inside their heads. The present-tense narrator may be omniscient but hides much from readers who are encouraged to infer motives from the behavior, facial expressions, and gestures of characters.[41] Esther Summerson, the past-tense narrator, also holds back much information but does tell readers more of what they need to know. For characters and readers alike, *Bleak House* is a puzzle – or more accurately, multiple puzzles – that must be solved on the basis of clues.

Dickens provides clues in the form of correspondences and duplications between characters and situations, weather conditions (e.g., fog, mist, sunlight), and his extensive use of metaphor and metonymy. One thing frequently stands for another, as a rag and a bottle shop do for the Court of Chancery. These relationships are in plain sight but are only signs to alert, imaginative, and reflective readers who dismiss little as noise and are able to make the right inferences from what they read. The same game occurs within the novel as characters look for hidden meanings in the documents so many of them craft or read. Like readers, Dickens' characters struggle to find and read signs and are frequently misled in both respects.

Bleak House characters search for signs in the first instance to learn about themselves. They want to know to whom they are related and what connections they might have or make with people who can help them. Esther and Richard stand to make great financial gain by establishing their illegitimate or legitimate parental relationships. Tulkinghorn and Guppy seek information about others as a means of gaining power or wealth. Most look for signs in documents associated with Jarndyce and Jarndyce. Tulkinghorn, Sir Leicester's legal advisor is "the high-priest of noble mysteries" and "an oyster of the old school, whom nobody can open."[42] He is a trained reader of documents and obsessively pursues the secret of his client's wife in the hope of protecting him. He keeps his secrets and peruses documents in his chambers by candlelight at night with a glass of vintage port at hand. Most of the other characters are de facto detectives trying to ferret out secrets or struggling to keep them.

Ironically, unlocking secrets – or thinking one has – does not often lead to desired ends. Mrs. Snagsby, wife of the law-stationer, wrongly concludes that her husband has been unfaithful and is Jo's father. Guppy's discovery of Lady Dedlock's secret does not make Esther any more willing to marry him. Bucket's impressive effort, which Dickens recognizes "as nothing short of miraculous," fails to save Lady Dedlock.[43] Tulkinghorn discovers Lady Dedlock's secret but is murdered before this knowledge can do him any good. The reader is also encouraged to become a detective and, like the novel's characters, is at times deliberately misled by the author.[44] The biggest mystery of all – Jarndyce and Jarndyce – is never solved by characters or readers – or the author. The metaphorical fog that filled the Court of Chancery at the outset of the novel is just as thick as its conclusion.

Characters and readers alike struggle to make sense of themselves or the plot because – as in the real world – it is difficult to distinguish signals from noise. Signals, moreover, lose their meaning, or take on different ones, in the process of discovery or interpretation. The attorneys handling Jarndyce and Jarndyce further obfuscate their meaning when they act to advance their own, often hidden, ends. Toward the end of the novel, John Jarndyce exclaims: "what shall we find reasonable in Jarndyce and Jarndyce! Unreason and injustice at the top, unreason and injustice at the heart and at the bottom, unreason and injustice from beginning to end – if it ever has an end – how should poor Rick, always hovering near it, pluck reason out of it?"[45]

Jarndyce and Jarndyce is the thread that links together the various characters in *Bleak House*. It also allows Dickens to address society at the macro level. The lawsuit consumes the lives and fortunes of the litigants as it works its way, at a snail's pace, through the Court of Chancery. This is no rhyme or reason to the procedures of the court or, often, to the behavior of the litigants as there is little hope that the case will be resolved in their lifetimes. Richard Carstone is typical. A ward of the Chancery, for whom the case was "the curtain" of "his cradle."[46] The ever-growing mass of documents associated with the case makes it all the more impenetrable. *Bleak House* is generally read as supportive of the ongoing effort to streamline and reform English legal procedures, and this was certainly one of Dickens' goals. I believe that Dickens also chose to write about the law because it was an appropriate vehicle for exploring the nature of reason and cause in the modern world.

Reason exists for Dickens but almost invariably in the form of instrumental reason in thrall to self-interest. Self-interest in turn is motivated by the passions for wealth, status, and marriage – the last goal often a means of achieving the first two. We never really learn about the origins and outcome of Jarndyce and Jarndyce, but we observe the beginning of another possible suit: the action Sir Leicester Dedlock wants to bring against his neighbor Boythorn over a contested walkway at the border of their respective estates. The dispute is inconsequential as neither man regularly uses the walkway and it could easily be shared. His anger aroused, Leicester defames Boythorn and describes him to Tulkinghorn as "an extremely dangerous person in any community." He rejects out of hand his lawyer's suggestion that they avoid court and find a compromise solution.[47] Boythorn in turn describes Sir Leicester as "Sir Arrogant Numskull."[48]

In Dickens' novels, reason is rarely used for moral betterment, in the sense of building character and shaping goals, as conservatives and liberals alike in the Victorian era insisted it should be. Like Hume before him, Dickens rejects these goals as unrealistic. It is not how people behave, and, for reasons we will examine momentarily, Dickens thinks it is that much less likely in the modern world. His pessimism and scorn for moralists of any political coloring were not lost on contemporary critics, and it is one of the principal reasons why they warned that reading him would offer bad role models and make people less interested in more worthy literature.

Dickens has a complex relationship to Hume when it comes to cause. He is interested in immediate cause when describing the behavior of his characters. He does not portray resemblance and contiguity as the source of their causal inferences. Their search is more positional than causal. They want to know to whom they are related or connected or through whom they might wield influence. The answers they seek, largely in documents, are not envisaged as a part of a causal chain but rather as knowledge that is present, hidden, and waiting to be revealed – or so they think.

Bleak House and other Dickens' novels suggest that, if there are causes, they are hidden, at considerable remove from the present, and difficult, even impossible, to discover. They are also irrational in the sense that they are not attributable to people acting thoughtfully in pursuit of their interests. Rather, they are a product of something his characters refer to as "the system." Gridley from Shropshire describes the Chancery Court as part of "the system."

The system! I am told, on all hands, it's the system. I mustn't look to individuals. It's the system. I mustn't go into Court, and say, "My Lord, I beg to know this from you – is this right or wrong? Have you the face to tell me I have received justice, and therefore am dismissed?" My Lord knows nothing of it. He sits there to administer the system.[49]

Once *Bleak House* characters become enmeshed in the legal process, they become more like objects and less like people – something to be manipulated for the ends of others. Would-be manipulators lose control of their lives as the system intrudes more and more into their once private and secure worlds.

Jarndyce and Jarndyce is a synecdoche for the system. Over time, the lawsuit has become so complicated that nobody really understands it. Most of those involved have lost sight of the ultimate aims of plaintiff and defendant and focus instead on short-term legal maneuvers and filings, which assume a life of their own. The descendants of the agents who initiated the suit, or defended themselves against it, are now scores of people. They too have been reduced to varying degrees to objects on whom the system acts and preys. They have lost their freedom and purse. The only beneficiaries are members of "the system," judges, lawyers, beadles, and the like, whom cases like Jarndyce and Jarndyce sustain.

Outcomes – if they ever emerge from the Court of Chancery – are the product of interactions among numerous actors, many of them constrained or guided by their institutions and their often-arcane procedures. Outcomes are the result of mysterious, even unfathomable, processes of aggregation, most of which are out of sight. The same is true in the world of fashion. "Both the world of fashion and the Court of Chancery," Dickens suggests, are things "of precedent and usage."[50] What is true of fashion is true of society at large; social outcomes of all kinds are the unpredictable result of interactions among numerous people. We can know something about the rules that govern their behavior but little in advance about its product. Such outcomes are what we might call today emergent properties. In such situations, the concept of cause, as some philosophers have come to understand, loses most of its meaning and utility.[51]

Dickens' imagery reinforces this understanding of cause. Consider the iconic account of the effects of industrialism offered in *Hard Times*:

Seen from a distance in such weather Coketown lay shrouded in a haze of its own, which appeared impervious to the sun's rays. You only knew the town was there, because you knew there could have been no such sulky blotch upon the prospect without a town. A blur of soot and smoke, now confusedly tending this way, now that way, now aspiring to the vault of Heaven, now murkily creeping along the earth, as the wind rose and fell, or changed its quarter: a dense formless jumble, with sheets of cross light in it, that showed nothing but masses of darkness.[52]

Dickens draws our attention to soot, not people, for whom it is a stand-in. Like soot particles, people are disaggregated, appear uniform at a distance, and move, if not randomly, in response to outside forces. The soot hides the city and its inhabitants. Dickens opens *Bleak House* with a related image: thick fog rolling up the Thames that obscures our view of London and its Inns of Court. The fog is thickest in the chambers of the Court of Chancery. Evan Horowitz suggests that "Unlike the soot in *Hard Times*, which is so thickly negative and so baleful to all coherence, this fog seems to compose a kind of integument, a thin tissue binding the city together. Bleak House's fog ... is both a metaphor for incoherence and a testament to incipient solidarity."[53] I see no hint of solidarity in this fog. Nor do I see it, like the soot, as a synecdoche of an urban population that lives cheek by jowl. Dickens has us view the city and its soot from afar. In contrast to the fog, he does not suggest that it is unevenly distributed but rather that it is concentrated in legal London and most of all inside the judge's chambers. This is a physical impossibility, which the reader recognizes but accepts because of the dramatic way it drives home both the confusion that reigns in the law courts and how the courts' workings are hidden from the public and reader alike, and perhaps from some of the participants as well.

What links the two images most effectively is what they have to say about causation. The fog is a micro metaphor because it directs our attention on the Inns of Court – not London more generally – the Court of Chancery, and, finally, the darkened judge's chambers. Our focus is on individuals, their separation from one another and confusion, and perhaps how their decisions and the basis on which they are made are obscured, not only from public view but also from the so-called light of reason. The soot offers us a macro and undifferentiated image of London. Its courts, businesses, society are all obscured from view. The soot and smoke move about seemingly at random as the wind changes direction. It is no use trying to explain or predict this movement, and the same is true for what goes on in the city shrouded underneath.

From the vantage point of the twenty-first century, this understanding of cause is unproblematic. We are accustomed, although not at all happy about, the extent to which our lives are moved and shaped by events of which we have no control and struggle to understand. It is one reason why conspiracy theories proliferate in the postindustrial world. They purport to explain the inexplicable by reducing it to the concerted, if hidden, actions of others who advance their interests at our expense. More sophisticated people have come to see the social world as complex, open-ended, and nonlinear. They may search for immediate causes of certain events but are also likely to inquire into their causes. They understand many of its outcomes as emergent properties, a concept coined by G. H. Lewes in 1875. He was a British empiricist who used John Stuart

Mill's example of the properties of water not being reducible to those of hydrogen and oxygen.[54]

Liberal Victorians especially saw reason and morality as closely connected: the one reinforced the other. Many conservatives, drawing on the Platonic and neo-Platonic formulation of reason, shared this belief. Liberals also held that reason and morality were encouraged by society and the positive role models it offered.[55] Dickens appears to reject these beliefs and expectations outright. *Contra* liberals, he depicts society as offering largely negative role models. Richard Carstone, a ward of the Chancery, and one of the early subjects of Esther Summerson's narrative, offers a nice example. Richard, we are told, had many good qualities but had been educated "in no habits of application and concentration." "The system" had guaranteed that his good qualities were undeveloped as it rewarded dash, confidence, and quick but superficial performance of tasks. The Chancery suit did not help either, as it inculcated in him "the careless spirit of a gamester, who felt that he was part of a great gaming system."[56]

The few characters who act on the basis of morality are often children. Charley Neckett in *Bleak House*, who describes herself as "over thirteen," is an orphan who supports and looks after her two siblings, one of them an infant. Her fingers are white and wrinkled from all the washing she does to earn money to keep the three of them alive. Others feel sympathy and forgive them their rent, give them washing, or contribute clothes and food.[57] Charley's selflessness is not a function of reason – she is too young and too uneducated to have developed this faculty. Her commitment to her siblings derives from the love she feels toward them, which has not yet been corrupted by society. Others feel varying degrees of sympathy toward her and her wards and respond accordingly. Charley and those who support her are the embodiment of the sympathy that Smith and Hume described as a universal human emotion and made possible by our ability to put ourselves in the situation of others. Emotions, not reason, for Dickens too are the source of selflessness and human solidarity.[58]

Sympathy and selflessness may involve reflection but it is not their catalyst. It is aroused by the sight of people who are suffering and in need of assistance. In Humean terms, they provide us with powerful images, stimulate our imagination, and may move us to act in selfless ways. Sympathy, moreover, is the product of social interaction, not solitary reflection. The latter is generally how material and other interests are calculated and strategies designed to advance them. Dickens suggests that both kinds of motives are difficult to infer in the absence of knowledge of the context in which actors find themselves. Even then, they may not respond as we think they should if their hearts and minds are closed to outsiders.

Dickens began his professional life as a reformer and arguably ended it as an escapist. Victorian novelists foregrounded social abuses in conscious efforts to promote change. *Bleak House* and *Hard Times* can be read as responses to the ugly reality of industrial Britain, the country's antiquated legal and political system, liberals' misplaced belief in reason, the mechanical and flawed doctrine of utilitarianism, and the heartlessness of laissez-faire economics. *Bleak House* was begun in 1851, the same year as the Chancery Reform Act was passed. Legal reform was in part a response to the growing power of the positivist tradition in law but also a response to changing conditions.[59] The novel offers little in the way of legal arguments or reasoning and relies instead on dramatization and the emotions this arouses to win support for reforms. Dickens was roundly criticized for this approach by jurist Leslie Stephens and fellow novelist Anthony Trollope. Dickens in turn was less optimistic than they were about the ability of reforms to do more than change "the system" at the margins. Patrick Bratlinger describes his move to realism as a response to this recognition.[60]

Dickens' realism went hand in hand with an emphasis on imagination over logical argument, sympathy over reason, and a search for the ways in which people made their lives more meaningful or pleasurable by the exercise of their imaginations and tapping into instincts not yet suppressed by "the system." Kieran Dolin calls Dickens a "sentimental radical."[61] Like Disraeli, Evan Horowitz maintains, Dickens came around to the belief that "the social conflicts of industrial life could be solved by means both public and private, through politics and ideology but also romance and reproduction."[62] Horowitz may overstate Dickens' optimism but his novels certainly oppose utility and statistics with the irreducible and immeasurable. Fog, soot, and smoke can be read in this light. They are terrible by-products of industrialization, but, as playful and powerful images, they might help us take refuge from this reality, or at least put it in perspective.

Dickens' commitment to imagination begins and ends with his own. He is not a good psychologist at the conscious level, but he is very capable of understanding what it is like for people who confront the massive inertia and opaqueness of institutions and the repressed realms of their psyche. The novels know more than Dickens knows, both politically and psychologically.[63] His solution – to the extent he has one – is regressive. Good folk should seek refuge in their small communities and aspire to extend them outwards to encompass their neighbors, giving up as much as possible on institutions. Ethically, they must resemble Charley Neckett and recognize responsibility for those around them. Esther gives voice to this sentiment when she keeps talking about not being Mrs. Jellyby dreaming of Africa but doing her duty to those in front of her and winning some local love. If everybody does this, society would work.

Trollope

Anthony Trollope was long considered a popular but shallow writer. His novels are about the gentry and their associates and are nostalgic in their depiction of country squires and clergymen. Their plots mostly revolve around money and marriage, often combined in complicated ways.[64] Henry James reviewed unfavorably four Trollope novels. In the first review, of *Miss Mackenzie* in 1865, he wrote: "Life is vulgar, but we know not how vulgar it is till we see it set down in his pages."[65] Trollope is read more generously today, perhaps in part because nostalgia is more appealing. In 2014, a *Guardian* article ranked his *How We Live Now* number 22 of the best 100 novels.[66] A year later, on Trollope's 200th anniversary, the newspaper ran a story in which prominent religious, political, and literary figures identified their favorite Trollope novel and explained why they were drawn to it.[67]

These different assessments reflect different aesthetics. In the late Victorian era, many critics worried that popular literature was destructive of high culture and only gave their approbation to writers of whose style and characters they approved.[68] This perspective became deeply entrenched in British academic life and would find its most extreme statement in F. R. Leavis' 1948 book, *The Great Tradition*. Leavis vaunted the writings of Jane Austen, George Eliot, Henry James, and Joseph Conrad and wrote dismissingly of Charles Dickens – "a mere entertainer" – Laurence Sterne, and Thomas Hardy.[69] The rebellion against the received wisdom prompted rejection of the very concept of the canon and the rise of cultural studies and with it a radical reevaluation of Victorian and contemporary literature.

My turn to Trollope is motivated by a different concern: I am interested in what he has to say about reason and cause. This focus might encourage renewed respect for Trollope on the grounds that he was a writer who addressed fundamental epistemological and ethical questions in a thoughtful way.

Trollope was an extraordinarily prolific author, writing forty-seven novels between 1847 and 1884.[70] I draw on a number of them *en passant* but concentrate on two of the so-called Palliser novels, *Phineas Finn* (1869) and *Phineas Redux* (1874). More than the rest of his corpus, they explore reason, cause, and their relationship. They do so in the context of parallel investigations of what society and the law courts regard as evidence, how they assess it, and how they reach judgments. Contrary to the conventional Victorian wisdom that regarded society as fickle and the law courts as more rigorous, Trollope depicts them as remarkably similar in their functioning. Juries make judgments more or less like society does, which is not surprising as they are drawn from society. Legal professionals – barristers and judges – are smarter, better trained, and more sophisticated but make inferences in the same way as ordinary people do. They are Humean in the sense of being influenced more by custom and imagination than reason.

Liberal understandings of society from Boswell emphasize the positive tension between individuals and their society. The latter offers role models, allowing individuals to emulate them or mix and match qualities observed in different people. Through an iterative process of imitation, role-playing, reflection, and self-fashioning, people become possible role models for others.[71] Trollope follows Dickens in his rejection of this optimistic understanding of society but develops his critique differently.

Like Dickens, Trollope was fascinated by the law. He knew more than his senior contemporary about how the courts worked and barristers argued. Trollope's knowledge came from observing county courts and his almost daily practice of writing legal-style reports. He studied the law assiduously on his own time and prided himself on his knowledge. He was opposed to the adversarial system of law, which he did not believe advanced the cause of justice. His treatment of multiple trials in his novels suggests that writers are better than lawyers at getting at the truth and making fair judgments. Trollope encourages his readers to believe that they could do the same. In *John Caldigate*, he offers the aside that "Judge Bramber could not quite yet make up his mind. It is hoped that the reader has made up his, but the reader knows somewhat more than the judge knew."[72]

Trollope's interest in the law influenced the structure of his novels. His plots are trial-like and propelled not so much by action as by the "testimony" of their characters. Documents of various kinds are often central to his novels and characters attempt to affirm their validity or discredit them and to interpret them in ways consistent with their interests. Dialogue resembles examination and cross-examination, with characters attempting to elicit and interpret evidence and readers encouraged to exercise their judgment. *Orley Farm* revolves around testimony about a forged will. Characters weigh in for and against the accused and pose questions about the forgery to one another, informally at first, but toward the dénouement they testify on the witness stand in a criminal trial. Although guilty, Lady Mason is not convicted of forgery because the prosecution fails to ask the right question of the key witness, Brigit Bolster. Moulder, a commercial traveler, draws out the truth from her in an informal conversation that offers a striking contrast to the court proceedings. It is another instance of Trollope showing that novels and their characters are better than barristers and courts at eliciting vital truths.

There is, of course, something ironic about the structure of *Orley Farm* and *Phineas Redux*. Trollope opposes the adversarial system, and has his doubts about the common law system more generally, but adopts its procedures and conventions to structure his novels. There is also something underhanded about the ability of Trollope's characters to consistently show up the legal system. Their success is an artifact of the novel and its plot, deliberately constructed by the author to produce this result.

Phineas Finn recounts the rise in political influence, social standing, and the romantic aspirations of its eponymous hero. In *Phineas Redux*, Finn, now a respected member of Parliament, undergoes an unexpected reversal and is tried and acquitted for a murder he did not commit. He is set free because of the evidence unearthed at great effort and expense by Madame Max Goesler, whom he subsequently marries. What is really on trial in the novel is society and the legal system, and Trollope expects the reader to find them both guilty beyond a reasonable doubt.

Following Finn's arrest, his friends stick by him as they believe him incapable of murder. Emotions of the best kind shape their response. Emotions also govern those most convinced of his guilt and hoping he will be hanged. They already dislike or distrust Finn, or simply seek revenge as in the case of Bonteen's widow. Very few people are torn between their emotions and the seeming facts of the case. Most people who do not know him – including many of his constituents in Taskerville – are convinced of his guilt simply because he has been arrested and charged. Trollope writes:

It was the condemnation of those who had known him that was so terrible to him; the feeling that they with whom he had aspired to work and live, the leading men and women of his day, Ministers of the Government and their wives, statesmen and their daughters, peers and members of the House in which he himself had sat; that these should think, after all, he had been a base adventurer unworthy of their society![73]

After Finn is acquitted, parliament, society, and the general public lionize him. Finn understands both judgments as unreasonable as they are based on emotions or self-serving calculations and the willingness of people to accept and mimic in a thoughtless way the opinions of others. Finn ends the novel a celebrity but a troubled one.

Trollope follows Hume more closely than Dickens in his portrayal of reason and cause. As noted, Hume downplays the role of reason in making inferences. They are based on the vividness of impressions: "All kinds of reasoning consist in nothing but a *comparison*, and a discovery of those relations, either constant or inconstant, which two or more objects bear to each other."[74] Thinking consists of a finite set of simple manipulations and takes the form of weak impressions. The more abstract these impressions, the "more faint and obscure" they become.[75] "In short," Hume insists, "all the materials of thinking are derived either from our outward or inward sentiment: The mixture and composition of these belongs alone to the mind and will. Or, to express myself in philosophical language, all our ideas or more feeble perceptions are copies of our impressions or more lively ones."[76]

When we make causal inferences, Hume attributes them to resemblance and contiguity. When things touch or connect or follow closely on one another, we think of them as contiguous. When one event regularly follows another, we assume a causal connection. Natural relations prompt the imagination to make "union or cohesion" among sensory impressions and create categories in which to organize them. Philosophical relations build on these categories and the concepts we use to make comparisons. They include resemblance, proportion in quantity or number, degree in any quality, and contrariety.[77] A causal connection is a natural relation, but causation the concept is a form of philosophical reasoning that goes "beyond the evidence of our memory and senses."[78] Many beliefs are self-evident, "natural" impressions. They do not require "exercise of thought, or any action, properly speaking."[79]

Humean-style inference accounts for the false identification of Finn as the murderer of Mr. Bonteen, a party whip who had questioned his trustworthiness. The police arrest Finn on the basis of circumstantial evidence. He argued with Bonteen just prior to the murder, brandished what could have been a murder weapon outside the club, and headed home in the same direction and only moments after Bonteen's departure. Equally important was the testimony of Lord Fawn who reports seeing a man running up the alley – away from the murder scene – wearing a jacket like Finn's. He later tells the people he thought it was Finn. On the basis of Lord Fawn's uncertain testimony, the case against Finn is considered strong enough to bring to trial. Police and prosecutor admit to relying regularly on circumstantial evidence for convictions. Plausibility rather than proof is the key to conviction, and the jacket and Lord Fawn's identification of Finn as the man wearing it are sufficient to establish it.[80] For most people, the mere arrest of a suspect by the police is a good presumption of their guilt.

Mr. Chaffanbrass, the barrister defending Finn in the Old Bailey, does not dispute any of the facts and questions only two witnesses. The first is a well-known novelist who saw Finn come out of the club. He teases the novelist about stealing his plots from the French and both agree that French crime writers are good judges of human nature. They further agree that murders in these novels, and, by inference, those in real life, are planned well beforehand. Macbeth, Lady Macbeth, and Iago are cited as examples. This line of reasoning casts some doubt on Finn as the murderer since the provocation came only minutes before Bonteen's murder.

Lord Fawn is the other witness Chaffanbrass questions. Under cross-examination, it becomes evident that he engaged in backwards reasoning, as has almost everyone who believes Finn guilty. Fawn assumes that Finn was the murderer and thus that the man he saw running was accordingly Finn. In O. J. Simpson's murder trial his defense attorney argued that "if the gloves don't fit you must acquit." Chaffanbrass relies on the same tactic. Finn is asked to put on the jacket identified as the one worn by the man running away from the murder scene. It clearly does not fit and Lord Fawn becomes confused. He is reduced to a pathetic figure on the witness stand, where he is made to stand rather than keep sitting on the VIP bench. Under further pressure from Chaffanbrass, he backs away from his earlier identification of Finn. More evidence subsequently is unearthed pointing at the guilt of Mr. Emilius, but he is never tried for the murder.

In Trollope's novels and in Victorian society – and, no doubt, today as well – attorneys and judges have unreasonable confidence in the court system. Defense lawyers in *Phineas Finn* – but probably in Victorian England too – believe that nineteen out of every twenty people hanged for murder are guilty. They pull this base rate out of the air, and it presumably reconciles them to the cases they lose. They also believe in deterrence without any evidence; one attorney regrets that forgery is no longer a capital offense and confidently asserts that people are more likely to steal and cheat in its absence.

Also revealing are the beliefs of the prosecuting and defense attorneys. They do their best not to inform opinions about the innocence or guilt of their clients as they believe they would interfere with their professional responsibilities. One works to convict and hang Finn and the other to get him off. Chaffanbrass, who wins the case, cannot prevent himself from believing Finn is guilty. The two lawyers are consciously playing roles and value their performance above any truth. The attorneys mirror what happens in parliament and the press. Quintus Slide, a newspaper publisher, is offered as the most extreme example. He curries favor, bribes informants, lies outright, and does anything else he thinks will sell newspapers. In the course of the two Phineas Finn novels, he moves from taking money from the Liberals to taking it from the Conservatives. Similar to the members of these parties, he convinces himself he is a true servant of the people.

Society is no different. Trollope's characters seek approval in the court of public opinion to advance their parochial goals. Like prosecutors and defense attorneys, they devise strategies toward this end. The truth is largely irrelevant. They try to tell stories that people will believe, which is more likely when their narratives are fact-based; but they do not have to be to succeed. People are often more willing to believe lies than the truth when it suits their needs and supports their existing beliefs about other people or how the world works.

Trollope offers a radical take on English society and its core institutions. They may be rule-based but those rules do not serve their intended purpose and certainly do not produce justice. Even the law – especially the law – suffers from this problem. It is allegedly based on procedures that evolved over centuries to make trials fairer, elicit relevant evidence, make sure that it is given careful evaluation, and that justice is served. Law is valued because of its rules, their explicit nature, and the presence of a judge to enforce them fairly. James Boyd White observes that "the more technically and logically satisfactory the statements within a set of rules, the more those rules must fail to express what the situation thus regulated really holds."[81] Trollope grasped this contradiction and makes it central to his treatment of the trial and related events outside the courtroom. The novel's drama is due as much to events in the courtroom as those outside. The most important of the latter are the murder and Madame Goessler's trip to Prague in search of evidence about the real murderer. The reader knows more than the judge, attorneys, and jury and is in a better position to render a just verdict.

The reader's knowledge of the facts of the case highlights another irony. Trollope knows the truth because he has created it and so does the reader because he has led them to it. The competition between law and fiction is in no way a fair one. The legal system only looks bad because of what we know independently of what the common law and its adversarial system have managed to ferret out. Trollope recognizes this imbalance and holds his punches to sustain his critique of common law; he allows Finn to be found innocent. A guilty verdict would not be credible given what the reader knows.

The leading characters reinforce Trollope's more general disillusionment with the social, political, and legal order. They drive home to the reader the great difference between legal or social justice and real justice, and also between a parliament that acts on the behalf of the people or of its members:

When some small measure of reform has thoroughly recommended itself to the country, – so thoroughly that all men know that the country will have it, – then the question arises whether its details shall be arranged by the political power which calls itself Liberal, – or by that which is termed Conservative. The men are so near to each other in all their convictions and theories of life that nothing is left to them but personal competition for doing of the thing that is to be done.[82]

Later in the novel, Trollope is more critical: "What does it matter who sits in Parliament? The fight goes on just the same. The same falsehoods are enacted. The same mock truths are spoken. The sane wrong reasons are given. The same personal motives are at work."[83]

Finn is a "natural" character in the sense of having a strong and appealing personality whose behavior shows no sign of affectation or subterfuge. Parliament and London life make him adopt roles that alienate him from himself and the world in which he has grown up. A defining moment comes when the Tories introduce a bill to disestablish the Church of Ireland. This was formerly a key objective of the Liberals, who now oppose it because they want the Tory government to fall. Finn won his seat in part by campaigning for disestablishment, something he fervently supports. He is under great pressure to vote with his party, and his refusal to do so – in contrast to most other Liberals in his position – turns the powerful Mr. Bonteen against him.

Out of office, Finn returns to Ireland where he finds its society parochial and his youthful love constraining. He yearns to return to London, and Trollope later admitted he felt the need to kill off his wife in the act of childbirth to free him.[84] Finn secures a new posting in London. He retains his unaffected character, easygoing affability, and commitment to hard work and gains the approbation of prominent social and political figures. One cannot help but suspect that Trollope has created the kind of persona he aspired to be himself.

Finn's character is subject to a second test after the trial. He is deeply depressed because of the gap he understands has opened up between his natural, Rousseau-like self and the social self he has consciously fashioned. The contrast between the two selves becomes more extreme and intolerable when the status of celebrity is forced on him. He wants desperately to return to his former self but discovers that it is impossible.[85] As Mozart suggests in *Così fan tutte* – and I argue in *Politics and Ethics of Identity* – role-playing transforms people, often in ways they do not anticipate.[86] Through self-fashioning, Finn has become a different person and must remain one, in limbo between the old self he yearns for and the new self with which he feels uncomfortable. He remains in parliament, although never aspires to high office. To the extent he finds fulfillment, it is in his marriage to Madame Goesler.

Madame Max Goesler is the other outsider. Finn is from Ireland and a Catholic. Madame Max is from Vienna and is described as "this half-foreigner, this German Jewess, this intriguing feminine upstart."[87] Like Finn, she is intelligent and physically attractive; but she is as calculating as Finn is natural and uses her social skills to gain admission to the highest levels of British society. The elderly Duke of Omnium proposes to her and leaves her some of his finest jewels, which she refuses to accept. She wins Finn's respect and love by remaining steadfast in her belief in his innocence and using her intelligence, resources, and linguistic skills to track down a witness who can help identify the real killer. Her intelligence, self-discipline, and beauty consistently work to her advantage, but only because she behaves in accord with the values and rule package of the British elite. Those who are envious denounce her behind her back as a foreigner and a Jew, and they are invariably people who fail to live up to their proclaimed values.

In the disestablishment episode, Trollope builds on historical fact. He folds it in to the novel to create a moral dilemma for Finn but also to demonstrate the calculating and self-serving nature of party politics. The goal of doing something worthwhile for the country always takes a back seat to gaining and retaining power. Despite the abrupt about-face of the two major parties, it is striking how few defections there are on either side of the House. The Bonteens and Ratlers – the party whips – are men with no principles beyond party loyalty – what Weber would later call *Fachmenschen*. They have limited imaginations and use and abuse their authority to enforce conformity. At the other end of the spectrum are politicians like Plantagenet Palliser who achieve high office but get nowhere with their reforms. Planty Pal, as he is known, wants to introduce a partially decimalized coinage but cannot muster sufficient support for his project even when he becomes prime minister. Successful politicians, like successful barristers and journalists, cannot rely on raw power; they must mobilize ideas that arouse emotions. Decimalization is a dead end for this reason.

The six Palliser novels carry a powerful social and political message. They portray a political system with both parties committed to the preservation of the social order. Whig and Tory are "so near to each other in all their convictions and theories of life that nothing is left to them but personal competition for the doing of the thing that is to be done."[88] Trollope was a partisan Whig and described himself as an "advanced conservative liberal."[89] As he thought both parties did the right thing in the end, what bothered him most about the political system was what he regarded as its utter hypocrisy.

The novels expose the liberal belief in the positive tension between society and the individual and suggest, as did continental Romantics, that society imposes a straitjacket on people. Rather than helping them become themselves, it stands in their way. The problem becomes more acute the higher up one ascends the social ladder. Women are especially constrained and compelled to marry, or deny their preferred beaus for the wrong reasons, and suffer greatly as a result.

Reason and cause everywhere take a back seat. People as individuals, and society as a collectivity, make emotion-based judgments. Even when Trollope's characters try to reason, they generally draw false inferences about the character, motives, and actions of others. They rarely turn their reason inwards to examine themselves. For Trollope's characters, reason is instrumental reason. In Hume's colorful phrase, it is nothing more than "the slave of the passions."[90] Characters calculate what they must do, or how they must behave, to achieve desired ends. Instrumental reason often works against them. It blinds them to the ways in which other people make judgments, as it continually does to Quintus Slade, the muckraking journalist. It can also reduce their likelihood of achieving their goals because others see them as cold and calculating. Bonteen and Ratler aspire to higher office but will never achieve it for this reason.

Success invariably requires successful performances, whether in society, the House of Commons, or court. One must make a good impression on others. The ability to do this is a major source of influence for worthy people like Madame Goesler and Phineas Finn and for villains like Augustus Melmotte in *How We Live Now* (1875), who uses his money and charm to enter society and defraud investors who trusted him. In *The Prime Minister* (1875), Ferdinand Lopez, another foreigner and Jew, defrauds investors and marries the lovely Emily Wharton. He has befriended her brother to get into his club and meet his sister. Appearance, not reason, determines how most people responded to both villains, and this in turn enables their schemes. Nothing drives home this point so effectively as the Duke of Omnium, uncle of Plantagenet Palliser. He is among the most respected of aristocrats because he is nothing but performance. He holds no office, performs no services, has no goals, womanizing aside, but is held out as a role model for others.

Performance in these several fora also requires good storytelling. Chaffanbrass understands that jurors are less likely to be persuaded by reasoned argument than they are by a vivid show. He achieves this effect with his "you must acquit if the jacket doesn't fit" ploy. Finn gains respect in parliament when he makes a good speech. It is well-structured and contains a good argument, for which precedents and evidence are mustered. Finn is successful not because of what he says but how he says it. When reputed orators speak, Liberals and Conservatives crowd their benches and outsiders, the visitors' gallery. Reasoned argument in parliament is a form of display. Decisions take place behind closed doors and are made on the basis of other criteria.

As reason plays such a nugatory role in people's behavior and judgments we must look elsewhere for causes. Trollope finds them in the character of people; they are respectable or cads. Hardly anybody falls into the gray areas between. For the most part, his characters get what they deserve in life. The principal exceptions are upright women who make bad marital choices – albeit for reasons of necessity or parental pressure – and suffer long-term consequences.

Trollope's morality tale might be attributed to his own sense of ill ease with the inferences his novels suggest. They reflect his astute observations of Victorian life but are in conflict with his image of himself as a self-made man who succeeded through virtue, talent, and hard work. He presumably also hoped that the extraordinary popularity of his fiction reflected its quality and was not a product of some fickle and unwarranted public judgment. Trollope wants very much to believe that success and failure are attributable to moral excellence. Men and women get ahead in life because they are likeable, have appropriate values, and act like gentlemen and gentlewomen.[91] Phineas Finn and Madame Goesler attest to this view of life. Virtue is more important than class or religion – as Trollope believed it was in his case. The Irish Catholic Phineas Finn and the Viennese and Jewish Madam Goesler are accepted by the aristocracy because they are charming, display appropriate élan, and uphold their core values. Acceptance by the aristocracy is an end in itself for some of his characters and for others opens the door to success in politics, business, and marriage.

Collins

Wilkie Collins was born in London but lived in France and Italy with his family and learned both languages. He was a friend of Dickens, who served as his mentor, encouraged him to write, and collaborated with him, primarily on plays. His best-known novels are *The Woman in White* (1859), *No Name* (1862), *Armadale* (1866), and *The Moonstone* (1868). Many critics consider the last to be the first English detective novel. My analysis will draw primarily on *The Woman in White* and *The Moonstone*.

The Woman in White is described as a "sensation novel" by contemporary critics. Matthew Rubery gives this definition:

Sensation fiction drew on a variety of popular forms including melodrama, domestic realism, newspaper reports, Newgate novels, and gothic tales. The gripping plots of these novels involved scandalous events including murder, adultery, bigamy, fraud, madness, and sexual deviance often perpetrated by seemingly moral and upright individuals in familiar domestic settings.[92]

This genre offered a sharp contrast with so-called Victorian realism, in which the key feature of identity is moral character. In sensation novels, characters "are defined by a plot of identification that attends most closely to documenting the material facts of physical embodiment."[93] This contrast may be exaggerated as class and character are important identifiers for Collins, just as they are for Dickens and Trollope. Walter, Laura, and Marian are above reproach in every respect; it is their commitment to one another and to truth that motivates their investigations.

Trollope found Wilkie Collins' novels unsatisfying because they were all about plot.[94] Thackeray stayed up all night to finish it, and Gladstone canceled a theater engagement to do so.[95] *The Woman in White* was such a sensation that all kinds of merchandise with its name were sold, including perfumes and cloaks. Dances were also named after it.[96] Reviewers were more likely to agree with Trollope. *The Times* described the plot as ingenious but did not think sensation novels or cabinet making "a high art."[97]

The narration bears a close resemblance to a trial in that the multiple narrators or witnesses tell only what they know from firsthand experience and observation and are largely unaware of the meaning of their testimony. The reader must sift through their testimony and put it in the right context to make sense of it. This method dramatizes the elusive nature of truth and may encourage thoughtful readers to wonder if there is such a thing.

The mystery begins when Walter Hartright, a young art teacher, gives directions in London to an obviously distressed woman clad entirely in white. A policeman subsequently informs him that she has escaped from an asylum. Walter then takes up residence in a Cumberland country estate, where he is employed as a drawing master. What follows is a typically convoluted Victorian plot. Walter falls in love with Laura Fairlie, one of his pupils, who reciprocates his affections. She bears a striking resemblance to the woman in white. Laura is engaged to another man. Walter leaves the country for a time and Laura marries Sir Percival Glyde and takes up residence at his Hampshire estate, along with his Italian companion, Count Fosco. Glyde tries unsuccessfully to coerce Laura into signing a document that would, in effect, give him complete access to her marriage settlement. Walter returns and, by various means, he and Laura's half-sister, Marian, discover that Glyde is not a count, the woman in white, Anne Catherick is the illegitimate child of Laura's father, and that Fosco has switched the identities of Anne and Laura. He also learns that Fosco is a notorious conman who is then killed by Italian nationalists. Laura's true identity is revealed, she and Walter marry, and their son inherits Glyde's estate.

Like many Dickens and Trollope novels, *The Woman in White* revolves around deception. Documents are forged and others hidden, and people turn out not to be whom they pretend to be. Discovery of the truth takes the form of uncovering documents that reveal the true identity or character of people and bring about dramatic changes in their status, wealth, or freedom. Discovery is never inadvertent but the product of assiduous and astute detection, usually, but not always, by amateurs. The amateurs are invariably more effective at this game than the police or courts. Collins takes discovery and transformation to new levels. Glyde and Fosco are outright scoundrels who profit from carefully constructed false identities. To sustain their ruse they must incarcerate one woman and switch the identities of two others. The woman in white assumes her own disguise once free, but for benign reasons. In sharp contrast to *Bleak House*, discovery is meaningful and enables good people to get the rewards they deserve.

The Moonstone is the first English novel to foreground forensic science. The novel's plot has many parallels with *The Woman in White*. There is a core mystery that must be solved; an attractive and wealthy woman with multiple suitors, one of whom is honorable and the other corrupt; dramatic and unpredictable twists and turns in the plot based on discoveries; resolution through the remarkable efforts at detection by the worthy suitor and those who aid him; and a happy ending with the marriage of hero and heroine.

The plot is driven by the disappearance of a gem brought back from India by a soldier who leaves it to his niece Rachel Verinder. Indian jugglers appear at her residence and maintain a dark, enigmatic, and seemingly evil presence until the dénouement. The Moonstone is stolen from Rachel's bedroom, and suspicions fall on a servant, the Indians, and Franklin Blake. He was entrusted with transporting the gem from London to Rachel in time for her eighteenth birthday party and falls in love with her. Rosanna Spearman, one of the estate's servants, commits suicide and leaves behind a confession. The Indians had no access to the house but are after the gemstone, which was stolen by Rachel's uncle from a holy temple. Sergeant Cuff, a famous London detective, makes some headway in his investigations but cannot discover the gem or identify its thief, and the parties involved disperse.

Franklin returns to Rachel's Yorkshire estate with the hope of solving the mystery and redeeming himself in her eyes. He makes common cause with Ezra Jennings, assistant to Dr. Candy. They discover that Dr. Candy was furious with Franklin for his disparagement of medical science and sought revenge by slipping him a large dose of laudanum at dinner on the night the Moonstone disappeared. Moved by his concerns over the safety of the gem and his own nervous irritations, Franklin entered Rachel's room in a trance, removed the gem, and stashed it in a safe place. He accidently brushed against her bedroom door on his way out, which explains the stain on his night-robe. Later, in London, the two amateur sleuths discover that Godfrey Ablewhite, Rachel's attorney and other suitor, embezzled the contents of a trust fund in his care. Blake ran into him outside of Rachel's bedroom and gave him the gem to be returned to safe storage at his father's bank. Instead, Ablewhite pledged it as security for a loan to prevent his insolvency. He is murdered and the Indians get possession of the Moonstone, return home, and restore it to the temple from which it had been stolen.

Like Dickens and Trollope, Collins suggests that novels can make discoveries and promote justice in ways courts cannot. The preamble of *The Woman in White* offers a critical take on the law. *The Moonstone* dramatizes this critique. The local police detective is arrogant and incompetent and dismisses as an irrelevancy a seemingly innocuous smudge in the fresh paint on Rachel's bedroom door. Sergeant Cuff, a perceptive precursor of Sherlock Holmes, considers it an important clue and, indeed, it is the first step in solving the mystery.

Rachel Verinder recognizes the source of the stain and wrongly concludes that Franklin is a thief and has befriended her for nefarious reasons. Rosanna Spearman, the maid who found the smear, who is in love with Franklin, also concludes that he is the thief and commits suicide. Franklin refuses to believe the written confession she left behind and is dismissed for his naiveté by Mr. Bruff, the pompous family solicitor. Mr. Bruff explains that he has looked at Rosanna Spearman's confession as evidence "from a lawyer's point of view." He suggests that Blake was misguided by his emotions and "pitied the poor creature, and couldn't find it in your heart to suspect her. Does you credit, my dear sir – does you credit."[98] In Dickens, Trollope, and now in Collins, emotions have a positive valence and often guide people to truths they would never discover merely through the application of reason. Reason can blind people, as it consistently does in *The Moonstone*. The fault is not inherent in reason but in the way in which it is applied. Collins comes across as very Humean.

Collins wants us to recognize that so-called facts can reveal the truth or stand in the way of its discovery. They only take on meaning in context, and these contexts are by no means self-evident. Lawyers and courts rarely go beyond Humean-style inference. They focus on resemblance and contiguity and make unwarranted inferences on the basis of them. This line of reasoning leads to the simplest explanations of events and responsibility and also the ones most likely to be believed by ordinary people, who reason the same way. Lawyers and juries think alike. So too do ordinary people but they are often more affected by emotions. Lord Chiltern explains to his wife that the attorney general "can prove that the man was killed with some blunt weapon, such as Finn had; and he can prove that exactly at the same time a man was running to the spot very like to Finn, and that by a route which would have been his route, but by using which he could have placed himself at that moment where the man was seen."[99] Lady Chiltern, his wife, and formerly in love with Finn, nevertheless remains confident that he is innocent.

Credible firsthand witnesses are the gold standard of Victorian legal evidence. Trollope has Chaffanbrass gain acquittal for Phineas Finn by demonstrating that the principal witness against him is not reliable. Collins takes his attack on eyewitness testimony a step further by demonstrating that credible witnesses can be deceived and material evidence deceiving. Rachel was awake when Franklin entered her room and she saw him leave with the gem. She also correctly identified the nightgown with the paint stain as his. She trusts her eyes and the confirming evidence and rejects out of hand his subsequent explanation of events: "I don't believe you *now*! I don't believe you found the nightgown, I don't believe in Rosanna Spearman's letter, I don't believe a word you have said. You stole it – I saw you. You affected to help the police – I saw you! You pledged the diamond to a money-lender in London – I am sure of it."[100] There is, of course, another irony here in that Franklin, who is unaware that he stole the gem while in a trance, is nevertheless telling the truth about his motives and efforts to discover the thief. He is as unreliable as a witness as he is effective as a detective.

Sergeant Cuff's inquiry is offered as the benchmark against which others must be measured. He too relies on reason and material evidence but avoids simple Humean inference. He does not reject resemblance and contiguity but they are only the starting points of his inquiry. He seeks to put eyewitness accounts, material evidence, and the inferences they suggest into a broader perspective. For a start, he must follow the kinds of procedures associated with courts: collect and assess evidence and elicit the testimony of witnesses. Sergeant Cuff confides to the reader:

I am to keep strictly within the limits of my own experience, and am not to inform you of what other persons told me – for the very sufficient reason that you are to have the information from those other persons themselves, at first hand. In this matter of the Moonstone the plan is, not to present reports, but to produce witnesses. I picture myself a member of the family reading these pages fifty years hence. Lord! what a compliment he will feel it, to be asked to take nothing on hearsay, and to be treated in all respect like a Judge on the bench.[101]

The reader is asked to behave the same way and to render a verdict not only on the case at hand but also on the legal system.

Cuff understands the motives are opaque and not easily inferred on the basis of the available facts and testimony of others; but it is Franklin Blake who does the spade work to unearth them. Rosanna Spearman's confession and suicide are not what they first appear; nor, as we have seen, are his own testimony and behavior. Both have acted for reasons that defy easy inference. The reasons must be discovered by digging deeper, unearthing new facts and interviewing new witnesses, and imagining likely scenarios. Franklin Blake uses reason but only solves the mystery by turning to enactment. Franklin's gifts in this regard distinguish him from the other characters; but he also differs by virtue of his extensive foreign travel and education. He is described as having many jarring sides to his character. "He had his French side, and his German side, and his Italian side – the original English foundation showing through, every now and then." He has, at least in part, liberated himself from the more confining aspects of English culture that stand in the way of his using imagination, emotions, and role-playing that, along with reason, are essential to solving the mystery.

Humean inference, so central to how people and courts reach judgments, looks for what Aristotle called efficient causes. These are the events that precipitate whatever it is that we are seeking to explain. The lesson of *The Moonstone* is that immediate cause may appear to provide a good explanation but it is not necessarily the correct one. Sergeant Cuff and Franklin Blake are successful because they look beyond immediate causes and attempt to construct a causal chain of actions and motives that may go back multiple steps. In the end, Franklin Blake is able to construct a picture of what happened that relies on a number of independent causal chains that come into confluence on the night of Rachel's birthday party.

Franklin's principal motive is protecting the gem, and he is presumably more intent on doing this than he otherwise might be because of his growing affection for Rachel. Fully in control of his own faculties, he would never have stealthily entered her room to remove it and put it in a safer place. He does so in a trance and that is because of having been drugged by Dr. Candy. It was in no way foreordained that Dr. Candy would have laudanum with him or that he would have an exchange with Franklin about the value of Western medicine that so deeply angered him.

It was also pure chance that Franklin met Godfrey Ablewhite in the hallway after leaving Rachel's bedroom. Had his judgment not been impaired by the laudanum, it is unlikely that he would have given him the jewel for safekeeping; and, absent his impending bankruptcy and public exposure, Ablewhite would have had no reason to take the Moonstone and use it to secure a loan. These events were highly contingent and independent, as each was the product of its own causal chain. Equally contingent was their confluence on the evening of Rachel's birthday party.

Cause is not a very helpful concept in understanding the theft and removal of the Moonstone to London. At best, we can identify a number of causes, each of which is necessary but insufficient in and of itself to have brought about the theft and disappearance of the Moonstone. It is the overall configuration that is responsible, so it makes no sense to look for a single or efficient cause. The causal puzzle does not end here. Human motives lie behind each of the actions in our multiple causal chain. They are responsible for all the events on the night of the theft and for actions that led to those events. Ablewhite, for example, is driven by greed and it has put him in the desperate situation that provides the motive for him to use the Moonstone as collateral. These motives are opaque and would not readily come out in court or be apparent to an outside student of the case. Franklin Blake is able to fathom them and piece the story together only because he is the agent of an omniscient author.

Collins leaves us in no doubt about the difficulty people have in recognizing their own motives. In a conversation with Miss Clack, Godfrey Ablewhite compares his grasp of his motives to those of a child:

Let me appeal, my dear Miss Clack, to your experience of children ... A child pursues a certain course of conduct. You are greatly struck by it, and you attempt to get at the motive. The dear little thing is incapable of telling you its motive. You might as well ask the grass why it grows, or the birds why they sing. Well! in this matter, I am like the dear little thing – like the grass – like the birds. I don't know why I made a proposal of marriage to Miss Verinder. I don't know why I have shamefully neglected my dear Ladies. I don't know why I have apostatized from the Mother's-Small Clothes. You say to the child, why have you been naughty? And the little angel puts its finger into its mouth, and doesn't know. My case exactly, Miss Clack![102]

Emotions turn out to be as important as reason in cracking the case. Love and rejection prompt Franklin Blake's commitment to ferret out the truth. Ezra Jennings, his able assistant, is moved by dislike for Dr. Candy and his desire to do something positive before he dies. Emotion not only drives the investigation; it enables empathy, which offers insight into other's minds and motives. Emotion and reason combine to lead the investigators where neither would alone.

In this connection, we must also consider the trance states that feature so prominently in the novel. The conventional wisdom regards them as the ultimate antithesis of reason. Early on, the Indians, posing as jugglers, pour ink on a young boy's hand to put him in a trance so he can provide them with information about the whereabouts of the Moonstone. The Europeans are unimpressed and Franklin dismisses their turn to the unconscious as so much "hocus-pocus" of the East.[103] Later, of course, he will steal the Moonstone in a trance, and resolution of the mystery depends on knowing what he did while in this altered mental state. Ironically, the Indians induce the trance in the hope of eliciting the truth. Westerners – Dr. Candy – use trances to hide it. The prominence of trance states prompts another important lesson, voiced by Franklin Blake, who proclaims: "We must all become objects of inquiry to ourselves."[104] Single perspectives and eyewitness accounts, he concludes, are deeply suspect.

Conclusion

Cause and reason have a complex relationship. If people act rationally, it is easier to discover the reasons for their behavior. As we will see in the next chapter, Max Weber argues that the starting point of any analysis of cause is to ask what a rational person, given the information they had, would have done in the circumstances. Weber understands that people do not always act rationally, so proposes to use reason as an ideal type: a theoretical benchmark against which to compare and evaluate the behavior we observe. He recognizes that rationality is only useful as an analytical tool if behavior does not deviate too much from the ideal type. If everyone behaved irrationally – acted, that is, in ways that made attainment of their goals less rather than more likely – some other analytical framework would have to be devised. Using rationality as a template requires prior knowledge of people's motives and expectations. A foreign policy that risked war with a more powerful state might appear irrational to an outside observer but perfectly rational to leaders convinced that a crisis would forestall an even more serious foreign threat and strengthen their hand at home.[105]

For Weber, as for Hume, reason is purely instrumental; it enables people to pursue their goals in an efficient manner. Dickens, Trollope, and Collins question the rationality of people and the use of reason to study their behavior and its cause. Their characters do not necessarily seek rational ends, do not behave rationally in their pursuit, and have imperfect knowledge of their own motives. Rational strategies, when adopted, may not be the most efficient way of pursing desired ends. In part, this is because of what reliance on reason communicates to others about their character or goals. It is also a function of aggregation. People never act alone but in conjunction with others. Their interaction, as in Jarndyce and Jarndyce, can produce outcomes that most neither anticipated nor desired.

Dickens is sensitive to all of these problems surrounding reason and its uses. His novels offended some critics in the first instance because they portrayed the lives of lower-class deviants with some sympathy. Equally offensive was his depiction of them as no more or less rational than their upper-class "betters." Wealth, education, church attendance, and good role models do not necessarily build character or make people more reflective or rational. The destructive lawsuits and other ill-fated initiatives of his elite characters are motivated by anger, generally ill-considered in the face of their likely consequences, and pursued in the face of sage advice by trusted advisors. Lower-class characters, who live closer to the edge, are sometimes, of necessity, more calculating that their superiors and better able to stand back emotionally from their decisions. Dickens offers no evidence that they are any more successful in attaining their goals. Fagin ends up with a noose around his neck, but he had calculated the odds correctly, reasoning that there was only a low probability of this happening to someone who led the kind of criminal life he did.

Dickens is particularly interested in the aggregation problem. Although he certainly does not distinguish explicitly between actor and system levels of analysis, *Bleak House* is not alone among his novels in suggesting that understanding actor motives and behavior tells us relatively little about the outcomes of their behavior. Again, he does not say so, but his invocation of "the system" and his metaphors of "fog" and "soot" certainly suggest that looking for cause is something of a fool's errand. Knowledge of the system and its rules is often little help in explaining outcomes because even tightly regulated systems like the courts are affected by the private goals and whims of those who are governed by them or their enforcers.

Trollope also attributes behavior and outcomes to some degree to "the system" that governs the courts, parliament, and society. They influence, if not shape, people's goals and the means by which they pursue them. The "system" encourages them to behave in ways at odds with their better inclinations or natures. The institutions of which the English are most proud – parliament, the courts, and the Church of England – are the biggest offenders. They focus people's efforts on career advancement, often achieved at the expense of others. The legal system and parliament all but force people into zero-sum contests in the form of adversarial proceedings and elections. To succeed, lawyers, barristers, politicians, and prelates must resort to calculated strategies that often work against, even undermine, the proclaimed purposes and values of their respective institutions.

Trollope offers Plantagenet Palliser as his counterexample to make his point even more graphically. Planty Pal is deeply committed to the public welfare but does not succeed because he relies largely on reasoned arguments, not behind-the-scenes deals. Ironically, he becomes prime minister – the office most politicians dream of – because he is so unambitious that he is acceptable to diverse and warring factions of his party. His success in reaching the top of what Disraeli called "the greasy pole" only makes him more miserable.

Trollope's Palliser novels suggest that the most important causes are products of institutions like the courts, parliament, and society. They socialize people into desiring certain ends and using certain means to achieve them. They provide an underlying explanation for much behavior, although not necessarily for the outcomes to which it leads. We find no resonance in Trollope of Hume's notion of constant conjunction and immediate cause. He does, however, agree that people draw inferences on the basis of resemblance and contiguity, and this is indeed why Lord Fawn mistakenly identifies Phineas Finn as the murderer. Here, as elsewhere, Humean-style inferences are shown to be misleading. The true murderer, Emilius, is identified by means of a more scientific inquiry conducted by Madame Goesler. Emilius claimed to have been locked inside his lodgings the night of the murder, but Madame Goesler travels to Prague and finds the locksmith who made him a copy of the key to let himself out of the house where he boards. This contributes to the dismissal of the case against Finn but is insufficient evidence to bring Emilius to trial.

Wilkie Collins offers the most radical critique of reason and cause. People at every level of society fail to behave rationally. The exceptions in *The Moonstone* are Sergeant Cuff and Rosanna Spearman. The former fails to solve the mystery and the latter is considered mentally disturbed by the other characters. Motives that explain behavior are hidden from the characters themselves, let alone from those hoping to solve the mystery. Franklin Blake is unaware that he has stolen the diamond while drugged and sleepwalking. In the end, he needs his own actions explained to him, although not in realizing how contrary they are to the end he seeks. Rachel Verinder was convinced of her lover's guilt on the grounds of resemblance and contiguity. Like Trollope, Collins shows us how misleading such inferences can be – but with a twist. They point the finger – correctly in this instance – at the true thief but mislead her about his motives. Franklin sought to protect Rachel and her diamond by removing it to a safe place.

Collins attempts to deflate European pretensions of being superior to the East because of their commitment to reason versus superstition. Victorian stereotypes held that the East was mysterious and irrational, in contrast to the enlightened West, where most behavior was rational, more transparent, and explicable. In *The Moonstone*, the reverse is true. The English are often motivated by selfishness, insecurity, and, sometimes, extreme greed that shows no respect for the life and property of others. Mr. Candy laces Franklin Blake's drink with laudanum for his criticism of Western medicine. Colonel Herncastle obtained the diamond around which the plot revolves in India by murder and theft. More normal English people are still moved more by passion than by reason. Rachel Verinder and her suitor are cases in point. Gabriel Betteredge looks for guidance to all of life's problems in his copy of *Robinson Crusoe*. This is another version of the ancient practice of soothsayers, who read fortunes from knuckle bones or entrails. The English people, Collins is suggesting, are emotional, irrational, and superstitious – indeed, not far removed from their uncivilized ancestors. Godfrey Ablewhite turns out to be a most ironic name.

The Indians offer a sharp contrast. From their first appearance as jugglers, who are dismissed as pathetic figures by the Europeans, they show themselves to be rational, calculating, steadfast, selfless, imaginative, and plucky. They possess the characteristics the English unreasonably attribute to themselves. They succeed in retrieving the diamond and returning it to India to the temple to which it belongs. In doing so, they right a major wrong of imperialism. Collins would explore imperialism in other works. *The Frozen Deep*, published in 1856, dramatizes the class exploitation on which imperialism depends. *Armandale*, published in 1866, examines the criminal legacy of British slave ownership in the Caribbean.

The three novelists question the rationality of people; the feasibility of determining their motives; and the difficulty of using them, when known, to explain their behavior. Many people, perhaps most, do not act rationally. To understand their behavior, we must turn to individual psychology and folk wisdom, as Collins does, or institutions and society, as Dickens and Trollope do. Either is an uncertain path as it often requires inside knowledge, unearthed by a good detective. Outcomes in turn cannot be explained or predicted even on the basis of good knowledge of actor behavior. Once aggregated through "the system," they are an emergent property.

Trollope arguably insists even more on this kind of knowledge. He might be said to find cause in character. Over time, your experience of people reveals their character and what they are capable and incapable of doing. Collins excels in sensory distractions and Trollope is better at portraying social learning. Collins is only interested in institutions as a vehicle for understanding society. Trollope is very much concerned, personally, professionally and artistically, in the relationship between social knowledge and institutional functioning. His Palliser novels foreground his hope that good interpersonal relations can keep institutions honest. He is more pessimistic in later novels.

Dickens, Trollope, and Collins turn the concept of cause on its epistemological head. Their contemporary John Stuart Mill thought reason and cause could unlock secrets of the social world and generate knowledge useful in improving it. These novelists portray a Victorian England in which reason and cause are not closely linked and inquiry based on them does not explain human behavior and is certainly not the basis for reform. The search for reason and cause is nevertheless productive in that its use as a template – along the lines that Weber would later suggest – helps us to expose some of the complexities of Victorian society and institutions and their consequences for people of all classes. They lead us away from *epistēmē* (scientific knowledge) as the goal of inquiry and toward that of *phrōnesis* (practical knowledge).

Notes

1. Dickens, *Bleak House*, chap. 24. As there are so many editions of *Bleak House*, I use chapter rather than page numbers to make it easier for readers who may want to look up these quotes.
2. Engels, *Condition of the Working Class in England*, p. 28.
3. Mill, "Spirit of the Age."
4. Russell, "On the Notion of Cause"; Lebow, Constructing *Cause in International Relations*, chap. 1.
5. Ben-Yishai, "Trollope and the Law."
6. Maine, *Ancient Law*, p. 20.
7. Dicey, *Lectures on the Relation between Law and Public Opinion*, p. 377.
8. Lynch, *Economy of Character*, pp. 107–151; Armstrong, *How Novels Think*, pp. 7, 16–18, 43–59.
9. Armstrong, *How Novels Think*, pp. 54–56, 79–80.
10. Durkheim, *Rules of Sociological Method*, pp. 97–104.
11. Bakhtin, "Forms of Time and the Chronotope in the Novel."
12. Lebow, *Politics and Ethics of Identity*, chap. 4.
13. Schramm, "Victorian Novel and the Law."
14. Watt, *Rise of the Novel*, p. 31.
15. Clarke, *Language and Style of Anthony Trollope*, p. 136.

16. Collins, *Woman in White*, p. 5.
17. Sutherland, *Victorian Fiction*, p. 151.
18. Vincent, *Literacy and Popular Culture in England*, p. 217; Hammond, *Reading, Publishing, and the Formation of Literary Taste in England*, p. 28.
19. Altick, *English Common Reader*, p. 231.
20. Trollope, "On English Prose Fiction as a Rational Amusement."
21. Ibid.
22. Gettelman, "Early Victorian Novel and Its Readers."
23. Eliot, *Essays of George Eliot*, p. 27.
24. Gettelman, "Early Victorian Novel and Its Readers."
25. Duncan, *Scott's Shadow*, p. 29.
26. Oliphant, "Novels," *Blackwoods* 102 (September 1867), p. 257, quoted in Gettelman, "Early Victorian Novel and Its Readers," p. 124.
27. Altick, *English Common Reader*, pp. 132–133.
28. Brantlinger, *Reading Lesson*, p. 16.
29. Stewart, *Dear Reader*; Gettelman, "Early Victorian Novel and Its Readers"; John, "Introduction"; Guy, "Politics and the Literary."
30. Eliot, *Middlemarch*, p. 17.
31. Jones, *Powers of the Press*, p. 87; Robinson, "Victorian Novel and Reviews."
32. Atherton, *Defining Literary Criticism*, p. 4; Delany, *Literature, Money and the Market*, p. 106.
33. Quoted in Pykett, "Collins and the Sensation Novel."
34. Robinson, "Victorian Novel and Reviews"; Taylor, "Trollope and the Sensation Novel"; Pykett, "Collins and the Sensation Novel."
35. Wiener, *Reconstructing the Criminal*, p. 9; Thomas, *Detective Fiction and the Rise of Forensic Science*, p. 63.
36. Lebow, *Politics and Ethics of Identity*, chaps. 1 and 8, for a discussion of the liberal identity project and its connection with civil society.
37. Mill, "Bentham."
38. Ibid.
39. Collins, *Dickens and Crime*, p. 17.
40. Dickens, *Bleak House*, chap. 1.
41. Miller, "Introduction."
42. Dickens, *Bleak House*, chaps. 42, and 10.
43. Ibid., chap. 2.
44. Miller, "Introduction."
45. Dickens, *Bleak House*, chap. 60.
46. Ibid., chap. 35.
47. Ibid., chap. 12.
48. Ibid., chap. 18.
49. Ibid., chap. 1.
50. Ibid., chap. 2.
51. Holland, *Emergence*, pp. 6–7; Goldstein, "Emergence as a Construct"; Goodwin, *How the Leopard Changed Its Spots*; Lebow, *Cause in International Relations*, chap. 1.
52. Dickens, *Hard Times*, p. 111.
53. Horowitz, "Industrialism and the Victorian Novel."

54. Lewes, *Problems of Life and Mind*, vol. 2, p. 412.
55. Lebow, *Politics and Ethics of Identity*, chap. 1, on this point.
56. Dickens, *Bleak House*, chap. 17.
57. Ibid., chap. 15.
58. See the previous chapter on Hume for discussion.
59. Bratlinger, *Spirit of Reform*; Kestner, *Protest and Reform*; Gallagher, *Industrial Reformation of English Fiction*.
60. Bratlinger, *Spirit of Reform*, p. 1.
61. Dolin, *Critical Introduction to Law and Literature*, chap. 4.
62. Horowitz, "Industrialism and the Victorian Novel."
63. Thanks to Dorothy Noyes, private communication, for this insight.
64. Lansbury, *Reasonable Man*, chaps. 6–13 on this point.
65. Quoted in Michie, "Odd Couple."
66. Robert McCrum, "The 100 Best Novels: No 22 – The Way We Live Now by Anthony Trollope (1875)," *Guardian*, February 17, 2014, www.theguardian.com/books/2014/feb/17/110-best-novels-way-we-live-now-trollope (accessed October 9, 2017).
67. "To Celebrate Anthony Trollope's 200th Anniversary, Writers Choose Their Favourite Novel," *Guardian*, April 11, 2015, www.theguardian.com/books/2015/apr/11/anthony-trollope-200th-anniversary-writers-favourite-novel (accessed October 9, 2017).
68. Trollope, *Autobiography*, p. 318.
69. Leavis, *Great Tradition*. He later revised his evaluation of Hardy.
70. Catherine Pope, "List of Trollope's novels," http://blog.catherinepope.co.uk/list-of-trollopes-novels/ (accessed October 11, 2017).
71. Lebow, *Politics and Ethics of Identity*, chaps. 1, 8.
72. Trollope, *John Caldigate*, vol. 2, chap. 27.
73. Trollope, *Phineas Redux*, p. 432.
74. Hume, *Treatise of Human Nature*, 1.3.2.2.
75. Hume, *Enquiry Concerning Human Understanding*, 2.9.
76. Ibid., 2.5.
77. Hume, *Treatise of Human Nature*, 1.3.11.
78. Hume, *Enquiry Concerning Human Understanding*, 4.4.
79. Hume, *Treatise of Human Nature*, 1.3.2.2.
80. Trollope, *Phineas Redux*, chap. 62, pp. 441–448 for Fawn's testimony and cross-examination.
81. White, *Legal Imagination*, p. 240.
82. Trollope, *Phineas Finn*, p. 236.
83. Ibid., p. 487.
84. Trollope, *Autobiography*, p. 257.
85. Trollope, *Phineas Finn*, pp. 459–461.
86. Lebow, *Politics and Ethics of Identity*, chap. 4.
87. Ibid., p. 464.
88. Trollope, *Phineas Redux*, chap. 33; Halperin, *Trollope and Politics*; Cohen, "Palliser Novels."
89. Trollope, *Autobiography*, chap. 16.
90. Hume, *Treatise of Human Nature*, 2.3.3.4.

91. Lansbury, *Reasonable Man*, p. 76, on this point.
92. Rubery, "Sensation Fiction" *Oxford Bibliographies*, www.oxfordbibliographies.com/abstract/document/obo-9780199799558/obo-9780199799558-0062.xml?rskey=I1Oook&result=1&q=sensation+fiction#firstMatch (accessed August 4, 2018).
93. Thomas, *Detective Fiction and the Rise of Forensic Science*, p. 63.
94. Trollope, *Autobiography*, p. 258.
95. Ackroyd, *Wilkie Collins*, p. 90.
96. Ibid.
97. Ibid.
98. Collins, *Moonstone*, pp. 338–339.
99. Trollope, *Phineas Finn*, p. 437.
100. Ibid., p. 355.
101. Ibid., p. 197.
102. Ibid., p. 258.
103. Ibid., p. 52.
104. Collins, *Moonstone*, p. 357.
105. Lebow, *Between Peace and War*, chaps. 4–5, for elaboration and documentation.

6   Max Weber

The early twentieth century is my third era of epochal change. By the end of the nineteenth century, when Weber wrote, industrialization, urbanization, and state building had transformed western Europe and the United States. Local economies were increasingly dependent on, if not fully incorporated into, national ones. Canals, railroads, and turnpikes connected towns and cities, making possible the rapid transportation of people and goods. Newspapers, literacy, and public education stimulated the growth of civil society, which came to be recognized as an important power in its own right. A better informed and more involved public demanded more political influence in an age when government intruded into and regulated the lives of people in a way it never had before.

There were equally dramatic developments in science and engineering, medicine, art, literature, and philosophy. Some of them appeared to challenge long-held and fundamental beliefs about the world. They were responsible, Weber thought, for the "demystification" (*Entzauberung*) of the world. Many people felt their anchors had been set loose and struggled to understand these changes and the implications for their lives. Toward this end, economics, sociology, political science, and public administration emerged as specialized disciplines. They were expected to provide some insight into the direction and consequences of these and future developments. In an era of rapid, if not revolutionary, change, cause became a more important conceptual tool than ever before. It also became more difficult to trace and establish.

Social scientists and popular writers were increasingly drawn to two divergent strategies for understanding cause. Many searched for deep, underlying explanations, which usually took the form of processes, that would account for key features of modern society. For their master variables, they turned to environment (Taine), biology (Spencer), and economics (Marx). Their accounts were reductionist, often determinist, and invariably smuggled in values while claiming to be purely scientific analyses of society. All these formulations significantly reduced the power of agency – and in an era in which the individual and their alleged uniqueness were increasingly valued. Such explanations nevertheless had appeal for multiple reasons. Social Darwinism justified domestic and international hierarchies, self-serving beliefs like racism and the moral inferiority of the poor, and conscription, armaments, and imperialism. Marxism justified opposition to these policies and the hierarchies responsible for them and promised a better world to the mass of oppressed workers.

These various "isms" empowered believers by providing them with inside knowledge about how the world worked. For much the same reasons, evangelical religions prospered and continue to today, especially among the disadvantaged or those opposed to social change. Conspiracy theories also empowered believers. They too offered simple explanations for complex events and, by doing so, restored belief in cause. Marxism and cruder forms of evangelical Christianity attributed all evil to capitalists or the devil and promised paradise when they were overthrown.[1]

The second generic strategy all but give up on cause. In lieu of looking to the past for underlying processes or structures to explain present conditions, it focused on the present and on the most immediate precedents of outcomes of interest. Such approaches, which came to dominate in economics and, later, in sociology and political science, were rooted in Humean causation. They searched for regularities in the expectation that they would enable predictions. Their proponents recognized the difference between association and cause and many paid lip service to cause; the search for associations was often characterized as a first and necessary step to the discovery of cause. However, most scholars in this tradition dispensed with cause, which they thought problematic to establish and unnecessary in any case for purposes of prediction. They believed they were being scientific and following practices that had proven wonderfully productive in the physical sciences. In reality, they misread Hume, who, we have seen, was interested in how ordinary people behaved. He intended constant conjunction as the basis for social science. They also misread the physical scientists, who developed thicker understandings of cause that emphasized the processes and events responsible for outcomes, or moved away from cause altogether as a concept that impeded their development.[2]

Weber fell into neither of these traps. He rejected outright theories that made far-reaching claims and were generally teleological and ignored the role of culture and agency. He had no more respect for regularity theories because he believed that most outcomes of interest were context-dependent. He also thought the half-life of any regularity would be short once it became known and people took it into account. Weber struggled to formulate an approach to the world that would be causal and generalizable and recognize the critical roles of culture and reflection. He was very much in the interpretivist tradition but committed to methods that he regarded as rigorous and scientific.

I argue elsewhere that Weber developed his approach to knowledge in the context of controversies between historicists and positivists, and historicists and neo-Kantians.[3] He built on these traditions while attempting to finesse what he saw as their limitations. The result was a definition of knowledge as causal inference about singular events that uses the individual as its unit of analysis, relies on ideal types, and employs counterfactual thought experiments to probe putative causes. For many reasons, this approach is no "silver bullet" but represents an imaginative and fruitful attempt to chart a more rewarding path toward knowledge in what Weber, following Wilhelm Dilthey, called "cultural sciences" (Geisteswissenschaften).

Weber's approach, I contend, has unresolved tensions. The most important is the contradiction between his recognition of the subjective nature of the values and interests that motivate research and his insistence on the objective means by which it might be conducted. Facts and values are not so easily reconciled, and Weber came to understand that they influence, if not determine, the questions we ask, the methods we choose to research them, what we consider relevant evidence, and the inferences we draw from it. Weber was unambiguous in his recognition that all research questions are subjective; we can look at reality in myriad different ways, and those we choose to reflect our commitments, station in life, and problems that engage our attention. All social knowledge is inescapably cultural and local in nature.

I begin this chapter with a short overview of Weber's life that identifies some of the connections between his epistemology, the substantive questions he researched, and his political commitments. I then elaborate his approach to cause. Like Hume, he regarded cause as artifice but still the most useful concept for making sense of the social world. Cause and reason were closely linked in his mind, but in a procedural way. Neither people nor their practices and institutions were particularly rational, but theories about them had to meet this condition. They had to be logically consistent and explicit about their assumptions and any deductions based on them. Nevertheless, reason, like all concepts, was culturally specific. Weber's reliance on it was another way, he recognized, in which his approach to social science was a product of his time and place.

It followed that causal claims could never be considered truth claims. They are subjective understandings that are at best consistent with the methods and evidence used to formulate them. Like Humean constant conjunctions, the goal of causal inference was to help people cope with the world. Accordingly, the only external means of evaluating causal claims was their utility. In this sense, Weber was like his contemporaries, the American pragmatists, and both were in the Humean tradition.

I conclude with a critique of Weber's epistemology. I identify unresolvable tensions that have to do with the concepts he chose to work with; the difficulty, really impossibility, of using so-called objective methods to make subjective inquiries; the kind of inquiries that they allow; and problems of practical evaluation. His approach to social science nevertheless has much to recommend it.

Biography

Max Weber was born in 1864 into a politically active family. His father was a politician and a member of the National Liberal Party, most of whose members had moved from opposition to support of Bismarck during the three wars of German unification. His mother was deeply pious and estranged from her husband. Max Jr. was close to her but rejected her religion and was secular from a young age. He contracted meningitis at two and took several years to recover. In the aftermath, he was keen to demonstrate his intelligence, as feeble-mindedness was thought to be a long-term consequence of the disease.[4]

Weber studied law at Heidelberg University but took courses in history, economics, and philosophy and read widely on his own. He swilled prodigious amounts of beer as a member of a student fraternity. He did his military service in 1883–1884. He then took up a legal internship, resumed his studies, and, in 1889, published his *Habilitationsschrift* on Roman agrarian history. In 1892–1893, he designed and ran a survey of agrarian conditions in the East Elbian region of Prussia. This experience turned him against the landowning aristocracy and encouraged, or revealed, his hostility to Poles. He taught briefly in Berlin and, in 1894, at the age of thirty, was called to a full professorship in economics at the University of Freiberg.[5]

The year before receiving his professorship, Weber married Marianne Schnitger, a distant relative. They had a close relationship but seemingly no sexual intimacy.[6] Max was a depressive and suffered a near nervous breakdown between 1898 and 1902. Following his partial recovery – he would suffer recurrent bouts of depression – he developed an abiding interest in Protestant aestheticism. He came to regard Lutheranism as a German curse, although he insisted that it made Germans more sensuous and *gemütlich* than their Puritan-influenced Anglo-American counterparts. In 1904, he joined Edgar Jaffé and Werner Sombart as editor of *Archiv für Sozialwissenschaft und Sozialpolitik* and wrote his objectivity essay for its opening issue. That year, he also published the first part of *The Protestant Ethic and the Spirit of Capitalism* and spent three months visiting the United States.

In 1905, he learned to read Russian and wrote a commentary on the Russian Revolution.[7] Over the course of the next few years, he founded the German Sociological Association and authored a series of studies on subjects as diverse as religion, the economy, the city, and bureaucracy, all of which would see posthumous light in *Economy and Society*. When World War I broke out, he was an enthusiastic supporter of Germany and aided the war effort by managing a military hospital in Heidelberg for a year.[8] His study of Chinese religion was published in 1915, and he worked hard on what he envisaged as a multivolume study of the economic ethics of the great world religions.

Weber gradually became disenchanted with the German military and its foreign policy. He wrote essays for the *Frankfurter Zeitung* opposing territorial annexation on moral and political grounds and unrestricted submarine warfare for strategic reasons, and he voiced support for political reforms, including universal suffrage. In March 1916, he sent a memo to the foreign office and twenty parliamentarians warning that unrestricted submarine warfare would bring the United States into the war.[9] He favored a strong, popularly elected, American-style president to offset parliamentary divisions and the state bureaucracy. He helped to found the liberal German Democratic Party.

In 1918, Weber joined Heidelberg's worker and social council. He served as an advisor to the Confidential Committee for Constitutional Reform, which drafted the Weimar Republic's constitution. He nevertheless described socialist politicians as "grumpy old men" (*griesenhafte Nörgler*). He was even more opposed to socialist revolutionaries like Rosa Luxemburg, whose agitation he dismissed as a "bloody carnival."[10] He was not at all displeased by the assassination of Kurt Eisner, the organizer of the short-lived socialist revolution in Bavaria that overthrew the Wittelsbach dynasty.[11] In the spring of 1918, he strongly defended the rapacious Treaty of Brest-Litovsk that the German Supreme Command imposed on Bolshevik Russia. He believed the Russians harbored a strong hatred of Germany and considered it in the national interest to weaken the country.[12]

Weber subsequently served on the German delegation to Paris and opposed ratification of the Treaty of Versailles. He came close to supporting the stab-in-the-back (*Dolchstoss*) legend propagated by right-wing German nationalists.[13] Democratic Party officials rejected his nomination as a candidate for the Reichstag. Frustrated with politics, he taught for a year at the University of Vienna and then in Munich, where he directed the country's first institute of sociology. In Munich, he wrote and presented his essays on science and politics as professions and was the target of protests from students on the far right and far left. He died of pneumonia in June 1920 at the age of fifty-six. His widow, Marianne, prepared *Economy and Society* for publication in 1921–1922.

Weber inherited his liberalism and nationalism from his father. He was six years old at the time of the Franco-Prussian War but it made a lasting impression on him. According to Marianne Weber: "the naïve belief in the justice of the German cause; the joyful seriousness of a belligerent nation willing to make sacrifices in order to gain the position of a great power; then the overwhelming victory celebrations and the proud exaltation over the finally achieved unity of the Reich – all this the child absorbed alertly, and he was shaped by it for life."[14] In the post-unification decades, Weber experienced the intense nationalism of the German middle class and came to disapprove of its unhealthy worship of the Prussian military. When World War I broke out, he was pessimistic about the outcome when England came in on the side of France and Russia but happy to be alive and experience a conflict that would be "great and wonderful."[15]

Weber became a more committed liberal as an adult, influenced in part by his reading of Wilhelm von Humboldt and John Stuart Mill. He subscribed to Mill's conception of an open, agonistic, scholarly world and intellectual community as essential to intellectual progress. He opposed the consensus among his colleagues that professors should be above politics but still champion the "national cause." Weber believed the claim of being apolitical was a nefarious way of justifying German nationalism that had a chilling effect on free thought and speech within the university. He reached out to anarchists and socialists, including Ernst Toller, Robert Michels, Ernst Bloch, and Georg Lukács, men the academy rejected because of their political beliefs.[16]

Weber outgrew his Polish prejudice. At a 1910 meeting of the Social Policy Association, he protested against a colleague's effort to define nations in racial terms. He strongly opposed anti-Semitism. He collaborated with Jewish colleagues, supervised Jewish students, and struggled to find them good positions – unsuccessfully in the case of Georg Simmel, whom he very much wanted as a colleague in Heidelberg. Weber imagined what an intellectual joy it would be to teach a seminar composed entirely of Jewish, Polish, and Russian students.[17] He was guilty of other forms of racism. In April 1917, he fell hook, line, and sinker for the general staff's propaganda about the need to defend the country against the mongrel forces of the allies. In one of his *Frankfurter Zeitung* articles, he proclaimed that "Germany is fighting for its very life against an army in which there are negroes, Ghurkas and all manner of barbarians who have come from their hiding places all over the world and who are now gathered at the borders of Germany, ready to lay waste to our country."[18]

German professors exploited World War I to reassert their cultural leadership by depicting the conflict as a struggle between German *Kultur* and Western "civilization." Although a supporter of the war effort, Weber refused to sign the October 1914 "Manifesto of the Ninety-Three" that defended the German invasion and occupation of Belgium. He distanced himself from what he denigrated as "zoological nationalism." He nevertheless thought that German participation in the war served a higher purpose, that of upholding an alternative to "the autocracy of Russian officialdom on the one hand and the conventions of Anglo-Saxon 'society' on the other." Taking his cue from Herder, he warned that a German defeat would reduce the cultural diversity of humankind.[19]

Weber's nationalism was undeniably extreme. At the war's end, at a student meeting in Heidelberg, he urged students to resort to the methods of the 1905 Russian Revolution so "that the first Polish official who dares to enter Danzig is hit by a bullet."[20] He told another group of students,

Only a scoundrel could still go around in his student colors at a time when Poles rule German cities in the east. Put your caps and bands away and give up this *feudal nonsense*, which does not fit these times and is of no use to anyone ... He who is not willing to employ revolutionary methods in the regions where a German irredenta will emerge, and to risk scaffold and prison, will not deserve the name of nationalist in the future.[21]

Weber was deeply committed to human rights, whose origins he traced back to the struggle for freedom of religion waged by English dissenting sects.[22] Although not a socialist, he maintained close ties to the socialist intellectuals of the SPD and rejected conservative efforts to cast the socialists as enemies of the nation. His 1906 essay on Russia commented favorably on local governance and Russian liberals, whom he compared to the members of the 1848 Frankfurt Parliament.[23] His efforts on behalf of the Weimar constitution sought to ensure a plurality of political views and impose some controls on the bureaucracy. Had he lived, Weber would have remained a strong supporter of Weimar, unlike so many German intellectuals who were disdainful and aloof or outright opposed. He almost certainly would have opposed Hitler and the Nazis in an outspoken and courageous manner. Like so many Germans, he shared their nationalism, imperialism, Darwinism, and racism – albeit in an attenuated form. Had Weber lived, one hopes that Hitler's rise to power and dictatorship would have compelled him to confront the contradictions between his nationalism and liberalism and to come down strongly on the side of the latter.

Fin de Siècle

Weber lived most of his life in what we have come to view in retrospect as Europe's golden age. Many educated Europeans of his era believed in material, cultural, and ethical progress and were self-confident about their place in society and their countries' role in the world. Other artists and intellectuals rejected this "bourgeois" certainty as delusional, were alienated from their culture, and had deep forebodings about the future. In Germany, historian Heinrich Treitschke and philologist-philosopher Friedrich Nietzsche gave voice to this pessimism. Weber straddled this divide, as he did so many others.[24] He saw the state as a progressive instrument and was an unabashed German nationalist. He nevertheless followed Nietzsche in believing that the gods had departed from European skies, compelling individuals to invent their own.

Nietzsche focused on Europe's underlying cultural crisis, and Weber on its political and epistemological manifestations.[25] In a disenchanted world, there was no certainty of any kind, not only about values but also about scientific knowledge. Weber warned:

> Even though the light of *ratio* may keep advancing, *the realm of what may be known will still remain shrouded in unfathomable mystery*. That is why *Weltanschauungen* can never be the product of progressive experience and why the highest and most stirring ideals can become effective for all times only in a struggle with other ideals that are just as sacred to others as our ideas are to us.[26]

Because beliefs are arbitrary, people need to convince themselves of their validity and often do so by warring with those espousing different beliefs.

Weber recognized the need for people to make choices but he did not believe they were necessarily free ones. Like other nineteenth-century sociologists – most notably, Marx and Durkheim – Weber came to accept the powerful role of society in influencing the beliefs of individuals and, more importantly, in shaping their underlying values and understanding of the world. Probing and elaborating this relationship became the major substantive focus of Weber's research and found expression in his study of the world's great religions and their political, social, and economic consequences for their believers. He published *The Protestant Ethic and the Spirit of Capitalism* in 1905, *The Religion of China: Confucianism and Taoism* in 1915, *The Religion of India: The Sociology of Hinduism and Buddhism* in 1915, and *Ancient Judaism*, published posthumously in 1920.[27]

The Protestant Ethic and the Spirit of Capitalism maintains that capitalism arose in Europe in part because of how the Calvinist belief in predestination was interpreted by English Puritans. Official doctrine held that people could never know whether they were among the elect. Weber argued that this uncertainty was psychologically difficult for people. To ease their anxiety, Puritan leaders began assuring coreligionists that, if they did well in their businesses – and used the fruits of their labor for worthwhile ends – they could take their success and virtue as unofficial signs of being among god's elect and the saved. This belief led to the pursuit of financial success beyond what one needed simply to live combined with frugality, what Weber calls the "spirit of capitalism."[28] Over time, the habits associated with the spirit of capitalism lost their religious significance, and rational pursuit of profit became a goal in its own right, and not just for Puritans.

Talcott Parsons famously – and erroneously – claimed that two major streams of thought – idealism and positivism – converged in the thought of Marshall, Pareto, Durkheim, and Weber.[29] He called this new synthesis about human behavior the "voluntaristic theory of action" and thought it superior to either of its components. It conceived of sociology as scientific but also idealist in its support of human agency and freedom. It nevertheless recognized a wide range of social constraints. People were free but only in limited ways. Whereas earlier positivists had stressed biological and environmental constraints, the later sociologists emphasized cultural norms and values. Their synthesis allowed for meaningful generalizations while rejecting the social determinism of Marx, Taine, and Spencer. Parsons claimed that "A revolution of such magnitude in the prevailing interpretations of human society is hardly to be found occurring within the short space of a generation, unless one goes back to about the sixteenth century."[30]

Morton G. White, H. Stuart Hughes, and Henry Steele Commager all remarked on this fin-de-siècle transformation. Morton White also adopted the metaphor of revolt.[31] There was undeniable rejection of idealism but an equally strong reaction against positivism, but one that retained its commitment to the scientific method. H. Stuart Hughes described the transformation as a revolt not only against positivism but also against reason and, with it, a heightened concern for subjectivity and recognition of the importance of the unconscious.[32] Only in the case of Weber did Hughes accept Parsons' finding of convergence.[33]

Thomas Haskell contends that Parsons overstates the degree of convergence, and Hughes the extent of rebellion; but there can be little doubt, he maintains, that the 1890 were a decade of profound intellectual change.[34] Major sociologists and philosophers rethought the nature of modern society. Weber, Émile Durkheim, Vilfredo Pareto, Ferdinand Tönnies, and Alfred Marshall led the way in Europe, and Charles Sanders Peirce, William James, and John Dewey in the United States. For Dewey and the pragmatists, the enemy was the early nineteenth-century positivism of Bentham and, subsequently, of John Stuart Mill and John Austin.[35] Positivism, of course, continued to flourish, notably in Marxism, the mechanistic psychology of Jacques Loeb, and the behaviorism of Ivan Pavlov and John Watson. Watson treated the mind as purely epiphenomenal.[36]

The European sociologists and American pragmatists were committed to causal accounts of the social world. It was one of their reasons for rebelling against idealism and positivism. Idealist accounts of cause propounded deep, underlying frameworks, mystical in nature, like the Absolute, the World Spirit, and emanationism. Neither their ontology nor their mechanisms were amenable to empirical evaluation or application. In the social sciences, positivist approaches in economics increasingly took the form of what today we call regularity theories. Their proponents showed little interest in cause, that is, in the mechanisms or process that might be responsible for any regularities they discovered. Weber, in particular, thought such approaches misguided because they ignored culture, context, and reflexivity. Marxism might be said to lie somewhere in between these extremes; it embraced cause, sought it at a deeper level than most positivists, but was nevertheless unacceptable to Weber, Durkheim, and many other sociologists because of its teleology and materialism. They regarded it as more a political than scientific project and one, moreover, that reduced culture, ideas, and agency to mere epiphenomena.

The so-called transformation of the 1890s was not just a reaction against idealism and positivism. It was more fundamentally a response to changing circumstances. People in western Europe and the United States were living in an increasingly urbanized and industrial world, changing in unpredictable ways, and one, moreover, in which traditional social norms and beliefs no longer appeared to provide useful guidance.

Cause was no longer something reserved for poets, philosophers, and historians to speculate about but increasingly central to the everyday lives of ordinary people. They began to think in causal terms more than their predecessors had because they acted less habitually, less in response to their knowledge of the right way to behave, and more in pursuit of their perceived interests. They had to "game" situations and make forecasts of how others would respond to their initiatives, and vice versa. These forecasts were causal in nature. In 1790, 95 percent of the US population lived on small farms or settlements with a population of less than 2,500. By 1890, 35 percent of the population was urban, and most of the majority that still lived on the land were increasingly affected by distant market forces.[37] Knowledge about the local community and integration within it was no longer sufficient for managing one's life. Its economy, politics, and even social values were increasingly influenced by remote developments.[38] For this reason, virtually all students of the nineteenth-century transformation stress the word "interdependence."[39]

Thomas Haskell contends that, in an urban, increasingly interdependent society, "prediction and explanation (or retrodiction) are critically important tasks, because change is pervasive and ceaseless: little can be taken for granted. But by the same token, prediction and explanation are exceedingly difficult tasks, because nothing moves independently."[40] "Where all is *inter*dependent, there can be no '*in*dependent variables.'"[41] Causation becomes "tentative" and "probabilistic." An effect can have many causes, and a single causal chain, even if it can be established, may not tell us all that much. Efficient causation loses its power as the loci of causes becomes increasingly distant. The more cause recedes, the more difficult it is to trace. People's immediate environment "is drained of vitality" and they suffer a corresponding loss of self-importance and self-confidence.

The causal problem and its consequence are particularly grave in a society that stresses individualism and self-fashioning. For practical and psychological reasons, people have strong incentives to "solve" the problem of cause. As noted, some sought to resolve it by escaping into the realm of conspiracy theories, and others by embracing accounts of the world that explained everything in terms of single causes such as class struggle or the conflict between god and the devil, and promised to make it right in the end. Sociologists sought more complex and less determinate explanations that recognized the importance of material conditions and ideas as well as agency. Max Weber was the most interesting and influential of the sociologists when it came to probing the meaning of cause.

Weber and Knowledge

Talcott Parsons studied with Alfred Weber in Heidelberg and was deeply drawn to his brother's writings. He incorrectly represented Weber as a structural-functionalist, just as Edward A. Shils, H. H. Gerth, and C. Wright Mills would, with no more justification, depict him as a positivist.[42] Frederick Beiser insists that Weber is a neo-Kantian and that the philosophy of Windelband, Rickert, and Lask "found its ultimate fulfilment in Weber's methodology."[43] Guy Oakes singles out Rickert for attention, arguing that Weber's conceptual vocabulary is largely drawn from his work.[44] Fritz Ringer argues that Weber was neither a positivist nor a neo-idealist but what he calls a "causalist." The major influences on him, he contends, were Karl Menger, Georg Simmel, Johannes von Kries, and Gustav Radbruch.[45]

Weber is open to so many interpretations in part because he drew on multiple scholars and traditions to formulate his approach to knowledge.

Elsewhere, I situate it in his response to controversies between historicists and positivists, and historicists and neo-Kantians. Weber sought to build on these traditions while finessing their drawbacks and limitations.[46] His approach is best understood as a response to these ongoing controversies in German history and social science.[47] He developed compelling critiques of both schools but acknowledged their distinctive contributions to the study of history, economics, and politics. The second controversy, which receives little attention in the English-speaking world, pitted neo-Kantians against historicists. Here too, Weber borrowed heavily from both traditions. The result is an approach to knowledge understood as causal inference about singular events that uses the individual as its unit of analysis, rationality as an ideal type, and counterfactual thought experiments to evaluate putative causes. It represents an imaginative and fruitful attempt to chart a more rewarding path toward knowledge in what Weber, following Dilthey, called the "cultural sciences."

In his "Objectivity" essay, Weber goes back to Kant's assertion that concepts are the only theoretical means for intellectual mastery of the empirical world. Weber follows Kant in arguing that what we study is dictated by subjective choices: "one can, in fact, 'rationalize life' from a vast variety of ultimate reference points."[48] In contrast to Kant, and in accord with historicist thinking, Weber's approach to knowledge is firmly anchored in the study of singular events.[49] He does not restrict singular to the individual but includes the actions of individuals, groups, institutions, or nations and one-off developments like the emergence of capitalism. He further acknowledges that understanding can refer to the average intended meaning of sociologically mass phenomena.[50] The explanation of such phenomena is the appropriate goal of the cultural sciences.

Drawing on the argument of his friend and colleague Georg Simmel, Weber endorsed the division of the law-like sciences (*Gesetzeswissenschaften*) from the sciences of "reality" (*Wirklichkeitswissenschaften*).[51] The former seek regularities and laws, and the latter knowledge of particulars. The sciences of reality are the cultural sciences (*Kulturwissenschaften*), so called by the Baden neo-Kantians. For Weber, they encompass history and the social sciences, disciplines that share a common interest in the concrete aspects of the world.[52] This is what Wilhelm Windelband called *Ereigniswissenschaften*, best rendered in English as idiographic knowledge of singular events and patterns.[53] By this means, Windelband sought to downplay the role of empathy and focus attention on the individuality of events.

Weber was dubious about the search for social laws and was convinced that any that were found would be of limited utility. In "Roscher and Knies," he reasons that "laws of nature" would, of necessity, be highly abstract and would exclude all "historically contingent" considerations.[54]

In "Objectivity," he argues that rules at best offer only general insights because real-world developments are shaped by context, agency, chance, or what appears to us as chance. In the social world, the more general a concept is, the more it "leads us *away from* the richness of reality, since it must be as abstract as possible – that is contain a *minimum* of substance – to incorporate what is common to as many phenomena as possible."[55]

The same problem exists at the level of singular events. In "Objectivity," Weber follows Rickert and Simmel in describing the social world as composed of a "meaningless infinity" of events that are only "endowed with meaning and significance from a *human* perspective."[56] Once singled out, no event or development can be treated exhaustively because it can be subdivided into an infinite number of components. The social world is a seamless web of human actions, interactions, and consequences. To make sense of it, we impose meaning by inventing categories of event types and imagining possible connections among them. Event types and events are objects of study and imagined connections among them we frame in terms of cause. Only a finite part of this reality can become the subject of scientific attention, and all the criteria we use for selection are subjective.[57] We cannot reduce reality to any conceptual scheme or set of schemes. *Pace* Rickert, Weber acknowledges a *hiatus irrationalis* between concepts and reality. The latter is always concrete, idiosyncratic, and qualitative. It follows that we cannot use laws to organize reality but must be guided by our particular interests.[58]

Reality can be described only through our categories and the judgments we make about "causal *necessity*." Such judgments restrict our attention to certain features of an event or development. "These elements are the only ones we consider" when "we 'abstract' from an infinite number of others, which have to be, and can be, left aside as 'unimportant.'" There are no rules for making these choices. They reflect our cultural values, individual interests, and social and political commitments. The choices people make differ within and across generations. Researchers not only ask different questions but also use different concepts and event categories to seek answers.[59]

Weber is untroubled by this diversity and subjectivity because the goal of social science is not to produce universal truths but rather insights of practical value. He recognizes that all historical disciples – and this includes the social sciences – "are constantly confronted with new questions by the ever-advancing flow of culture."[60] Categories and questions evolve with the result that "reality" constantly changes. Our understanding of "reality" is also reshaped by our research questions, concepts, and findings. The history of the social sciences is accordingly "in constant flux between the attempt to order facts intellectually by means of concept formations" and the "breaking down" of these schemas – "because of the broadening and displacement of the scientific horizon – of the mental images that have been arrived at in this fashion" and the creation of "new conceptions on this altered basis." All social knowledge is accordingly "transient."[61]

Weber became almost poetic when contemplating this situation. He concludes his "Objectivity" essay with the observation that concepts gradually lose their appeal.

> At some point, the coloring changes: the value of perspectives formerly applied unreflectively grows uncertain, the way forward fades in the twilight. The light emanating from the great cultural problems has faded. Science searches for a new standpoint and conceptual framework to contemplate the course of events from the summits of thought. Only those stars can impart meaning and direction to its work.[62]

Intellectual evolution of this kind, while not necessarily progressive, is socially healthy because it keeps societies from becoming ossified, as Weber believes was the case in China. Most importantly, change in scholarly understanding is "tied up with a shift in the practical cultural problems and assumes the *form* of a cultural critique."[63] Critique in turn has the potential to promote changes in beliefs and practices.

Weber does not share the expectation, common to many historicists and positivists, that good research can lead to better – that is, more accurate – conceptualizations of "reality." In "Objectivity," he writes: "*There is no* absolutely 'objective' scientific analysis of cultural life … *independent* of special and 'one-sided' points of view." These arise not only from our particular research interests but from how we select and order what we call facts. The goal of social science is to acquire "knowledge of relationships that are significant from the individual point of view." We must "keep the *limits* of their validity in mind."[64]

This limitation was all the more essential in light of the breakdown of the fundamental value consensus in Western society. Weber used the term *Eigengesetzlichkeit* to characterize the distinctive compartmentalization that modernity had promoted. "We are put into different life-circles, each governed by different laws."[65] Religion, politics, art, science, sports, and sex have become increasingly independent activities governed by their own evolving norms. They provide no grounding for ethics and, indeed, often generate clashing ethical imperatives. Conflicts within and across these and other social domains are inevitable and there is no possible logical resolution to them. A science of culture must rest on some values, and they are a matter of choice for researchers.[66]

Weber's ontological commitment is to the individual. He describes individuals and their behavior as the units of sociology because it is the only thing that is subjectively understandable. States are often personified as a matter of convenience, but their policies consist of the actions of multiple individuals and must be understood as such.[67] Individual behavior is also determinative of long-term macro processes and developments. In *The Protestant Ethic and the Spirit of Capitalism*, he attributes the rise of capitalism in terms of value and behavioral shifts in people. Individuals hold beliefs and are the units of social behavior. For this reason, Weber did not believe that we could reduce our analysis to lower levels of analysis or extend it to higher ones.

Cause

Weber's epistemology is anchored in the belief that social knowledge is by its nature subjective. However, it is not arbitrary. It can be constructed to allow "empirical reality to be *ordered intellectually* in a valid manner." By valid order, Weber means a causal account. *Pace* Hume, he insists that cause is what distinguishes history and social science from chronicles. Chronicles record events, possibly in temporal order, but make no connections between and among them. History and social science are above all interested in these connections. Their narratives select and describe phenomena on the basis of their connections and attempt to demonstrate, or at least argue, that one or more of them are responsible for others.[68]

To make causal inference, we must posit event types and identify events that arguably fit within the categories we create. Typologies of event types enable comparative study and nomological understandings in the form of imperfect regularities. Weber understands these associations as imperfect because events have many causes and we can identify and study only some of them. Moreover, the context in which they unfold will differ across "cases," making them far from fully comparable.

Weber, like Hume, is adamant that "cause" and "effect" are human creations, not features of the world. Causal inference relies on reason to discover regularities but also on emotions to develop empathetic understandings of actors and their motives. It is inescapably rhetorical in nature. Causal narratives can nevertheless be evaluated on the basis of their logical consistency, available empirical evidence, and what Weber calls the "rules of experience" (*Erfahrungsregeln*). By rules of experience, he means other imperfect empirical generalizations in which we and our readers have some degree of confidence. It can also take the form of what he calls "common sense," which is more or less the same thing: some consensus about the likely outcome of particular actions in particular contexts.[69] Researchers can never prove their causal claims but can convince others to accept them. They are most likely to succeed when they can demonstrate that their inferences are based on shared assumptions about the world.[70]

Weber encourages us to construct narratives around imagined causal chains. He frequently uses the words *Verlauf* and *Ablauf* to describe what is understood as a progression of seemingly related actions and events. These actions and events may be causally linked or manifestations of some underlying process. Either way, the narrative form encourages us to think about what connects actions and events. Weber rarely uses the word "mechanism" but this is what he implies.

Causal narratives confer another advantage. They allow us to access deeper levels of explanation. To reach this level of understanding "we have to refer back to other, equally individual configurations" that might account for the phenomenon in question. We must then try to explain these configurations.[71] With diligence, and some luck, Weber believes, we may reach underlying cultural explanations. He offers the example of market transactions, which he considers significant and worthy of study because they are nearly ubiquitous. This was not always the case, so we want to know what changed in the values of Western society to understand "the cultural significance of the money economy." These changes enabled the growth of a money economy and gave it its "significant" and "distinctive" character.[72]

To address the problem of culture, Weber invented the concept of the "ideal type." Its meaning is hard to pin down because his understanding and use of ideal types evolved in the course of his career.[73] He devised the concept initially to replace intuition as a means of understanding the behavior of societies with different values and worldviews. Ideal types of this kind have no external validity because they do not correspond to any historical reality. He offered his typology of authority as an example.[74] Weber subsequently reformulated ideal types to give them more of an empirical connection to the world. He now described them as an analytical accentuation of aspects of one or more attributes of a phenomenon to create a mental construct that will never be encountered in practice but against which real-world approximations can be measured. Such ideal types were not intended as a basis for comparison but a schema for understanding a specific culture or situation and by these means singular events.[75]

Both kinds of ideal types are "pure constructs of relationships." They are neither hypotheses nor in any way accurate representations of reality. An ideal type is a "mental image that is not historical reality and certainly not 'true' reality; still less is it meant to serve as a schema *into* which it would be possible to fit reality as a *specimen*." Rather, it represents a synthesis of many phenomena that remove all variation to create a parsimonious and consistent "mental image." Weber offers the examples of individualism, imperialism, feudalism, mercantilism, and the so-called Marxist laws of capitalist development. Weber is clear that ideal types can never be used to gain a holistic understanding of a subject or problem. They are always perspectival.[76]

Weber considers ideal types a necessary tool for identifying key characteristics of cultures that can explain their distinctive patterns of behavior. In causal narratives, ideal types can presumably function as either starting or end points. In *The Protestant Ethic and the Spirit of Capitalism*, the ideal type of capitalism is Weber's end point in the sense that it is what he seeks to explain. He constructs Protestantism as another ideal type and uses it to account for what made capitalism possible. He connects the two with a causal narrative.

If Weber were alive today, he would react strongly against the way in which ideal types have been interpreted by positivists who assert that only "generalities" count as knowledge.[77] The Weberian approach to social science regards generalizations as without merit unless they are explicitly rooted in particular cultural understandings. They are inapplicable elsewhere and will break down in societies where they are relevant when these understandings change. Ideal types and the values they incorporate nevertheless allow us to explain aspects of cultures of interest to us – for example, ancient Egypt or modern China – even though we have no direct historical relationship with them as we do with the Romans and ancient Greeks. Ideal types are fundamental to social science because they allow us to formulate and investigate research questions that go beyond the actual chain of actions and values in which we might be entrenched.

Weber understands cause in terms of ends–means relationships. He assumes that all social or political behavior is intended to serve particular ends. He describes motives as reasons and explanations for behavior. We begin causal analysis by trying to ascertain the motives of actors. Weber defines a motive as "a complex of subjective meaning that appears to the actor or observer as adequate ground for the conduct in question."[78] We can advance a claim for causal understanding "when the observable action and the motives have been correctly apprehended and their relationship is made meaningfully comprehensible."[79] Weber identifies four kinds of motives: "purposeful rational" (*zweckrational*) is calculated behavior "adequate" to achieve an intended goal; "value rational" (*wertrational*) arises from normative commitments; "traditional" or "habitual" action is made with reference to accepted norms and practices; and "affective" action, which is prompted by the emotions.[80] What is rational therefore depends on the actor's perspective. So-called objective rationality exists only in the realm of technique, and even here there are reasons to question it. Life is about meaning, and meaning is found through reasoning, but reason cannot provide the values that give life meaning.

"Purposefully" rational action comes the closest to Weber's ideal type of "right rationality" (*Richtigkeitstypus*). It is "the a priori" of all reason-based and interpretative understanding.[81] It is a mode of logic for understanding the world, or acting in it, that makes use of abstract concepts like induction, deduction, causation, and ideal types. We must be very careful in the attribution of rationality and irrationality. We must assess the rationality of an action in terms of its underlying logic of social action. Nothing is either rational or irrational but only becomes so when examined from a specific "'rational' *standpoint*." According to Weber:

> A simple sentence should stand at the center of every study that delves into "rationalism." It must not be forgotten that one can in fact "rationalize" from a vast variety of ultimate vantage points. Moreover, one can do so in very different directions. "Rationalism" is an historical concept that contains within itself a world of contradictions.[82]

Right rationality is subjective because it depends on what we think would have constituted rational behavior. This in turn hinges on what motives we think are in play, what ends actors sought, and what course of action had the best chance of producing them. All these judgments, even when evidence-based, require leaps of inference.

The closer any action conforms to right rationality, the less need there is to introduce "psychological considerations" to comprehend it. The identification of "irrational" processes (*sinnfremd*) and their analysis also start with reason. We must "determine how the action would have proceeded in the limiting case of purposive and right rationality" and then account for the variation.[83] The construction of a "purely rational course of action" functions here as an ideal type that provides a clear and unambiguous – but a purely theoretical – account of a causal relationship. Weber repeatedly warns that rationality is nothing more than "a methodological device." It does not require, nor is it intended to suggest, "a belief in the actual predominance of rational elements in human life."[84]

To illustrate his method, Weber uses the examples of Frederick II (the Great) in the Seven Years' War and generals Moltke and Benedek in the 1866 Austro-German War. "To explain the campaign of 1866," he writes in his *Grundbegriffe*, it is indispensable to construct imaginatively how each general, given fully adequate knowledge of his own situation and that of his opponent, would have acted." We then compare this ideal type reconstruction with how the generals actually behaved and attribute any deviation "to such factors as misinformation, strategic errors, logical fallacies, personal temperament, or considerations outside the realm of strategy."[85]

Weber recognizes the difficulty of determining motives, let alone their source. They are often opaque, feigned, unconscious, and, we could add, intransitive and unrecognized by actors. Behavior can be motiveless when it is habitual and not in any way the result of reflection. "In the vast majority of cases," Weber concedes, "action takes place in dull semi-consciousness or unconsciousness."

Although Weber is concerned with singular causation, he insists that it requires comparative analysis. Even the most plausible motivational account of a motive or behavior is never more than a hypothesis until evaluated against a "progression" of external behaviors. We must make causal inference in comparative context by studying an act against previous actions by the same individual and others in similar circumstances. Weber further warns that not all rational behavior will appear rational to us, especially if is motivated by beliefs (e.g., placating the gods will bring rain) that we do not grasp or accept. He offers a six-step continuum from right rationality to "wholly incomprehensible" behavior.[86]

This brings us to the final step of causal analysis: making and evaluating inferences. As noted, Weber believes that there is a near infinity of causes for any event, so we need to identify what we consider to be the most promising antecedents of phenomena of interest to us. Toward this end, we utilize available nomological knowledge and intuition, supplemented by our "common sense" understanding of how the world works. Where a result was brought about by a complex of antecedent conditions that made it "objectively probable," its "cause" should be considered "adequate" with respect to the "effect." A contributing factor that was not "adequate" Weber calls an "accidental cause."[87]

To determine whether antecedent conditions were "objectively probable" and "adequate," we turn to counterfactual thought experiments. Here Weber draws on the probability theory of Karl Knies and the legal analysis of Gustav Radbruch.[88] Radbruch sought to determine malfeasance or criminal responsibility by asking what the likelihood was that some negative outcome would have occurred in the absence of the agents or conditions alleged to be responsible. In Weber's reformulation, we are instructed to ask if "elimination ... or alteration" of the putative cause could "according to general rules of experience" have led to a different outcome.[89] Social scientists, like judges, must work backward from what they want to explain to possible causes. By removing one possible cause at a time and asking what might have happened in its absence, we can evaluate its relative importance for an outcome.

Weber's approach is based on the assumption that a phenomenon of interest is contingent and not overdetermined. If the latter, we are likely to find multiple relevant causes and it will be difficult to determine their relative responsibility because the same outcome would appear to have occurred in their absence. Weber was most interested in the question of responsibility when considering possible forks in history. He uses the Battle of Marathon as an example because Eduard Meyer, whose work he critiques in the "Objectivity" essay, maintains that it was a decisive turning point in history. To assess Meyer's claim, we need to conduct counterfactual experiments to get some idea of what courses of action other probable actors might have pursued and the outcomes to which they might have led.[90] Only if we think there is a real possibility of meaningful variation is it worth examining the possible consequences of alternative outcomes.[91]

Counterfactual thought experiments help us understand the kind of causes responsible for an outcome of interest by giving us some idea about how far the behavior in question departed from what we would expect under conditions of perfect rationality. These deviations can be attributed to pressures and constraints on actors, lack of information, cognitive failings, or emotional commitments. In this connection, I cited Weber's use of this method to evaluate the strategies of Frederick William IV during the Seven Years' War and generals Moltke and Benedek during the Austro-Prussian War of 1866. In the absence of an ideal type template – in this instance, perfect instrumental rationality – we would find it much more difficult to determine these possible causes and make the case for their relevance.

The two kinds of counterfactual exercises Weber advocates are useful in identifying two kinds of cause. The first is rational in the sense of it being a logical and practical means of achieving a given end. It is the product of the kind of cost calculus made by intelligent and unconstrained actors. The second is context- or agent-specific due to pressures or constraints interfering with pure instrumental rationality. Presumably, most real-world actions need to be explained with reference to both kinds of cause because actors are to varying degrees rational but also pressured and constrained.

Weber recognizes that he has not solved the causal problem by any means. In his defense of *The Protestant Ethic and the Spirit of Capitalism* against the criticism of Felix Rachfal, he introduces the concept of *Wahlverwandtschaft* (elective affinities), which he never really defines.[92] He asserts the existence of these affinities between Calvinism and capitalism. At one point, he uses the *Adäquanzbeziehungen* (adequate relations) – also left undefined – as an equivalent but suggests that it implies some form of causal or constitutive relationship.[93] *Wahlverwandtschaft* might be considered his line of retreat when he was unable to show a causal connection by other means but strongly believed such a connection to be present.[94]

Critique

I preface my critique of Weber with the observation that any approach to social knowledge is by definition both subjective and flawed. My critique is nevertheless a friendly one, because I think, that unlike positivism, Weber's ontology and epistemology are, if not fundamentally sound, at least based on reasonable assumptions about the social world and the quest for knowledge about it. Identifying the problems with his approach is a necessary step toward improving it. It also highlights tensions that any approach must address, resolve, or finesse.

Individual Actors. The starting point of any critique is Weber's ontology. His chosen unit of analysis is the individual, because all social behavior is ultimately reducible to that of individuals. He is right, of course, and by no means alone in focusing on individuals and their behavior. Most modern-day constructivists follow Weber in believing that the core goal of interpretivist approaches is to fathom the reasons people have for acting as they do. This is a feasible but elusive goal, even when adequate evidence is available. The first problem is getting inside their heads. We often infer motives from what people confide in others about them; but what they say may not reflect what they think their motives are but rather what they think others want to hear. Prior to the Cuban missile deployment Nikita Khrushchev told the foreign minister he was doing it to deter an American attack, the defense minister that he wanted to restore the strategic balance with the United States, and his son-in-law Alexei Adjubei that his goal was to make Kennedy feel vulnerable and thus, he hoped, pave the way for an improvement in relations. We also know that he wanted to get even with Kennedy for having deployed Jupiter missiles in Turkey.[95] We really don't know why Khrushchev acted as he did. The best we can do is offer an inference based on what he told others and consistent with his past modus operandi.

The second problem is that people do not always behave rationally, especially when the decisions they confront involve serious risks or hard choices among competing goals. People rarely rank their reasons for behaving as they do and are likely to convince themselves that they do not need to make trade-offs.[96] When facing risk, they are likely to defer decision as long as possible, shift the burden of responsibility to someone else, and, if they must act, deny, distort, discredit, or explain away information that suggests their chosen course of action is likely to fail.[97] German policymaking in 1914 and Khrushchev's Cuban missile deployment are well-documented examples.[98]

The third problem is the open-ended nature of the social world. People rarely make decisions in isolation. They face multiple problems that involve multiple decisions and generally perceive that their decisions on one issue or problem will have consequences for others. They engage in admittedly flawed, but usually complex, calculations that are difficult, indeed impossible, to reconstruct from the outside unless we know exactly what problems are on their mind, their order of importance – or at least which have been most recently primed – and how they evaluate – if they do – the trade-offs involved. Even good evidence and robust method may not provide us access to the reasons people have for acting.

Aggregation. Even if we had access to the reasons people have for acting, they would tell us little about the consequences of their behavior. Individuals may be a good entry point for analyzing the social world, but to understand outcomes of interest to us we need to know something about the aggregation effects of their decisions and behavior. These effects, which are found at a higher level of social aggregation, invariably involve interaction among multiple actors and may result in outcomes neither envisaged nor desired by any of them.

Adam Smith coined his "invisible hand" and Hegel the "cunning of reason" to account for system-level outcomes that are the product, but not the intention, of self-interested behavior by individual agents.[99] Following the pioneering work of Friedrich Hayek, emergent properties has become an increasingly important field in economics and political science.[100] In sharp contrast to much research in the social sciences that is confined to one level of analysis, emergent properties is interested in connections across them. Outcomes at the system level are the result of the ways in which the consequences of behavior are mediated by rules at one or more levels of aggregation. These rules can be unknown, making it difficult to compare systems in the absence of numerous iterations of interactions based on real interactions or simulations. Yet, even if discovered, rules do not represent cause as that term is understood by Weber or most contemporary philosophers.

We accordingly face a double quandary. We must address the aggregation problem and, if we do, it may not take the form of causal analysis. Sometimes, we can identify mechanisms and processes that are responsible for outcomes of interest. Weber attempts this in his effort to link Protestantism – and Calvinism in particular – with capitalism. Protestants required believers to follow a secular vocation with as much zeal as possible. This led to the accumulation of capital. Most sects, but especially Calvinists, condemned as sin spending hard-earned money on luxury goods. Gifts to churches were also limited because most Protestant sects abhorred icons and other visual displays. Donations to the poor or to charity were generally frowned on as poverty was seen as the product of laziness and other moral failings. Money was accordingly invested, which, Weber argued, gave an important boost to nascent capitalism.[101]

Comparative Analysis. Even if correct, the so-called Protestant work ethic and capital investment are only two of a suite of conditions that were critical, or at least important, to the development of capitalism. Weber's account is incomplete in the absence of knowledge of these other conditions. More to the point, he fails to follow his own method and use comparative analysis to evaluate his claims. In the 1960s, I discovered a hitherto ignored pamphlet by the nineteenth-century English radical Richard Cobden that attempts what today we call an intra-case comparison.[102] Before Weber did, Cobden theorized a relationship between Protestantism and capitalism. To test it, he devised a measure of economic development and compared the levels of development across Swiss cantons. He divided them into predominantly Protestant, predominantly Catholic, and confessionally mixed. He found the Protestant cantons to be the most developed, the Catholic cantons the least, and the mixed in between.

Counterfactual comparisons, as Weber suggests, are also important tools. Victoria Tin-bor Hui used this strategy to examine state formation in China and Europe. She identifies a series of processes common to both regions and uses China as a "real world counterfactual" to evaluate state formation in Europe, and vice versa.[103] Kenneth Pomeranz uses Europe as a counterfactual case to understand why China did not have an independent industrial revolution.[104] These experiments are based on the assumption that similar causal mechanisms operate in diverse contexts where they may have different consequences. By examining the differential impact of these mechanisms and the extent to which they were determined by local conditions, scholars in this instance attempt to identify different trajectories of historical development.[105] The Pomeranz study demonstrates the additional creative potential of counterfactual experiments. By controlling for circumstances considered vital to an outcome – in this case, the colocation of iron and coal in Britain and parts of the continent, and rivers that allow transport of raw materials to markets – investigators are encouraged to identify other conditions that might have impeded or helped to bring about the outcome in question.[106]

If suitable mechanisms and processes can be found to connect multiple underlying conditions to an outcome, we can construct a causal narrative. We can make this narrative more compelling if we also conduct good counterfactual experiments to buttress our claims. We may use what Weber called "minimal rewrite" counterfactuals: small, plausible changes in history that succeed in either untracking the course of events or demonstrating that history would have developed more or less as it did despite multiple counterfactual efforts to divert it from its path. I have used the Sarajevo assassination toward the first end, arguing that, in its absence, there is good reason to suppose that Europe might have avoided a continental war in the first decade of the twentieth century.[107] Frank Harvey has done the latter; he has tried to show that various rewrites of American politics, including the election of Al Gore as president in 2000, do not prevent the 2003 invasion of Iraq.[108]

So-called miracle counterfactuals are also useful for Weberian purposes. They violate our understanding of what is "realistic," or even conceivable, but they are valuable when they allow us to reason our way to the causes and contingency of real events, or the dynamics that govern them. The utility of miracle counterfactuals does not depend on their realism but on the analytical utility of the alternative worlds they create.[109] Counterfactuals of this kind have a distinguished lineage. Euclid used one to prove that there are an infinite number of prime numbers and Newton to attempt to demonstrate that the universe could not be infinite with regularly distributed and fixed stars. If these conditions held, Newton reasoned, the sky would not be blue.[110] Tin-bor Hui and Pomeranz rely on miracle counterfactuals and use them appropriately for their analytical purposes.

Noncausal Analysis. Weber insists that there is no social science without causal analysis. He rejects noncausal approaches out of hand and has in mind descriptive history, or history that smuggles in causal inference and for that reason does it badly. However, to explain system-level effects, we may need to go beyond individual actors and causal analysis. System-level effects can be the consequence of processes that help to account for the aggregation of individual behavior. Weber works on this assumption. They can also be the result of the ways in which a system – or society – brings about a certain degree of convergence through selection, by rewarding certain kinds of behavior and punishing others; by encouraging conscious adaptation by actors; or by imitation, which may or may not be adaptive.[111] Weber also relies on selection effects, most notably to explain investment, but it might also be attributed to conscious adaptation or imitation. He neither identifies nor distinguishes among these several mechanisms.

Modeling and simulation might be regarded as tools that parallel and complement counterfactual analysis. They can evaluate causal narratives by noncausal means. Since Weber's time, simulation has emerged as an alternative approach to scientific knowledge. For most of the twentieth century, good theories were considered to be those that used linear equations to describe the evolution of continuous quantities. Information technology has enabled a discrete on/off approach to phenomena that are rule-governed. It inspired a search for simple rules – algorithmic systems – which, when repeatedly applied, generate complex, system-level patterns. Beginning in biology, this approach spread to physics and then to the social sciences. It has since become more sophisticated by moving beyond binary coding to fuzzy sets, and from reductionist accounts to multi-level explanations.

Modeling could be combined with Weberian causal analysis by building a model or simulation based on assumptions and mechanisms derived from causal narratives. Millions of worlds might then be generated to see the extent to which they resembled the ones for which the causal narratives sought to account. Modeling and simulation were not tools available to Weber. If he were alive today, he might see their utility in accounting for system-level outcomes.

Structure and Agency. For Weber, there is an inevitable tension between structure and agency. Weberian structures are cultural and, like their material counterparts, have the potential to provide underlying explanations for important singular developments like capitalism, the state, and democracy. Even these system-level outcomes must take account of agency. The subjective understandings of actors, their parochial goals, their propensities for risk-taking, and their networks and opportunities can be important, perhaps even decisive, for the timing and location of these singular developments.

When we move to discrete events like the outcomes of elections, the onset of economic crises, or wars or their absence, agency is arguably more important. It can determine whether these events occur or what form they take, not just their timing and location. The end of the Cold War is a case in point. George Breslauer and I imagine East–West relations without Gorbachev, Reagan, or Bush and, by doing so, make the case for the determining role of leaders. We identify other leaders that might have come to power and consider the most plausible policies they would have pursued toward each other's country. This leads us to a wide range of possible scenarios in the late 1980s, from intensification of the Cold War to its resolution on terms that might have allowed for the continued existence of the Soviet Union. Both the end of the Cold War and the particular outcome it produced were highly dependent on leaders.[112]

Explanation in social science must invariably take place at two levels. Underlying accounts can never do more than described conditions, mechanisms, and processes that make some outcomes more likely than not. Whether they happen or not, how and when they happen, and also their consequences will depend on context. Good causal narratives build in underlying and immediate causes and also the extent to which the latter are independent of the former.[113] Weberian analysis is equally applicable to both levels of analysis. Weber was not only interested in underlying causes, but recognized the importance of context in shaping outcomes. It is one of the reasons why he described many important outcomes as singular events. He theorized that particular cultural configurations shape the context in which they occur. There is no reason why the same kind of approach to cause cannot be used to analyze more discrete events or to provide more comprehensive causal narratives by linking underlying to more immediate levls of causes. In *Constructing Cause in International Relations*, I attempt to show how this can be done.

Reason

As noted, Weber proposes a fourfold typology of social action: "purposeful rational" (*zweckrational*) is calculated behavior "adequate" to achieve an intended goal; "value rational" (*wertrational*) arises from normative commitments; "traditional" or "habitual" action is made with reference to accepted norms and practices; and "affective" action is prompted by the emotions.[114]

This typology represents a major substantive insight, something unusual for Weber in his methodological writings. The other steps of his research strategy – ideal types, rationality, and counterfactuals – are purely abstract formulations. It is in some ways the most important part of his research strategy. Weber envisages it as the initial step in empirical research. We must determine the basis of the rationality that motivates the actors we study. Surprisingly, given its centrality to his epistemology, the concept of typology nevertheless lacks clarity because of its piecemeal construction and evolution in the course of Weber's writings. Another problem is his fairly loose and sometimes interchangeable use of such key words as *Rationalismus*, *Rationalität*, and *Rationalisierung*.[115]

The typology is substantive in a second sense. The four logics have personal and social determinants and the latter are the product of particular cultural configurations. They vary across cultures and epochs. The typology further implies that different motives are transformed into behavior by different mechanisms and have different implications for social and political cohesion.[116] They give rise to different ways of life (*Lebensführungen*) and cultures. Weber is very clear that the logics for social action do not imply any kind of linear development. All four kinds of rationality were evident throughout history. So-called primitive man could be just as means–end rational as modern people, although early humans probably used ends–means rationality more in conjunction with religion and other forms of value rationality.

Weber offers no benchmarks or protocols for determining the kind of behavior we confront. Protocols are an essential requirement if the typology is to have any empirical utility. They are also essential to avoid circularity. In their absence, researchers will be tempted to infer a logic of action from the behavior they observe. They will also do what Weber strongly opposed: rely on "empathetic understandings" of the kind espoused by Dilthey. Historicists portrayed empathetic understanding as the product of intuition made possible by the innate gifts of the researcher and years of intimate study of a people and their epoch. Weber accepted the need to replicate the mindsets of actors and attempted to do so himself with Calvinists and other Protestants he considered responsible for capitalism. However, in the absence of any method for developing and justifying claims of empathetic standing, the method of empathy rested on a shaky and entirely subjective foundation. There were no grounds for privileging one scholar's account of motives over another's.[117]

Weber had a more fundamental objection to the historicist reliance on empathy. He wanted to separate intuitions from "the logical structure of cognition" and devise appropriate methods for making causal inferences. He coined the term *rationale Evidenz* to signify something that has the appearance of being true or correct. He sought to distinguish himself and his method from Dilthey's and to provide a more scientific basis for the *Verstehen* approach by introducing logical and empirical tests for inference. He nevertheless remained adamant that explanation generally required empathy as well as reason.[118] It is surprising, therefore, that he failed to take the next essential step and to specify means for determining which motives were at play.

This would not have been an easy task. It requires measures independent of the behavior we are trying to explain. It is further complicated by the possibility that people act on the basis of more than one logic at a time or misjudge which one actually motivates them. Normative commitments may lead to habitual behavior, making it difficult for the actor or observer to distinguish between the two. More problematic is calculated instrumental behavior that actors convince themselves is normatively motivated. Some analytical concepts, like anxiety, lend themselves to measures independent of the behavior they are invoked to explain. We can determine anxiety levels by measuring perspiration, heartbeat, or the cognitive complexity of actor comments and speeches. Inferring logics of behavior might suggest looking more broadly at the actors in question. How have they behaved in the past and especially in similar situations? Yet this does not really solve the problem because how do we know what motivated them in these other occasions?

At best, we can look at what actors say about themselves and the world. This is problematic, for reasons already noted, but can still sometimes be fruitful. Alexander and Juliette George authored a fascinating psychobiography of Woodrow Wilson, arguing that he made many key political decisions on the basis of value rationality. They infer this from his actions, arguing that purposeful- and value-based behavior were at odds and his choices in these situations reveal his motives. To avoid circularity, they try to support their analysis by drawing evidence from his speeches, conversations, and letters. They also look at patterns in his behavior and, with them, the conditions where he is more likely to opt for one logic over another. They further rely on how actors close to him judged his motives.[119]

Rationality. Weber finesses the logic of action problem by focusing only on *Zweckrationalität*: purposeful, calculated behavior. It most closely approaches his ideal type of "right rationality" (*Richtigkeitstypus*).[120] It is goal-oriented, and actors accordingly acknowledge the importance of instrumental rationality and try to make use of it.

Weber's strategy still leaves us with a problem, if not a contradiction. In the *Grundbegriffe*, Weber insists that ideal types help us to understand the motives of actors. This is difficult to reconcile with his insistence on understanding motives from the actor's point of view. Admittedly, some ideal types attempt to capture or build on commonly shared motives, but many do not. Injudicious use of ideal types or of the logic of *Zweckrationalität* is little different from "assuming" motives and rational behavior the way present-day rationalists do.[121]

Weber defends his assumption of rationality on practical grounds; we must assume some actor rationality for purposes of analysis. It is a methodological ideal type and, like other ideal types, provides a benchmark for assessing actual behavior. The logic of *Zweckrationalität* nevertheless threatens to blur the distinction between rationality as an ideal type and rationality as something that informs real-world behavior. Weber tries to sustain the distinction but also comes close to eliding it when he defines purposeful rational behavior as that which "is exclusively oriented towards means which are (*subjectively*) considered to be adequate for the attainment of purposeful goals which are (*subjectively*) unambiguously comprehended."[122]

The more an individual's deliberations "have not been obfuscated by 'external' constraint[s] or irresistible 'affects,'" the more readily they submit to an ends–means analysis. He recognizes that this condition is rarely met in practice, but we must still try to use what evidence we have about actors, their goals, and their behavior to try to make the latter "fit into a model of rational action."[123] Weber is trying hard to finesse a dilemma. In the absence of instrumental rationality, social behavior would be entirely unpredictable and societies could neither form nor function.

Weber nevertheless warns us against attributing too much rationality to actors. What is important is that the researchers function in terms of rationality. They have to be sensitive to errors of judgment and common types of errors (*Irrtumstypus*) that routinely distinguish real-world from rational actors. Wearing his Kantian hat, Weber conceives of the world as one of logical behavior and causal "necessity" but in which such necessity is never more than a guide. He was also willing to admit that there is more unpredictability in human behavior than in the weather.[124] This admission is not easy to square with his Kantian belief in the world as something made accessible by reason – or with his epistemological need to avoid too great a gap between rationality as an ideal type and rationality as a description of behavior.

Weber had a dismissive attitude to psychology. The psychology he rejected was the "touchy-feely" kind that Dilthey advocated. Psychology has made enormous strides in the postwar era, and much useful work has been done in using its concepts and experimental methods to understand foreign policy and international relations. Psychological research demonstrates severe limits to rational decision-making, especially in high-risk decisions, those in which they would have to make trade-offs between important values, or those in which actors perceive there are no good choices.[125] Weber, I believe, would be receptive to this work because it employs a transparent logic of argument and is subject to the same kind of evaluation as any research rooted in rationality. Some psychological research addresses the deviation from rationality that Weber very much expected to characterize real-world, as opposed to ideal type, politics.

Evaluation. The final stage of Weber's strategy for social science involves evaluation. How can we defend the plausibility of our causal narratives? In addition to the usual rules of logic and evidence, Weber invokes "rules of experience" (*Erfahrungsregeln*). What are rules of experience if not a fancy compound word for the conventional wisdom; and what reason do we have for supposing that the conventional wisdom makes sense – or is always the appropriate yardstick? Perhaps with the problem in mind, Weber suggests that *Erfahrungsregeln* be supplemented by nomological understandings that take the form of imperfect regularities.

Neither benchmark meets Weber's proclaimed standard for robust methods. The conventional wisdom is often wrong, even when seemingly supported by scientific research. During the Cold War, deterrence was consistently confirmed tautologically by American scholars and policymakers. Rather than believing that deterrence failed because it is a flawed strategy that risks provoking the very behavior it seeks to prevent, they concluded that it had not been practiced forcefully enough. It was only after the end of the Cold War, when it became possible – alas, for a brief time only – to get access to Soviet records, including Politburo minutes, did this truth became evident.[126] There is now compelling evidence from studies of Cold War crises that document how deterrence threats led Soviet – and American – leaders to pursue more confrontational policies for fear of otherwise being seen as weak by the other side. For political and psychological reasons, the belief in the efficacy of deterrence nevertheless remains the conventional wisdom in the American national security establishment – and among many academics.[127]

Even when the conventional wisdom is valid, it may be an inappropriate benchmark for understanding behavior. Relying on the conventional wisdom is a classic source of intelligence failures. The United States and other Western powers imposed an asset freeze and then an oil embargo on Japan in July–August 1941 in the hope of moderating Tokyo's policies. These actions were in fact the catalysts for Japan's decision to go to war. Its leaders feared that the embargo would deprive them of the means of continuing their struggle against China and would ultimately put them at the mercy of their adversaries. It accordingly fostered a mood of desperation in Tokyo, an essential precondition for the attack on Pearl Harbor that followed.[128]

The Japanese decision to attack Pearl Harbor was another strategic decision based on wishful thinking. The Japanese military settled on a limited war strategy because they knew that it was the only kind of war they could hope to win against the United States, given the latter's superior economic and military power. They convinced themselves that a successful counterforce strike against US naval units in the Pacific would convince Washington to withdraw from the Western Pacific and give Japan a free hand in the region. The American reaction was, of course, nothing of the kind. Public opinion in the United States was enraged by Japan's "sneak attack" and intent on waging war against the country à l'outrance.[129]

It is notoriously difficult to reconstruct from the outside the motives and calculations of actors. Motives and the rank ordering of goals are often opaque and existing evidence may support diametrically opposed readings of them. Efforts to understand China's foreign policy provide a nice contemporary example; judgments of scholars and policymakers run the gamut and it is sometimes difficult to fathom that they are talking about the same country.[130] As the above examples nicely illustrate, actors sometimes do not undertake anything like a serious cost calculus, or, if they do, they factor in the rosiest estimates of how others will respond to their initiatives. This is true in everyday life, national policy, and international relations. Bias can be equally pronounced on the part of outsiders' attempts to understand their motives and behavior. Analysts rely on that conventional wisdom, which may not be wisdom at all but a set of arbitrary assumptions that at best reflect our personal – or national – experiences and cultural and other assumptions. To the extent that we make inferences on the basis of them, we risk imposing our understanding of the world on others, which is likely to mislead us about their motives and calculations.

In medieval epistemology, science (*Scientia*) is knowledge of universal truths. Thomas Aquinas used the term *opinio* to refer to beliefs that could not be proven by demonstration. The term came to be used for beliefs that arose from reflection, argument, and disputation.[131] It ultimately gave way to nomological knowledge based on demonstration. Its present-day successor is conventional wisdom. Sensing its subjectivity, Weber wanted inference about motives to meet the test of demonstration. His descendants make similar appeals, for example to distinguish good counterfactuals from bad ones.[132] Yet there is no established nomological knowledge in the social sciences and certainly not in those branches of it that address politics. This has not prevented some social scientists from asserting the existence of such knowledge, but these are rhetorical, not scientific, claims.

Conclusions

Weber's ends–means approach to cause rests on rationality. This limits its applicability to all the logics of action that Weber identifies. It assumes that actors to some degree exercise reason and, more importantly, that researchers can determine the kinds of choices that instrumentally rational behavior would have produced in any given situation. I have argued that these are unsupportable epistemological assumptions. The same problem arises in evaluating causal narratives. Counterfactual analysis is helpful in probing the assumptions on which different arguments rest but certainly cannot provide definitive answers in most instances because it is difficult, and sometimes impossible, to know with any certainty how others would have responded to an actor who behaved differently.[133]

We need to recognize that causal analysis is as much an art as a science. Historical knowledge and empathetic ability are as essential as qualitative and quantitative skills. I think Weber understood causation this way and it is why he gives empathy equal billing to reason in his causal nexus. It is certainly not the conventional wisdom in contemporary social science, which ignores empathy to focus entirely on reason. As causal arguments can never be demonstrated, they are nothing more than rhetorical claims and put a premium on "selling" our narratives to relevant audiences. They will appeal more to the extent they are based on the conventional wisdom.[134] So there is no escaping the inherent subjectivity of social science and its inherent risk of circularity.

Max Weber first took up the question of method in his contribution to a *Festschrift* for Karl Knies, his predecessor in the chair of economics at Heidelberg. He subsequently wrote about method because it raised issues too important to be ignored. At the same time, he maintained a jaundiced view about methodology as a field of study. "Methodology can never rise above self-reflection about the means that have *proven useful* in practice; one does not need to be explicitly aware of those means in order to produce useful work just as one does not need knowledge of anatomy to walk 'correctly.'"[135] This may have been a throwaway line. If intended seriously, it only applies to fields where there is a consensus about what constitutes good practice. It does not hold where there are competing understandings of science, how it is conducted, and for what ends. We must follow Weber's example of engaging fundamental issues of epistemology to make informed choices about our research.

The most important tension in Weber is between fact and value. He believed that empirical science and value choices inhabit different domains. Our value commitments motivate our research, but our findings must be evaluated on the basis of criteria independent of these values. He acknowledged the subjectivity of scholarly interests, not just political ones, and of the concepts and methods used to study human behavior. He regarded social knowledge as limited by time and place: "*There is no* absolutely 'objective' scientific analysis of cultural life ... *independent* of special and 'one-sided' points of view." These points of view reflect our particular research interests but more fundamentally how we select and order what we call facts. The goal of social science is to acquire "knowledge of relationships that are significant from the individual point of view." We must "keep the *limits* of their validity in mind."[136]

For Weber, the tension between fact and value has been greatly intensified by modernity. By foregrounding instrumental rationality and encouraging people, organizations, and states to think and plan in terms of it, it correspondingly reduces their focus on the ends these means are intended to serve. As instrumental rationality becomes dominant, substantive rationality recedes. For Weber, as for the great philosophers of the past, reason was a means of discovering the good or appropriate life. Paradoxically, instrumental reason attempts to substitute efficiency and order for the values that might more successfully promote the good life. In effect, *Zweckrational* substitutes for *Wertrational*. It is the fundamental reason why modernity threatens to be so dehumanizing.[137]

The Vienna Circle tried and failed to solve this problem by deriving logical warrants for assessing truth claims, and their project was of little interest to scientists in any case. We have come to realize that good science is what good scientists think it is at any given moment and that their understandings are field-specific and labile.[138] The social reality of science shifts the burden of validation away from procedures to the normative commitments of practitioners. They must be open-minded, pluralist, and, above all, fair-minded. Science rests on ethical values, yet these values are culturally dependent, open to interpretation, and recognized as constantly evolving.

Our values guide not only our choice of subjects and research methods but also how we evaluate our findings and their significance. Weber worried that these values were smuggled in rather than brought to bear in a transparent way. "One finds value judgments being made everywhere without compunction ... But it is the exception rather than the rule for the person making a judgment to clarify *in his own mind*, and for others, the ultimate subjective core of his judgments, by which I mean the *ideals* on the basis of which he proceeds to judge the events he is observing."[139] Weber warned that many social scientists, especially economists, assume norms of economic efficiency and productivity and fail to distinguish between "what is" (*das Seiende*) and "what ought to be" (*das Seinsollende*).[140]

Weber too has difficulty in distinguishing the "is" from the "ought." He assumed that the state is the central political fact and that its preservation and growth is a first-order concern. He accordingly supports what Germans of his day called the primacy of foreign policy (*Primat der Außenpolitik*). His scientific study of politics is based on this assumption and his belief that competition *à outrance* among classes, peoples, and states is an unavoidable fact of life. Weber differed little from Marx in his belief that states had to compete for markets. His commitment to the state led him to castigate German politicians of all parties for using narrow, self-interested instrumental reason in lieu of the national interest.[141] He considers their behavior irrational, but this is only evident from his point of view, not from theirs. Weber acknowledged his value commitments in his scholarship but understood that this was not a solution to the problem. If we start with different values and goals, we are likely to ask different questions, find different answers, and assess their meaning and significance in light of different metrics. Science can be objective only in the narrow sense of research concepts, design, and findings being consistent with and following the researcher's value commitments.

I believe Weber was more interested in a different kind of consistency, one that has more to do with our lives than with our research. Throughout his life, he was deeply concerned with the development and expression of individualism, especially his own. Liberalism's emphasis on the value and sanctity of the individual was what attracted him to it as a worldview. To develop as an individual, one had to commit to consistent values and aspire to act in accord with them. Weber tried hard to do this in his private life, scholarship, university professorship, and politics.

Tracy Strong draws an interesting parallel between Weber and Freud.[142] Both men considered the unmasking of illusions (*enttäuschen*) the fundamental goal of their science. Like Freud, Weber sought to strip away personal illusions. He insists that scholars require "relentless honesty" to make proper use of ideal types, which are the vehicle for making knowledge claims in the social sciences. Ideal types identify the "meaningful traits of a culture."[143] To fathom these traits, we must do more than what Clifford Geertz described as "soak and poke."[144] We must first understand our culture, as it is the starting point of the analysis of any other. This in turn demands honest self-reflection and understanding and the recognition of the extent to which we are largely products of our culture and our position in it.

Weberian ethics requires something more difficult still. Marianne Weber reports that, when her husband was asked what his scholarship meant to him, he replied: "I want to see how much I can bear."[145] Strong interprets this as a reference to his belief that because our world is demystified, it no longer makes sense; all former certainties have lost their hold on us. We must accept that we cannot make sense of the world and come to terms with its meaningless, as far as we can. This is unsettling and painful and we are always tempted to try to make the world cohere. Only by resisting this temptation can we hope to create the kind of ideal types that can at least help us understand how the world became the way it did.

There is an interesting parallel between Weber's conception of ethics and his ideal types. From his "Objectivity" essay on, Weber is clear that ideals have always been and always will be in conflict. There is no way to resolve this conflict, nor to resolve the conflict between the ethics of conviction and responsibility. At best, people can make choices among competing values. To do this effectively, they must be as candid as possible with themselves about the motives behind their behavior or policy choices.

The two ethics can be considered vehicles for probing one's intentions and the values on which they rest. They are as much a starting point for introspection as they are for policy analysis. The same can be said of Weber's approach to scholarship. Good scholarship depends on the questions we ask, the methods we use to find answers, the way in which we collect and evaluate evidence, and the inferences we make from it. This in turn depends on understanding our social and political commitments, our position in society, and, indeed, the position of our society relative to others. We must look inward before we can look outward.

For Weber, scholarship and life are closely intertwined. He seeks neither escape nor happiness but identity through scholarly commitment. Here too, the ideal type is the key. As Strong notes, it provides the analytical answer for the scholar the same way the phrase *Hier stehe ich* (Here I stand) does for the Lutheran – a phrase Weber uses at the outset of his "Profession and Vocation of Politics" essay. Ideal types make the world known to us and help us discern what can reasonably be done within it. It is a Kantian conception but not inferred by reason. It is the product of historical sociology.[146]

We come to the ironic realization that objectivity is available only to scholars who recognize their utter subjectivity and understand that *wissenschaftliche Wahrheit* (scientific knowledge) is a product of a given culture and their position within it, not a feature of the world. The connection between science and personal development is an intimate one.

Notes

1. Lebow, *Politics and Ethics of Identity*, chap. 6, on the striking similarities between Marx and Engel's communism and certain forms of evangelical Christianity.
2. Lebow, *Constructing Cause in International Relations*, chap.
3. Lebow, "Weber's Search for Knowledge."
4. Weber, *Max Weber*, pp. 32–33.
5. Weber, "Nation State and Economic Policy."
6. Radkau, *Max Weber*, passim, for Weber's love life in and out of marriage.
7. Weber, "Zur Lage der bürgerlichen Demokratie in Russland" [On the State of Constitutional Democracy in Russia].
8. On Weber during the war years, see Weber, *Max Weber*, chap. 16; Mommsen, *Max Weber and German Politics*, chap. 7.
9. Weber, "Der verschärfte U-Boot Krieg" [Unrestricted Submarine Warfare], pp. 146–154.
10. Weber, "Parliament and Government in Germany under a New Political Order," pp. 130–271.
11. Radkau, *Max Weber*, pp. 506–510.

12. Weber, *Russian Revolutions*, p. 264.
13. Weber, *Max Weber*, chaps. 17–19; Mommsen, *Max Weber and German Politics*, pp. 283–331; Radkau, *Max Weber*, pp. 504–505.
14. Weber, *Max Weber*, p. 40.
15. Ibid., pp. 412, 521–522; Mommsen, *Max Weber and German Politics*, pp. 190–282, on Weber and World War I.
16. Toller did not pursue an academic career. Dahlmann, "Max Weber's Relation to Anarchism and Anarchists"; Mommsen, *Political and Social Theory of Max Weber*, chap. 6, on Weber and Michels.
17. Radkau, *Max Weber*, pp. 432–436.
18. Weber, "Parliament and Government in Germany under a New Political Order"; Weber, *Russian Revolutions*, p. 225.
19. Weber, "Zwischen zwei Gesetzen" [Between Two Laws] and "Deutschland unter den Europäischen Weltmachten" [Germany under the European Great Powers] speech in Munich, October 22, 1916, p. 30.
20. Weber, *Max Weber*, p. 631.
21. Report of the *Heidelberger Tageblatt*, in ibid., pp. 631–632.
22. Weber, "Zur Lage der bürgerlichen Demokratie in Russland."
23. Ibid. Weber acknowledged the influence in this regard of his friend political scientist Georg Jellinek.
24. On Weber's methodological positions, see Ringer, *Max Weber*, chap. 3; Lebow, "Weber's Search for Knowledge"; Jackson, "Production of Facts"; Guzzini, "Max Weber's Power."
25. Weber read Nietzsche and subscribed to his "ethic of human dignity" [*Vornehmheit*] but made only one reference to him in his letters. Ringer, *Max Weber*, p. 241.
26. Weber, *Max Weber*, p. 325.
27. Weber, *Protestant Ethic and the Spirit of Capitalism* and *Sociology of Religion*.
28. Ibid., *Protestant Ethic and the Spirit of Capitalism*, p. 6.
29. Parsons, *Structure of Social Action*, pp. 51–74, 77–82.
30. Ibid., p. 5.
31. White, *Social Thought in America*.
32. Hughes, *Consciousness and Society*, chap. 2.
33. Ibid.
34. Haskell, *Emergence of Professional Social Science*, p. 7.
35. White, *Social Thought in America*, chaps. 2–3, 7.
36. Loeb, *Mechanistic Conception of Life*; Watson, "Psychology as the Behaviorist Views It."
37. US Census Bureau, "1800–1990: Changes in Urban/Rural U.S. Population," www.seniorliving.org/history/1800–1990-changes-urbanrural-us-population/ (accessed February 23, 2018).
38. Ibid., pp. 33–36.
39. Ibid., p. 28.
40. Haskell, *Emergence of Professional Social Science*, p. 13.
41. Ibid.
42. Gerth and Mills, *From Max Weber*, p. 44.
43. Beiser, *German Historicist Tradition*, p. 511.

44. Oakes, *Weber and Rickert*.
45. Ringer, "Max Weber on Causal Analysis" and *Max Weber*.
46. Lebow, "Weber's Search for Knowledge" on the *Methodenstreit* and the dispute between historicists and neo-Kantians and Weber's response.
47. Ibid.
48. Weber, *Protestant Ethic and the Spirit of Capitalism*, p. 98.
49. Ibid., pp. 76–77.
50. Weber, "Conceptual Exposition," p. 9. He also mentions laws but notes that they offer a purely theoretical understanding because people act in accord with them "only in unusual cases."
51. On Weber and Simmel, see Frisby, "Ambiguity of Modernity."
52. On Weber and the neo-Kantians, Oakes, *Weber and Rickert*.
53. Windelband, "Geschichte und Naturwissenschaft."
54. Weber, *Roscher und Knies*, pp. 4–5.
55. Weber, "Die Objektivitätsozialwissenschaftlicher und sozialpolitischer Erkenntnis" [Objectivitist Social Science and Social Political Knowledge] (hereafter Objektivität).
56. Ibid.; Rickert, Grenzen der naturwissenschaftlichen Begriffsbildung, pp. 102–119, 197–200; Simmel, *Über soziale Differenzierung: Sozialogische und psychologische Untersuchungen* [On Individual and Social Forms: Sociological and Psychological Investigations], chap. 1.
57. Weber, *Protestant Ethic and the Spirit of Capitalism*, p. 77.
58. Weber, "Objektivität," pp. 170–172.
59. Ibid.
60. Ibid., p. 206.
61. Ibid., pp. 181–183.
62. Ibid., p. 214.
63. Ibid., pp. 170, 183–184. John Stuart Mill also contrasted the West with what he called "Chinese Stationariness."
64. Ibid., pp. 170, 181–182.
65. Weber, *"Vocation and Profession of Politics."*
66. Weber, "Objektivität," pp. 212–214.
67. Weber, "Conceptual Exposition," p. 13.
68. Weber, "Objektivität," pp. 172–178.
69. Ibid., pp. 178–180.
70. For a contemporary version of this approach to causation, see Lebow, *Constructing Cause in International Relations*.
71. Ibid., for a derivative approach.
72. Ibid., pp. 175–178.
73. Jackson, "Production of Facts"; Mommsen, "Ideal and Pure Type," pp. 121–132.
74. Ibid. and Weber, "Conceptual Exposition," p. 20.
75. Weber, "Objektivität," pp. 190–195; Jackson, "Production of Facts."
76. Ibid., pp. 190–193, and "Conceptual Exposition," pp. 19–20.
77. Jackson, "Production of Facts" voices the same objection.
78. Weber, "Conceptual Exposition," p. 12.
79. Ibid.

80. Weber, "Roscher und Knies," pp. 67–69, 126–131.
81. Weber, "Objektivität," pp. 170–172, and "Kritische Studien," pp. 276–280.
82. Weber, *Protestant Ethic and the Spirit of Capitalism*, p. 98.
83. Weber, "Kritische Studien," pp. 276–280.
84. Weber, "Conceptual Exposition," pp. 6–7.
85. Weber, "Roscher and Knies," p. 130, for Frederick William IV; and "Causal Exposition," p. 21, for the Austro-Prussian War and quote.
86. Weber, "Conceptual Exposition," pp. 9–21.
87. Ibid. and "Kritische Studien," p. 286.
88. Knies, *Statistik als selbständige Wissenschaft*; Radbruch, *Lehre von adäquaten Verursachung* [Theory of Adequate Causation].
89. Weber, "Kritische Studien."
90. Ibid., pp. 274–275.
91. For examples, Hanson, "Themistocles at Salamis," and Strauss, "Salamis without Themistocles, and the West without Greece."
92. Weber, *Protestant Ethic and the Spirit of Capitalism*, p. 109. In 1904–1905, H. Karl Fischer and Felix Rachfal wrote the first major reviews of *The Protestant Ethic and the Spirit of Capitalism* in the *Archiv für Sozialwissenschaft und Sozialpolitik* and the *Internationale Wochenschrift für Wissenschaft, Kunst und Technik* and provoked a choleric reply from Weber. For an abbreviated English version of Weber's reply, see "A Final Rebuttal to a Critic of Capitalism."
93. Weber, *Economy and Society*, vol. 1, 1.7 (pp. 11–13 in the English edition).
94. I am indebted to Jens Steffek for this point.
95. Lebow and Stein, *We All Lost the Cold War*, chap. 2.
96. Jervis, *Perception and Misperception in International Relations*, pp. 128–143.
97. Janis and Mann, *Decision Making*.
98. Lebow, *Between Peace and War*, chap. 4; Lebow and Stein, *We All Lost the Cold War*, chap. 4.
99. Smith, *Inquiry into the Nature and Causes of the Wealth of Nations*, 4.2.4 and 9; Hegel, *Lectures on the Philosophy of World History*, 3.2.§37.
100. Axelrod, *Evolution of Cooperation*; Cederman, *Emergent Actors in World Politics*; Epstein and Axtell, *Growing Artificial Societies*; Jervis, *System Effects*.
101. Weber, *Protestant Ethic and the Spirit of Capitalism*, chap. 4.
102. Cobden, *England, Ireland and America*.
103. Tin-bor Hui, *War and State Formation in Ancient China and Early Modern Europe*; Wong, *China Transformed*.
104. Pomeranz, *Great Divergence* and "Counterfactuals and Industrialization in Europe and China."
105. Elster, *Political Psychology*, p. 5; Tarrow, "Expanding Paired Comparison"; McAdam, Tarrow, and Tilly, *Dynamics of Contention*.
106. Lebow, *Forbidden Fruit*, chaps. 2–4, on this point.
107. Ibid., chap. 3.
108. Harvey, *Explaining the Iraq War*.
109. Lebow, *Forbidden Fruit*, chap. 2.
110. Newton reasoned that the energy reaching us from an individual star is E/r^2, where r is the distance of the star, and E is the average energy radiated by each star, and if the density (d) of stars in the universe is constant, the

number of stars would be d r^3. The total energy produced by these stars would grow in a linear fashion with r, and rise to infinity in an infinite universe – neither we nor the earth would exist. Hence, the density of stars must decrease or the universe must be finite.
111. Lebow, "Evolution, Adaption, and Imitation in International Relations."
112. Breslauer and Lebow, "Leadership and the End of the Cold War."
113. Lebow, *Forbidden Fruit*, Conclusions.
114. Weber, "Roscher und Knies," pp. 67–69, 126–131.
115. Kalberg, "Max Weber's Types of Rationality," on this point.
116. On the latter point, Lebow, *Rise and Fall of Political Orders*.
117. Weber, "Roscher und Knies," pp. 88–89.
118. Weber, "Conceptual Exposition."
119. George and George, *Woodrow Wilson and Colonel House*.
120. Weber, "Objektivität," pp. 170–172, and "Kritische Studien," pp. 276–280.
121. Weber, *Economy and Society*, p. 22.
122. Weber makes this argument most extensively in "Profession and Vocation of Politics."
123. Weber, "Roscher und Knies," pp. 67–70.
124. Ibid., pp. 127–131.
125. Lebow, *Between Peace and War*, chaps. 4–6; Stein, "Calculation, Miscalculation, and Conventional Deterrence I," and "Calculation, Miscalculation, and Conventional Deterrence II"; Lebow, "Miscalculation in the South Atlantic."
126. Lebow, *Between Peace and War*, chaps. 4–6; Stein and Lebow, *We All Lost the Cold War*.
127. Hopf, *Deterrence Theory and American Foreign Policy in the Third World*; Stein and Lebow, *We All Lost the Cold War*; Lebow, *Avoiding War, Making Peace*, chaps. 1, 7; Press, *Calculating Credibility*.
128. Hattori Takushirō, *Dai-tōa sensō zenshi* [Complete History of the Great East Asia War] rev. ed. (Tokyo, 1965), p. 111, quoted in Iriye, "The Failure of Military Expansionism"; Iriye, *Second World War in Asia and the Pacific*, pp. 146–180; Pelz, *Race to Pearl Harbor*, pp. 212, 219–223, 223–226. Ike, *Japan's Decision for War*, for the records of Japanese decision-making.
129. Roper, "Polling and Pearl Harbor," December 1, 2016, https://ropercenter.cornell.edu/blog/polling-and-pearl-harbor.
130. Zhang and Lebow, *Rethinking Sino-American Relations*.
131. Hacking, *Emergence of Probability*, pp. 20–22.
132. Tetlock and Belkin, "Counterfactual Thought Experiments in World Politics"; Fearon, "Causes and Counterfactuals in Social Science."
133. For a discussion of this problem, Breslauer and Lebow, "Leadership and the End of the Cold War."
134. Lebow, *Constructing Cause in International Relations*, for elaboration of this claim.
135. Weber, "Kritische Studien."
136. Weber, "Objektivität," pp. 170, 181–182.

137. Weber does not treat modernity at length in any of his writings. Rather, his thoughts on the subject must be inferred from paragraphs and pages in diverse writings, making them open to quite different interpretations.
138. Popper, "Epistemology without a Knowing Subject" and *Logic of Scientific Discovery*; Kratochwil, "Evidence, Inference, and Truth as Problems of Theory Building in the Social Sciences."
139. Weber, "Nation State and Economic Policy," pp. 18–19.
140. Weber, "Objektivität," pp. 149–155.
141. Lebow, "Weber and International Relations."
142. Strong, "Entitlement and Legitimacy" and "Weber and Freud."
143. Weber, "Objektivität," pp. 190–195.
144. Geertz, *Local Knowledge*.
145. Weber, *Max Weber*, p. 678.
146. Strong, "Entitlement and Legitimacy" and "Weber and Freud."

7   Thomas Mann and Franz Kafka

In the late nineteenth century, cause became more difficult to trace but also more important given the pace of change and the need to understand and adapt or, some hoped, master it. Social scientists, writers, and other intellectuals were confronted with difficult choices. They could devise new methods to establish cause or find new means of organizing inquiry into their societies. Max Weber was committed to causal narratives and brought considerable analytical skill and imagination to the task.

Thomas Mann and Franz Kafka went in the opposite direction. Neither thought cause easy to establish or of much use in negotiating life. Mann wrote realist fiction that emphasized impressions, emotions, and the knowledge and commitments they could promote. Weber and Mann nevertheless share much in common. Weber attempted to integrate intuition with causal analysis and, by doing so, transcend the limitations of both approaches. Mann described his approach to knowledge as dialectical; he believed that feeling and reflection must combine to produce deeper understandings of oneself and one's society. Both turn to narratives as preferred vehicles of enlightenment.

Kafka straddles Romanticism and Modernism. His critique of modernity is darker and more compelling than that of either Weber or Mann. He depicts government and the legal system as arbitrary institutions of oppression. He also has a more jaundiced view of reason and cause. They cannot explain the world or right injustice because they are another form of enslavement. Here, Kafka is closer to Nietzsche.

For Weber, cause was the key to understanding and coping with a rapidly changing world. Kafka, following Hume, believed that people, by their very nature, thought in causal terms. He sought to demonstrate just how frustrating and inappropriate this kind of reasoning was in modern society. Like Weber, Kafka was fascinated by bureaucracy. Weber regarded it as the most important and far-reaching instantiation of the rational-legal authority that he considered the quintessential feature of modernity. He thought it empowering but also dehumanizing.

Kafka also regards bureaucracy as a defining feature of the modern age but evaluates its consequences with an even more jaundiced eye.

Weber attributed the downside of bureaucracy to the very rationality that made it so powerful and effective. For better and worse, it treated people alike and had the potential to deprive them of their individuality. Kafka emphasized its pathology, which he attributed to its lack of transparency and freedom from democratic oversight. For Weber, bureaucracy performs tasks in accordance with the law and directives from higher political authority. For Kafka, bureaucracy is a law unto itself. It seeks to preserve and extend its power and buttress the authority and self-esteem of its officials. For both writers, bureaucracy offers insight into cause, just as cause offers insight into bureaucracy. Their thoughts about this relationship lead them in opposing directions, analytically and politically.

Thomas Mann

Thomas Mann was born in Lübeck in 1875 and died in Zurich in 1955. He was the scion of a Hanseatic family, a class and background he portrayed in his first novel, *Buddenbrooks*. His older brother Heinrich was a radical writer and three of his six children – Erika, Klaus, and Golo – became important writers. Mann was in Switzerland when Hitler came to power in 1933, broke with Hitler in 1936, and went to the United States when war broke out in 1939. He returned to Switzerland in 1952.

In the course of his long career, Mann wrote novels, novellas, short stories, social criticism, and essays. In 1929, he was awarded the Nobel Prize in literature. His highly symbolic and often ironic fiction explores the psychology of artists and intellectuals. Mann began writing *The Magic Mountain* in 1913. He was inspired by his wife's extended stay at a sanatorium in Davos, Switzerland, where she was successfully treated for a lung complaint. Mann visited her and made the acquaintance of the doctors and many of the patients in this cosmopolitan institution. Like Hans Castorp, the novel's hero, he was diagnosed as having a wet spot in his lung. Repelled by what he described as the "profiteer's smile" on the doctor's face, he promptly fled the clinic and resumed his life in Munich.

Mann initially envisaged a novella along the lines of *Death in Venice*, which, at the time, he was preparing for publication. He later acknowledged that he intended it as "a humorous companion piece to *Death in Venice*."[1] That novella reveals Mann's fascination with the death wish, what Freud called *thanatos*. It pits order, based on rules and self-discipline, against the Dionysian pleasure principle, which finds expression in drink, sensuality, and disorder. Freud and Mann portray this tension as universal, although, with some distance from their era, we might better view it as a particularly bourgeois and German understanding of life.

Mann's writing was abruptly interrupted by the outbreak of World War I. In its aftermath, he sought to use *The Magic Mountain* as a vehicle for exploring European bourgeois society and how civilization carried the seeds of its own destruction. Like Freud, he discusses bourgeois attitudes to health, illness, sexuality, and mortality and their broader social and political consequences. *The Magic Mountain* was radically revised, expanded, and finally published in two volumes in 1924. World War I and antibiotics put sanatoria out of business. Mann is describing an earlier world, though one that is still vivid in his memory.

The Magic Mountain is a difficult work to read and interpret. It aspires to realism, but its realism often comes across as ironic. It has numerous symbolic undertones that prompt understandings and inferences seemingly at odds with its realism. Mann recognized the elusiveness of his text but offered few clues about how to approach it. Late in life, he compared his novel to a piece of music. It is "composed" like a symphony with multiple movements and themes. It is "a work in counterpoint, a thematic fabric; the idea of the music motif plays a great role in it." It had to be "listened to" more than once to understand how the parts formed a whole.[2]

Nietzsche maintained that music exists in a realm that is beyond and before all phenomena. Language and the concepts its spawns can never capture its cosmic symbolism because language itself is a symbol. It can have superficial contact with music – it can describe its structure, rhythm, instrumentation, and evolution – but it cannot disclose its innermost heart. That reveals itself to us directly, unmediated by language.[3] Music can accordingly produce a higher form of enlightenment than language.

Mann was undoubtedly familiar with Nietzsche's analysis of music and had something similar in mind. Although he communicates in words, he wants to mimic music in structure and effect. Like Wagner's operas, *The Magic Mountain* uses a leitmotiv to establish continuity between past and future and the sanatorium and the "flatland" below. Mann further emulates music by trying to evoke pleasure and enlightenment by means of sensations and emotional responses. Reflection is, of course, required, to grasp the structure of the novel and the way in which its themes are developed and interact. It can intensify the pleasure and understanding that come from engaging the text. This process nevertheless differs profoundly from texts whose meanings are primarily found in their arguments.

Mann and Weber. Mann's narrative about European culture on the eve of World War I is distinctly noncausal and accordingly structured very differently from Weber's avowedly causal account of Protestantism and the rise of capitalism. Weber posits a cause – Protestantism – and the values and practices it promoted – savings and profit-making investments – and an effect – capitalism. He elaborates the chain of logic connecting the two. Mann does nothing of the kind. He paints portraits of the diverse inhabitants of the Magic Mountain sanatorium and describes their relationships, and the ways they change, or do not, over the course of their stay. He uses two characters – Settembrini and Naphta – to make the case for opposing approaches to life and disease. They argue endlessly about their respective positions and neither in any way yields to the other.

Weber makes explicit the methods that underlie his analysis of Protestantism and other religions and expounds on them at some length in other writings. He believes this kind of transparency is essential to good causal analysis and scholarship more generally. Mann keeps his methods hidden from readers, as most writers do. He may not be fully aware himself of how he went about constructing his novel. This may also be true of Weber to some degree, as great social science, like great writing, consists of more than the application of procedures.

Despite their different projects and approaches, there are some interesting and important parallels in how Weber and Mann frame and structure their inquiries. Most notable is their mutual turn to abstraction. Weber invented the concept of the ideal type as a kind of "mental image that is not historical reality." Rather, it represents a synthesis of many phenomena that remove all variation to create a parsimonious and consistent concept. Weber offers the examples of individualism, imperialism, feudalism, mercantilism, and the so-called Marxist laws of capitalist development. Weber is clear that ideal types are always perspectival.[4] He considers ideal types a necessary tool for identifying key characteristics of cultures that can explain their distinctive patterns of behavior. In *The Protestant Ethic and the Spirit of Capitalism*, Weber uses two primary ideal types: Protestantism and capitalism. Each represents a pared-down highly stylized characterization of a complex, diverse, and constantly changing phenomenon.

Mann's sanatorium is certainly not an ideal type. It is nevertheless a pared-down and highly stylized representation of pre–World War I European society, a microworld in which emotions and responses can be isolated and examined. As with ideal types, this artificial construct is the starting point for a complex narrative that folds in context and agency to tell a complex story with the purpose of providing insight into the real world. Weber and Mann are not all that far apart in how they structure their inquiries.

The Magic Mountain. The Berghof "*bei uns hier oben*" (with us on high) is physically distant from society. Hans Castorp feels this isolation acutely in the last stages of his train and carriage journey to the sanatorium, where he has come to visit his cousin Joachim. "Home and regular living, lay not only far behind, they lay fathoms deep beneath him, and he continued to mount above them" – literally and figuratively – into a world of "phantasmagorical world of towering peaks."[5] In Hans, this produces "a sense of the impoverishment of life and gave him a slight attack of giddiness and nausea."[6]

The Berghof is populated by a representative sample of Europeans and patients from further afield. All but the physicians and staff suffer from varying degrees of consumption. Hans quickly discovers that "It is a sort of substitute existence." After six months, people lose touch with the outer world and its ideas and concerns. The novel deliberately attempts to convey this feeling to the reader. According to Mann: "it depicts the hermetic enchantment of its young hero within the timeless, and thus seeks to abrogate time itself by means of the technical device that attempts to give complete presentness at any given moment to the entire world of ideas that it comprises."[7] This psychological as well physical distance is nicely signaled home by the book Hans has brought with him: *Ocean Steamships*. He tries on several occasions to read it and then gives up as his former life as a naval engineer loses all meaning.[8]

The sanatorium has a rigidly structured life. "The daily routine was clearly articulated, carefully organized; one fell quickly into step, and by yielding oneself to the general drift, was soon proficient."[9] Almost every hour of the day is taken up by meals, lectures, veranda rests in wraps, walks, and examinations. Time is the organizing principle of modern life, as it is of the sanatorium. It nevertheless loses most of its meaning in the Berghof because of the repetitive nature of its routine, more or less unchanging in the days of the week, months of the year, and, for many, for years on end. This leads to a sharp contrast between the way time is understood by the doctors who run the institutions and by the patients who are its residents. For the former, it is a scientific tool. For the latter, time "has nothing whatever to do with reason, or with the ordinary ways of measuring time; it is purely a matter of feeling."

Mann highlights the differences between objective and subjective time. It is most evident in music, which, the narrator notes, is measured by beats. There are frequent concerts at the Berghof, where some insignificant march that is seven minutes long provides pleasure in part because of the way it divides time and, by doing so, makes you more aware of its passage. It arouses anticipation of what comes next and enjoyment of the gap between this realization and the expected sounds.[10] Music, the narrator tells us, "quickens time, she quickens us to the finest enjoyment of time; she quickens – and in so far she has moral value."[11] Pleasure can also be derived from divorcing oneself entirely from time and recognition of its passing. "The settled citizens preferred the unmeasured, the eternal, the day that was forever the same."[12]

Berghof residents were able to foreground time when listening to music but otherwise largely banish it from their lives. Joachim describes young adults at the sanatorium as free and liberated from all considerations of time. They indulge in "just a sort of loafing about and wasting time; life is only serious down below."[13] Joachim informs the newly arrived Hans that "Our smallest unit is the month."[14] For many patients, this appears to be a psychological defense mechanism. Dwelling on the passage of time is of little utility in the sanatorium, where the stay may be prolonged and survival in question. Patients need to live for the moment; by divorcing themselves from time, they enhance the enjoyment of the moment and distance themselves from thoughts about their illness and the course it may run. For Mann, timelessness is another way of distinguishing Berghof residents from flatlanders. In the world below, time is of the essence, especially for the bourgeoisie, whose pace has been quickening in contrast to the slowing down of time for sanatorium residents. Those below are so caught up in their schedules that they have little time to reflect on the meaning of their existence or indulge in passions not germane to moneymaking and advancement.

Readers of *The Magic Mountain* are very much encouraged to put time aside; it is the only way to engage a 700-plus-page novel. Like the patients they encounter in its text, readers are invited to enter into a world not in thrall to human time – artificial divisions of hours, days, weeks, months, and years – or its natural counterpart – changes in flora and weather that accompany the seasons. To the extent they succeed, they become more aware of the way the environment influences people and better able to empathize with the concerns and feelings of the novel's characters. Time is closely connected to reason, and Berghof residents learn more by feeling than reflection, and to do so they must first free themselves from time. So should readers, the novel suggests.

Hans Castorp. Our young hero has trained as an engineer and is about to begin an apprenticeship in a shipyard. He is healthy and comes to the Berghof for a short stay to visit his cousin Joachim, who has been diagnosed with a lung condition and has become a long-term resident.

Hans and Joachim do not use first names or the familiar pronoun with each other. They succeed in achieving most of what they attempt but are not in touch with their motives and rarely think about the consequences of their behavior. They are totally apolitical in a world in which Hans' friend, the self-identified humanist Settembrini, proclaims, and seemingly with good reason, that everything is political.

Castorp is "an unassuming young man," "a still unwritten page," and "by nature and temperament passive."[15] He describes himself as someone "of retiring disposition" and "a disinterested spectator" of what goes on around him.[16] He is "quite without arrogance; yet a larger arrogance, the pride of caste and tradition, stood written on his brow and in his sleepy-looking eyes, and voiced itself in the conviction of his own superiority."[17] He is a stereotype of Germans, especially north Germans and Prussians. Mann would later contend that "the German reader recognized himself in the simple-minded but shrewd young hero of the novel. He could and would be guided by him."

Castorp develops and matures in a way he would not have in the flatland. He is exposed to death on a regular basis, lives cheek-to-jowl with fellow sufferers from diverse backgrounds and countries, listens to heated debates about life and disease between Naphta and Settembrini, and falls in love. Mann maintains that heightening (*Steigerung*) is a fundamental theme of the book. Hans "is really a supple-minded hero, the young scion of good Hamburg society, and an indifferent engineer."[18] "But in the hermetic, feverish atmosphere of the enchanted mountain, the ordinary stuff of which he is made undergoes a heightening process that makes him capable of adventures in sensual, oral, intellectual spheres he would have dreamed of in the 'flatland.'"[19] He is incapable of expressing his enlightenment in words. Mynheer Peeperkorn, a late arrival at the sanatorium from the Dutch East Indies, describes him as a young man "of fluent little phrases." "Your tongue runs on," he tells Castorp, "it springs over stock and stone, and rounds off all the sharp corners. But satisfactory – no."[20]

Castorp learns in a distinctly Humean way: he experiences strong impressions that, for him, have greater vivacity than ideas. His ideas are largely derivative of these impressions.[21] "Hans Castorp, who knew naught of affairs of state, and whose formless, uncritical judgments were rather the fruit of mere lively perceptions. Yet they persisted into later life, as the elements of a perfectly conscious memory-picture, which defied expression or analysis, but was none the less positive for all that."[22] Mann tells us that "All the characters suffer this same process; they appear to the reader as something more than themselves – in effect they are nothing but exponents, representatives, emissaries from world, principalities, domains of the spirit."[23] By this means, a novel, rooted in realism, bridges to symbolism.

Mann further explains that "sickness and death, and all the macabre adventures his hero passes through, are just the pedagogic instrument used to accomplish the enormous heightening and enhancement of the simple hero to a point far beyond his original competence." Hans Castorp "in the course of his experiences, overcomes his inborn attraction to death and arrives at an understanding of a humanity that does not, indeed, rationalistically ignore death, nor scorn the dark mysterious side of life but takes account of it, without letting it get control over his mind." "What he comes to understand," the author writes, "is that one must go through the deep experience of sickness and death to arrive at a higher sanity and health; in just the same way that one must have a knowledge of sin in order to find redemption."[24] It is this notion of disease and death as a necessary route to knowledge, health, and life that makes *The Magic Mountain* a novel of *initiation*.[25]

Other Characters. There are numerous patients in the Berghof. Some leave because they are cured, others "visit" the real world for periods of months, even years, and still others are wheeled out to be buried in the graveyard below. The rooms of those who died are quickly cleaned and disinfected and made ready for new arrivals. No mention is made of the deceased. Hans Castorp is rebuffed when he tries to talk about death at dinner.[26]

Joachim is an officer candidate and his life revolves around his profession. He is committed to uphold his honor as a soldier and a German. The depth of his commitment contrasts sharply with the shallowness of his reflections about why he has these commitments, his choice of profession, or other aspects of his life. His failure to interrogate and understand his motives is a general phenomenon in the Berghof and, Mann appears to suggest, of Europeans more generally. In contrast to Hans, Joachim never really comes to understand his emotions. He is driven by them but not in any way in control of them. For this reason, he leaves the Berghof before he is fully cured, returns to his regiment, succumbs to an infection, and dies.

Dr. Behrens aside, the most reflective characters are Lodovico Settembrini and Leo Naphta. Settembrini, a fellow patient, espouses democracy, tolerance, and human rights. He often finds Castorp sitting in the dark and finds the need to throw the light switch on before their conversations. He compares himself to Prometheus, alleged to have given humans fire and enlightenment. His mentor, Bolognese poet Giosuè Carducci, wrote a hymn to a different bringer of light: Lucifer. Settembrini does his best to shake Castorp from his morbid fascination with death and disease. He warns him without success against his growing feeling for Clawdia Chauchat.

Settembrini, aging, ill, but mentally alert, makes explicit the connection between disease and war. "Disease has nothing refined about it, nothing dignified." Naphta's conception of disease, he insists, is pathological, or at least tends in that direction."[27] He opposed any "spiritual backsliding in the direction of that dark and tortured age" that Naphta admires.[28] Mann admits that Settembrini "is sometimes a mouthpiece for the author, but by no means the author himself." Naphta describes Settembrini as an exemplar of *Zivilisationsliterat* (pre–World War I German intellectuals committed to political and cultural renewal and tolerance). Mann originally conceived of him as a caricature of the liberal-democratic novelist, of whom his own brother Heinrich was a leading example. After the war, Mann himself became a committed supporter of the Weimar Republic, and Settembrini increasingly took on the authorial voice.

Naphta is a Jew from eastern Europe whose father was crucified in a pogrom. He became a Marxist but then converted to Catholicism and became a Jesuit. Mann acknowledged that he was intended as a parody of Hegelian-Marxist philosopher George Lukács.[29] Naphta is a counterpoint to Settembrini in his passionate defense of religion, nationalism, and god and his derision of reform and democracy.[30] Like Dr. Krokowski, he believes that disease is an external manifestation of a deeper psychological cause. Unlike Krokowski, he revels in it. "Man's unhealthiness is what makes him man," he proclaims. "Man is distinguished by his spirit, and it is enhanced, even made possible by disease. Disease and death are a form of nobility."[31] For this reason and others, Naphta exclaims, "War would come and be a good thing."[32] He implores "the eagle to strike and rip apart his prey with his claws." Joachim agrees with Naphta that, in a future war, no limit should be imposed on the shedding of blood. Naphta's name may be revealing. It is close to "Naphtha," in German and English a liquid hydrocarbon that was often used as the catalyst for starting larger fires.

Hans is not sure what to make of Settembrini. "But after all, it's worth listening to, he talks so well; the words come jumping out of his mouth so round and appetizing – when I listen to him – I keep seeing a picture of hot round rolls in my mind's eye."[33] Hans is right on the money. Settembrini and Naphta live in their imaginary worlds of pure but opposing ideologies. Neither is willing to engage the real world, where compromise, messiness, and irreconcilable conflicts over values are the order of the day. At best, they are taking refuge from this world and making themselves and their ideas irrelevant to it. At worst, they encourage the kind of simple thinking – albeit couched in complex arguments or flowery rhetoric – that helps to promote the destructive conflicts that Naphta welcomes. Settembrini's sunnily optimistic, nineteenth-century liberal idea of reason proves inadequate as an intellectual and heuristic tool, but then Naphta's approach leads quite literally to self-destruction. Mann is left with the challenging task of balancing the two approaches and possibly integrating them at a deeper level, as some critics believe he does in the "Snow" chapter.

Body and Soul. Mann's realism is most pronounced in his description of tuberculosis and how it is diagnosed and treated. His Dr. Behrens reduces the libido and love to vesicular responses. Mann also presents the conventional view of tuberculosis whose sufferers were romanticized. They were said to attain higher levels of spiritual refinement through their fevered lives and proximity to death. Consumption was also associated with intensified desires, especially sexual ones, and the spiritualization of death.[34] Dr. Behrens reports that his young patients quickly lose interest in everything but flirtation and temperature.[35] A number of them have affairs, with each other or outsiders. Hans and Joachim are shocked by a Russian couple next door who make joyous and noisy love during the day. Hans reasons with some disgust that they must see each other naked. The patients also indulge in culinary orgies. Almost everyone appears for the two breakfasts that are served and cannot wait for chocolate nights, when they sample diverse concoctions and debate their relative merits.[36]

The novel creates related tensions between body and soul, science and art, and reason and feeling. They are explored in debates between Settembrini and Naphta, comparisons of photographs and portraits, different approaches to life and love by patients, and their reasons for remaining in, departing from, or alternating between life in the flatland and in the Berghof. For our purposes, the most revealing tensions are between art and science. They highlight Mann's own ambivalence about the role of science and the utility of reason and cause.

Mann focuses on cause in the physical and biological worlds because they were considered more amenable to explanation than their social counterpart. His characters raise many causal questions that appear unanswerable, at least by the science of the time. They include the origin of the universe, of life, and of disease. People speculate about their causes, and their failure to find compelling answers raises questions about the utility of science and creates space for mystical perspectives.

Medicine is presented as a causal science and the raison d'être of the Berghof. Its doctors use the latest methods of diagnosis and treatment and patients pay substantial fees in the hope of being cured. The novel suggests that diagnosis and treatment are very hit-and-miss. Dr. Behrens and his colleague, Dr. Krokowski, offer diametrically opposed understandings of the causes of disease. Behrens attributes tuberculosis and its various manifestations to biological, chemical, and physical causes. He explains that the reddish flush on the face of patients is a by-product of heightened oxidation and that this in turn is attributable to soluble toxins released by bacteria. The effects of on the body raise as many questions as understanding the process answers. Krokowski insists that organic disease is entirely a secondary phenomenon that arises from psychological disturbances and tensions within the person.[37]

Diagnosis relies in the first instance on the sound elicited by palpitations of the chest, front and back, with the help of a stethoscope. Troubling sounds from the chest cavity invite X-ray examinations. Then comes the Gaffky test, which determines the level of bacilli in the blood. Each of these methods is problematic. Listening and interpreting chest palpitations is more an art than a science and so it appears is the reading of X-ray plates and the results of the Gaffky test. Both give rise to lots of false positives and negatives. There are bacilli in Hans Castorp's blood but Behrens is not worried about them.[38] Joachim's test is also indeterminate. Behrens admits that it could mean something or nothing.[39] There is no way of knowing. At best, "It was a question of probabilities."[40] Settembrini wonders aloud if these tests offer proof of anything since they all depend on highly subjective readings by the doctors.[41] Medicine, he implies, is more art than science.

The ubiquitous thermometers provide another example. Patients are required to take and record their temperatures several times a day. Settembrini observes that they are possessed of two ideas: "temperature, and then again temperature."[42] These readings interfere with their other activities, as they must remain still for minutes at a time. Joachim cannot talk when the thermometer is in his mouth.[43] His temperature returns to close to normal but he is far from cured. Hans' temperature goes up and down, and these variations turn out to be meaningless. Thermometers are one more instrument, together with the rigid routine, that reduce the body to an object. It suggests, and perhaps Mann intends, an analogy to a military organization.

The recovery or death of patients is largely random. Efforts at treatment are at best primitive: dry, rarefied air, rest, and high caloric intake. In the sixteenth century, Machiavelli compared politics to medicine: "doctors tell us about tuberculosis: in its early stages, it's easy to cure and hard to diagnose, but if you don't spot it and treat it, as time goes by it gets easy to diagnose and hard to cure."[44] Little has changed at the Berghof. The false positives are invariably in cases with few if any symptoms. Deaths occur in advanced cases where diagnosis is certain and treatment ineffective.

Mann uses medicine to explore the similarities and differences between science and art. He suggests that they are superficially mirror opposites but at a deeper level may be expressions of similar impulses. Conveniently, Behrens is an artist as well as a doctor. He makes portraits of people with X-ray machines and with paintbrushes. Castorp is struck by the realism of the portrait he has made of Clawdia Chauchat. Behrens describes the techniques he has used to give the impression of real skin and softness of the female face and body. The two portraits are connected in Castorp's mind by the shadow of her breasts on the X-ray plate.

X-rays are nevertheless portrayed as the ultimate dehumanizing device. They reduce subjects to mere things to be stripped naked, deprived of their dignity, posed, irradiated, and examined. They are a black art – literally – as they only work in the absence of light in the visual spectrum. Behrens explains: "We must first accustom our eyes ... We must get big pupils, like a cat's, to see what we want to see ... We must banish the bright daylight and its pretty pictures out of our minds."[45] The conventional association of light with en*light*enment is reversed but also questioned, because X-rays are not nearly as efficacious as the medical profession pretends.

X-rays can also be viewed as art. Hans Castorp cherishes an X-ray of his inamorata, Clawdia Chauchat, that he carries with him at all times. It reveals her skeleton but also the shadows of her organs and breasts. His attachment to this image personalizes it and transforms it into something of emotional and erotic significance. X-rays expose illness and corruption that might prove deadly. Yet Clawdia Chauchat's X-ray inspires Hans and heightens his sense of life. Mann uses Castorp to show, à la Freud, the close connection between the seemingly opposed forces of eros and thanatos.

Dr. Krokowski elaborates this tension in his discourse on the seeming polarities of sex and chastity and life and death. Nature has allowed women to arouse sexual and emotional passions in men as they are necessary to preserve the species, but both genders find it difficult to cope with them. Illness is the product of the tensions they generate and can be understood as a manifestation of love.[46] Physiological problems accordingly have psychological causes that arise from "the dark tracts of the human soul."[47] Tuberculosis might be understood this way, and Mann appears to suggest that this is the case with Castorp. He repressed his love for his childhood friend Pribislav Hippe, which may have been a cause of his earlier tuberculosis infection. Now he is in love with Clawdia but still repressing his feelings. He stays in Davos because of her and his long dormant infection flares up. His temperature rises and falls as a function of his interactions with her.

Freud would later make a more general argument about repression and its effects, attributing World War I to the extreme degree to which bourgeois society repressed natural instincts.[48] Krokowski is no Freud. His version of psychiatry leads to séances and efforts to communicate with the dead. This might be regarded as transgression of the most important binary of all: that of life and death.

War and Cause. Early in the novel, Joachim compares Hans' visit to Odysseus descending into Hades. Hans objects that he has ascended great heights to be here, but Joachim dismisses his descent as "an illusion."[49] Readers are primed to question the traditional hierarchy of heaven and hell, and good and evil as well. Late in the novel, the Berghof turns into a mild version of hell. There is "A rising temper, acute irritability. A nameless rancor. A universal tendency to envenomed exchange of words, to outburst of rage – yes, even to fisticuffs."[50] The breakdown of relations in the sanatorium parallels that among European states and peoples in 1914. In the final chapter, Hans Castorp goes into battle and Mann gives readers the impression that he is killed. Earlier, he had been amazed by the sight of his skeleton, which he presciently compared to seeing a dead man.[51]

The torpor that characterizes residents of the sanatorium until the end of the novel and the uproar at the end are related. The great stupor induced by the monotony of life in the Berghof encourages frivolous occupations and, finally, the great irritability (*grosse Gereiztheit*) that it produces. The absence in prewar Europe of the kind of spiritual fulfillment that makes for a satisfied life generates anxiety and unrest that find release in aggression in the Berghof but also in the flatland. Castorp feels this compulsion even if he does not understand it. "It seemed to him that 'all this' could come to no good, that a catastrophe pending, that long-suffering nature would rebel, rise up in a storm and whirlwind that would break the great bond that held the world in thrall; snatch life beyond the 'dead point' and put an end to the 'small potatoes' [*Sauregurkenzeit*] in one terrible Last Day."[52]

The transformation in mood and the ending of *The Magic Mountain* are perplexing. Mann gives us no reason or hint why interpersonal relations should suddenly deteriorate in the Berghof. Perhaps this sudden change is intended to be as inexplicable as its counterpart in the flatland? To the extent that we read the former as a synecdoche of the latter, Mann may be suggesting that the great catastrophe is beyond rational explanation.

An alternative reading starts with the recognition that – quantum mechanics aside – there is action at a distance. In the social as in the physical world, we need some mechanism connecting an object and that which is acting on it, in this case, changes in the flatland and their manifestations in the Berghof. Mann does not provide one. The other possibility is that they have independent but parallel causes. This line of argument would begin with the assumption that tuberculosis is a stand-in for the social-psychological-spiritual disease afflicting European culture.[53] Mann, after all, did reconceive the novel after the war, rejecting its initial framing in favor of one that allowed him to grapple with the intellectual and cultural conditions that made the Great War possible. Tuberculous, as noted, was thought to intensify all kinds of passions, which makes it a suitable metaphor.

Passions prompt intolerance and aggression. We get a hint of this at *Walpurgisnacht* and see more it with the fight between the anti-Semite and Jewish residents and then in the duel between Naphta and Settembrini. For most of *The Magic Mountain*, these protagonists argue fiercely but treat one another with respect; their intellectual differences never become personal. Their dialogue is reminiscent of Plato's *Republic*, where intense exchanges involving Socrates and the sons of men who fought on opposing sides in the Athenian civil war build friendships. What matters in the *Republic* is not the arguments that Socrates or any of his interlocutors make but the personal relationships their dialogues establish. As Thucydides has Pericles explain in his funeral oration, friendship (*philia*) is the basis of civic solidarity.[54] Yet the friendship between Naphta and Settembrini cannot endure. As their arguments became sharper, and the differences in their positions and temperaments more apparent, their inner tensions and contradictions rise more to the fore. Naphta succumbs to Thanatos and uses the duel as a vehicle to kill himself.

The kind of solidarity that Naphta and Settembrini seemed to construct is absent among other residents of the Berghof. At best, they share some kind of weak "we" feeling, a common identity based on their residence in the sanatorium that distinguishes them from flatlanders. It is perhaps not unlike the "European" identify of flatlanders when they confront non-Europeans but regrettably absent when they interact with one another. This is mirrored in the Berghof dining room. Residents are assigned tables for dining; there was no free seating and relatively little social interaction before or after dinner across tables. Seating assignments were made largely on the basis of nationality, which was functional because it put people together who spoke the same language. Each table develops something of a collective identity and negative stereotypes of people at other tables. The Russians, for example, sit at two tables, one of which is referred to as "the good Russian table" and the other as "the bad" one. Even those at the good table are regarded with suspicion. Experiments at the core of social identity theory indicate that groups created to perform even the most menial tasks develop positive in-group feelings and negative out-group feelings.[55] The obvious inference is that something similar has happened; people identify not as Europeans or Berghof residents but as members of tables and nations.

National, regional, and gender stereotypes abound. Castorp and Ziemssen are described by Mann as typical north Germans. Settembrini is a southerner and different in temperament and outlook. Clawdia Chauchat has Mongol eyes that are said to reveal much about her character. The "good" and "bad" Russian tables are said to be differentiated on the basis of their behavior but no evidence is provided. Both tables, as noted, are treated as Russians by others, that is, as Europeans who are not quite European. Gender stereotypes are rife but frequently violated. There are many Jewish patients, judging by their last names, and at least one man is identified as such. He is subjected to anti-Semitic insults by another patient and comes to blows with him. In this respect, too, the Berghof is representative of the world below.

Mann conveys a perhaps deliberate ambiguity in treating causes. In the science of medicine, there is a most uncertain relationship between so-called cause and effect. Putative causes can have diametrically opposed effects, as the mountain air and other treatments do with tuberculosis. Other causes are hidden, difficult to fathom, and difficult to represent.

The Magic Mountain suggests that bourgeois repression, national and ethnic stereotypes, and the growing imbalance between reason and emotions are the underlying causes of World War I. As in the Naphta and Settembrini relationship, reason has triumphed over emotions. It has stifled the kind of learning necessary to sustain friendship and tolerance but has also put intolerable stress on the psyche that finds release in aggression directed against others and the self. Mann says about Hans Castorp that he "comprehended then with his mind, if not with his sympathies, which would have meant even more."[56] He cannot find the cause of Clawdia Chauchat's behavior because, unlike Herr Albin, "he is not in touch with his emotions."[57] In his efforts to explain fever, Hans says "one involuntarily tries to find an emotion which would explain, or even half-way explain the goings-on."[58] Mann values empathy over causal understanding, in keeping with the Dilthey and the German historicist tradition.

Mann would subsequently change his mind when he observed the triumph of emotion over reason in late Weimar and the Nazi era. He never formally repudiated the underlying assumptions of *The Magic Mountain*, which ends in an aporia. Mann came around to recognizing the importance of reason and emotion but said little to nothing about how they should be related and inform one another. The problem here may be one of path dependency. Starting from scratch he might have written a different novel but working with the large text he had already produced there were only so many changes and additions he could reasonably make or add.

Mann stands in sharp contrast to Weber who recognized the importance of empathy but thought it too subjective a foundation for inquiry. At best, empathy could generate insights that lead to the construction of ideal types or propositions. It was a stepping stone to causal narratives that were rational, in the sense of being internally or logically consistent and externally consistent with available evidence. Weber was very much interested in the process that led from empathy to insight to ideal types and propositions, although he complained bitterly about having to take time off from his substantive investigations to write about it.

The Magic Mountain appears to be noncausal on multiple levels. Nothing much happens in the course of the novel. Hans Castorp remains in the sanatorium for seven years all but cut off from developments in the world below. His horizon is limited to the patients and staff of the Berghof, a cast of characters who, with a few exceptions, remain relatively constant. Clawdia Chauchat comes and goes, and the occasional patient leaves for good, some feet first. The most significant events in the lives of the sanatorium residents are improvements or decline in their health, developments which, we have seen, defy causal explanation. So do other developments and behavioral patterns, or at least no explanations are proffered. Among these mysteries are Clawdia Chauchat's penchant for allowing the dining room door to slam behind her, the division of Russian tables into good and bad, the choices people make about affairs vs. celibacy, and Naphta's shifting commitments in philosophy and religion.

The narrative focuses on the emotional growth and changing self-realizations of characters, most notably, Hans Castorp. He nevertheless makes uncertain progress. There is an unbridgeable gulf in understanding between him and his inamorata. Her door slamming in the dining room infuriates Hans but delights Herr Albin. Albin interprets it and her direct gaze as indicative of the sickness of the young and their lack of restraint to which he responds positively. Castorp is offended by both but later becomes more accommodating of her behavior as he becomes emotionally involved with her. Is this new empathy due to dissonance reduction; as he loves her – or thinks he does – her behavior must be seen as acceptable, even pleasing? Or, is it due to the north German Hans beginning to loosen up and allow himself to express and appreciate emotion?[59] These are unanswered questions and ones Mann might think best left this way. What matters is that our hero has grown emotionally.

Yet it is superficial growth because his infatuation with Clawdia Chauchat is hormonally driven. His relationship with her remains distant, superficial, and unreciprocated. Hans is unreflective about this attachment, and the more so as he becomes consumed by it. Here too, perhaps, a comparison is intended with the world below. The biggest parallel is, as noted, the use of disease as a synecdoche for social evils. Doctors and patients alike look into the body to understand its ills. They do not meet with success and nor does Mann when he looks into his isolated, ideal-type society. At best, there are vague hints about the similarities and contrasts between the sanatorium and Europe on the eve of World War I.

The focus on Hans Castorp's development suggests that we read *Der Zauberberg* as a *Bildungsroman*. Mann characterized it as such in a 1938 lecture at Princeton.[60] *Bildungsroman* is a literary genre that focuses on the psychological and spiritual growth of the protagonist in the transition from youth to adulthood.[61] The term was coined by philologist Karl Morgenstern in 1819 and prominently brought to the attention of the German reading public at the end of the nineteenth century by Wilhelm Dilthey. Dilthey was a pioneer of the interpretivist and historicist traditions, in which Mann was steeped.

The *Bildungsroman* focuses on individuals, although certainly does not ignore the settings in which they mature. The protagonist typically achieves maturity in the course of conflict with his society. He – the protagonists up to the time of Mann were men – finds resolution and maturity by accepting the values of society and being embraced by it in return. In *The Magic Mountain*, Mann presents Castorp not so much in conflict with German society but as its quintessential product.

A man lives not only his personal life, as an individual, but also, consciously or unconsciously, the life of his epoch and his contemporaries. He may regard the general, impersonal foundations of his existence as definitely settled and taken for granted and be as far from assuming a critical attitude toward them as our good Hans Castorp really was; yet it is quite conceivable that he may, nonetheless, be vaguely conscious of the deficiencies of his epoch and find them prejudicial to his own moral well-being.[62]

As this insight is offered early in the novel, Mann appears to be priming us for a deeper explanation for Castorp's personal development and perhaps using Hans to offer insight into his society. The individual is a product of the Zeitgeist and especially a young man like Castorp who lacks any strong will or desire to distinguish himself or oppose his family and peers. An era that lacks hope and prospects limits those of its generation. Hans' early love for Hippe and the patches on his lung may have been the organic expression of sexual repression, which in turn was a product of Victorian values. They shaped his response to Clawdia Chauchat and life more generally and, in the end, led him and others of his generation to embrace death as anonymous warriors. Abnormality in this society is latent in the healthiest of young men as it is in Hans Castorp.

Kafka

Franz Kafka was born in Prague in 1883 into a middle-class Jewish family. His parents were said to have spoken a Yiddish-inflected German, referred to pejoratively as *Mauscheldeutsch*. He and his siblings were encouraged to speak High German as it was a prerequisite for upward mobility. He trained as a lawyer, was awarded his doctoral or law degree in 1906, and performed an obligatory year of unpaid service as law clerk for the civil and criminal courts. He was subsequently employed by an insurance company; his job involved investigating personal injury claims filed by industrial workers. Kafka had to write in his spare time. He became engaged to several women but never married.

In 1915, in the midst of World War I, Kafka received a draft notice. His insurance company successfully arranged for a deferment on the grounds that his work was essential government service. He nevertheless tried to join the army in 1917 but was rejected for medical reasons after being diagnosed with tuberculosis. A year later, he was pensioned off because of his illness. He spent the rest of his life in sanatoriums and died in 1924 at the age of forty. Kafka shared many of Hans Castorp's experiences, but in real life.

Kafka numbered among "his true blood brothers" Goethe, Dostoevsky, Flaubert, Gogol, Franz Grillparzer, and Kleist.[63] He spoke and read Czech and developed an abiding interest in its literature. He immersed himself in Yiddish and Jewish culture after seeing a Yiddish theater troupe perform in October 1911.[64] He was, however, ambivalent about his Jewishness. At one point he exclaimed: "What have I in common with Jews? I have hardly anything in common with myself and should stand very quietly in a corner, content that I can breathe."[65]

Kafka straddled Romanticism and Modernism. Thomas Mann greatly admired his style, which he described as "conscientious, curiously explicit, objective, clear, and correct."[66] Few of Kafka's works were published during his lifetime. A collection of stories *Contemplation* (*Betrachtung*) and "The Transformation" (*Die Verwandlung*) appeared in literary magazines and attracted scant attention. Kafka ordered that his unfinished works be destroyed, among them his novels *The Trial* (*Der Process*), *The Castle* (*Das Schloss*), and *Der Verschollene* (translated as both *Amerika* and *The Man Who Disappeared*). His friend Max Brod ignored Kafka's wishes and had them published posthumously.

The Castle. The village where the story is set is remote and covered by deep snow when K. arrives. There is no sign of the castle above: "fog and darkness surrounded it, not even the faintest gleam of light suggested the large Castle. K. stood for a long time ... gazing upward into the seeming emptiness."[67] The castle would become visible when the weather improved but it remains invisible in a figurative sense. From the outset, the reader is primed to understand the castle and the town and its inhabitants as signifiers of the powerful and powerless.

K. discovers that the closer he approaches to the castle the less impressive it appears. It was "distinctive only because everything perhaps was built of stone, but the paint had long since flaked off, and some of the stone seemed to be crumbling."[68] The main part of the cast is "a monotonous, round building."[69] Carriages come and go from the castle to the wider world but the town's inhabitants stay put. The arrival of the surveyor K. is something of an anomaly; townspeople are initially distant, if not hostile. The exception is Frieda, a young woman who takes him to bed and becomes his fiancée. She later leaves him for a young townsman. By the end of the story, K. is isolated, unpaid, and unemployed. The plot, to the extent there is one, revolves around K.'s efforts to contact authorities in the castle. They have summoned him to do a job but he never succeeds in finding out what it is exactly they want him to do. He is not paid for the time he has put in or reimbursed the expenses he has incurred. His efforts to contact the castle are rebuffed, an enigmatic conversation aside with one of its officials whose responsibilities are far removed from land management.

There are subplots about the townspeople. There is also a family that has no relations with anyone else, having been expelled from town because their daughter resisted the sexual advances of a castle official. They are isolated and abandoned by townspeople once the castle makes it known they are viewed with disfavor. Some critics see an analog here to anti-Semitism.

K.'s professional training carries over into his personal life; he uses reason and logic to understand his situation and the social life of the town. It does not take him very far. Reasoning must start from some substantive assumptions, and those he brings to his situation are largely inappropriate. Reason therefore leads him astray. He makes many false attributions, just as townspeople routinely misinterpret his behavior and motives. This is particularly evident with respect to the castle, where K.'s understandings diverge from those of the townspeople. He revises his provisional suppositions on the basis of new information – what today would be called a Bayesian updating – but gets no closer to the truth – whatever that is – in his understanding of either town or castle. Townspeople start from largely shared assumptions and assimilate what little information they have to these assumptions, confirming them tautologically.

In a world in which assumptions may be inappropriate, information scarce, and motives hidden, cause is difficult, if not impossible, to fathom. The problem is equally evident in castle and town, although they differ greatly in the amount of information about them available to an outsider like K. The castle is truly unknowable, only bits of information leak out about what goes on inside. Nobody knows who is in charge as there appear to be layers of outer offices through which it is impossible to pass to reach the inner sanctum, even for those who work there. The castle resembles a black hole, and, like Hawking radiation, some information leaks out, most of it in the form of rumor from people who have visited the castle or work as messengers for it. We might understand the castle as representative of the modern world and the ways in which our lives are affected, if not shaped, by hidden, unknowable forces.

The castle's seemingly official point of contact is Herr Klamm. He makes periodic appearances in the town but remains elusive and unapproachable and will not speak to anyone. Like the other castle officials in the novel, his actual area of expertise is never mentioned. Nobody knows what he does, although his rulings appear to shape the town. K. consistently tries and fails to secure a meeting with Klamm, whom he hopes can resolve his problems or act as an intermediary to someone in a position of authority in the castle. His failure drives home to K. "the extent to which one's official position and life" are "so intertwined that it sometimes seemed as though office and life had switched places."[70] In German, *klamm* is "clammy" or "damp" and, in its noun form, means "gorge" or "ravine." The latter meaning seems fitting given the physical and social divide separating town and castle. In Czech, *klamm* means "illusion," which is also apropos.

K. has all kinds of relations with townspeople, ranging from hostile confrontations through social intercourse to physical intimacy. The motives of townspeople are difficult to fathom because they are often the product of long, generally unknown histories of the people in question or their families. Without this recondite knowledge, it is impossible to know why people do the things they do. Commonsense analogies based on prior social experience are generally misleading. Consider K.'s two assistants, who come across as idiots and slackers, but turn out to be anything but. K. struggles to understand people and their situations and turning to others for advice is of little help. Everyone gives different explanations for the behavior of Frieda, the assistants, the innkeeper, and Barnabas the messenger. It is not at all clear to K. or the reader who is right and who is manipulating him and for what ends.

There is a very low level of trust in the town. Individual and family security seems to derive from good relations with the castle. People also claim and establish status by this means. Frieda's standing rises once she has an affair with Klamm – if indeed she does. There is a clear class divide in town, and the novel views the world through the eyes of the lower class. They are the most vulnerable to the vagaries of the castle and most dependent on protection and support from others. Their vulnerability becomes the source of authority for their social superiors in the castle. They need to do little to benefit townspeople to maintain this authority. The one boon they provide is a gift of a fire engine to the town. At the presentation ceremony, Sortini, the low-ranking official sent by the castle to oversee the presentation, makes a pass at Amalia, Barnabas' sister, and is rebuffed. He starts nasty rumors about her, and she and her family are disgraced for their seemingly causing bad relations with the castle.

The novel offers a powerful critique of the class structure and of anti-Semitism, the latter suitably disguised. It is quite modern in some ways in its take on women. They are just as intelligent and scheming as men but required, given their lower social status, to use sex to advance their status and interests. It also offers a powerful indictment of bureaucracy. The castle is divided into numerous offices, each with specific responsibilities. Presumably, this organizational scheme developed piecemeal in response to circumstances but, once in place, does not change even if external circumstances do. The people who staff its many offices seem to have been randomly assigned to them, without any prior consideration of their qualifications. The chairman explains to K. "they could just as easily have fallen like snowflakes, given how little thought went into assigning them."[71] Department A and Department B appear responsible for summoning K. as a surveyor but only after months and years of sending files back and forth, losing most of them, and demonstrating other kinds of incompetence.

The mayor of the town, or chairman (*Dorfvorsteher*), is fat, friendly, and insignificant. He is an agent of Herr Klamm from the castle. He explains to K. that he is not really needed as a land surveyor and offers him the job of school janitor. According to the chairman: "One of the operating principles of the authorities is that the possibility of error is simply not taken into account. The principle is justified by the excellence of the entire organization and is also necessary if matters are to be discharged with the utmost rapidity."[72] In practice, the organization's decisions are riddled with errors and take forever to be made. To safeguard against error there are "control agencies." Over the course of time, they have come to supplant agencies with substantive functions. "Of course, they aren't meant to find errors, in the vulgar sense of that term, since no errors occur, and even if an error does occur, as in your case, who is to say it is an error?"[73]

The chairman describes K.'s case as a minor matter but one by virtue of the zeal of an official that became a major concern. This is not atypical as "the ordinary cases, that is those without so-called errors, create a far greater quantity of admittedly much more productive work."[74] The zeal of the official was in response to suspicions that surveying could have significant consequences for land ownership, and some accordingly believed that some dirty deal had been secretly concluded. It is not made evident how such concerns arose in a bureaucracy that makes no errors and is carefully supervised by other bureaucrats. Controversy never came into the open and a decision was finally made. "When a matter has been deliberated on at great length," according to the chairman, "it can happen, even before the deliberations have ended, that suddenly, like lightning, in some unforeseeable place, which cannot be located later on, a directive is issued that usually justly, but nonetheless arbitrarily, brings the matter to a close."[75] From the outside, and even from within the castle, there is generally no way of knowing which official reached the decision and on what grounds.

In K.'s case, the file on him has been mislaid and efforts to go through file cabinets and boxes are to no avail. "A pity," the chairman exclaims, "but of course you already know the story, we no longer need the file."[76] The castle is something like an onion, with layers under layers protecting the core. The officials in the outer layers have only limited access to the next layer in and distribute files with no particular logic or recognizable purpose. The narrator observes, with some irony: "So he [K.] hadn't noticed the difficulties under which the distribution of files had taken place, which were actually incomprehensible, for after all, each gentleman serves only the cause, never thinks of personal gain, and therefore had to work with all his strength to ensure that the distribution of files, this important, essential work, proceed quickly, easily, and without error?"[77]

K.'s case is a typical example of how the castle functions. It violates every ideal of the *Rechtsstaat* and bureaucracy as idealized by Weber – a subject to which we will return. Here, I want to comment on the implications of the castle's functioning for reason and cause.

Neither K. nor the chairman understands how the castle works. Firsthand observation by K. and long experience with the castle by the chairman convince them that most of the officials who work there are equally in the dark. There is no logic that can serve as a basis for inferences about what matters achieve importance; who considers them; what, if any, evidence is gathered; who makes decisions and on what basis; and why some decisions are publicized and others not. The flow of files and the chain of command seem to have little connection. Kafka does not give us the impression that everything is random but rather that there may be some underlying, but unknowable, logic that governs the castle. Its source is so hidden and protected that castle officials are also in the dark, making it unlikely, if not impossible, that they will act in accord with this logic. Procedures and self-interest are accordingly given free rein and interact in ways that are unknowable and inexplicable. If the castle is intended to represent modern government, especially government in authoritarian regimes, Kafka has hit the nail on the head.

Weber posits close links between cause and reason. Rational models help us infer cause. They rest on assumptions about how the world works that allow the construction of chains of logic, consistent with evidence, that link goals and behavior and behavior and outcomes. We must start by asking what values and goals actors have and what actions would, in the circumstances, effectively serve those values and ends. When there is variation between what they do and what we consider rational, we need to rethink our understanding of actor goals and values. If we are satisfied with this analysis, we must look to other factors to explain the variance. They might include concerns and issues to which the one in question has been subsumed, external pressures that we did not recognize at first, or their failure to carry out a rational assessment. Irrationality can have cognitive or motivated causes.[78]

Kafka may never have read Weber but still offers a powerful critique. He agrees that causal analysis depends on rational models and their fit with social reality. His character K. is a good rational analyst. He starts with reasonable, provisional assumptions: he has been summoned for a job and will be given the information and access he needs to complete it; officials are responsible and responsive; and he can infer the motives of townspeople from his general understanding of social life and human nature. These assumptions and his observations form the basis for an initial series of inferences that turn out to be incorrect. We understand why he fails and continues to do so: it has to do with his commitment to rational analysis. Given the way the castle and the world work, it stands in the way of understanding, let alone the attribution of cause. Cause is not a very useful concept and can be costly to those who seek it.

The Trial. This novel offers many parallels with *The Castle* in its focus on the secret functions of government, the inaccessibility of those in power, and the unfortunate fate of their heroes. *The Trial* ends with the death of Joseph K., and *The Castle* with K.'s abandonment by his lover and marginalization by town and castle. Both men are victims of circumstances over which they have no control.

The novels differ in their setting: a major city versus an isolated village. Both venues serve their purposes well. The village under the shadow of the mysterious castle allows a sharp division between rulers and ruled.

The rulers are situated physically above the rule, in a location barely visible from below. It suggests a comparison with Olympus or heaven in its sharp separation of deities from humans. The sweaty mortals below must honor and submit to the never-seen gods above them. As with Homer's gods, people in town are their playthings. Denizens of the castle summon nubile women for their sexual use and love affairs with gods confer status on them.

The city bustles with commercial life and young people pursuing careers and seeking their fortunes. It is as changeable as the village is fixed in its roles and fates of those who fill them. The justice system, not government as a whole, is the focus of the story. As in *The Castle*, people, including our hero, meet with only the lowest members of the court system. They too expect sexual favors from women and force themselves on them if necessary. Senior judges, like high officials in the castle, are never seen and are held in awe by townspeople and lower court officials. Defendants and lawyers try to reach them, the same way K. does with castle officials, but with no more success. Their petitions are either unread or not acted on, to their great frustration.

This is a more significant failing in *The Trial* because criminal justice – even more than ordinary administration – is supposed to function according to well-established and transparent procedures that protect the rights of all parties. Criminal proceedings especially are expected to guarantee a fair trial, in part by giving defendants access to the charges and evidence against them, the right to mount a defense, and the right to call and interrogate witnesses. Their failing is also more significant because of what is at stake. For K. in *The Castle*, it is the surveying job he has agreed to perform. Joseph K. has agreed to nothing, is suddenly arrested, and discovers that his freedom and then his life are at risk.

For these and other reasons, the law is the ideal institution for Kafka's purposes. He depicts the police, court, judiciary, and bar as dysfunctional, corrupt, secretive, and unprofessional in the extreme. These failings are evident at every level of their interaction, beginning with the officials who come to arrest Joseph K. They are thugs who arrive unannounced, proclaim that he is under arrest, and help themselves to his breakfast. They offer to buy him a replacement meal but it is clear they would pocket most of the money. Without permission, they take over a neighbor's apartment and steal her underwear. Joseph K. never learns the nature of the charges against him.

The courthouse is in an old warehouse in a rundown part of town. Defendants wait in a poorly ventilated, unlit, and stuffy room with lawyers crowded above them in a gallery whose low ceiling makes them crouch. Defendants and lawyers alike are deprived of their dignity and treated more like prisoners. Joseph K. is at last brought before an examining magistrate who looks through his notebook and says: "You're a house painter?" Joseph K. explains that he is a chief financial officer at a large bank. Other people in the room, some of them court officials, burst out laughing. Joseph K. complains to the magistrate that this error and the response to his effort to set the record straight "is characteristic of the way these entire proceeding against me are being conducted."[79]

Joseph K. goes on to denounce the justice system as an organization "that not only engages corrupt guards, inane inspectors, and examining magistrates who are at best mediocre, but that supports as well a system of judges of all ranks, including the highest, with their inevitable, innumerable entourage of assistants, scribes, gendarmes, and other aides, perhaps hangmen."[80] Its purpose "consists of arresting innocent people, and introducing senseless procedures against them, which for the most part, as in my case, go nowhere." Joseph K. is right about everything, of course, but not about his judgment regarding his own case. The system is more nefarious than even he believes.

Hi uncle, a prominent lawyer, recognizes that trials like his "are lost from the start."[81] He nevertheless urges Joseph not to leave town to escape the proceedings. It will be seen as flight and draw in his relatives and "drag them through the mud."[82] Like everyone else involved in the process, his uncle puts his interests above those of Joseph K. Leni, his father's servant, with whom he has a sexual liaison, tells him that "he can't defend himself against this court, all you can do is confess. Confess the first chance you get."[83] He reasonably ignores her advice, which probably would not have saved him in any case. Joseph K. learns from a painter that, as far as he knows, there has never been an acquittal. "A single hangman," he suggests, "could replace the entire court."[84] He later encounters a priest who, for some inexplicable reason, seems to be privy to the deliberations of the court. He tells Joseph "I fear it will end badly. They think you're guilty."[85] "But I'm not guilty," he exclaims. "It's a mistake."[86] "But that's how guilty people always talk," responds the priest.[87]

His lawyers are shady characters; one of them admits that others consider them "shysters." He is told he must file petitions with the court but the lawyer acknowledges they are unlikely to be read or acted on, and possibly misplaced. "They are simply put in the file with a note that for the time being the hearing and surveillance of the accused were much more important than anything put in writing."[88] Court records, he explains, "and above all the writ of indictment, are not available to the accused and his defense lawyers, so that in general it's not known ... what the first petition should be directed against, and for that reason it can only be by chance that it contains something of importance to the case."[89] The defense "is not actually countenanced by the Law, but only tolerated."[90] "They want to eliminate the defense as far as possible; everything is to be laid on the defendant himself."[91] The most lawyers can do is bribe people and pay them for information.[92]

Lower court officials are venal and sexually abusive and higher court judges are unknown and inaccessible. The law, previous judgments, and legal opinions are all secret.[93] So too are the proceedings against Joseph K. Neither he nor his lawyer is present at his trial or sentencing. The first he learns about them is when he is accosted by two men and taken to a deserted quarry for his execution.

The only instance of judicial responsiveness is to Joseph K.'s complaint about the guards who arrested him. He tells the magistrate examining him that the system is corrupt. The guards "try to steal the shirts off the backs of arrested men, inspectors break into strange apartments," and property is removed and taken to depositories "where the hard-earned goods of arrested men are rotting away, if they haven't already been stolen by pilfering officials."[94] The guards are disciplined for their theft by being flogged in a storeroom at his bank.[95] One of them explains to Joseph K. that "it's a tradition that undergarments belong to the guards, it's always been that way, believe me; and you can see why, what difference do such things make to a person unlucky enough to be arrested."[96] They complain to Joseph about the difficulty of supporting themselves without engaging in bribery and theft and how it is tolerated, even encouraged, by the system. This scene further highlights its corrupt nature.

Kafka and Weber. Kafka's courts and public administration are sharply at odds with the expectations we have of how modern institutions should function. This is especially true in the German-speaking world where the *Rechtsstaat* has long been an ideal and where court and public administration are expected to perform logically and fairly. Their deviance is further heightened by the seeming efficiency of the transportation and banking systems. Max Weber took the *Rechtsstaat* as close to a reality, when it was better described as an ideal type. He depicted bureaucracy as a key feature of modernity and expression of the "formal rationality" that gained traction because of its efficiency. He nevertheless considered bureaucracy stifling to human creativity in the first instance because it imposed rules to govern as much behavior as possible. Rules had to be simple to be understood and were likely to be enforced in a heavy-handed way. They reduced the authority and independence of individuals and, as circumstances changed, ultimately stood in the way of efficiency and common sense.

Weber feared that ordinary citizens would live in "a steel-hardened cage" of serfdom, helplessly, like the fellahin in ancient Egypt. Bureaucracy also threatened to reorient people's loyalties by narrowing their horizons to those of their institution. In the absence of deeper ethical commitments, bureaucracy would impose its own values on people. The *Kulturmensch* (man of culture) would give way to the *Fachmensch* (occupational specialist). For the latter, the only ethical yardstick would be the interests and power of the organization. Quoting Nietzsche, Weber predicted "the 'last men'" would be "specialists without spirit [and] sensualists without heart."[97]

Kafka regards bureaucracy in an equally jaundiced light but largely because it does not behave as Weber suggests. Bureaucracy and the justice system are irrational. Instead of restraining human passions, they give them free rein. They are a holdover from the Middle Ages, or even earlier times, when rule was arbitrary, if not cruel and exploitative. Justice in turn was primitive; people were tortured to extract confessions and punished by decapitation, hanging, garroting, or drawing and quartering. *The Castle*'s setting in a backward village dominated by an ancient castle further highlights the medieval connection.

For Kafka, modernity has allowed older, dysfunctional patterns of behavior to endure. There is no evidence that Kafka intended his novels as a critique of the Soviet Union or Nazi Germany. *The Trial* was written before either came into existence and *The Castle* in the early days of the former. The latter nevertheless represents a powerful *avant la lettre* indictment of both regimes. Gustav Janoch, a youthful disciple, asked Kafka if his writings were "a mirror of tomorrow." Kafka reportedly closed his eyes, rocked back and forward on his chair, and replied: "You are right. You are certainly right. Probably that's why I can't finish anything. I am afraid of the truth."[98]

Stories. Kafka's stories are also set in irrational, frightening, and unpredictable worlds in which individuals are at the mercy of forces they do not comprehend? "The Metamorphosis" is perhaps the most famous and most dramatic of these stories. Gregor Samsa lives in his parents' apartment, expects to rise early in the morning, pack the samples he has carefully laid out before going to bed, and make an early train out of the city. Instead, he wakes up to discover he has been transformed into a large beetle-like insect. He is mentally unchanged and struggles to make sense of and control his new body. He does not want to frighten his family so stays in his room. They begin to worry when he does not appear and a messenger from his firm comes looking for him. Samsa ultimately shows himself, horrifies his parents, but seems to reach an accommodation with his sister. Over the course of the following days, she brings food into the room and cleans it while he hides under the bed. When alone, he looks out the window to connect with the wider world, learns what food is acceptable to an insect, and enjoys the pleasure of hanging head down from the ceiling. His attempt to make gradual contact with his family prompts his terrified father to throw an apple at him that lodges in his carapace, the cook and the lodgers to leave, and his sister to turn against him. He starves to death in his room and is disposed of by the charwoman.

"In the Penal Colony" is an equally chilling story more closely connected to *The Trial*. An explorer visits a penal colony whose prisoners lead a depressing, undernourished, and servile life. He is invited to watch the execution of a prisoner whose job it was to stand watch outside the bedroom of an officer during the night and salute his door from the outside every hour. Caught napping, he is sentenced to death by the officer-judge-executioner without any trial. The execution device is an elaborate machine invented by the former commandant. It carves words, like "justice is served" in script on the man's body. Each circling of the machine inserts the needles a tiny bit deeper into the man's body, which is rotated so the script can cover his chest and back. This torture continues for six hours, with a gag inserted in the prisoner's mouth to muffle his screams until he dies from loss of blood. The needles still continue to write until the words are deeply inscribed. People watch the execution and children are brought close up to look at the face of the executed man, who is finally dumped into a pit. Modern technology has brought medieval torture to a higher level of sophistication.

Such torture, the story suggests, can only be sanctioned in a penal colony far away from ordinary civilization. The officer in charge of executions defends it as not only the legacy of the prior commandant but as a practice that teaches victims and onlookers alike about the nature of justice. Even here, it seems, there is opposition, as the new commandant, the officer reasons, has asked the visiting explorer to watch the proceedings to elicit his disgust as part of his campaign to end the practice. The new commandant has a more nefarious purpose, because the officer is suddenly substituted for the condemned prisoner – surprisingly, without resistance on his part – and strapped into the machine.

The officer about to be executed has complained bitterly about the new commandant's refusal to authorize funds for replacement parts for his complicated machine. It falls apart as his body is being written upon; wheels come flying out of its innards and roll toward the pit. Because of this malfunction, the officer dies a more merciful death as the failing machine collapses on top of him and drives a spike through his forehead. It is a welcome, if bizarre, form of justice and one that rests on values and practices no different from those of the ex-commandant and his faithful officer executioner. The explorer must flee for his life and is chased back to his ship by the former prisoner and a soldier. Modern values triumph – just barely – suggesting, perhaps, that we are not as far away from the Middle Ages as we would like to believe.

Kafka might be read against Sophocles. The reversal of executioner and executed is reminiscent of the kind of peripeteia we find in Oedipus. More fundamentally, Kafka's novels and stories, like Sophocles' plays, use dramatic reversals of fortune to explore fate and the unsuccessful struggle of people to figure it out, let alone game it. Like Oedipus, who ultimately comes to accept his fate, so do some of Kafka's characters. This is true of Joseph K., Gregor Samsa, Georg Bendeman, and the executed officer. "Before the Law" (*Vor dem Gesetz*) also involves reversal and acceptance. A man has spent years standing before a guarded gate attempting to gain admission to the law. At the end of his life, the doorkeeper takes pity on him and explains that "No one else could ever have been admitted here, since this gate was made only for you, and now I am going to shut it."[99]

Unlike Oedipus, Kafka's characters give no evidence of becoming wiser in the process and offering lessons to us. Their acceptance of their fates only arouses greater fears in us. Kafka's view of life is undeniably tragic and recognizes that denizens of the modern world are just as vulnerable as their predecessors. In sharp contrast to the expectations of the Enlightenment, technological advances and institutional reforms may only succeed in making human beings more vulnerable.

Before turning to a general discussion of reason and cause in Kafka, I want to discuss his story that most directly addresses these concepts. "The Great Wall of China," published in 1919, is about the building of the Wall, the reasons behind it, the way it was constructed in piecemeal fashion, and how the populace was mobilized to support the project. The narrator, an imaginary Chinese of the era, tells us about a comparison that was made to the Tower of Babel.

The narrator tells us that the Wall was ostensibly built to keep out barbarian marauders. He also reports that its piecemeal construction made the Wall and China porous to tribal incursions. He suggests that these incursions were in no way a real problem because China is so vast that invading horseman would soon dissipate and exhaust themselves as they penetrated the country. So why was the Wall built? The masons who are constructing it are separated by many layers of bureaucracy from the emperor and mandarins who surround him. The mandarins are unapproachable and their decrees are difficult to interpret. China is presented as a vast version of the castle in which the population tries to read the tea leaves, so to speak, to fathom the wishes of those whose decisions influence, if not determine, what they do with their lives and how they gain status.

Mobilization of the masses, and with it the provision of purpose to many lives, may not be an aim of the emperor but merely an unintended consequence. Those at the top – in the castle, Joseph K.'s country, or the emperor – may have power that verges on the absolute. They may have correspondingly little understanding of the meaning and consequences of their decisions. Here too, we have a parallel with World War I.

Reason and Cause

In Chapters 2 and 3, I suggest that cause became more important but also more difficult to trace in fifth-century Athens. Sophocles and Thucydides responded differently to this conundrum; the former sought to find ways of living without causal attribution and the latter looked for deeper understandings of cause. Mann and Kafka adopt variants of the Sophoclean strategy, while Weber follows Thucydides.

Mann and Kafka show important similarities with Sophocles. Chief among these is the two-level take they provide on fate and cause. They foreground the understandings their characters have, which are often counterproductive or self-serving. Their texts also offer more detached and sophisticated readings. Kafka's characters nevertheless differ from Sophocles in that they do not succumb to the temptation to interpret reality in accord with their practical or psychological needs. K. and Joseph K. are eminently reasonable people. Their failure to make sense of the world is also our failure.

Sophocles invariably provides some seeming explanation for the fates of his heroes and heroines. It is usually a curse that arises from earlier violation of nomos. Efforts to escape fate often bring it about, as Oedipus most dramatically demonstrates. I noted in Chapter 2 that many ancient Athenian theatergoers may have accepted this explanation and not had any difficulties accepting a curse with transgenerational consequences.

Kafka offers no explanations for anything that happens to his heroes. With the exception of Georg Bendeman, they are neither cursed nor the descendants of people who were. They appear not only blameless but good personal and professional role models. K. is a committed surveyor attempting to carry out his professional responsibility. Georg is a loving and caring son. Joseph K. is a conscientious bank official, and Gregor Samsa works hard as a traveling salesman to support his parents and sister. When tragedy strikes, they maintain their values and attempt to act in ways to minimize its consequences to themselves and others. Samsa remains considerate to the end of the feelings and sensitivities of his parents and sister. His acts of thoughtfulness and self-restraint ironically help bring about his murder by his frightened and uncomprehending family.

Sophocles' explanations are essential to the lessons his plays might be said to offer about how life should be understood and lived. Whether it is a curse or more immediate willful behavior, the cause of tragedy is always serious violation of nomos. We can question the links between the remote past and the present action but we are still encouraged to look for broader social explanations for tragic outcomes. By offering no explanation, Kafka leads us to a total aporia. The fragility of life, social standing, and self-esteem is a feature of the world from which there is no escape and no possible way of protecting oneself against through either ethical behavior or wisdom. It is a denial not just of the Enlightenment but of the Judeo-Christian tradition; and perhaps even of the ways in which the human mind is constructed.

Mann and Kafka are convinced that cause in the modern world is so complex and so far removed in its multiple original causes – if such things exist – to be largely unfathomable. World War I undoubtedly validated this perspective for them and many of their readers. It was catastrophic, made no sense, and its causes, beyond the most immediate ones, were unknown. So too were the motives of the policymakers difficult at the time to fathom. Mann, however, tackles the problem of World War I. His explanation is more hinted at than argued and not terribly persuasive because he offers no mechanism to explain the sudden transformation in relations in the Berghof or flatland below.

Ancient Greeks conceived of four kinds of knowledge: *technē*, *phrōnesis*, *epistēmē*, and *sophia*. *Technē* was equated with practical knowledge of the kind that allows people to fashion things or grow crops, win athletic competitions, and reach concrete goals. Plato's Socrates applied *technē* more broadly to the social realm. He maintains that dialectic – in contrast to sophistic rhetoric – is the true art of politics because it facilitates meaningful discourse.[100] In his search for knowledge, Socrates professed to be greatly impressed by the genius of craftsmen (*technikos*). Some of them nevertheless presumed to know everything or thought themselves capable of judging everything on the basis of their specialized knowledge.[101] Modern social science aspires to produce knowledge in the form of *epistēmē*. As understood by Aristotle, *epistēmē* consists of propositions and theories that facilitate explanation and prediction.[102]

Aristotle thought politics was more an art than a science and the relevant category of knowledge *phrōnesis*. He defines *phrōnesis* as practical reason or prudence and describes it as arising from reflection about the consequences of our behavior and that of others.[103] It is a form of general knowledge but always concerned with particulars. It can help us make happier lives for ourselves by leading us to more appropriate goals and means to achieve them. It is more useful than *epistēmē* to policymakers both as a source of policy guidance and as a means of critically examining their goals and means.

The highest form of knowledge is *sophia*. Plato defines *sophia* as the kind of knowledge that should be possessed by the rulers of his republic. It "takes counsel about the city as a whole as to how it would best order its relations to itself and to other cities."[104] Such knowledge is difficult to come by, for, as Aristotle points out, the more comprehensive and universal something is, the harder it is to know because the further away it is from our senses.

Max Weber is committed to the enterprise of *epistēmē*. He sought to develop methods that would provide explanations of singular events and patterns of behavior. Mann and Kafka, like Sophocles, are more focused on *phrōnesis*. Readers of their works might gain insights into themselves, the world, and fate through encounters with fictional characters and their lives. We learn from tragedy, Aristotle suggests, because we empathize with its heroes and experience shock and consternation when they undergo a reversal in fate. As we are not directly involved, and accordingly experience their fates vicariously, our shock is considerably less than theirs. Like a vaccine that produces immunity by having the body respond to an attenuated form of a disease carrying virus, tragedy provides just enough stimulation for us to reflect on the fate of tragic heroes and the causes of their reversals.[105]

Notes

1. Vaget, "Making of *The Magic Mountain*," for a good account of the origins of the novel.
2. Mann, *Reflections of a Nonpolitical Man*, p. 232; "Making of Magic Mountain."
3. Nietzsche, *Birth of Tragedy*, sections 1 and 3.
4. Weber, "Objektivität," pp. 190–193, and "Conceptual Exposition," pp. 19–20.
5. Mann, *Magic Mountain*, p. 6.
6. Ibid.
7. Ibid.
8. Ibid., p. 162.
9. Ibid., p. 112.
10. Ibid.
11. Ibid., p. 412.
12. Ibid.

13. Ibid., p. 50.
14. Ibid., p. 57.
15. Ibid., pp. 105, 35, 65.
16. Ibid., p. 541.
17. Ibid., p. 141.
18. Mann, "Making of Magic Mountain."
19. Ibid.
20. Mann, *Magic Mountain*, p. 605.
21. Hume, *Treatise of Human Nature*, 1.1.3.1, 1.3.7.5, 1.4.7.3.
22. Mann, "Making of Magic Mountain," p. 24.
23. Ibid.
24. Ibid.
25. Ibid. Mann is referring to Nemorov, "Questor Hero," who suggests that *The Magic Mountain* is similar to the Holy Grail romances and Goethe's Wilhelm Meister. The seeker of the grail arrives at a sacred castle and must survive frightening and dangerous initiation rites.
26. Mann, "Making of Magic Mountain," pp. 289–290.
27. Ibid., p. 96.
28. Ibid., p. 97.
29. MacIntyre, *Against the Self-Images of the Age*, pp. 60–69; Vaget, "Making of The Magic Mountain."
30. Mann, *Magic Mountain*, pp. 464–465.
31. Ibid., p. 592.
32. Ibid., p. 690.
33. Ibid., p. 99.
34. Sontag, *Illness as Metaphor*, pp. 7, 14, 34.
35. Mann, *Magic Mountain*, 196.
36. Ibid., p. 416.
37. Ibid., p. 219.
38. Ibid., p. 416.
39. Ibid., p. 418.
40. Ibid., pp. 414–416, 634, 635.
41. Ibid., p. 386.
42. Ibid., p. 234.
43. Ibid., p. 158.
44. Machiavelli, *Discourses on Livy*, book 1, chap. 3.
45. Mann, *Magic Mountain*, p. 386.
46. Ibid., pp. 124–125.
47. Ibid., pp. 665–681.
48. Freud, *Civilization and Its Discontents*.
49. Mann, *Magic Mountain*, p. 56.
50. Ibid., p. 682.
51. Ibid., p. 216.
52. Ibid., p. 634.
53. Ibid., pp. 663–665.
54. Thucydides, *Peloponnesian War*, 2.36–44.

55. Tajfel, "Social Categorisation, Social Identity and Social Comparison"; Tajfel and Turner, "Social Identity Theory of Intergroup Behavior"; Tajfel, *Human Groups and Social Categories.*
56. Mann, *Magic Mountain*, p. 103.
57. Ibid., p. 196.
58. Ibid., pp. 70–71.
59. Ibid., p. 123.
60. Reed, *Thomas Mann*, pp. 226–274, for the case of regarding *The Magic Mountain* as a *Bildungsroman.*
61. Swales, *German Bildungsroman from Wieland to Hesse.*
62. Mann, *Magic Mountain*, p. 32.
63. Stach, *Kafka*, p. 362; Gray, *Franz Kafka Encyclopedia*, pp. 74, 273.
64. Koelb, *Kafka*, p. 32.
65. Kafka, *Diaries*, January 8, 1914.
66. Quoted in Updike, "Foreword."
67. Kafka, *Castle*, p. 1.
68. Ibid., p. 5.
69. Ibid.
70. Ibid., p. 58.
71. Ibid., p. 62.
72. Ibid., pp. 62–74.
73. Ibid., pp. 64–65.
74. Ibid., p. 66.
75. Ibid.
76. Ibid., p. 70.
77. Ibid., p. 283.
78. Lebow, "Weber's Search for Knowledge."
79. Kafka, *Trial*, p. 44.
80. Ibid., p. 50.
81. Ibid., p. 94.
82. Ibid.
83. Ibid., p. 106.
84. Ibid., p. 154.
85. Ibid., p. 212.
86. Ibid., p. 213.
87. Ibid.
88. Ibid., p. 113.
89. Ibid.
90. Ibid.
91. Ibid., pp. 113–114.
92. Ibid., p. 114.
93. Ibid., pp. 154, 157–158.
94. Ibid., pp. 50–51.
95. Ibid., pp. 81–87.
96. Ibid., p. 81.
97. Weber, *Protestant Ethic and the Spirit of Capitalism*, p. 178, quoting Friedrich Nietzsche, *Ecce Homo.*

98. Quoted in Updike, "Foreword."
99. Kafka, "Before the Law."
100. Plato, *Gorgias* and *Republic*, 509d, 531d–534c.
101. Plato, *Apology*, 22c–d.
102. Aristotle, *Nicomachean Ethics*, 114b3–7.
103. Ibid., 1139a29–1141b20.
104. Plato, *Republic*, 428c12–d13, also 429a1–3.
105. Aristotle, *Poetics*, book 6.

8 Conclusions

> No one any longer knows who will live in this casing and whether entirely new prophets or a mighty rebirth of ancient ideas and ideals will arise at the end of this tremendous development. Or, however, if neither, whether a mechanized ossification, embellished with a sort of rigidly compelled sense of self-importance, will arise.
>
> – Max Weber[1]

I have sought to demonstrate that reason and cause are neither objective nor universal. Like all concepts, they are culturally and historically specific. They take on meaning in context and their appeal and content have changed significantly over the course of Western civilization. They undergo reframing in response to changing social conditions and especially those that generate psychological stress. The concepts of reason and cause are rightly considered central to science and social science. However, our understanding of them shifts more in response to external social developments than it does to those within disciplines. This relationship provides more evidence that social science is "social." The substantive and psychological problems we confront not only determine what we choose to study but how we study it.

My thesis is a radical one but only because of the long-standing pretense that there is something called the scientific method that stands proudly outside the subjective values, competing worldviews, and clashing interests that shape the social world. This is a comforting illusion and a useful one too because it has helped science gain high status and a degree of institutional independence. For both reasons, "social science" has sought to present itself as a science and has to a remarkable degree succeeded in convincing others of its self-proclaimed status.

Even someone as astute and self-aware as Max Weber initially bought into this belief. His famous fact/value distinction has been read by many as foundational to this view that social science methods are objective means of analyzing the social world and evaluating propositions about it. Weber later came to appreciate the subjective nature of methods. By the end of his life, he recognized that our culture, beliefs, social position, and intellectual and political projects determine the questions we ask and also influence the concepts and methods we use to research them, what we consider relevant evidence, how we evaluate it, and the inferences we draw from this evaluation. He rejected the supposition that we could analyze subjective questions with objective methods.[2]

Weber believed that the tension between fact and value was greatly intensified by modernity. By foregrounding instrumental rationality and encouraging people, organizations, and states to think and plan in terms of it, modernity reduces their focus on the ends these means are intended to serve. As instrumental rationality becomes dominant, substantive rationality recedes. For Weber, as for the great philosophers of the past, reason was a means of discovering the good or appropriate life. Instrumental reason substitutes efficiency and order for the values that might more successfully promote the good life. *Zweckrationalität* substitutes for *Wertrationalität*. It is the fundamental reason why modernity threatens to be so dehumanizing.

We have belatedly come to recognize that analytical concepts are subjective, have histories that give them multiple meanings, and are constantly reshaped to support intellectual and political projects. This process has been nicely documented with the state, power, and hegemony, among other concepts.[3] I do something different with reason and cause in this book. I do not offer a genealogy so much as snapshots of them in three periods of epochal change. Moreover, I am more interested in how they are used than defined.

My approach is justified by the longevity and centrality of reason and cause. They are not inventions of modern politics or social science, as are the territorial state, class, balance of power, interdependence, and almost any other analytical concept used in economics, psychology, and political science. They have been with us throughout human history, although not theorized until classical Greece. Reason and cause differ in another way from most other analytical concepts. They have a punctuated history in lieu of a continuous one. They were used before they were theorized, which is the opposite of most concepts. They were subsequently theorized and retheorized, and in disparate discourses.

Reason has been framed by philosophers and, more recently, by social science as a meta-concept. It is regarded as something prior to, independent of, and enabling of any all analytical concepts. From its very beginning, philosophy used reason as its language of discourse and intellectual justification. Cause is an analytical concept but has a status close to that of reason because it is seen as so fundamental to inquiry. Despite much evidence to the contrary, many philosophers continue to assert that it is a feature of the world and even, in the words of J. L. Mackie, "the cement of the universe."[4] Recognition that reason, like cause, is a human artifact is extremely threatening to philosophy and social science. Not surprisingly, there is great reluctance to acknowledge their subjectivity and its consequences.

Inquiry into reason and cause begins in literature. Homer wrote epics that explored cause, and Virgil had something to say on the subject in the Augustan age. Fifth-century Athenians used literature, and tragedy in particular, to explore the meaning of reason and cause and the possible consequences of relying on them to negotiate life. In the eighteenth century, debates about cause were found primarily in philosophical discourses. In the twentieth century, cause became a central concern of philosophers of science, who developed a discourse of their own that was heavily influenced by mathematics and physics. In the nineteenth and twentieth centuries, various writers also explored reason and cause in novels and stories. These disparate discourses do not for the most part speak to one another, and those who developed or continue to engage them show little interest in treatments outside their preferred domain.

To my knowledge, this is the first book that attempts a comparison of reason and cause across epochs and discourses. I did so with several aims in mind: first, to show how treatments of reason and cause in these different discourses can be analyzed in an intellectually meaningful and profitable way; second, to use these comparisons to show just how culturally and temporally embedded our understandings of these concepts actually are; third, to look for comparisons across epochs to discover patterns of responses to changing conditions; and, finally, to use these comparisons to assess contemporary understandings of the concepts of reason and cause.

The opening section of this chapter reviews my findings, period by period and author by author. Earlier chapters emphasize the similarities and differences between or among thinkers and writers of the same era. The major exception is my comparison of Homer and Sophocles. David Hume was born a century earlier than Dickens, so my chapter on Dickens, Trollope, and Collins compares adjacent eras: Enlightenment and Victorian Britain. The remainder of the chapter makes comparisons across the epochs my earlier chapters address.

The Greeks

I began my investigation with Homer, who is foundational not only to Greek culture but to Western civilization. Homer, or the bards responsible for his epics, wrote some time in the late eighth or early seventh centuries, just as the polis was emerging. The *Iliad* and the *Odyssey* are set in what we call the late Bronze Age and depict a society of aristocratic, warrior-based honor society. The *Iliad* pioneers the use of immanent critique to show how the very values that enable and sustain such a society also threaten its destruction. This is most evident with *xenia* (guest-friendship) and honor but is equally true of friendship, kingship, and hierarchy.

The *Iliad* provides an account of the origins and course of the parallel conflicts between Greece and Troy and Achilles and Agamemnon. The violation and honoring of *xenia* are the most important underlying cause of the Trojan War. The emergence of hierarchies of ascribed and achieved status pits Agamemnon against Achilles. Homer suggests that both kinds of conflict are nearly inevitable in warrior-based honor societies. Honor codes impose elaborate rule packages on high-status actors that require them to hold in check a range of human emotions and drives. The greater the need for self-restraint, the more likely it is that some actors will violate the rules, especially in the face of great temptations like Helen. Kingship is inherited, and not every king is capable of ruling wisely or being the best warrior. When these functions diverge, as they do in the *Iliad*, rivalry, if not acute conflict, is likely between those who occupy these roles. Warrior-based honor societies require wars, and especially wars against other societies with similar values, so warriors can achieve *aristeia* (excellence). War and its carnage arouse deep emotions, most notably those of anger and revenge. When this happens, honor-based conflicts can easily descend into contests of unrestrained violence.

If we read the *Iliad* and *Odyssey* literally, the gods are powerful actors and humans their playthings. The denizens of Olympus are depicted as an immortal, extended family of sexually charged, jealous, and squabbling adolescents who intervene regularly in human affairs for the crassest of motives. They do so to get back at other gods, to support people who honor them or to whom they are physically attracted, or simply for their amusement and self-gratification. A more figurative reading understands the gods as stand-ins for inner conflicts and reflections of people and metaphors for chance, luck, and other unpredictable yet often determining features of life. Either interpretation reveals a Homer committed to a causal narrative, often with events that appear anomalous made explicable by attributing them to the gods.

The literal reading would have Homer understand cause as a feature of the world and someone able to see behind and beyond what is visible to others. He finds cause in the reasons people and gods have for acting as they do. Reasons appear to be sufficient cause because they are responsible for behavior and outcomes. When these outcomes are not those that actors desire, it is because more powerful people or gods intervene. The figurative reading leads to a more problematic and uncertain understanding of cause.

It suggests the gods must be invoked because without them many important events cannot otherwise be explained. It follows that cause might not be a feature of the world but a human conceit that is so important that it is necessary to invent the gods to sustain it.

The literal approach to the *Iliad* and *Odyssey* most assuredly resonated widely throughout the ancient Greek world. It taps into what David Hume described as a compelling psychological need to see the world as explicable and at least in part controllable. Such a belief reduces anxiety over uncertainty and vulnerability and provides the self-confidence to face life and its challenges. The hope of godly intervention is presumably one of the oldest sources of religion. People were mystified, baffled, and frightened by nature and hostile people. They were desperate to find some way of protecting themselves from storms, fires, floods, crop failures, disease, infertility, stillbirths, and marauders. They personalized these events, convincing themselves that they were not random but deliberate actions by spirits they could not observe but might placate and even enlist in their support.

By the late fifth century, there were many intellectually sophisticated people in Athens and elsewhere in Greece. Among intellectuals, Herodotus may have been atypical in believing in divine will and its consistent fulfillment. Thucydides considers prophecies worthless and is scornful of people who believe in them. Euripides is even more dismissive.[5] Prophecies take the form of prediction and most oracular utterances were sufficiently ambiguous enough to allow for a seeming outcome and its opposite. The most famous example is Croesus' reading of the Delphic oracle's prophecy that, if he crossed the Halys River and attacked Persia, he would destroy a great empire. It never occurred to him that the empire in question might be his own.[6]

The Homeric gods must have appeared increasingly incredible as they were juvenile in their behavior, unable to control their emotions, and rarely even-handed enforcers of justice. Yet dispensing with them left humans alone in a hostile world in which there was no longer any cosmic order on which norms and justice were thought to depend. This dilemma would resurface in the Enlightenment and give rise to its own set of culturally conditioned responses.

Sophocles is sensitive to, or perhaps representative of, the skepticism associated with the fifth-century proto-Enlightenment. Cause for Sophocles remains elusive, as does almost everything in his corpus. There appears to be an intended parallel between his plays and his life: the more we think we understand key features of either, the more we succumb to dangerous illusions. Nevertheless, we cannot do without cause because, to get on in the physical and social worlds, we need some understanding of how they work. For Sophocles, these beliefs are of questionable validity. We face a quandary: disillusionment about gods and cause can incapacitate us while unquestioning belief will almost certainly mislead us. The most sensible approach to life, Sophocles appears to suggest, is one that hovers uneasily between belief and skepticism, clarity and obscurity, self-confidence and doubt, search for causes and answers and acceptance of what has happened.

Tragedy is a response to the more complex life of the polis, especially a large, democratic one like Athens, where individuals had more choices. Understanding how society worked was essential to making the right choices, whether in the family, business, law courts, or politics but so too was a heavy degree of skepticism about one's ability to do this. This was because the interdependent nature of society, the greater difficulty of fathoming the motives and goals of others, the often determining importance of context, and the ways in which all of these consideration were subject to rapid and unpredictable change made all action uncertain in its consequences.

If Homer can be read at two levels, so can Sophocles. His plays foreground what his characters think has brought about their fates. They invariably accept personal responsibility for good outcomes and deny it for bad ones. They shift responsibility for the latter to those who have cursed them and the gods they have enlisted to help them. Causes and their mechanisms are hidden and problematized in Sophocles in a way they are not in Homer. This seems more in keeping with the experience, and perhaps expectations, of his fifth-century audience. In contrast to Homer and Aeschylus, the gods do not appear in Sophoclean tragedies. Like curses, they are invoked by people to explain plagues and tragic outcomes. Sophoclean plays encourage thoughtful audiences to distinguish his beliefs from those of his characters. He compels these audiences to make their own causal inferences.

Sophocles' plays uphold traditional values, including belief in the gods. They are present in the background of most plays, never appear or speak directly, and their wishes and judgments – if they have any – become known second- and thirdhand through the voices of people. In contrast to Homer, his gods give the appearance of intervening on the side of justice. In every instance, human agency brings prophecies to fruition. Oedipus' unsuccessful efforts to avoid killing his father and bedding his mother are only the most dramatic example. Sophocles' plays suggest that actors make free choices and are largely responsible for their fates. He attributes their choices to pride, envy, ambition, and fear and bad outcomes to behavior that violates nomos.

Agency is more meaningful in Sophocles than in Homer. It is also more problematic. Characters who act on the basis of their emotions invite tragic outcomes. This is independent of whether these emotions are worthy ones – as they are for Oedipus and Antigone – or contemptible – as with Laius and Creon. Reason should be increasingly relevant in a world where people must devise appropriate strategies rather than rely on traditional routines, but it appears to be equally fallible as Oedipus so dramatically demonstrates. His efforts to reason his way through the Sphinx's riddle save Corinth and win him a kingship but also help to fulfill the prophecy he is trying so desperately to escape. Emotion and reason are presented as another false binary. Successful people rely on some combination of both, never one or the other alone. Aristotle would later theorize this relationship and argue that good decisions involve appropriate emotions and good instrumental reasoning.[7] Recent work in neuroscience offers support for his argument.[8]

Sophocles develops two perspectives on cause: descriptive and analytical. The first is what his characters think about cause and how they use it to make sense of the world and formulate responses to the problems and challenges they confront. The second is how audiences are encouraged to ponder the reasons why his characters act as they do and bring about fates they sought to avoid. Here too, there is a tension but a productive one. Audience reflection in response to emotional arousal, the latter arising from involvement with the characters in the play, encourages learning. This is why Aristotle thought tragedy valuable. For Sophocles and Aristotle – and for Thucydides, I contend – tragedy is a vehicle to teach people how to live in a world in which cause is difficult to understand and the social environment unpredictable and more difficult still to control.

Thucydides wrote a history but refused to self-identify as a historian. In offering his account of the Archidamian and Peloponnesian Wars as "a possession for all time," he wanted readers to focus on the universal human and political insights his work conveyed.[9] A generation later, Aristotle would insist that poetry is superior to history because "poetry speaks more of universals and history of particulars."[10] Thucydides never claimed to be a poet but did structure his account as a tragedy, a discourse until then exclusive to poets.

Thucydides' turn to tragedy encouraged readers to compare his narrative not only to Herodotus but also to Aeschylus, Sophocles, and Euripides. It allowed him to foreground the role of hubris, agency, and fate and explore the ways in which goal-seeking behavior can bring about the outcomes actors are desperately seeking to avoid. There is an obvious parallel in his narrative between Athens and Oedipus. The relationship cuts two ways as Sophocles wrote *Oedipus Turannus* in 429 and may have meant Oedipus to represent Athens.[11]

Thucydides is more explicit about cause than Sophocles. He uses the concept to order his narrative and appears to assume that readers will find this a natural structure or at least a familiar one. Like Sophocles, he does not refer to any gods but tells us that peoples and leaders routinely look to them for explanations. Thucydides finds the causes of social outcomes in the beliefs, judgments, and behavior of political actors.

Sophocles and Thucydides create causal sequences. *Oedipus Turannus* consists of one primary sequence that focuses on its eponymous hero, his choices and actions, and how they bring about the fate from which he is trying to escape. Thucydides also focuses on actors and their behavior but embeds them in multiple causal sequences that explore cause at the individual, societal, and system levels of analysis.[12] This is a key feature of his accounts of the Archidamian and Peloponnesian Wars and the Sicilian expedition. Thucydides describes behavior at the individual level that has consequences for the polis and at the polis level that affects the wider Greek world. The changing political culture of Athens and the breakdown of order in Hellas, and with it the transformation of the rule-based competition for honor into a free-for-all struggle for power, are what today we call emergent properties. This concept is implicit in Homer and Thucydides but would not be explicit until Vico, Mandeville, and Smith in the eighteenth century.[13]

If Sophocles offers a double perspective on cause, Thucydides might be said to offers a triple one because he also tells us how actors attempt to manipulate others' understandings of cause to further their own ends. Thucydides' actors have considerable freedom to construct causal narratives or forecasts based on them because they live in more complex societies where the future is more opaque than it was in the *oikos* and more so still in an expanded regional political system with many cities with diverse interests and commitments. Given the uncertainty of the future, there are more competing narratives and greater emphasis on the rhetorical skills necessary to sell them. They are especially important, if not determinant, in democracies like Athens. They also assume a life of their own. Over the course of Thucydides' narrative, what political actors say in their speeches is increasingly at variance with what they appear to believe; there is something of a progression in this regard from Pericles' funeral oration to the Mytilenian and Sicilian debates. It is no exaggeration to claim that causal stories in the form of forecasts become important causes in their own right.

Sophocles and Thucydides distinguish between reason and reasons. The former is what actors rely on to "game" life in a world in which behavior for individuals and cities is less constrained by traditional norms and expectations and more a matter of choice. Instrumental reason is accordingly more important in classical Greece than it was in the age of Homer. Sophocles' tragedies and Thucydides' history nevertheless indicate that many, if not most, people are not especially rational in their decision-making. They are consistently overconfident in their predictions of how others will respond and have correspondingly inflated expectations of success. They have difficulty understanding how others see them and the world and frame their interests and ignore or downplay chance and accident, both of which play a big role in shaping fictional and historical outcomes. Wishful thinking is often a product of hubris but is just as often a form of motivated error. Political actors make forecasts consistent with and supportive of their goals, and they deny, distort, ignore, or explain away information threatening to them. The two forms of distortion are reinforcing because powerful actors are the people most likely to pursue risky policies and practice denial.[14]

Reasons are the explanations people give for their behavior and that of others. For Sophoclean and Thucydidean actors, they are generally self-serving when about themselves and often incorrect when about others. Instrumental reasoning, gaming of situations, and public rhetoric at odds with private calculations make it much more difficult to establish cause because it requires observers to reconstruct the often hidden or disguised goals and calculations of multiple actors. Part of Sophocles' genius is his ability in the short format of plays to provide us with enough information and incentives to attempt this task. Thucydides also attempts to get into the heads of key actors, reconstructs their understandings, and makes them central to his compelling nonlinear narrative. Like Sophocles, he provides us with clues in the form of speeches, actions, parallels, and the deeper structure of the text that encourage us to do the same.

Thucydides takes uncertainty to another level through his examination and emphasis on aggregation effects. Depending on the circumstances, the same behavior can lead to diametrically opposed outcomes. This is because the chains of events they set in motion are affected by other decisions and events independent of them and often unforeseeable. The mechanisms that mediate between action and consequences are equally opaque and vary according to circumstance, so the relationship between policies and outcomes is rarely evident beforehand – or after the fact – despite what actors may believe. Causal analysis is essential in fifth-century Greece, but, as Sophocles and Thucydides demonstrate, it is a risky and uncertain enterprise. Attempts to reason through a problem can obfuscate as much as clarify.

David Hume

The Scottish Enlightenment produced a score of original thinkers, two of them – David Hume and Adam Smith – among the most influential intellects of the eighteenth century. Both men wrote theoretical works but also addressed policy matters. Many political leaders of the era were well-educated and familiar with their writings; their ideas accordingly resonated in political and economic as well as philosophical circles. Both men had a serious interest in cause and went in different directions with it in their inquiries. Limitations of space forced me to address only one of these figures and I chose Hume because his idea of constant conjunction is an important intellectual justification for regularity theories. They in turn are the dominant approach in contemporary social science.

Following a tradition that begins with Thucydides and extends through Weber, Adam Smith looks for thick explanations of cause. Like Thucydides, he is interested in system-level phenomena and explains them as unintended consequences of individual behavior. Economic development is the product of people motivated by need and greed.[15] These mechanisms, operating at the state level, also require appropriate conditions at the state level, which Smith's successors enumerate.[16] Most important are security of tenure and possessions, sanctity of contract, and civil stability. John Stuart Mill would invoke them to explain why, in their absence, Ireland's agricultural development had stagnated while England's had developed.[17]

One of the most important ways in which Smith most resembles Hume is in the extent to which they were misinterpreted. Smith was misread as a supporter and father of laissez-faire capitalism, which he certainly was not. Capitalism unchecked by government would, in his view, lead to the kind of tyranny and oppression that characterized most European colonies.[18] Hume, I have argued, is no more foundational to regularity theories than Smith is to laissez-faire capitalism.

This kind of distortion is hardly surprising. Epistemologies, paradigms, and methods benefit from founding "fathers."[19] Realists grossly misread Thucydides, Hobbes, and Rousseau toward this end, liberals do the same with Locke and Kant, and positivists with Hume and Weber. They cherry-pick quotes out of context, read only sections or works they think supportive of their positions, distort what they read, and, in the case of Weber, produce misleading translations. Misrepresentations of Hume and Smith endure because economists for the most part do not read Smith and social scientists rarely engage Hume. Political theorists have provided defensible interpretations of these texts but they are rarely read by those who believe they are engaging in "normal" science. Once these epistemologies, paradigms, and approaches are well-launched, drilling holes in their bottoms usually has little effect. They have enough intellectual momentum, institutional backing, and former students who have made careers on the basis of what they have been taught to ignore even the most penetrating rebuttals.

Critiques of epistemologies, paradigms, and approaches can still get under the skin of their advocates, as the "New Hume" debate reveals. Galen Strawson and other philosophers were driven to counter the claims of those who read Hume as arguing that causation is merely a shorthand people use to make sense of the world. As I relate in Chapter 4, they have tried to reinterpret him as a "realist," as someone who believes cause to be a feature of the universe. In doing so, they seek in the first instance to legitimate the long-standing philosophical project of finding a logically consistent and universally applicable formulation of cause. They also hope to validate efforts by the physical, biological, and social sciences to develop theories that map successfully onto the world.

Hume rejects out of hand traditional moral philosophy because it is rooted in the Christian belief that god made humankind in his image, with the ability to grasp his presence and conduct themselves in accord with his desires. Hume will have none of this faith-based reasoning. He starts from the premise that human beings are not so different from other animals and closely resemble them in their thought processes. Reason in his view is just as likely to lead us away from morality and the divine. To the extent that humans behave well toward one another, it is largely due to their emotions.

Hume rejects philosophy as a waste of time. Rather, we should learn about people from experience and observation. We should ask how people come to believe in the importance, indeed the necessity, of such things as cause and justice? What kinds of beliefs, aesthetic judgments, and behavior are universal, and why are others specific to particular cultures? In method, too, Hume is radical as he rejects abstract reasoning in favor of experimentation in the expectation of creating "the science of human nature."

Hume asserts that external objects and experiences become known to us by the impressions they evoke. Some make a more forceful impression on the mind than others, leading Hume to distinguish between "strong" and "faint images" or impressions. Another difference between them is temporal; strong impressions are more likely to be immediate ones and faint ones are those called up from memory. However, some of these latter impressions can still be very vivid.[20] All ideas, however, are faint impressions as they are derivative of strong impressions and based on our secondary reflections about them. Vividness is the most important characteristic of an impression, and the more vivid something is the more attentive we are to it. Sensory impressions, not rational reflection, determine our beliefs. Hume's argument finds ample resonance in cognitive psychology, where experiments indicate that immediacy and vividness greatly increase credibility.[21]

Hume maintains that observation and introspection reveal that imagination is the source of our beliefs, religion, metaphysics, morals, and identities.[22] The more people turn to reason, the more befuddled they become. Reason can lead us not only astray but into violent conflicts based on ideological differences. Emotions also cut both ways. Individual and civil order is most likely when there is a "prevalence of the calm passions over the violent."[23] Anger, hate, and envy are violent passions inimical to order and in need of controlling. This is best accomplished by the calm passions, especially benevolence and sympathy.

Hume is interested in causation because he believes it central to how we think about the world and the "hard case" for a theory of the mind that downplays the role of reason. He attempts to show that we infer cause in a manner little different from other animals. He does not deny the existence of complex forms of reasoning but is interested in ordinary people and how they think and act.

Hume begins by arguing that "identity," by which he means discrete objects and phenomena, and "contiguity," defined as nearness, are "natural" impressions that require no thought.[24] On this basis, he constructs his definition of cause as "An object precedent and contiguous to another, and where all the objects resembling the former are plac'd in like relations of precedents and contiguity to those objects, that resemble the latter."[25] Events that occur in "a regular order of contiguity and succession" constitute a "constant conjunction."[26]

Cause is a philosophical relation that builds on a natural one. It involves more than direct observation and primary impressions. It is the product of vivid secondary and tertiary impressions. The responsible mechanisms are custom and imagination. Once established, a belief creates expectations about the world. This is attributable in the first instance to the belief and secondarily to the fact that, once it is established, alternatives become more difficult to imagine.[27] Belief in cause leads to other beliefs. We become convinced that the future will resemble the past and that everything has a cause. Once we make repeated connections between putative causes and effects, this kind of reasoning becomes habitual. Viewing the world in causal terms confers a survival advantage.[28] It alerts us to danger and enhances our ability to satisfy our passions.[29] Hume thinks like a modern-day cognitive psychologist as he understands cause as an important and useful heuristic. He goes further and suggests that causal inference is not only a cognitive bias but a motivated one.

Hume tries unsuccessfully to limit his analysis of cause to mind. All the cognitive processes he describes are based on impressions from our body or the external world. In their absence, we could not have the secondary and tertiary impressions that constitute concepts and beliefs. He further assumes that constant conjunctions occur often enough in the world for them to make vivid impressions on people and prompt the concept of cause. There is accordingly some degree of homology between our cognitive processes and the physical world. Hume never admits this relationship, in large part, I suspect, because he is keen to distinguish himself from Locke, who insists on it.

There are few constant conjunctions in the real world but many regularities. If, as Hume suggests, people routinely exaggerate the likelihood of regularities on the basis of those they observe, constant conjunction is more a product of the mind than of the world.[30] We impose a degree of order on the world that is unwarranted, if useful. For this reason, Hume, I contend, considers his understanding of cause useful in coping with daily life but certainly not an appropriate foundation or goal for scientific inquiry.

Hume famously declared that reason is "the slave of the passions." This assertion constitutes a radical rejection of the dominant view of moral philosophers, ancient Greek and Christian alike, that reason had the ability to constrain the passions. Hume does not deny the existence of complex forms of reasoning; he praises Newton for his calculus and discoveries about the physical world. He relies on reasoning to construct a model of the mind that all but excludes reason as the source of learning or social order. He aims to expose and discredit theories that stand in the way of useful learning and progress.

Hume is a radical not only in his era but in ours. His rejection of moral philosophy and what today is called realism put him at odds with many contemporary philosophers. He was ahead of his time in trying to build a human psychology on observation but his project stalled because he attempted this in advance of the development of statistics. He thought one could come to general understandings on the basis of studying individuals but recognized that he had no means of distinguishing idiosyncratic or uncommon insights, feelings, beliefs, or understandings from more general ones, let alone those that might acquire the status of laws.

Hume's understanding of cause did not respond to the need, felt by many people, for better tools to understand and control their world. At best, it suggested that we might make some progress in this direction by understanding how the majority of people formed opinions and beliefs, including causal ones. Although there is no evidence that they read Hume, Dickens, Trollope, and Collins developed remarkably similar understandings of how people form opinions and beliefs. They demonstrate in detail how erroneous, misleading, and even counterproductive, Humean inference can be.

Victorian Novelists

Dickens, Trollope, and Collins are several generations younger than Hume and witnesses to the full-blown emergence of civil society and the industrial revolution. Like Sophocles and Thucydides, they lived in an age where interdependence was making cause more important but also more inaccessible.

Dickens develops an early and prescient critique of the concept of cause that questions its value as an analytical concept to meet the challenges of everyday life. Like Hume, he turns to introspection and observation for evidence and embodies his insights in his characters. Humean-style causal inference does not get them very far in Victorian society. Dickens goes a step beyond Hume, who could not solve the problem of induction. Dickens sought, and achieved to his satisfaction, validation of his insights through his appeal to readers. They bought and read his novels in large numbers, considered his characters and their behavior realistic, and made him the bestselling author of the nineteenth century.

Dickens develops his critique of reason and cause through his engagement with criminal deviance and the legal system. Most of his novels involve crimes against property or persons. His offenders invariably face human or divine justice in the form of disgrace, prison, hanging, or death from natural causes. He shows that neither criminals nor judges behave rationally. They are often blinded by dishonesty, hypocrisy, and even more by self-deception. Reason for Dickens is the slave of passions for wealth, status, and marriage, with the last usually being a means toward achieving the first two ends. Reason is rarely used for moral betterment, in the sense of building character and formulating worthwhile and attainable goals, as Victorian conservatives and liberals alike insisted it should. Like Hume, Dickens rejects these goals as unrealistic and considers reason as more a barrier than a gateway to them.

Dickens has a complex relationship to Hume when it comes to cause. He is interested in immediate cause when describing the behavior of his characters. He does not indicate resemblance and contiguity as the source of their causal inferences. For characters in *Bleak House*, causal search is most often positional. They want to know to whom they are related or connected and through whom they might wield influence. They mostly search for answers in documents and envisage knowledge as something that is present but hidden and waiting to be revealed.

Bleak House is not alone among Dickens' novels in suggesting that, if there are causes, they are obscure, at considerable remove from their putative effects, and difficult, if not impossible, to fathom. They are also irrational in the sense that they are not attributable to people intelligently pursuing their interests. Rather, they are a product of something his characters refer to as "the system." Once *Bleak House* characters become enmeshed in the legal process, they become more like objects and less like people; they are manipulated to serve the ends of others. However, these manipulators, or would-be manipulators, lose control of their lives as the system they try to game intrudes more and more into their once private and secure worlds.

Jarndyce and Jarndyce, the lawsuit at the center of *Bleak House*, is a synecdoche for the system. Over time, the suit has become so complicated that nobody understands it. Most of those involved have lost sight of the ultimate aims of plaintiff and defendant and focus instead on short-term legal maneuvers that assume a life of their own. The descendants of the agents who initiated the suit or defended themselves against it now number scores of people. They too have been reduced to varying degrees to objects on whom the system acts and preys. They have lost their freedom and purse. The only beneficiaries are members of "the system," judges, lawyers, beadles, and the like, whom cases like Jarndyce and Jarndyce handsomely sustain.

Outcomes – if they ever emerge from the Court of Chancery – are the product of interactions among numerous actors working at cross-purposes and determined by institutions with arcane procedures. They are the result of mysterious, even unfathomable, processes of aggregation, most of which are out of sight. This is equally evident in the world of fashion. We can know something about the rules that govern the behavior of courts or society but little in advance about what they produce in the way of judgments. In such a world, the concept of cause loses most, if not all, of its meaning and utility.

Trollope follows Hume more closely than Dickens in his conception of reason and cause. In *Phineas Finn*, Humean-style inference based on identity and contiguity leads to the mistaken arrest of Finn for the murder of Mr. Bonteen, a party whip who had questioned his trustworthiness. The police arrest Finn on the basis of circumstantial evidence. He argued with Bonteen just prior to the murder, brandished what could have been a murder weapon outside his club, and headed home in the same direction as the victim and only moments after his prior departure. Finn was identified – incorrectly – as running away from the murder scene. Police and prosecutor admit to relying regularly on circumstantial evidence. Plausibility rather than proof is the key to conviction, and, for most people, the mere arrest of a suspect is a good presumption of his guilt.

Under cross-examination, it becomes evident that Lord Fawn, the man who thought he saw Finn fleeing the murder scene, has engaged in backward reasoning – as has almost everyone who believes Finn guilty. Fawn assumes that Finn was the murderer and thus that the man he saw running was accordingly Finn. In O. J. Simpson's murder trial, his defense attorney argued that "if the gloves don't fit you must acquit." Chaffanbrass relies on the same tactic. Finn is asked to put on the jacket identified as the one worn by the man running away from the murder scene. It clearly does not fit and Lord Fawn becomes confused. He is reduced to a pathetic figure on the witness stand. Under further pressure from Chaffanbrass, he backs away from his earlier identification and Finn is acquitted.

Society is no different. Trollope's characters seek approval in the court of public opinion to achieve their parochial goals. Like prosecutors and defense attorneys, they devise clever strategies toward this end. The truth is largely irrelevant. They try to tell stories that people will believe, which is easier to do when they are factual. However, people are more willing to believe lies than the truth when it suits their needs or supports their preexisting beliefs about other people or how the world works.

Reason and cause everywhere take a back seat. People as individuals and society as a loose collective routinely draw false inferences about the character, motives, and actions of others. They rarely turn their reason inwards to examine themselves. One of the ironies of Trollope's novels is that characters who are truly rational and calculating are no more successful in gaining desired ends than those who are not. Their reliance on rationality blinds them to the ways in which other people make judgments and encourages others to see them as cold and calculating. As reason plays such a nugatory role in people's behavior and judgments, we must look elsewhere for causes. Trollope finds them in the character of people; they are respectable or they are cads. Hardly anybody falls into the gray areas between. For the most part, his characters get what they deserve in life. The principal exceptions are good women who make bad marital choices – albeit for reasons of necessity or parental pressure – and suffer long-term consequences.

Trollope's morality tale might be attributed to his own sense of ill ease with the inferences his novels suggest. They reflect his astute observations of Victorian life but are in conflict with his image of himself as a self-made man who succeeded through virtue, talent, and hard work. He presumably also believed that the extraordinary popularity of his fiction reflected its quality and was not the result of fickle and unwarranted public approbation.

Trollope wants us to recognize that so-called facts can reveal the truth or stand in the way of its discovery. They only take on meaning in context and these contexts are by no means self-evident. Lawyers and courts rarely go beyond Humean-style inference. In contrast to Dickens' characters, they focus on resemblance and contiguity and make unwarranted inferences on the basis of them. This line of reasoning leads to the simplest explanations of events and responsibility and also the ones most likely to be believed by ordinary people, who reason the same way.

Lawyers and juries think alike. They are also deeply affected by their emotions. Lord Chiltern explains to his wife that the attorney general "can prove that the man was killed with some blunt weapon, such as Finn possessed. And he can prove that exactly at the same time a man was running to the spot very like to Finn, and that by a route which would have been his route, but by using which he could have placed himself at that moment where the man was seen." Lady Chiltern, his wife, and formerly in love with Finn, remains confident that he is innocent.

Reliable firsthand witnesses are the gold standard of Victorian legal evidence. Trollope has Chaffanbrass gain acquittal for Phineas Finn by demonstrating that the principal witness against him is unreliable. Wilkie Collins goes a step further and shows that even reliable witnesses can be misleading. He further suggests that incontrovertible material evidence is equally suspect. Rachel was awake when Franklin entered her room and she saw him leave with the gem. She correctly identified the nightgown with the paint stain as his. She trusts her eyes and confirming evidence and rejects out of hand his subsequent explanation of events: "I don't believe you now! I don't believe you found the nightgown, I don't believe in Rosanna Spearman's letter, I don't believe a word you have said. You stole it – I saw you. You affected to help the police – I saw you! You pledged the diamond to a moneylender in London – I am sure of it." There is, of course, another irony here in that Franklin, who is unaware that he stole the gem while in a trance, is nevertheless telling the truth about his motives and efforts to discover the thief. He is as unreliable as a witness as he is effective as a detective.

Efficient cause explains little in this mystery. Outcomes are the product of complex, independent, but interacting causal chains. Emotion more than reason is the primary motivation of each of them. Franklin is driven by love, Ablewhite by greed, Ezra Jennings by dislike for Dr. Candy and his desire to do something positive before he dies. Positive emotions are a source of empathy, which offers insight into others' minds and motives. Emotion and reason together lead the investigators where neither would alone.

Dickens, Trollope, and Collins challenge the rationality of people and the use of reason to study their behavior and cause more generally. Often their characters do not seek rational ends, do not behave rationally in their pursuit, and have imperfect knowledge of their own motives. Nor are rational strategies, when pursued, necessarily the most efficient way of achieving desired ends. In part, this is because of what this communicates to others about the character or goals of the people who use them. It is also a function of aggregation. People never act alone but in conjunction with others. Their interaction, as in Jarndyce and Jarndyce, can produce outcomes that most neither anticipated nor desired.

Dickens, like Thucydides, is particularly interested in the problem of aggregation and, in particular, in the ways in which people in pursuit of their goals can collectively produce an outcome none desired or foresaw. In *Bleak House*, Dickens' invocation of "the system" and his foreground metaphors like "fog" and "soot" suggest that looking for cause is all but futile. Nevertheless, rule-based systems like the courts are deeply influenced by the goals and opinions of those who staff them.

Trollope's Palliser novels indicate that the most important underlying causes are the legal system, parliament, and society. They socialize people into desiring certain ends and using certain means to achieve them. We find no resonance in Trollope of Hume's notion of constant conjunction and immediate cause. People make inferences on the basis of resemblance and contiguity, and this is indeed why Lord Fawn mistakenly identifies Phineas Finn as the murderer. Here, as elsewhere, Humean-style inferences are shown to be misleading. The true murderer, Emilius, is discovered by means of a more scientific inquiry conducted by Madame Goesler.

Wilkie Collins offers the most radical critique of reason and cause. English people at every level of society behave irrationally. The exceptions in *The Moonstone* are Sergeant Cuff and Rosanna Spearman. The former fails to solve the mystery and the latter is considered mentally disturbed by the other characters. Motives that explain behavior are hidden from the characters themselves, let alone from those hoping to solve the mystery. Franklin Blake is unaware that he has stolen the diamond while drugged and sleepwalking. In the end, he needs his own actions explained to him, although not in realizing how contrary they are to the end he seeks. Rachel Verinder was convinced of her lover's guilt on the grounds of resemblance and contiguity.

Like Trollope, Collins shows us how misleading such inferences can be – but with a twist. They point the finger – correctly in this instance – at the true thief but mislead her about his motives. Franklin sought to protect Rachel and her diamond by removing it to a safe place. Collins effectively reverses the stereotypes of Europeans and Asians. The English believed Indians to be irrational. In *The Moonstone*, the English are emotional, selfish, insecure, grasping, and superstitious.

John Stuart Mill thought that reason and cause could produce useful social knowledge. Dickens, Trollope, and Collins depict a Victorian England in which they explain little and are no foundation for reforms. Their failure led us to devalue *epistēmē* (scientific knowledge) and upgrade *phrōnesis* (practical knowledge).

Max Weber

Weber was fully acquainted with the historicists and positivist traditions and drew on both while attempting to circumvent their limitations. He defined knowledge as causal inference about singular events that uses the individual as its unit of analysis, relies on ideal types, and employs counterfactual thought experiments to probe putative causes.

Weber believed that social knowledge is inescapably subjective but not arbitrary. It is ordered intellectually by the concept of cause. Following Hume, he insists that history and social science are distinguished from chronicles by their selection and description of events or processes on the basis of their connections and attempt to demonstrate that some of them are responsible for others.[31] Like Hume, he is adamant that "cause" and "effect" are human creations, not features of the world. Causal inference relies on reason to discover regularities but also on emotions to develop empathetic understandings of actors and their motives. Causal claims are inescapably rhetorical in nature.

The first step in causal inference is to create event types and identify events that fit within these categories. Typologies of this kind enable the search for regularities. Weber recognizes that these associations are always imperfect because events have many causes and we can identify and study only some of them. The context in which they unfold will differ across "cases," making them far from fully comparable. Causal narratives can be evaluated on the basis of their logical consistency, available empirical evidence, and what Weber calls the "rules of experience" (*Erfahrungsregeln*). By rules of experience, he means other imperfect empirical generalizations in which we and our readers have some degree of confidence.[32] Researchers are more likely to convince others to accept their claims when they are based on shared assumptions about the world.[33] Causal inference risks becoming tautological; we accept as valid what is consistent with our beliefs and look for evidence to confirm them. Causal claims are accordingly best assessed in terms of their utility in helping us cope with the world.

Weber's preferred method of research is the construction of narratives organized around imagined causal chains. The actions and events that constitute these chains may be causally linked or manifestations of some underlying process. Causal narratives can lead us to deeper levels of explanation if we find causes for causes.[34] With diligence and luck, we may discover underlying cultural explanations, as Weber tried to do for capitalism.

To address the problem of culture, Weber invented the concept of the "ideal type." Ideal types have no external validity because they do not correspond to any historical reality.[35] He subsequently reformulated his concept to give ideal types some empirical connection to the world. He characterized them as analytical accentuations of some features of important phenomena against which real-world approximations could be measured. These ideal types were specific to a culture or epoch and useful for analyzing singular events.[36] As examples, Weber offers individualism, imperialism, feudalism, mercantilism, and the so-called Marxist laws of capitalist development. Ideal types can never provide a holistic understanding of a subject or problem. They are perspectival.[37] They can function as starting or end points of causal narratives. In *The Protestant Ethic and the Spirit of Capitalism*, the ideal type of capitalism is what Weber seeks to explain. He constructs Protestantism as another ideal type and tries to show via a causal narrative that it made capitalism possible.

Weber assumes that all social behavior is goal-seeking. We must accordingly begin causal analysis by trying to determine the motives of relevant actors.[38] We can construct a causal narrative "when the observable action and the motives have been correctly apprehended and their relationship is made meaningfully comprehensible."[39] Weber identifies four kinds of motives: "purposeful rational" (*zweckrational*) is calculated behavior "adequate" to achieve an intended goal; "value rational" (*wertrational*) arises from normative commitments; "traditional" or "habitual" action is made with reference to accepted norms and practices; and "affective" action, which is prompted by the emotions.[40] Each of these motives prompts different kinds of calculations and behavior and we must be careful not to impute any of these several motives to actors but instead reconstruct them on the basis of evidence and empathy. Nothing is either rational or irrational but "becomes so when examined from a specific 'rational' *standpoint*."[41] That standpoint is always the actor's perspective. So-called objective rationality exists only in the realm of technique, and even here there are reasons to question it. Life is about meaning, and meaning is found through reasoning, but reason cannot provide the values that give life meaning.

Weber recognizes that "In the vast majority of cases, action takes place in dull semi-consciousness or unconsciousness." We must nevertheless assume "purposeful rational" (*zweckrational*) on the part of actors and behavior that more or less conforms to his ideal type of "right rationality" (*Richtigkeitstypus*). It is "the a priori" of all reason-based and interpretative understanding.[42] It makes use of abstract concepts like induction, deduction, causation, and ideal types. "Right rationality" is subjective because it depends on what we think would have constituted rational behavior. This in turn hinges on what motives we think are in play, what ends actors sought, and what course of action had the best chance of producing them. Even when evidence-based, such judgments still require leaps of inference.

The closer any action conforms to right rationality, the less we need to turn to "psychological considerations" to comprehend it. The identification of "irrational" processes (*sinnfremd*) and their analysis also start with reason. We must "determine how the action would have proceeded in the limiting case of purposive and right rationality" and then account for the variation.[43] The construction of a "purely rational course of action" functions here as an ideal type that provides a clear and unambiguous – but a purely theoretical – account of a causal relationship. Weber repeatedly warns that rationality is nothing more than "a methodological device." It does not require, nor is it intended to suggest, "a belief in the actual predominance of rational elements in human life."[44]

Although Weber is concerned with singular causation, he insists that it must be approached by means of comparative analysis. Even the most plausible motivational account of a motive or behavior is never more than a hypothesis until evaluated against a "progression" of external behaviors. We make causal inferences by studying actions against previous actions by the same individual and other people in similar circumstances. Weber further warns that not all rational behavior will appear rational to us, especially if it is motivated by beliefs (e.g., placating the gods will bring rain) that we do not grasp or accept. He offers a six-step continuum from right rationality to "wholly incomprehensible" behavior.[45]

The next step of analysis is making and evaluating causal inferences. Weber believes that there is a near infinity of causes for any event so we need to identify the most promising antecedents of phenomena of interest to us. Toward this end, we utilize available nomological knowledge and intuition, supplemented by our "common sense" understanding of how the world works. When a complex of antecedent conditions combine to make an outcome "objectively probable," its "cause" should be considered "adequate" with respect to the "effect."[46]

To determine whether antecedent conditions were "objectively probable" and "adequate," we turn to counterfactual thought experiments. Weber instructs us to ask if "elimination ... or alteration" of the putative cause could "according to general rules of experience" have led to a different outcome.[47] Social scientists, like judges, must work backward from what they want to explain to possible causes. By removing one possible cause at a time and asking what might have happened in its absence, we can evaluate its relative importance for an outcome. Counterfactual thought experiments help us understand the kind of causes responsible for an outcome of interest by giving us some idea about how far the behavior in question departed from what we would expect under conditions of perfect rationality. These deviations can be attributed to pressures and constraints on actors, lack of information, cognitive failings, or emotional commitments.

Counterfactual exercises also help us tease out the kind of rationality that is involved in decisions and the context in which they are made. Weber distinguishes between cause that is rational because it is a logical and practical means of achieving a given end. It is the product of the kind of cost calculus made by intelligent and unconstrained actors. Actors are often affected by context-specific pressures or constraints that prompt deviations from what we might consider pure instrumental rationality. Political, economic, and social behavior needs to be explained with reference to both kinds of cause because even rational agents are to varying degrees pressured and constrained.

To recapitulate, Weber follows Hume in understanding cause as a human invention but one that is extremely useful in making sense of the world. He differs from Hume in his desire to use cause as the leitmotiv of scientific inquiry. He recognizes that such inquiry relies on artifice at every step. Rationality is the thread that makes causal narratives possible and, like cause, is not an attribute of the world but a human invention. Ideal types are another fiction, although, arguably, have a closer connection to the world. Some are abstractions of empirical observations. They do not map onto the world but can organize our study of it. Rationality might be considered an ideal type, but I think it more accurate to describe Weber's conception of it as something more abstract. It is not connected at all to the empirical world. Rather, like cause, it is an invention that makes possible the study of that world.

When Hume wrote of constant conjunctions, the examples he gave were from ordinary life. Close observation of the physical and social world and the sensations this created in the mind led to associations, one of which was the inference that two things were related because one almost always preceded the other. Constant conjunctions were valuable because they helped people to plan and act in more effective and efficient ways. Hume never describes imperfect conjunctions, but, presumably, these too had benefits. If trout like a particular location in a stream, it makes sense to fish there even if they were not always to be found. Weber also thought that cause had practical payoffs. As causal narratives were, by their very nature, no more than stories about the world, the only way of choosing among them was their utility. This leads to the radical conclusion that the ultimate judges of scientific propositions about the social world are not the scholars who formulated them but the policymakers and ordinary people who attempt to make use of them. Presumably, Weber imagines some kind of ongoing interchange between scholars and laypeople in which the latter make use of causal narratives developed by the former, and they in turn, update, revise, and develop new narratives, as a function of the feedback they receive.

My chapter on Weber identifies several problems with his approach. The first is his emphasis on individual actors. He makes this move because all social behavior is ultimately reducible to that of individuals. Most modern-day constructivists follow Weber in believing that the core goal of interpretivist approaches is to fathom the reasons people have for acting as they do. This is a feasible but elusive goal because it is so difficult to get inside the heads of people. Absent our ability to do this, we cannot determine which of Weber's four types of rationality are appropriate in any given circumstance to the actors we study.

The second and related problem is that people do not always behave rationally – that is, in terms of any of the kinds of rationality. Their motives are accordingly more difficult to infer. This is most likely to happen when the decisions people confront involve serious risks or hard choices among competing goals. They rarely rank their reasons for behaving as they do and are likely to convince themselves that they do not need to make trade-offs. When facing risk, they are likely to defer decision as long as possible, shift the burden of responsibility to someone else, and, if they must act, deny, distort, discredit, or explain away information that suggests their chosen course of action is likely to fail. People deviate from right rationality in ways that are significant enough to limit its utility as an ideal type.

The third problem is the open-ended nature of the social world. People rarely make decisions in isolation. They face multiple problems that involve multiple decisions and generally believe that their decisions on one issue or problem will have consequences for others. Weber is aware of these constraints but fails to acknowledge just how difficult it is from the outside to reconstruct their motives and thought processes, to determine what problems are on their mind, their relative perceived importance, and how they evaluate – if they do – the trade-offs involved. Even good evidence and robust methods may not provide access to the reasons people have for acting as they do.

Finally, there is the problem of aggregation. Even if we knew why people behaved as they did, this would tell us nothing about the consequences of their behavior. Individuals may be a good entry point for analyzing the social world but to understand outcomes of interest to us we need to know something about the ways in which behavior by multiple actors interacts and the outcomes to which it leads. They may be different from those envisaged or desired by the actors.

Weber believed that empirical science and value choices inhabit different domains. Our value commitments motivate our research but our findings must be evaluated on the basis of criteria independent of these values. If we start with different values and goals, we are likely to ask different questions, find different answers, and assess their meaning and significance by means of different metrics. Science can be objective only in the narrow sense of research concepts, design, and findings being consistent with and following the researcher's value commitments.

However, Weber acknowledged that our values guide not only our choice of subjects and research methods but how we evaluate our findings and assess their significance.

Weber worried that researchers smuggled in values rather than being transparent about them.[48] He thought economists guilty of doing this and of failing to distinguish "what is" (*das Seiende*) from "what ought to be" (*das Seinsollende*).[49] Weber also had problems in distinguishing the "is" from the "ought" and inadvertently assumed the objective validity of a series of political assumptions that undergird his analysis. These include competition *à outrance* among classes, peoples, and states, a belief in the existence of a national interest, and the primacy of foreign over domestic politics. Weber struggled to keep values distinct from facts and his inability to do so is further reason for questioning his belief that research methods might be objective and isolated from our values.

Mann and Kafka

Neither Thomas Mann nor Franz Kafka wrote causal narratives. They were convinced that cause in the modern world is so complex and so far removed in its multiple original causes – if such things exist – to be largely unknowable. Immediate causes, which often derive from human motives, are often equally problematic. World War I undoubtedly validated this perspective for both men. It was catastrophic, made no sense, and its causes, even its most immediate ones, were subject to extensive disagreement among policymakers, scholars, and journalists. Equally difficult to determine were the motives of those in power in 1914.

Mann and Kafka were disenchanted with reason or cause, although for different reasons. Mann considered the search for cause fruitless and unproductive. His narratives emphasize impressions, emotions, and the knowledge and commitments to which they lead. Kafka follows Hume in believing that people, by their very nature, think in causal terms. He seeks to demonstrate just how frustrating, inappropriate, and even dangerous this kind of reasoning is in the twentieth century.

The Magic Mountain is noncausal on multiple levels. Nothing much happens in the course of the novel. Hans Castorp remains in the sanatorium for seven years all but cut off from developments in the world below. His horizon is limited to the patients and staff of the Berghof, a cast of characters who, with a few exceptions, remain relatively constant. Residents improve or decline in health, developments that defy causal explanation. So do social developments and patterns, or at least no explanations are offered. These mysteries include Clawdia Chauchat's penchant for allowing the dining room door to slam behind her, the division of Russian dining tables into "good" and "bad," the choices people make about affairs vs. celibacy, and Naphta's shifting commitments in philosophy and religion.

Mann pays so much attention to the physical and biological worlds because they were considered, then as now, more amenable to explanation than social interactions. Medicine was among the most advanced of the practical sciences. Berghof doctors use the latest methods of diagnosis and treatment, and patients pay substantial fees in the hope of being cured. The novel suggests that diagnosis and treatment are hit-and-miss and that the recovery or death of patients is largely random. Medicine, Mann implies, is more art than science.

Mann cautiously explores cause in the social and political world. *The Magic Mountain* suggests that bourgeois repression, national and ethnic stereotypes, and the growing imbalance between reason and emotions are the underlying causes of World War I. Mann suggests that balance between is essential for accommodation and peace and also for understanding. Hans Castorp "comprehended with his mind, not with his sympathies, which would have meant even more."[50] Mann values empathy over causal understanding, in keeping with the Dilthey and the German historicist tradition, but believes that it must be combined with reason for good effects.

The focus on Hans Castorp's development suggests that we read *Der Zauberberg* as a *Bildungsroman*, and Mann characterized it as such in a 1938 lecture at Princeton.[51] In the *Bildungsroman*, the protagonist typically achieves maturity in the course of conflict with his society. He ends up assimilating the values of society and being accepted by it in return. In *The Magic Mountain*, Mann presents Castorp not so much in conflict with German society but as its quintessential product.[52] This social connection offers us a deeper explanation for Castorp's personal development. The individual is a product of the Zeitgeist, especially a young man like Castorp who lacks any strong will or desire to distinguish himself or oppose his family and peers.

Mann would subsequently rethink the relative importance of reason and emotions when he observed the triumph of emotion over reason in late Weimar and the Nazi era. He came to recognize the importance of both but said little to nothing about how reason and emotion should be related and inform one another. He offers a contract to Weber who respected empathy but rejected it as too subjective a foundation for inquiry.

Kafka engages cause more directly and can be read as an implicit critic of Weber. He agrees that causal analysis demands reasoned inquiry and inference. In *The Castle*, his principal character K. is a good rational analyst. He starts with reasonable assumptions: he has been summoned for a job and will be given the information and access he needs to complete it; officials are responsible and responsive; and that he can infer the motives of townspeople on the basis of his general understanding of social life and human nature. These assumptions and his observations form the basis for a series of inferences that are woefully incorrect. He updates his assumptions but still fails to understand or predict because the world of the castle is irrational. Reason stands in the way of understanding, as does the attribution of cause. Cause is not only unhelpful but costly to those like him who search for it.

The Trial also shows the frustration, but also danger, of relying on reason and causal analysis. Joseph K. is suddenly arrested but released, never presented with the charges against him, or given the right to appear in court. He discovers that his freedom and then his life are at stake. He is tried in absentia, picked up on a street, and executed in a deserted quarry. The police, court officials, his lawyers, and the judiciary are dysfunctional, corrupt, secretive, and unprofessional to the extreme. Joseph K.'s knowledge of his innocence and belief in the rationality and justice of the legal system help to bring about his death.

Max Weber is committed to the enterprise of *epistēmē*. He sought to develop methods that would provide explanations of singular events and patterns of behavior. Mann and Kafka, like Sophocles, are focused on *phrōnesis*. They are drawn to *phrōnesis* because of their tragic view of life. The less effective reason and cause are in understanding and controlling the world, the more humans are victims to tragedy. Encounters with fictional characters, their suffering, and fates can bring about emotional arousal and prompt reflection and learning. This cannot reduce tragedy but can provide insight into ourselves, the dark nature of the world, and acceptance of the undeserved fates it often imposes on people.

Cause and Change

Every historical epoch is singular. There are nevertheless processes, problems, and responses that span temporal and cultural divides and are worthy of our attention. This section of the chapter accordingly makes comparisons across fifth-century Athens, eighteenth-century Europe, and the early twentieth century. My analysis of thinkers and writers of these eras reveals certain similarities in changing conceptions of reason and cause and some of the reasons responsible for these changes.

In Sophocles and Thucydides, we see an early version of what Thomas Haskell calls "the recession of cause." The world of the polis was more complex than its predecessor, the *oikos*, and a large-size polis like Athens – upwards of 250,000–300,000 people lived in Attica – more complex still in its economic, political, and social relations. Late fifth-century Athens had bottom-up and top-down orders and a civil hierarchy distinct from familial ones.[53] The city assumed responsibilities that were once private, most notably for the determination and dispensing of justice. Cause was increasingly difficult to infer because outcomes were now more often the product of multiple interactions among many agents operating at different levels of aggregation.

The nineteenth century was an even more dramatic era of change. By the turn of the twentieth century, industrialization, urbanization, and state building had transformed western Europe and the United States and was making inroads in the Pacific rim. Local economies were increasingly dependent on, if not fully incorporated into, national ones. Canals, railroads, and turnpikes connected towns and cities and made possible the rapid transportation of people, goods, and ideas. Newspapers, literacy, and public education stimulated the growth of civil society, which came to be recognized as an important power in its own right. A better informed and more involved public demanded more political influence in an age when government intruded into and regulated the lives of people in a way it never had before. There were dramatic developments in science and engineering, medicine, art, literature, and philosophy. They challenged long-held beliefs about the world. Collectively, Weber thought, they were responsible for the demystification (*die Entzauberung*) of the world. People who felt their anchors have been set loose struggled to understand these changes and the implications for their lives.

Thomas Haskell contends that, in the course of the nineteenth century, the United States became an increasingly interdependent society. Explanation and prediction became critically important tasks in economic, political, and social life but also more difficult "because nothing moves independently."[54] Causation became "tentative" and "probabilistic" and lost much of its power as causes became increasingly distant and diffuse.[55] The local community declined in importance and people suffered a corresponding loss of self-importance and self-confidence.[56]

The project of the autonomous individual became more difficult to sustain in these circumstances. Victorian authors were among the first to challenge it on an empirical basis, showing how society was less the product of individuals than they were of it. Jane Austen novels made clear that, to make headway in the world, especially in the marriage market, people had to discipline themselves and act in accord with society's increasingly rigorous norms of presentation and comportment.

At mid-century, Dickens painted an even bleaker picture. "The system" intruded in almost every way in everybody's lives and was unknowable, unpredictable, and uncontrollable. The best one could do was to avoid making oneself more vulnerable than necessary but that was hard to do in the absence of knowledge about how "the system" worked and affected lives. Trollope described the irrational, although sometimes predictable, very Humean, ways, in which society and the law courts reached judgments. In *The Moonstone*, Wilkie Collins showed how events in far-off India could affect in decisive ways a rural household in the north of England. The widely read novels of these authors increase awareness of how individuals were at the mercy of social and economic forces that they did not understand and over which they had no control. They showed how this was true not only for those at the lowest rungs of society but also for those at the top.

Sociology provided further evidence and support for the power of social forces. For Marx, capitalism reduced human beings to objects, depriving them not only of a meaningful livelihood but of any satisfaction and self-esteem derived from their labor. Weber stressed the consequences of rationalization and its manifestation in bureaucracy. It was in the process of creating a "steel-hardened" cage that people might be reduced to the status of Egyptian peasants. Durkheim explored the nature of social control and the shift in the modern world from mechanical to organic solidarity. Modernity made people only superficially freer. Those who were free and cut off from meaningful social ties and identities suffered anomie, which Durkheim identified as a major cause of suicide. Weber remained deeply pessimistic about the future. Marx believed that mature capitalism created the conditions for its own overthrow and that it would be replaced a more humane socialism. Durkheim had high hopes that a *conscience collective* would develop, based on a widely internalized work ethic that would incorporate core liberal values of dignity and independence of the individual, equal opportunity for all, and a commitment to social justice.[57]

Anglo-American liberals and continental Romantics had stressed the primacy of individuals and the potential of self-fashioning, although they disagreed about whether this was best done in cooperation or conflict with society.[58] By the 1890s, the balance between the individual and society had been reversed in the minds of many influential writers and social scientists. People did not so much create society as they were its products – a view that remains dominant in social psychology.[59]

Haskell maintains that "Self-reliance and interdependence are mutually exclusive." Interdependence and the way it enmeshed individuals and limited their freedom constituted a serious challenge to the nineteenth-century American ideology of "rugged individualism."[60] It was, of course, an equal challenge to the liberal project in Britain. Haskell has a narrow materialist take on the causes of interdependence, which, in my view, is unconvincing.

Individual self-esteem was undercut by other developments, some of them purely intellectual. In the sixteenth century, the claims of Copernicus and Galileo that the earth revolved around the sun were threatening because they meant that earth and human beings were not the center of the universe. They challenged the Catholic Church's use of cosmology to justify earthly hierarchies. In the nineteenth and early twentieth centuries, the writings of Darwin and Freud had similar effects. Evolution implied that humans were descended from earlier animal species and not created unique and distinct by a deity. Psychiatry indicated that much of our behavior, and even thinking, was not so much a matter of free choice as it was of biology and the unconscious mind. Sociology, as noted, also challenged free will and self-fashioning by its emphasis on the social determinants of behavior and identity. Indeed, the discipline of sociology was a response to growing recognition that individual behavior was largely the product of external influences.

Recession of cause, moreover, only applies to opportunities and constraints created at a physical and social distance from individuals. Most economic and social interaction is local and between individuals, and it too, my texts suggest, became harder to fathom. In traditional societies, much behavior is role- and norm-based. Rule packages dictate how people should act in a wide range of political, economic, and social circumstances. In modern society, people have much more choice about how to behave in all these domains. One cannot assume their behavior but must predict it.

Choice allows – and encourages – people to game social encounters. To advance their interests, they may encourage others to believe they have motives and goals that they do not. They in turn must read the motives and intentions of others. Gaming involves deception and mutual, even multiple, deceptions greatly complicate the causal picture. Gaming, moreover, is not the behavior of only marginal actors. In a wide range of situations, people benefit from making strategic choices about ends and means (e.g., investments, partners, education, residence, profession) and at times mislead others about their assets, qualifications, intentions, and goals. Mathematical economics pioneered the study of this process. Oskar Morgenstern demonstrated that general equilibrium analysis depended on imperfect foresight and divergent expectations of actors.[61] He redefined economics as a game of expectations that might be understood through game theory and probability theory.[62] Intended to reduce the problem of uncertainty, economics may have intensified this dilemma by encouraging people, groups, and organizations to behave more strategically. Although, to be fair, this kind of deception had become prominent in the Renaissance.[63]

Cause is not only more difficult to trace and establish but knowledge about it is more necessary to negotiate everyday life. Mortgages, business decisions, investments, even education and holidays are influenced by, or may be dependent on, such things as interest rates, crop, stock, real estate, and airline prices, the cost of tuition, and the availability of scholarships and low interest loans. Fluctuations in prices, rates, and availability are difficult to predict, and more so when multiple agents try to game them.

Large swings in any of these things are almost invariably the consequence of developments in other domains with important knock-on effects. All of the postwar economic recessions were the product of developments outside the realm of economics. So too have key political developments been triggered or accelerated by economic and social developments. Interdependent worlds are more open-ended and non-linear, which makes explanation difficult and all but the simplest predictions difficult, if not impossible. It may seems likely that Americans in the 1890s, and their western European counterparts, while not fully understanding why cause was more difficult to attribute, nevertheless felt its resulting frustrations. For this and the other reasons noted, they felt less autonomous, less secure, more vulnerable, and had correspondingly lower esteem.

To summarize, I contend that writers, historians, philosophers, and social scientists find cause most problematic in eras where societies become more complex, more interdependent, and in which people have more choices about ends and means. It becomes more problematic still when people try to hide or misrepresent their motives or goals. Ironically, the quest for autonomy helped to undermine it, as it was an underlying cause of both conditions.

Complexity and interdependence appear to be tightly coupled. Both are products – and enablers – of larger, more stratified societies with more complex divisions of labor. They are also likely to possess economies of scale and more extensive trade within their own boundaries or outside of them. In fifth-century Athens and late eighteenth-century Europe – and more so in the nineteenth and twentieth centuries – complexity and interdependence went hand in hand with the kinds of intellectual changes that encouraged strategic behavior and deception. Shifts in people's thinking about their roles in society and the nature of political, economic, and social orders enhanced the perceived value of agency. Stress and anxiety arise when increased complexity and interdependence coincide with increased desires for autonomy, as they did in fifth-century Athens, the so-called Age of Enlightenment, and the later industrial era. Material and ideational changes are equally important and were mutually reinforcing.

People think causally when it appears to confer advantages in coping with the world. Causal inference accordingly becomes more important in the very conditions that make it more difficult. When people feel less confident about making causal inferences, they consider themselves less able to control or manage their environment and correspondingly more at risk. They feel insecure and vulnerable, and all the more so to the degree that their livelihood, status, or security depends on predictions that rely on causal inference. Their self-esteem also declines precipitously when they have been encouraged to define it in terms of successful agency and especially self-fashioning. People accordingly have strong practical and psychological motives to find ways out of this dilemma.

Responses

I identify four different generic strategies for coping with the causal dilemma. Strategies 1 and 4 are found in three of the historical periods I studied. Strategies 2 and 3 are modern and emerged in the Enlightenment and early twentieth century.

1. *Develop thicker explanations for cause and research methods appropriate to its discovery.* This strategy rejects prediction on the grounds that most outcomes in the social world are context-dependent. Instead, it develops general understandings that are useful starting points for narrative explanations and forecasts. Thucydides and Weber adopt this strategy.
2. *Acknowledge social complexity but look for simpler explanations that make use of master variables.* This strategy generally seeks underlying explanations for a wide range of developments and behavioral patterns. Master variables may be economic, geographical, sociological, or biological. Theories based on them are more likely to make predictions about patterns of behavior or transformations than about individual events. Rousseau, Comte, Marx, and Spencer embraced this strategy as does present-day evolutionary psychology.
3. *Deny social complexity and seek thin explanations for cause.* This strategy develops models for the purposes of explanation and prediction based on a few seemingly simple assumptions about people and the contexts in which they make decisions. Models at the individual or so-called system

level assume that actors will respond in the same way to system-level opportunities and constraints. Micro- and macroeconomics, rational choice, and other rationalist approaches exemplify this approach.
4. *Acknowledge the difficulty, if not the impossibility, of making causal claims.* This recognition can stimulate a search for other routes to social knowledge. Sophocles' turn to tragedy, Thomas Mann's emphasis on emotional learning, and agent-based models are illustrative of this strategy.

Strategies 1 and 4 make diametrically opposed bets about the utility of cause and the possibility of finding it. Strategy 1 stipulates that social science research must be causal in nature, although its proponents are often pessimistic about finding causes and more so about making predictions. Strategy 4 rejects the quest for cause as illusory and even dangerous. These strategies are at the opposite ends of the causal spectrum but united in their recognition that the search for cause is a very difficult enterprise. Strategies 2 and 3 refuse to recognize the complexity of the social world and represent escapes from reality. They are, of course, the dominant approaches within the academy.

Strategy 1. Max Weber is the best known advocate of "thick" causation. His approach rejects out of hand any search for universal laws or understandings that can be the basis for meaningful predictions. Weber recognized just how difficult cause was to establish but still insisted that causal narratives should be the goal of social science. His most significant innovation is the "ideal type." It is the most salient feature of an epistemology that seeks case-specific configurational explanations, recognizes the determining importance of culture and history, and understands knowledge as a form of value clarification rather than the foundation for rational courses of action.

Equally radical is Weber's insistence that theoretical concepts can never capture the essence of their objects of analysis. He recognizes, even embraces, a form of cultural relativity that links ideal types to the value commitments of the scholars who invent and deploy them. Politics is accordingly a realm in which reason can advise but not dictate and in which scholars can clarify social and political dilemmas but never resolve them.[64] For Weber, all truth claims are not only provisional but local, and there are no independent rational or logical systems capable of assessing them. They must be evaluated on the basis of their utility in clarifying contemporary problems and the policy and ethical choices associated with them.

Weber's epistemology frames the causal problem in terms of explanation, not prediction. Singular causation of the kind Weber advocates assumes that outcomes have causes but that even the most compelling causal accounts cannot predict when a similar event will occur or what outcome it will lead to if it does. At best, explanations are useful starting points for narrative forecasts but with the understanding that outcomes are always context-dependent.

Thucydides might be said to be the father of this epistemology. He is equally committed to causal narratives that search for causes at multiple levels of analysis. His account of the Archidamian and Peloponnesian Wars are structured around Greek tragedy, which he utilizes in a different way from Sophocles. Thucydides conceives of tragedy as a kind of ideal type. For Weber, ideal types are concepts (e.g., authority, rationality) or expressions of them (e.g., charisma, *Zwechrationalität*). For Thucydides, tragedy can be considered an ideal type storyline about hubris and its consequences. He depicts the alliance with Corcyra and the Sicilian expedition as miscalculations produced by hubris that led to tragic outcomes that were the polar opposites of those intended and expected.

Like Weber, Thucydides looks for deeper levels of cause and this is another reason why he turns to tragedy to structure his narrative. At every level of analysis he shows how difficult it is to establish cause. Thucydides explores the reasons people have for acting as they do and the means they use to persuade others to support them. His narrative and speeches indicate that it is not always easy to grasp the motives of individuals and more difficult still to understand why their decisions or policies resulted in the outcomes they did. Depending on the circumstances, the same actions can have diametrically opposed results. This happens because the chains of events they set in motion incorporate or prompt other decisions and actions independent of them, many of which are unforeseeable. Thucydides differs from Weber in the kind of knowledge he seeks. Weber aspires to *epistēmē* and Thucydides at *phrōnesis* and possibly, *sophia*. I will explore the implications of this difference at the end of this chapter.

Weber and his intellectual descendants – of whom I consider myself one – do not represent the only approach to thick cause. The most prominent alternative is philosophical or scientific realism.[65] It was developed by Rom Harré and Roy Bhaskar and further elaborated by Nancy Cartwright and C. B. Mart.[66] It assumes that the world is largely independent of us and differentiated in the sense of being structured, layered, and complex. These layers interact, making all systems open and subject to emergent properties.[67] Realists contend that the world should be understood as an ensemble of powers, propensities, and forces that explain complex interactions and events. Examples in physics include the spin, charge, mass, and decay of particles. Causal properties are said to confer "dispositions on particulars that have to behave in certain ways when in the presence or absence of other particulars with causal properties of their own."[68]

While causal properties are unobservable, scientific realists insist they are nevertheless a fundamental ontological category. Each causal property is expected to manifest itself in specific ways but can remain latent if not stimulated, enabled, or otherwise activated. Causal properties give rise to tendencies rather than fixed laws (e.g., the likelihood that states will balance against more powerful or threatening states), which, together with the open-ended nature of the world, explain why there are no constant conjunctions.[69] Scientific and critical realists are interested in the kinds of causal properties that exist and the mechanisms that make them manifest.[70] Their approach stands in sharp contrast to Humean association, in which the only relations that count are those of spatial and temporal contiguity. Causation is extrinsic to them and observed through cause-and-effect pairs of regularity.[71]

Critics of scientific realism – I count myself among them – contend that the causal powers research program says little to nothing about the features of things that are causally relevant or the conditions in which their latent powers become manifest. More importantly, it does not tell us how we would even begin to find answers to these questions.[72] Scientific realism accordingly skirts circularity. Realists reject this criticism and contend that causal properties can be established in laboratory experiments. This ties their research program to a method of inquiry that has only limited applicability to social relations.[73]

Strategy 2. In the nineteenth century, it became fashionable to propose sweeping monocausal explanations to account for key features of modernity. For master variables, Taine turned to environment, Spencer to biology, Hegel to the world spirit, and Marx to economics. Their accounts are reductionist, often determinist, and invariably smuggle in values while claiming to be purely scientific analyses of society. Formulations of this kind all but do away with agency and in an era when the individual and their alleged uniqueness and autonomy were increasingly valued. These theories nevertheless had wide appeal for multiple reasons. Social Darwinism legitimated domestic and international hierarchies, self-serving beliefs like racism, the moral inferiority of the poor, and conscription, armaments, and imperialism. Marxism justified opposition to these policies and the hierarchies responsible for them and promised a better world to the mass of oppressed workers.

Marxism downgrades agency – the success of socialism is inevitable for Marx and Engels – but nevertheless empowered activists to hasten its triumph. These several "isms" may also have been appealing because they enhanced the self-esteem of believers by providing them with inside knowledge about how the world worked. They restored their faith in cause by providing simple explanations for complex events and blaming evil in the world on conspiracies.[74] They reduced anomie by allowing believers to be part of a tight-knit, like-minded community; and they held out the prospect of a better life.

Strategy 3. Social scientists and philosophers have developed approaches to knowledge that attempt to finesse cause. One of the most influential mid-twentieth-century efforts was the deductive-nomological (DN) approach, developed by Carl Hempel and Paul Oppenheim. It stipulates that an event (*explanandum*) is only explained when it is the product of a deductive argument, whose premise (*explanans*) is a law-like statement and a set of initial or antecedent conditions. These conditions need to be made explicit as must the links between *explanans* and *explanandum*.[75]

The DN model is not causal because laws are not causes. It can, however, accommodate outcomes associated with observable statistical distributions. One of its principal drawbacks is that laws, by their very nature, are expected to be universal. This posed no problem for Hempel, who intended DN to be applied to the physical world. It is a crippling impediment in the social world, where, as Max Weber understood, culture is determinant and agents are reflective and motivated by their own subjective ends. The rules of one culture or era do not map onto others. Seeming laws are often undermined within cultures when conditions change. Knowledge of laws also has the potential to undermine them. Weber thought the "half-life" of any law would be short once it became known and people took it into account. Law-like analysis is only possible when scientists or engineers can create closed systems that allow only independent and dependent variables and restrict their predictions to system-level effects.[76] In open and nonlinear systems, this cannot be done.[77]

The most common representative of this strategy today is regularity theories. They search for correlations in the expectation of offering explanations and predictions. They represent "thin" approaches to causation because they say nothing about the causes of any correlations. Regularity theories are widespread, if not dominant, in economics, sociology, and political science. They claim, falsely, to be rooted in Humean causation.

Regularity theories appeal to social scientists for many reasons. They obviate the need to connect an antecedent to an effect by means of a mechanism or process and thus restrict research to observables. This removes any need to learn history, languages, or familiarize oneself with cultures – including one's own. Advocates of regularity theories recognize the difference between association and cause, and many pay lip service to the latter; the search for associations is routinely characterized as a first and necessary step to its discovery. However, most scholars in this tradition never search for causes, which they recognize as difficult to establish and, some claim, unnecessary for purposes of prediction. Philosopher J. L. Mackie praises the regularity approach on the grounds that it "has at least the merit that it involves no mysteries, no occult properties like necessity."[78] Most attractive of all, regularity theories hold out the prospect of prediction. If so, they would confer the same benefits as causal explanations but directly and without the intervening need to establish a more meaningful relationship between antecedent and consequent.

There are serious conceptual and empirical problems with regularity theories in social science. They depend on the discovery of constant conjunctions, or at least regularities strong enough to allow prediction with some degree of confidence. In the social world, constant conjunctions do not exist, and what regularities we do find are context-dependent and usually useless for purposes of prediction. Regularity theorists who recognize this problem search for deeper regularities to explain the variance, but these too invariably also turn out to be imperfect. This process can lead to an infinite redress. Regularity theorists generally assume that regularity and cause are features of the world. As Bertrand Russell long ago observed, they make arbitrary assignations of antecedent and consequent. Decisions about what constitutes an event and what makes events alike or different, and some of them members of the same class, require precise criteria. These criteria can only be derived from independent theoretical conceptions, and they in turn inevitably rest on metaphysical foundations. As Mackie proclaims, this is what regularity theorists desperately want to avoid.[79]

Rationalist theories also seek parsimonious formulations in the form of explanatory and predictive models. They reject Weber's all-important distinction between the rationality of a model and that of real-world actors. For Weber, as we have seen, all models of human behavior have to be rational in the sense of being logical and consistent. When applied to actors, rationality is an ideal type, and a complex one. Weber began with a typology identifying four kinds of rationality to categorize actors' goals. It is an ideal type because people are not always aware of the choices they make in this regard and adhere to these categories only in part. Next comes the use of rationality as a benchmark for analyzing and evaluating behavior within these categories. It too is an ideal type, as people are never fully rational for a range of reasons. Rationalist models collapse Weber's distinction of the several types of rationality in favor of a universal instrumental rationality. They further assume that all actors are instrumentally rational or can be treated as such.

Rationalist approaches assume in addition that actors are capable of "choosing the best means to gain a determined set of end."[80] Analysts determine what this choice is rather than trying to ascertain what actors think it might be. Their models generally require actors to have transitive preferences, engage in Bayesian updating, and resort to sophisticated forms of signaling to convey their preferences and resolve and to gain information about those of other actors. They must also assume that actors are free of ideological commitments, political constraints, and psychological pressures that would interfere with the application of pure reason to decision-making. In effect, rationalist models "solve" the causal problem by simplifying the world in highly unrealistic ways.

Rationalist theories are open to devastating criticisms. They have a naïve understanding of rationality because they assume it is independent of context and culture.[81] Early critics of game theory were quick to point out that instrumental reasoning required actors to make trade-offs between their goals and the risks they appeared to entail.[82] It is arbitrary to rely on any algorithm like "minimax," the standard choice of first-generation game theorists, to address these trade-offs. This problem has not been solved by later theorists, despite the elaborate alternatives to minimax they have developed. Nor can it be by its very nature. We must look outside the game to their motives, values, rationality, and risk-taking propensities of actors. They determine how they assess the relative importance of cooperation and conflict and the choices they think open to them. Rationalist theories build on arbitrary assumptions and arbitrary decision rules to produce arbitrary theories that not surprisingly reveal a poor fit with the social domains they purport to model.

Rationalist theorists dismiss these criticisms as beside the point because they make no pretense of describing real-world behavior. Alternatively, they fall back on the argument of economist Milton J. Friedman, who famously asserted that there need be no correspondence between the assumptions of a theory and reality. Not surprisingly, unrealistic assumptions make models incapable of predicting real-world outcomes.[83]

Rationalist models might still be useful if they could identify and analyze dynamics that shape actual behavior; this was the intended goal of Morgenstern and von Neumann, the creators of game theory. Such models might provide a template against which to measure and understand actual behavior, a goal that is not infrequently proclaimed. They fail to serve either end. The equilibria they find depend entirely on the assumptions built into the models. Different assumptions and causal logics lead to different equilibria. Without attempting to evaluate these models and their assumptions against real behavior, we cannot know which – if any – capture the dynamics of actual crises. The general lack of empirical inquiry by theorists renders them useless as templates.

Strategy 4. Adherents of this strategy develop noncausal routes to social knowledge. Sophocles uses tragedy toward this end and as an alternative form of knowledge. Dickens, Trollope, and Collins search for causes only to show how difficult they are to establish and how badly ordinary people and professionals go about this task. These authors resemble Sophocles in believing that many of the most important developments in our lives have inaccessible causes, that people search for them improperly and in the wrong places, and if they succeeded in finding causes they would be of limited practical use. This pessimism is most evident in Dickens. He is intent on showing how the search for cause is often not only futile but also counterproductive to those who engage in it. It can bring about a reversal in their fates, as it does for some of the characters of *Bleak House*, suggesting a presumably unintended parallel with tragedy.

The physical and biological sciences have moved increasingly in the direction of strategy 4. The long-standing goal of science to reduce higher-order phenomena to lower-order ones has given way for many to a new emphasis on how higher-order phenomena develop or emerge. In particle physics, randomness, indeterminacy, and path dependency have been embraced, and with them a reframing of explanation in bottom-up terms. In biology, the human genome was formerly considered the key to understanding the human phenotype. Now it is recognized only as a beginning. Environments in utero and after birth, life experiences, and other factors play an important role. The genome cannot predict in detail but is a starting point for a historical narrative. In these and other fields of science, traditional understandings of cause are increasingly finessed or rejected as downright inapplicable.[84]

These bottom-up approaches understand objects more as dynamical processes than as units. "Instead of particles all the way down," as Norton Wise puts it,[85] "it would be processes all the way up." Sometimes they are thought of as self-stabilizing systems, or components of them, a framing that I contend is inappropriate to social relations.[86] They encourage a radical rethinking of the nature of the scientific enterprise. The relationship between cause and effect changes in a nonlinear world where small changes can produce dramatic effects. The analysis of units increasingly gives way to a more global approach. Reductionism is understood to have reached its limits and no longer considered the *ultima ratio* of science. Finally, and perhaps most importantly, universality and theory independent of context are supplanted by a historical perspective, even in such sciences as physics.[87]

In the social sciences, agent-based models are the most prominent noncausal approaches to knowledge. In contrast to much research in the social sciences that is confined to one level of analysis, these models probe interactions across levels. Outcomes at the system level are the result of behavior at lower levels of aggregation. Many agent-based models seek to account for these outcomes in terms of rules that govern the aggregation of actor behavior. If discovered, these rules cannot be characterized as causes as that term is understood by Weber or most contemporary philosophers.

Agent-based models also work in reverse. They create environments, actors, and rules. These models are used to produce imaginary worlds and to discover how sensitive their outcomes are to changes in any of their parameters. They are sometimes employed to evaluate theories by creating worlds based on their assumptions to see the extent that the outcomes they generate approximate real-world ones. Actor behavior is determined by the model; actors pursue goals and follow rules that have been stipulated in advance, although it is possible to build in some randomization. Actor behavior is accordingly predictable but outcomes often are not. In many games, they vary significantly as a function of the initial conditions.

Agent-based models finesse cause, which is a perfectly legitimate thing to do given their goals. At best, they can identify initial conditions and rules associated with particular outcomes. Agent-based models also do their best to avoid engaging rationality. Rules imposed from the outside substitute for decisions made by actors so it is not necessary to consider what motivates them or whether or not they are instrumentally rational. Rules must be consistent but can be arbitrary. Those who design models can freely manipulate rules and conditions to get a better match with external reality. Of course, these fits are always at best partial because outcomes are context-dependent; they are influenced by what else is going on or shaping the environment. Agent-based models that have some explanatory value will have little to no predictive value if their outcomes are highly dependent on initial conditions or if the phenomena they seek to explain are open-ended in their causes.

Agent-based models bridge to Weber in two important ways. Along with game theoretic models, they might be described as ideal types. They are highly stylized depictions that are never found in the real world but can be used to provide insight into it. Like ideal types, they may best be used as starting points for narratives that fold in context, in the form of not only initial conditions but also other features of the world that have the potential to affect the outcomes in question. Rationalist models might be used the same way in theory but are generally not.

Weber looked to comparative and counterfactual analysis as a means of evaluating causal claims. Agent-based models and simulation can function as another kind of counterfactual analysis. They can evaluate causal narratives by noncausal means. For most of the twentieth century, good theories were considered to be those that used linear equations to describe the evolution of continuous quantities. Information technology has enabled a discrete on/off approach to phenomena that are rule-governed. It inspired a search for simple rules – algorithmic systems – which, when repeatedly applied, generate complex, system-level patterns. Beginning in biology, this approach spread to physics and now to the social sciences. It could be combined with Weberian causal analysis by building a model or simulation based on assumptions and mechanisms derived from causal narratives. Millions of counterfactual worlds could be generated to see the extent to which they resembled the ones for which the causal narratives sought to account. Modeling and simulation were not available to Weber. If he were alive today, he might find them useful in evaluating causal claims and accounting for system-level outcomes.

The Great Paradox

It should come as no surprise that regularity and rationalist theories dominate social science. Their advocates portray themselves as scientists and have convinced many people that economics or other disciplines that use their approaches should be regarded in a not dissimilar light from physics, chemistry, and biology. Regularity and rationalist approaches have colonized sociology, political science, and international relations where researchers expect, and often receive, increased status and remuneration.[88] This institutional account nevertheless begs the question of why and how these researchers have convinced funding agencies, the media, and the Nobel Institute – which created a prize in economics in 1968 – that what they do is science.

Part of the answer may lie in society's need to believe in prediction. The inclination to think causally may be "hardwired" into us because, as Hume suggested, it was traditionally an effective tool for coping with the world. Prediction is even more important in the modern world, where it also has become more difficult. This tension is a source of personal insecurity and anxiety. None of us are happy about the extent to which our lives are moved and shaped by events of which we have no control and struggle to understand.

Their modern economy is based on production of goods, provision of services, and their financing, distribution, and sale. These activities could not function without investment and judgments about likely demand.

They in turn rely on estimates of such things as interest and exchange rates, price of raw materials and labor, access to markets, and consumer wealth and confidence. These predictions are notoriously unreliable but nevertheless essential.

People need to convince themselves they can rely on professional or personal forecasts. In their absence, they may find it difficult to cope with the uncertainty and associated anxiety generated by business decisions that put them at risk. The emperor may have no clothes but people want to convince themselves that he is fully arrayed in fine raiment. Social scientists encourage this belief. Economists and fellow travelers in allied disciplines do their best to deny uncertainty and treat as much of it as possible as risk.[89] Uncertainty is a term for the unknowable and risk treated as unknowns about which robust probabilities can be established. Historians of these several disciplines have rightly described them as cheerleaders of scholarly progress.[90]

Reinforcing psychological and practical needs to banish uncertainty may be why people are so forgiving when economists and public policy experts routinely make bad predictions or give what turns out to be bad advice. Economists and others who make these predictions continually hold out the prospect of doing better in the future. In the late 1950s, when the first digital computers were being constructed, they and artificial intelligence were expected to enable this breakthrough. Decades later came big data, and a revival of artificial intelligence based on neural networks instead of symbolic logic holds out this promise.[91] Funding agencies, investors, and the media are repeatedly hoodwinked by these claims. Richard Bernstein rightly observes: "One could write the history of social science during the past one hundred years in terms of declarations that it has just become, or is just about to become, a scientific enterprise."[92]

Economists are not unlike haruspices or augurs who read entrails, observed the flight of birds, or went to shrines to receive ambiguously worded guidance from oracles. Soothsayers achieved high status in their societies but were at risk if their predictions failed – or if they succeeded, as Cassandra and Teresias were when their predictions were seen as threatening by those in power. Homer and Sophocles' seers are always on target because it is the poets' power to impart mantic capabilities to them. Practitioners of the dismal science and allied fields have been able to claim high status on the basis of their advice, although there is no evidence to suggest that it is any more successful than that of seers, shamans, or witch doctors. Social scientists are their secular counterparts and benefit greatly from society's need to believe that the future is in part foreseeable.

There is a still deeper explanation for this phenomenon. It has less to do with need for prediction and more with the need for order. The two are related, of course, because order facilitates prediction when it privileges certain kinds of behavior and responses and sanctions others. People also value order because of the security, material, and emotional benefits it provides.

People are likely to feel the need to defend top-down and bottom-up orders when either is threatened.[93] Much has been written about the insecurity of nineteenth-century bourgeois in western and central Europe and the kinds of rigorous constraints bottom-up orders imposed on members of its class. Freud thought that Victorian repression of sexual urges was indirectly responsible for World War I.[94] This may be something of a stretch but Victorian values undeniably prompted repression, anxiety, and rebellion. In the United States, historians have described the Progressive movement as in part a search for order.[95] World War I and the turmoil that followed in its wake made people more insecure and many sought refuge in more ordered societies.

The quest for order – and the rebellion against it – was evident in art philosophy, and literature. Flamboyant and decorative architecture and design, as manifest in art nouveau and its central European equivalent of *Jugendstil*, gave way to Bauhaus and modernist architecture. The Bauhaus sought order and simplicity in architecture and furniture and rejected all decoration, free form, and whimsy. The twelve-tone technique did something similar in music. It decreed that all twelve notes of the chromatic scale be sounded as often as one another in a piece of music without emphasis on any one note. It achieved this through the use of tone rows, rigid orderings of the twelve pitch classes. In eastern and southern Europe, existing or newly created postwar democracies gave way to right-wing authoritarian regimes that stressed traditional values, order, and uniformity.

In science, there was also an intensified search for order. American-born, Swiss-based Albert Favarger thought that precise measurement of time and making this available to everyone was a key to rebuilding society.[96] "Objectivism" came to dominant history and political science. Turn-of-the-century historians in the United States and in Germany wanted to separate "facts" from interpretations and policy recommendations and view history and social science as objective activities governed by a rigorous set of rules. Wesley Mitchell and, in the postwar era, Charles Merriam, would become its most prominent American adherents in history and pollical science.[97] Arguably, the pure theory of law, developed by Hans Kelsen in the early 1930s, was a legal counterpart.[98]

In philosophy, the Vienna Circle sought to impose order on science through the development of logic-based rules for making truth claims.

The emphasis on falsification and the DN approach to knowledge were outgrowths of their efforts. Positivism also provided the epistemological foundations for regularity theories and may be considered another expression of the perceived need for order and control.

Before and after World War I, the struggle that pitted rebellion against order was equally evident in art and literature. It would belatedly come to social science in the forms of poststructuralism, feminism, and postcolonial studies. This seesawing of order and rebellion is an expression of the rise and fall of confidence in top-down and bottom-up orders and of intensified support and opposition to them. There is always some degree of time lag and often longer in fields where one epistemology, style, or movement becomes powerful enough to perpetuate itself for some time through control over institutions responsible for training people, finding them jobs and rewarding grants, contracts, or commissions and publishing, displaying, or performing their works. In social science, the behavioral revolution led to the institutional dominance of a particular epistemology. Those committed to it have done their best to maintain their power and marginalize challengers.

Positivist and rationalist approaches are products of a particular moment in time. They have no claim to objectivity or universality and should be understood as largely psychological responses to the tensions between the drive for autonomy and the reality of interdependence. Those reasons remain and this undoubtedly contributes to the continuing institutional success of these approaches despite their failure to live up to their promises. Prayer survives for much the same reasons.

Where does this leave us? Strategies 2 and 3 are unpromising for all reasons I enumerated. Strategies 1 and 4 are more realistic and attractive. We should focus on both kinds of inquiry. Their common attribute is their search for *phrōnesis* in lieu of *epistēmē*. This can be accomplished by both developing and elaborating thicker conceptions of causation and at the same time reducing our dependence on causal analysis.

These enterprises pull in different directions but it is not inconceivable that we could find ways of bridging or combining them. Thicker approaches recognize just how difficult it is to establish cause and how all claims to have done so in the social world are rhetorical at best. Paradoxically, they engage cause more seriously than thin formulations but take it less seriously. Advocates of thick approaches nevertheless take it less seriously from an epistemological perspective. They are more inclined to believe that cause is a human invention rather than a feature of the world. This prompts the realization that cause is a means to an end and that end is helping us better negotiate the world. Any causal claims must be evaluated in terms of their practical value.

Building on Weber, I develop my own thick approach in *Causation in International Relations*. "Inefficient causation" looks for multiple chains of causation at multiple levels of social aggregation and uses comparative, historical, and counterfactual analysis to explore their interaction. I argue that such analysis can promote useful knowledge in the form of multiple causal accounts for phenomena, some of them reinforcing but others at odds. These different formulations offer starting points for narrative explanations and forecasts that take context into account.

In the longer term, any epistemology that competes with positivism and rationalism will only supplant them by responding more effectively to human needs – and convincing scholars and funding agencies that it does. It could also get a boost from external events that discredit positivism and rationalism or at least seriously call them into question. In contrast to the physical sciences, where paradigm shifts are largely a function of developments internal to the discipline or related ones, those in the social sciences are more the consequence of political, economic, and social developments.[99] In the decade after Ken Waltz published his *Theory of International Politics* in 1979, numerous critiques exposed the inadequacies of neorealism with relatively little effect.[100] Its all but total collapse in the early 1990s was attributable to the end of the Cold War and the breakup of the Soviet Union.[101] These events stood in sharp contradiction to the expectation of the theory. Equally important was the availability of alternative approaches to international relations, most notably constructivism and classical realism. They seemed to many scholars more relevant to the problems posed by the post–Cold War world. We must persevere with strategies 1 and 4 because their time may well come.

Tragedy

In this book and in my trilogy on political order, I turned to the ancient Greeks for inspiration.[102] One of their important attractions was that their poets, historians, and philosophers wrote before this scientific, humanist, artistic divergence. They pioneered different understandings of knowledge; Aristotle was able to describe four kinds, and I cannot think of any approach to knowledge not captured by his typology. They pioneered different genres to develop and express these several kinds of knowledge. In the process, history diverged from poetry, and philosophy from history and poetry. Later, in early modern Europe, the sciences diverged from philosophy. Fifth-century Greek thinkers and writers were nevertheless open to the insights of all kinds of inquiry and sought to benefit from other approaches while developing approaches and genres of their own. As we have seen, Thucydides framed his historical account of the Archidamian and Peloponnesian Wars as a tragedy. Plato scorned Homer but structured his *Republic* and many dialogues in ways that resembled poetry. Aristotle turned to tragedy to understanding how learning occurred.

These late fifth- and early fourth-century Greek writers drew closer together as they were moving apart. They established distinct identities for their genres and the kinds of knowledge they produced, but, at the same time, drew ideas, inspiration, modes of presentation, argument, and examples from other genres. This dialectical approach to genre and disciplinary identity mirrors the way young children establish identities as separate beings. Studies indicate that the healthiest children psychologically are those who draw closer to the parents and caregivers from whom they are separating. In *The Politics and Ethics of Identity*, I argue this holds true for social collectivities and political units as well.[103]

In modern times, *epistēmē* has had little contact with *phrōnesis* and *sophia* – the first the goal of social science and the last two the pursuit of the humanities and creative arts. Practitioners of these disciplines and activities have erected metaphorical walls between them, especially in the Anglosphere. By the 1960s, C. P. Snow was able to describe them as distinct and different cultures.[104] Those in search of knowledge could profitably copy the more catholic outlook of the ancients. They could try to overcome the firewalls erected between social science and the humanities without in any way sacrificing their distinct identities. This process can take several forms or levels. Ideally, this engagement should be mutual, but I limit myself here to what social science can gain by a fuller engagement with humanities.

At the substantive level, social scientists can benefit from insights of humanists. Consider, for example, the different takes on bureaucracy offered by Weber and Kafka, two of the authors featured in this volume; or the elaboration of Hume's critique of reason by Dickens, Trollope, and Collins. These novels offer different ways of thinking about key features of modernity and epistemologies developed to make sense of it.

At the conceptual level, social science approaches strive for clarity, logical consistency, and linearity. Many works of literature foreground the tensions inherent in these goals and the way in which attempting to resolve them can be counterproductive. In *The Rise and Fall of Political Order*, I turn to Shakespeare's *Troilus and Cressida* to explore different conceptions of order and show how looser, open-ended understandings that display and acknowledge unresolved tensions are better in the sense of being more useful.[105] In this volume, I show how Homer, Sophocles, and Thucydides turn to tragedy as a means of exposing tensions in Bronze Age and classical Greek societies and develop immanent critiques of them. Their insights and methods are arguably relevant to ours.

Social science for the most part seeks knowledge at the level of *epistēmē*. Good literature aspires to *phrōnesis* or even *sophia*. Interpretivist approaches to social science also for the most part seek *phrōnesis*. I do not think we should collapse the distinction among these several forms of knowledge or seek one kind in preference to others. Rather, I suggest that the pursuit of any kind of knowledge can benefit from familiarity with others. At the very least, it makes us aware of the limitations of the form of knowledge we seek. At best, it can actively assist in the pursuit of this knowledge.

Let me close where I began, with Greek tragedy. It is a literary tradition that begins with Homer and extends through Aeschylus and Sophocles to Thucydides. It is a more difficult approach to life than *epistēmē*. It is arguably at least as appropriate to the present day than it was to classical Greece. It recognizes the human desire to control the future but also the impossibility of doing this and the possibility that it can lead to unexpected and unwanted outcomes. It teaches us that it is a category error for people to mistake themselves for gods. We must learn to live with uncertainty and its possible negative consequences. Tragedy offers an understanding of life and politics that makes this possible but it takes considerable courage to embrace it.

Tragedy is an alternative to *epistēmē* in a world where human beings cannot effectively fathom causes, predict the future, or shape the world to better suit themselves. In ancient Greece, the *sōphrosunē*, or wisdom that it encouraged, may have bettered one's chances of avoiding tragedy. In today's world, it cannot and should not be a substitute for *epistēmē* but a complement or supplement. A tragic understanding of life offers a different perspective on the world and something of a corrective, or at least a cautionary tale, about the search for *epistēmē* and its consequences. Balancing *sōphrosunē* against *epistēmē* – and *epistēmē* against *phrōnesis* – may prove to be a most valuable and productive tension.

Tragedy is not only a form of knowledge but also a form of ethics. It roots its ethical lessons in its understanding of the world, and its epistemology in its conception of ethics. Goethe, no stranger to tragedies, observed that ultimately everything is ethical and it should be no surprise that this holds true for epistemology in general.[106] In the nineteenth century, there was nevertheless an understandable attempt to separate science and scientific inquiry from ethics. Some came to believe that science could provide the foundation for ethics. Both assumptions were, of course, self-serving delusions. Nietzsche astutely observed that "in the same measure as the sense for causality increases, the extent of the domain of morality decreases."[107] Weber made a similar claim in describing the triumph of science: "precisely the ultimate and most refined values have retreated from public life either into the transcendental realm of mystical life or into the brotherliness of direct and personal relations."[108]

Nietzsche and Weber's concerns are even more germane to our era. They teach us to regard with a jaundiced eye the claims of economics and public choice to be value free enterprises when in fact they furtively introduce efficiency as the benchmark for assessing policies. Social science more generally still believes that "facts" can be separated from values and often looks quite erroneously to Weber for justification of this claim. Tragedy drives home the extent to which facts and values are intertwined as is any search for meaning in the world. This earliest of discourses that probes that concept of reason and cause remains among the most prescient.

Notes

1. Weber, *Protestant Ethics and Spirit of Capitalism*, pp. 177–178.
2. Lebow, *Max Weber and International Relations*, chap. 3.
3. Greenfield, *Nationalism*; Bartelson, *Genealogy of Sovereignty*; Reich and Lebow, *Good-Bye Hegemony!*
4. Strawson, *Secret Connexion*.
5. Knox, *Heroic Temper*, p. 44; Veyne, *Did the Greeks Believe in Their Myths?*
6. Herodotus, *Histories*, 1.29–45 and 1.85–89.
7. Aristotle, *De Anima*, 1.1403a16–b2 and *Rhetoric*, book 2.
8. Lebow "Greeks, Neuroscience and International Relations."
9. Thucydides, *History of the Peloponnesian War*, 1.22.4.
10. Aristotle, *Poetics*, 9.1451.b5–7.
11. Knox, *Oedipus at Thebes*, pp. 23, 60–73, 99–106, 168.
12. Singer, "Level-of-Analysis Problem in International Relations."
13. Smith, *Wealth of Nations*, 4.2.4; Lewes, *Problems of Life and Mind*, vol. 2, p. 412.
14. Janis and Mann, *Decision Making*.
15. Smith, *Wealth of Nations*, 4.3.5.
16. Ibid. Smith favors "order and good government" but is dubious that governments, by their nature corrupt, are likely to do much to support economic development.
17. Mill, *England and Ireland*.
18. Smith, *Wealth of Nations*, 4.7.3.
19. Lebow, "Texts, Paradigms and Political Change."
20. Hume, *Treatise of Human Nature*, 1.1.1.1, 1.1.2.11, 1.4.3 and 6–7.
21. Ross et al., "Social Explanation and Social Expectation"; Tversky and Kahneman, "Extensional versus Intuitive Reason"; Tetlock and Lebow, "Poking Counterfactual Holes in Covering Laws."
22. Hume, *Treatise of Human Nature*, 1.3.10.8.
23. Ibid., 2.3.3.
24. Ibid., 1.3.2.2.
25. Ibid., 11.3.14.31. See also 2.3.1.18, 3.2.6–11.
26. Ibid., 1.3.6.2. 1.3.2.11.

27. Ibid., *Abstract*, 18.
28. Hume, Treatise of Human Nature, 12.23.
29. Ibid., *Abstract*, 4.
30. Hume, *Treatise of Human Nature*, 1.3.12.6–8.
31. Weber, "Objektivität."
32. Ibid., pp. 178–180.
33. For a contemporary version of this approach to causation, see Lebow, *Constructing Cause in International Relations*.
34. Ibid., for a derivative approach.
35. Ibid. and "Conceptual Exposition," p. 20.
36. Weber, "Objektivität"; Jackson, "Production of Facts."
37. Weber, "Conceptual Exposition," pp. 19–20.
38. Ibid., p. 12.
39. Ibid.
40. Weber, "Roscher und Knies."
41. Weber, *Protestant Ethic and the Spirit of Capitalism*, p. 98.
42. Weber, "Objektivität" and "Kritische Studien."
43. Weber, "Kritische Studien."
44. Weber, "Conceptual Exposition," pp. 6–7.
45. Ibid., pp. 9–21.
46. Ibid.; "Kritische Studien."
47. Ibid.
48. Weber, "Nation and Economic Policy."
49. Weber, "Objektivität."
50. Ibid.
51. Reed, *Thomas Mann*, pp. 226–274, for the case of regarding *The Magic Mountain* as a *Bildungsroman*.
52. Mann, *Magic Mountain*, p. 32.
53. On bottom-up and top-down orders, Lebow, *Rise and Fall of Political Orders*, chaps. 1, 9.
54. Haskell, *Emergence of a Professional Social Science*, p. 13.
55. Ibid., pp. 33–36.
56. Ibid.
57. Durkheim, *Division of Labor*, p. 407.
58. Ibid., chaps. 1, 8.
59. Ibid., chap. 1.
60. Ibid.
61. Morgenstern, "Time Moment in Value Theory" and "Perfect Foresight in Economic Equilibrium."
62. Neumann and Morgenstern, *Theory of Games and Economic Behavior*.
63. Lebow, *Politics and Ethics of Identity*, chaps. 1, 8.
64. Jackson, "Production of Facts."
65. Lebow, *Constructing Cause in International Relations*, for a review and evaluation of these approaches to knowledge.
66. Harré and Madden, "Natural Powers and Powerful Natures" and *Causal Powers*; Bhaskar, *Realist Theory of Science*; Cartwright, *Dappled World* and *Hunting Causes and Using Them*.

67. Bhaskar, *Scientific Realism and Human Emancipation*, p. 61.
68. Bhaskar, *Possibility of Naturalism*, pp. 15–16; Chakravartty, *Metaphysics for Scientific Realism*, p. 108.
69. Bhaskar, *Realist Theory of Science*, pp. 46–47.
70. Mumford, "Causal Powers and Capacities."
71. Beebee, "Causation and Observation."
72. Woodward, *Making Things Happen*, p. 357.
73. Wight, "They Shoot Dead Horses Don't They?"; Patomäki, *After International Relations*.
74. Lebow, *Politics and Ethics of Identity*, chap. 6.
75. Hempel, "Logic of Functional Analysis."
76. Cartwright, *Dappled World*, p. 50.
77. Woodward and Hitchcock, "Explanatory Generalizations"; Lebow, *Cultural Theory of International Relations*, chap. 1. Byrne and Uprichard, "Useful Complex Causality," for a more upbeat take.
78. Mackie, *Cement of the Universe*, p. 60.
79. Russell, "On the Notion of Cause."
80. Morrow, *Game Theory for Political Scientists*, p. 17.
81. Popper, *Logic of Scientific Discovery*, pp. 9–10, for the most sophisticated claim of this kind. He accepted that science was not independent of culture in the sense of what it was we sought to know. However, scientific objectivity could be separated from culture as it rested on reason and falsification.
82. Rapoport, *Strategy and Conscience*.
83. Friedman, "Methodology of Positive Economics"; Moe, "On the Scientific Status of Rational Models," for a critique.
84. Wise, *Growing Explanations* for a collection of essays that explores this development in physics, engineering, immunology, and computer science.
85. Wise, "Introduction."
86. Lebow, *Rise and Fall of Political Orders*, chap. 2.
87. Dalmedico, "Chaos, Disorder, and Mixing."
88. Bernstein, *Social Science in the Crucible*, pp. 19–22.
89. Knight, *Risk, Uncertainty, and Profit*, for the distinction between risk and uncertainty. For recent applications to social science, Katzenstein and Seybert, *Protean Power*; Lebow, "Nuclear Luck."
90. Howerth, "Present Conditions of Sociology in the United States"; Ross, *Origins of American Social Science*.
91. Henry Marsh, "Can We Ever Build a Mind?" *Financial Times*, "Weekend," January 12–13, 2019, pp. 1–2.
92. Bernstein, *Restructuring of Social and Political Theory*, p. 52.
93. On bottom-up and top-down orders, Lebow, *Rise and Fall of Political Orders*, chap. 1.
94. Freud, *Civilization and Its Discontents*.
95. Wiebe, *Search for Order*.
96. Cited in Einstein, *Ideas and Opinions*, pp. 322–323.
97. Smith, *Social Science in the Crucible*.
98. Kelsen, *Pure Theory of Law*, first published in 1934.
99. Kuhn, *Structure of Scientific Revolutions*.

100. Waltz, *Theory of International Politics* was published in 1979.
101. Lebow and Risse-Kappen, *International Relations Theory and the End of the Cold War*.
102. Lebow, *Tragic Vision of Politics, Cultural Theory of International Relations*, and *Rise and Fall of Political Orders*.
103. Mahler, *Human Symbiosis and the Vicissitudes of Individuation*, pp. 8–10; Bird and Reese, "Autobiographical Memory in Childhood"; Fivush, Bohanek, and Duke, "Integrated Self."
104. Snow, *Two Cultures*.
105. Lebow, *Rise and Fall of Political Orders*, chaps. 1, 10.
106. Goethe, *Autobiographical Schema of 1810*.
107. Nietzsche, *Daybreak*, p. 12. This is because seemingly successful causal inference destroys a myriad of other imagined possibilities. The real world is smaller than the imaginary and, when any of the imaginary diminishes or disappears, respect for authority and custom diminish or disappear.
108. Weber, *Science as Vocation*.

Bibliography

Abrams, D., G. T. Viki, B. Masser, and G. Bohner, "Perceptions of Stranger and Acquaintance Rape: The Role of Benevolent and Hostile Sexism in Victim Blame and Rape Proclivity," *Journal of Personality and Social Psychology* 84, no. 1 (2003), pp. 111–125.
Ackroyd, Peter, *Wilkie Collins* (London: Vintage Books, 2013).
Afflerbach, Holger, *Falkenhayn: Politisches Denken und Handeln in Kaiserreich* (Munich: Oldenbourg, 1994).
Afflerbach, Holger, and David Stevenson, eds., *An Improbable War: The Outbreak of World War I and European Political Culture Before 1914* (New York: Berghahn Books, 2007).
Allison, June W., "Sthenelaïdas' Speech: Thucydides 1.86," *Hermes* 112, no. 1 (1984), pp. 9–16.
Altick, Richard, *The English Common Reader*, 2nd ed. (Chicago: University of Chicago Press, 1957).
Anger, Suzy, "Naturalizing the Mind in the Victorian Novel: Consciousness in Wilkie Collins's *Poor Miss Finch* and Thomas Hardy's *Woodlanders* – Two Case Studies," in Rodensky, *Oxford Handbook of the Victorian Novel*, pp. 483–506.
Aristotle, *De Anima*, in Jonathan Barnes, ed., *The Complete Works of Aristotle*, 2 vols. (Princeton: Princeton University Press, 1984).
Aristotle, *Economics*, in Barnes, *Complete Works of Aristotle*.
Aristotle, *Nicomachean Ethics*, Barnes, *Complete Works of Aristotle*.
Aristotle, *Politics*, in Barnes, *Complete Works of Aristotle*.
Aristotle, *Rhetoric*, in Barnes, *Complete Works of Aristotle*.
Armstrong, Nancy, *How Novels Think: The Limits of Individualism from 1719–1000* (New York: Columbia, 2005).
Atherton, Carol, *Defining Literary Criticism: Scholarship, Authority, and the Possession of Literary Knowledge, 1880–2002* (Houndsmills: Palgrave Macmillan, 2005).
Augustine, *The City of God*, trans. Marcus Dods (New York: Modern Library, 1950).
Austen, Jane, *Emma* in *The Complete Novels of Jane Austen* (New York: Race Point, 2012).
Austen, Jane, *Pride and Prejudice* in *The Complete Novels of Jane Austen* (New York: Race Point, 2012).
Axelrod, Robert M., *The Evolution of Cooperation* (New York: Basic Books, 1984).

Bakhtin, Mikhail, "Forms of Time and the Chronotope in the Novel," in Caryl Emerson and Michael Holquist, eds. and trans. *The Dialogic Imagination* (Austin: University of Texas Press, 1981).
Bakker, Egbert J., "Verbal Aspects and Mimetic Description in Thucydides," in Egbert J. Bakker, ed., *Grammar as Interpretation: Greek Literature in Its Linguistic Contexts* (Leiden: Brill, 1997), pp. 7–53.
Balot, Ryan K., Sara Forsdyke, and Edith Foster, eds., *The Oxford Handbook of Thucydides* (Oxford: Oxford University Press, 2017).
Bartelson, Jens, *A Genealogy of Sovereignty* (Cambridge: Cambridge University Press, 1995).
Baxter, Donald L. M., "Hume on Space and Time," in Russell, *Oxford Handbook of Hume*, pp. 173–190.
Baxter, Donald L. M., "Hume's Theory of Space and Time in Its Skeptical Content," in Norton and Taylor, *Cambridge Companion to Hume*, pp. 105–146.
Bayle, Pierre, *Dictionary*, ed. Pierre Desmaizeaux, 2nd ed., 5 vols. (New York: Garland Press, 1984).
Beauchamp, Tom L., "Editor's Introduction," in Hume, *An Enquiry Concerning Human Understanding*, pp. 7–82.
Beebee, Helen, "Causation and Observation," in Beebee, Hitchcock, and Menzies, *Oxford Handbook of Causation*, pp. 471–497.
Beebee, Helen, "Hume and the Problem of Causation," in Russell, *Oxford Handbook of Hume*, pp. 228–247.
Beebee, Helen, *Hume on Causation* (Abingdon: Routledge, 2006).
Beebee, Helen, Christopher Hitchcock, and Peter Menzies, eds., *The Oxford Handbook of Causation* (Oxford: Oxford University Press, 2009).
Beiser, Frederick C., *The German Historicist Tradition* (Oxford: Oxford University Press, 2012).
Bell, Duncan, "Writing the World: Disciplinary History and Beyond," *International Affairs* 85, no. 1 (2009), pp. 3–22.
Bell, Martin, "Hume on Causation," in Norton and Taylor, *Cambridge Companion to Hume*, pp. 147–176.
Bell, S. T., P. J. Kuriloff, and I. Lottes, "Understanding Attributions of Blame in Stranger-Rape and Date-Rape Situations: An Examinations of Gender, Race, Identification, and Students' Social Perceptions of Rape Victims," *Journal of Applied Social Psychology* 24, no. 19 (1994), pp. 1719–1734.
Ben-Yishai, Alelet, "The Fact of a Rumour: Anthony Trollope's *The Eustace Diamonds*," *Nineteenth Century Literature* 62, no. 1 (2007), pp. 88–120.
Ben-Yishai, Alelet, "Trollope and the Law," in Dever and Niles, *Anthony Trollope*, pp. 155–167.
Berg, Stephen and Diskin Clay, "Introduction," in Burian and Shapiro, *Complete Plays of Sophocles*, vol. 1, pp. 193–210.
Bernstein, Richard, *The Restructuring of Social and Political Theory* (New York: Harcourt Brace Jovanovich, 1976).
Bhaskar, Roy, *The Possibility of Naturalism: A Philosophical Critique of Contemporary Human Sciences* (Brighton: Harvester Press, 1979).
Bhaskar, Roy, *A Realist Theory of Science* (Leeds: Leeds Books, 1975).

Bhaskar, Roy, *Scientific Realism and Human Emancipation* (London: Routledge, 2009).
Bird, Amy and Elaine Reese, "Autobiographical Memory in Childhood and the Development of a Continuous Self," in Sani, *Self Continuity*, pp. 43–54.
Bismarck, Otto von, "Speech of 9 February 1876," in *Gesammelte Werke*, vol. 11. (Berlin: Stollberg, 1925).
Borg, Dorothy and Shumpei Okamoto, eds., *Pearl Harbor as History: Japanese-American Relations, 1931–1941* (New York: Columbia University Press, 1973).
Brantlinger, Patrick, *The Reading Lesson: The Threat of Mass Literacy in Nineteenth-Century British Fiction* (Bloomington: Indiana University Press, 1998).
Bratlinger, Patrick, *The Spirit of Reform* (Cambridge, MA: Harvard University Press, 1977).
Breslauer, George and Richard Ned Lebow, "Leadership and the End of the Cold War: A Counterfactual Thought Experiment," in Herrmann and Lebow, *Ending the Cold War*, pp. 161–188.
Brod, Max, *Franz Kafka: A Biography* (New York: Schocken Books, 1960).
Browning, Robert, "Greek Abstract Nouns in *-sis, -tis*," *Philologus* 102 (1958), pp. 60–74.
Brubacker, Rogers, *The Limits of Rationality: An Essay on the Social and Moral Thought of Max Weber* (London: Routledge, 1991 [1984]).
Bruner, Jerome, "Life as Narrative," *Social Research* 54 (1987), pp. 11–32.
Brunt, Peter A., "Spartan Policy and Strategy in the Archidamian War," *Phoenix* 19 (Winter 1965), pp. 255–256.
Burger, J. M., "Motivational Biases in the Attribution of Responsibility for an Accident: A Meta-Analysis of the Defensive-Attribution Hypothesis," *Psychological Bulletin* 90, no. 3 (1981), pp. 496–512.
Burian, Peter and Alan, Shapiro, *Complete Plays of Sophocles*, 2 vols. (Oxford: Oxford University Press, 2009–2010).
Burian, Peter and Alan, Shapiro, "Foreword," in Burian and Shapiro, *Complete Plays of Sophocles*, vol. 1, pp. 5–38.
Burn, William L., *The Age of Equipoise* (New York: Norton, 1964).
Burton, John Hill, *Life and Correspondence of Hume*, vol. 1 (Edinburgh: William Tait, 1846).
Butow, Robert, *Tojo and the Coming of the War* (Stanford: Stanford University, 1961).
Byrne, David and Emma Uprichard, "Useful Complex Causality," in Harold Kincaid, ed., *The Oxford Handbook of Social Science* (Oxford: Oxford University Press, 2012), pp. 109–129.
Carlisle, Janice, "Novels of the 1860s," in Rodensky, *Oxford Handbook of the Victorian Novel*, pp. 337–356.
Cartledge, Paul, Paul Millett, and Stephen Tod, *Nomos: Essays in Athenian Law, Politics and Society* (Cambridge: Cambridge University Press, 1990).
Cartwright, Nancy, *The Dappled World* (Cambridge: Cambridge University Press, 1999).
Cartwright, Nancy, *Hunting Causes and Using Them: Approaches in Philosophy and Economics* (Cambridge: Cambridge University Press, 2007).
Cassin, Barbara, *L'effet Sophistique* (Paris: Gallimard, 1995).

Cederman, Lars-Erik, *Emergent Actors in World Politics: How States and Nations Develop and Dissolve* (Princeton: Princeton University Press, 1997).
Chakravartty, Anjan, *A Metaphysics for Scientific Realism: Knowing the Unobservable* (Cambridge: Cambridge University Press, 2007).
Clark, Christopher, *The Sleepwalkers* (London: Allen Lane, 2013).
Clarke, John, *Language and Style of Anthony Trollope* (London: André Deutsch, 1975).
Clausewitz, Carl von, *On War*, ed. and trans. Michael Howard and Peter Paret (Princeton: Princeton University Press, 1976).
Cobden, Richard, *England, Ireland and America*, ed. Richard Ned Lebow (Philadelphia: Institute for the Study of Human Issues, 1980).
Cockburn, Peter, *The Occupation: War and Resistance in Iraq* (London: Verso, 2007).
Cohen, Dorrit, "Telling Timelessness in *Der Zauberberg*," in Vaget, *Thomas Mann's* Magic Mountain, pp. 201–218.
Cohen, William A., "Trollope's Palliser Novels," in Dever and Niles, *Anthony Trollope*, pp. 44–57.
Collins, Philip, *Dickens and Crime* (London: Palgrave Macmillan, 1962).
Collins, Wilkie, *Armandale* (London: Penguin, 1995).
Collins, Wilkie, *The Frozen Deep* (London: Hesperus Classics, 2004).
Collins, Wilkie, *The Moonstone* (London: Penguin, 1998).
Collins, Wilkie, *The Woman in White* (Oxford: Oxford University Press, 1996).
Colón, Susan, *The Professional Ideal in the Victorian Novel: The Works of Disraeli, Trollope, Gaskell, and Eliot* (Basingstoke: Palgrave, 2007).
Connor, W. Robert, "Scale Matters," in Balot, Forsdyke, and Foster, *Oxford Handbook of Thucydides*, pp. 211–224.
Connor, W. Robert, *Thucydides* (Princeton: Princeton University Press, 1984).
Crane, Gregory, *Thucydides and the Ancient Simplicity* (Berkeley: University of California Press, 1998).
Dahlmann, Dittmar, "Max Weber's Relation to Anarchism and Anarchists: The Case of Ernst Toller," in Mommsen and Osterhammel, *Max Weber and His Contemporaries*, pp. 367–381.
Dalmedico, Amy Dahan, "Chaos, Disorder, and Mixing: A New Fin-de-Siècle Image of Science," in Wise, *Growing Explanations*, pp. 67–94.
Danto, Arthur C., *Narration and Knowledge* (New York: Columbia University Press, 1985).
Daston, Lorraine and Peter Galison, *Objectivity* (New York: Zone Books, 2007).
De Bakker, Mathieu, "Authorial Comments in Thucydides," in Balot, Forsdyke, and Foster, *Oxford Handbook of Thucydides*, pp. 239–256.
de Romilly, Jacqueline, *Les grands sophistes dans l'Athènes de Périclès* (Paris: Éditions de Fallois, 1988).
de Romilly, Jacqueline, *The Mind of Thucydides*, trans. Elizabeth Rawlings (Ithaca, NY: Cornell University Press, 2012 [1956]).
Delany, Paul, *Literature, Money and the Market: From Trollope to Amis* (Houndsmills: Palgrave Macmillan, 2002).
Dennett, Daniel, *Consciousness Explained* (Boston: Little, Brown, 1991).
Descartes, René, *Meditations on First Philosophy*, trans. J. Cottingham (Cambridge: Cambridge University Press, 1996 [1641]).

Détienne, Marcel, *The Masters of Truth in Archaic Greece*, trans. Janet Lloyd (Cambridge, MA: Zone Books, 1996).
Deutsch, Karl W. and J. David Singer, "Multipolar Power Systems and International Stability," *World Politics* 16 (1964), pp. 390–406.
Dever, Carolyn and Lisa Niles, eds., *Anthony Trollope* (Cambridge: Cambridge University Press, 2011).
Dicey, A. V., *Lectures on the Relation between Law and Public Opinion during the Nineteenth Century* (London: Macmillan, 1905).
Dickens, Charles, *Bleak House* (Oxford: Oxford University Press, 2008).
Dickens, Charles, *Hard Times for These Times* (Oxford: Oxford University Press, 1998).
Dicker, Georges, "Hume on the External World," in Russell, *Oxford Handbook of Hume*, pp. 249–268.
Diogenes Laertius, *Lives of Eminent Philosophers*, trans. Pamela Mensch (Oxford: Oxford University Press, 2018).
Dodds, E. R., *The Greeks and the Irrational* (Berkeley and Los Angeles: University of California Press, 1951).
Dolin, Kieran, *A Critical Introduction to Law and Literature* (Cambridge: Cambridge University Press, 2007).
Dover, K. J., "Appendix 2," in A. W. Gomme, A. Andrews, and K. J. Dover, *Historical Commentary on Thucydides*, 10 vols. (Oxford: Oxford University Press, 1945–1981), vol. 5.
Duncan, Ian, "*The Moonstone*, the Victorian Novel and Imperialist Panic," *Modern Language Quarterly* 55 (1994), pp. 297–319.
Duncan, Ian, *Scott's Shadow: The Novel in Romantic Edinburgh* (Princeton: Princeton University Press, 2007).
Durkheim, Émile, *The Division of Labor in Society*, trans. W. D. Halls (New York: Macmillan, 1984 [1893]).
Durkheim, Émile, *Rules of Sociological Method*, trans. W. D. Halls (New York: Free Press, 1982).
Eakin, Paul John, *How Our Lives Become Stories* (Ithaca, NY: Cornell University Press, 1999).
Eco, Umberto with Richard Rorty, Jonathan Culler, and Christine Brooke-Rose, *Interpretation and Overinterpretation* (New York: Cambridge University Press, 1992).
Ehrenberg, Victor, *Sophocles and Pericles* (Oxford: Oxford University Press, 1954).
Einstein, Albert, *Ideas and Opinions*, trans. Sonja Bargmann (New York: Bonanza Books, 1954).
Eliot, George, *The Essays of George Eliot*, ed. Thomas Pinney (London: Routledge, 1963).
Eliot, George, *Middlemarch* (London: Penguin, 2003).
Elster, Jon, *Cement of Society* (New York: Cambridge University Press, 2010).
Elster, Jon, *Political Psychology* (New York: Cambridge University Press, 1993).
Engels, Friedrich, *The Condition of the Working Class in England* (Oxford: Oxford University Press, 2009 [1845]).

Epstein, Joshua M. and Robert Axtell, *Growing Artificial Societies: Social Science from the Bottom Up* (Washington, DC: The Brookings Institution Press, 1996).

Euben, J. Peter, "Creatures of a Day: Thought and Action in Thucydides," in Terence Ball, ed., *Political Theory and Praxis: New Perspectives* (Minneapolis: University of Minnesota Press, 1977), pp. 28–56.

Evans-Pritchard, E. E., "Witchcraft," *Africa* 8, no. 4 (1955), pp. 418–419.

Fallows, James, *Blind into Baghdad: America's War in Iraq* (New York: Vintage, 2006).

Farrar, Lancelot L. Jr., *The Short-War Illusion: German Policy, Strategy and Domestic Affairs, August-December 1914* (Santa Barbara, CA: ABC-Clio, 1973).

Fearon, James, "Causes and Counterfactuals in Social Science: Exploring an Analogy between Cellular Automata and Historical Processes," in Tetlock and Belkin, *Counterfactual Thought Experiments in World Politics*, pp. 39–68.

Finley, Moses I., *The World of Odysseus*, 2nd ed. (New York: Viking Press, 1977).

Fischer, Fritz, *War of Illusions: German Policies from 1911 to 1914*, trans. Marian Jackson (New York: Norton, 1975).

Fisher, Mark and Kinch Hoekstra, "Thucydides and the Politics of Necessity," in Balot, Forsdyke, and Foster, *Oxford Handbook of Thucydides*, pp. 372–390.

Fivush, Robyn, Jennifer G. Bohanek and Marshall Duke, "The Integrated Self: Subjective Perspective and Family History," in Sani, *Self Continuity*, pp. 131–144.

Forde, Steven, *Ambition to Rule: Alcibiades and the Politics of Imperialism in Thucydides* (Ithaca, NY: Cornell University Press, 1989).

Forrest, W. G., *A History of Sparta, 1950–192 B.C.* (New York: Norton, 1968).

Forsdyke, Sara, "Thucydides Historical Method," in Balot, Forsdyke, and Foster, *Oxford Handbook of Thucydides*, pp. 19–38.

Fowler, Robert, ed., *The Cambridge Companion to Homer* (Cambridge: Cambridge University Press, 2004).

Fowler, Robert "The Homeric Question," in Fowler, *Cambridge Companion to Homer*, pp. 220–234.

Frank, Catherine, *Law, Literature, and the Transmission of Culture in England, 1837–1925* (Farnham: Ashgate, 2010).

Freud, Sigmund, *Civilization and Its Discontents*, trans. Joan Riviere (Garden City, NY: Doubleday, 1958).

Freud, Sigmund, "Dostoevsky and Parricide," trans. D. F. Tait., in Neil Hertz, ed., *Writings on Art and Literature* (Stanford: Stanford University Press, 1997), pp. 234–255.

Friedman, Milton J., "The Methodology of Positive Economics," in Milton J. Friedman, *Essays in Positive Economics* (Chicago: University of Chicago Press, 1953), pp. 3–43.

Frisby, David "The Ambiguity of Modernity: Georg Simmel and Max Weber," in Mommsen and Osterhammel, *Max Weber and His Contemporaries*, pp. 422–433.

Fudge, Erica, *Brutal Reasoning: Animals, Rationality, and Humanity in Early Modern England* (Ithaca, NY: Cornell University Press, 2019).

Galbraith, Peter W., *The End of Iraq: How American Incompetence Created a War without End* (New York: Pocket Books, 2007).
Galison, Peter, *Einstein's Clocks, Poincaré's Maps* (New York: Norton, 2003).
Gallagher, Catherine, *The Industrial Reformation of English Fiction, 1832–1867* (Chicago: University of Chicago Press, 1985).
Garrett, Don, "Reason, Normativity, and Hume's 'Title Principle'," in Russell, *Oxford Handbook to Hume*, pp. 32–53.
Garst, Daniel, "Thucydides and Neorealism," *International Studies Quarterly* 33, no. 1 (1989), pp. 469–97.
Garthoff, Ramond L., *Détente and Confrontation: American-Soviet Relations from Nixon to Reagan* (Washington, DC: Brookings, 1965).
Gaskin, J. C. A., "Hume on Religion," in Norton and Taylor, *Cambridge Companion to Hume*, pp. 480–514.
Geertz, Clifford, *Local Knowledge* (New York: Basic Books, 1983).
George, Alexander and Juliette George, *Woodrow Wilson and Colonel House* (New York, Dover Publications, 1964).
Gerth, H. H. and C. Wright Mills, *From Max Weber* (New York: Oxford University Press, 1958).
Gettelman, Debra, "The Early Victorian Novel and Its Readers," in Rodensky, *Oxford Handbook of the Victorian Novel*, pp. 111–128.
Gilbert, D. T. and P. S. Malone, "The Correspondence Bias," *Psychological Bulletin* 117, no. 1 (1995), pp. 21–38.
Gilpin, Robert, *War and Change in World Politics* (Cambridge: Cambridge University Press, 1981).
Goethe, Johann Wolfgang von, *Aus meinem Leben: Dichtung und Wahrheit*, 3 vols. (Stuttgart and Tübingen: Cotta, 1811–1814).
Golden, Herbert and Richard Pevear, "Introduction," in Burian and Shapiro, *Complete Plays of Sophocles*, vol. 2, pp. 3–22.
Goldstein, Jeffrey, "Emergence as a Construct: History and Issues," *Emergence: Complexity and Organization* 1, no. 1 (2001), pp. 49–72.
Gomme, A. W., *The Greek Attitude to Poetry and History* (Berkeley: University of California Press, 1954).
Goodwin, Brain, *How the Leopard Changed Its Spots: The Evolution of Complexity* (Princeton: Princeton University Press, 2001).
Graham, A. J., *Colony and Mother City in Ancient Greece*, 2nd ed. (Chicago: Ares Publishers, 1983).
Greenfield, Liah, *Nationalism* (Cambridge, MA: Harvard University Press, 1992).
Greenwood, Emily, "Thucydides and the Sicilian Expedition," in Balot, Forsdyke, and Foster, *Oxford Handbook of Thucydides*, pp. 160–178.
Greiner, Rae, "The Victorian Subject: Thackeray's Wartime Subjects," in John, *Oxford Handbook of Victorian Literary Culture*, pp. 27–44.
Grene, David, "To the Readers," *The Peloponnesian War: The Complete Hobbes Translation*, ed. David Greene (Chicago: University of Chicago Press, 1989), pp. i–xx.
Grennan, Eamon and Rachel Kitzinger, "Introduction," in Burian and Shapiro, *Complete Plays of Sophocles*, vol. 1, pp. 303–322.

Grenville, Anthony, "'Linke Leute von rechts': Thomas Mann's Naphta and the Ideological Confluence of Radical Right and Radical Left in the Early Years of the Weimar Republic," in Vaget, *Thomas Mann's Magic Mountain*, pp. 143–170.

Grethlein, Jonas, *Experience and Teleology in Ancient Greek Historiography: "Futures Past" from Herodotus to Augustine* (Cambridge: Cambridge University Press, 2013).

Grethlein, Jonas, *Greeks and Their Past: Poetry, Oratory, and History in the Fifth Century BCE* (Cambridge: Cambridge University Press, 2010).

Griffiths, Thomas L., David M. Sobel, Joshua B. Tenenbaum, and Alison Gopnik, "Bayes and Blickets: Effects of Knowledge on Causal Induction in Children and Adults," *Cognitive Science* 35, no. 8 (2011), pp. 1407–1455.

Grossman, Jonathan H., *The Art of Alibi: English Law Courts and the Novel* (Baltimore, MD: Johns Hopkins University Press, 2002).

Guthrie, W. K. C., *The Sophists* (Cambridge: Cambridge University Press, 1971).

Guy, Josephine, "Politics and the Literary," in John, *Oxford Handbook of Victorian Literary Culture*, pp. 65–82.

Guzzini, Stefano, "Max Weber's Power," in Lebow, *Max Weber and International Relations*, pp. 97–118.

Haakonssen, Knud, "The Structure of Hume's Political Theory," in Norton and Taylor, *Cambridge Companion to Hume*, pp. 341–380.

Hacking, Ian, *The Emergence of Probability: A Philosophical Study of Early Ideas about Probability Induction and Statistical Inference* (Cambridge: Cambridge University Press, 2006).

Hacking, Ian, *Rewriting the Soul: Multiple Personality and the Sciences of Memory* (Princeton: Princeton University Press, 1995).

Halperin, John, *Trollope and Politics: A Study of the Pallisers and Others* (London: Macmillan, 1977).

Hammond, Mary, *Reading, Publishing, and the Formation of Literary Taste in England* (Aldershot: Ashgate, 2006).

Hanson, Victor David, "Themistocles at Salamis," in Tetlock, Lebow, and Parker, *Unmaking the West*, pp. 47–89.

Harré, Rom, *The Principles of Scientific Thinking* (London: Macmillan, 1970).

Harré, Rom and E. H. Madden, *Causal Powers* (Oxford: Oxford University Press, 1975).

Harré, Rom and E. H. Madden, "Natural Powers and Powerful Natures," *Philosophy* 48 (1973), pp. 209–230.

Harris, James A., *Hume: An Intellectual Biography* (Cambridge: Cambridge University Press, 2015).

Harvey, Frank, *Explaining the Iraq War: Counterfactual Theory, Logic and Evidence* (Cambridge: Cambridge University Press, 2011).

Haskell, Thomas L., *The Emergence of Professional Social Science: The American Social Science Association and the Nineteenth-Century Crisis of Authority* (Baltimore, MD: Johns Hopkins University Press, 2000 [1977]).

Hays, Samuel P., *The Response to Industrialization: 1885–1914* (Chicago: University of Chicago Press, 1957).

Hegel, Georg Wilhelm Friedrich, *Hegel on Tragedy*, eds. Anne Paolucci and Henry Paolucci (Westport, CT: Greenwood Press, 1962).

Hegel, Georg Wilhelm Friedrich, *Lectures on the Philosophy of World History*, trans. H. B. Nisbet (Cambridge: Cambridge University Press, 1975).
Heinemann, Felix, *Nomos und Physis* (Darmstadt: Wissenschaftliche Buchgesellschaft, 1965).
Hempel, Carl G., "Logic of Functional Analysis," in Carl G. Hempel, *Aspects of Scientific Explanation* (New York: Free Press, 1965), pp. 297–330.
Heralitus, Fragment 119, in Hermann Diels and Walther Kranz, eds., *Die Fragmente der Vorsokratiker, Griechisch und Deutsch* (Berlin: Weidmann, 1951–1952).
Herodotus, *The Histories*, trans. George Rawlinson (New York: Knopf, 1997).
Herrmann, Richard K. and Richard Ned Lebow, eds., *Ending the Cold War* (New York: Palgrave Macmillan, 2003).
Herwig, Holger H., "Clio Deceived: Patriotic Self-Censorship in Germany after the Great War," *International Security* 12 (Fall 1987), pp. 5–44.
Herwig, Holger H., *The First World War: Germany and Austria-Hungary, 1914–1918* (London: Arnold, 1998).
Holland, John H., *Emergence: From Chaos to Order* (New York: Basic Books, 1998).
Hoopes, Townsend, *The Limits of Intervention: An Inside Account of How the Johnson Policy of Escalation Was Reversed* (New York: David McKay, 1969).
Hopf, Ted, *Deterrence Theory and American Foreign Policy in the Third World, 1965–1990* (Ann Arbor: University of Michigan Press, 1994).
Hoppen, K. Theodore, *Mid-Victorian Generation, 1846–1886* (Oxford: Oxford University Press, 1998).
Hornblower, Simon, "The Religious Dimension to the Peloponnesian War, or, What Thucydides Does Not Tell Us," *Harvard Studies in Classical Philology*, 94 (1992), pp. 169–197.
Hornblower, Simon and Charles Stewart, "No History without Culture," *Anthropological Quarterly* 78, no. 1 (2005), pp. 269–277.
Horowitz, Evan, "Industrialism and the Victorian Novel," in Rodensky, *Oxford Handbook of the Victorian Novel*, pp. 357–375.
Hosoya, Chihiro, "Miscalculation in Deterrence Policy: Japanese-U.S. Relations, 1938–194," *Journal of Peace Research* 2 (1968), pp. 79–115.
Howerth, Ira W., "Present Conditions of Sociology in the United States," AAA PSS5 (1984), pp. 260–269, cited in Dorothy Ross, *The Origins of American Social Science* (Cambridge: Cambridge University Press, 1991), p. 131.
Hughes, H. Stuart, *Consciousness and Society: The Reorientation of European Social Thought, 1890–1930* (New York: Knopf, 1958).
Hume, David, *An Abstract of a Book Lately Published: Entitled, A Treatise of Human Nature* (Oxford: Oxford University Press, 2005 [1740]).
Hume, David, *An Enquiry Concerning Human Understanding*, ed. Tom L. Beauchamp (Oxford: Oxford University Press, 1999).
Hume, David, *An Enquiry Concerning the Principles of Morals*, ed. Tom Beauchamp (Oxford: Oxford University Press, 1998).
Hume, David, *Enquiries Concerning Human Understanding and Concerning the Principles of Morals*, ed. P. H. Nidditch (Oxford: Oxford University Press, 1975).

Hume, David, *The History of England: From Charles I to Cromwell*, vol. 1 (Philadelphia: Lippincott, 1901).
Hume, David, "A Kind of History of My Life," in Norton and Taylor, *Cambridge Companion to Hume*, pp. 515–521.
Hume, David, "My Own Life," in Norton and Taylor, *Cambridge Companion to Hume*, pp. 522–530.
Hume, David, "Of Civil Liberty," in Hume, *Essays, Moral, Political, and Literary*, ed. Eugene Miller, rev. ed. (Indianapolis: Liberty Fund, 1994), pp. 87–96.
Hume, David, "Of the Association of Ideas," in Hume, *An Inquiry Concerning Human Understanding*, ed. Charles W. Hendel (Indianapolis: Bobbs-Merrill, 1955), section iii.
Hume, David, "Of the Balance of Power," in Hume, *Political Essays*, pp. 154–160.
Hume, David, "Of the Rise and Progress of the Arts and Sciences," in Hume, *Political Essays*, pp. 58–77.
Hume, David, "Of Some Remarkable Customs," in Hume, *Political Essays*, pp. 179–185.
Hume, David, *On the Immortality of the Soul* (Adelaide: University of Adelaide, 2015), https://ebooks.adelaide.edu.au/h/hume/david/of-the-immortality-of-the-soul/.
Hume, David, "On the Study of History," in Eugene F. Miller, ed. *Essays: Moral, Political, and Literary* (Indianapolis: Liberty Classics, 1885), pp. 563–568.
Hume, David, *Political Essays*, ed. Knud Haakonsen (Cambridge: Cambridge University Press, 1994).
Hume, David, *A Treatise of Human Nature*, eds. David Fate Norton and Mary J. Norton (Oxford: Oxford University Press, 2000).
Hume, David, *A Treatise of Human Nature*, ed. P. H. Nidditch, rev. 2nd ed. (Oxford: Oxford University Press, 1978).
Ienaga, Saburo, *The Pacific War, 1931–1945* (New York: Pantheon, 1978).
Ike, Nobutaka, ed. and trans., *Japan's Decision for War: Records of the 1941 Policy Conferences* (Stanford: Stanford University Press, 1967)
Ikenberry, G. John, *Liberal Order and Imperial Ambition* (Cambridge: Polity, 2006).
Inkster, Ian, Colin Griffin, Jeff Hill, and Judith Rowbotham, eds., *The Golden Age: Essays in British Social and Economic History, 1850–1870* (Burlington: Ashgate, 2000).
Iriye, Akira, "The Failure of Military Expansionism," in James William Morley, ed., *Dilemmas of Growth in Prewar Japan* (Princeton: Princeton University Press, 2015), pp. 107–138.
Iriye, Akira, *The Origins of the Second World War in Asia and the Pacific* (New York: Longman, 1987).
Iser, Wolfgang, *The Implied Reader* (Baltimore, MD: Johns Hopkins University Press, 1974).
Jackson, Patrick Thaddeus, "The Production of Facts: Ideal-Typification and the Preservation of Politics," in Lebow, *Max Weber and International Relations*, pp. 79–96.
Janis, Irving L. and Leon Mann, *Decision Making: A Psychological Analysis of Conflict, Choice, and Commitment* (New York: Free Press, 1977).

Jervis, Robert, *Perception and Misperception in International Relations*, rev. ed. (Princeton: Princeton University Press, 2017).
Jervis, Robert, *System Effects: Complexity in Political and Social Life* (Princeton: Princeton University Press, 1997).
Jervis, Robert, Richard Ned Lebow, and Janice Gross Stein, *Psychology and Deterrence* (Baltimore, MD: Johns Hopkins University Press, 1984).
John, Juliet, "Introduction," in John, *Oxford Handbook of Victorian Literary Culture*, pp. 1–26.
John, Juliet, ed., *The Oxford Handbook of Victorian Literary Culture* (Oxford: Oxford University Press, 2016).
Joho, Tobias, "Thucydides, Epic, and Tragedy," in Balot, Forsdyke, and Foster, *Oxford Handbook of Thucydides*, pp. 587–604.
Jones, Aled, *Powers of the Press: Newspaper, Power, and the Public in Nineteenth-Century England* (Aldershot: Scolar Press, 1996).
Jones, Edward E, and Victor A. Harris, "The Attribution of Attitudes," *Journal of Experimental Social Psychology* 3, no. 1 (1967), pp. 1–24.
Jones, Peter, "Hume on the Arts and 'The Standard of Taste': Texts and Contents," in Norton and Taylor, *Cambridge Companion to Hume*, pp. 414–446.
Kafka, Franz, "Before the Law," in Kafka, *Complete Stories*, p. 3.
Kafka, Franz, *The Castle*, trans. Mark Harnan (New York: Schocken Books, 1998).
Kafka, Franz, *The Complete Stories* (New York: Schocken Books, 1972).
Kafka, Franz, *Diaries 1910–1923* (New York: Schocken Books, 1988).
Kafka, Franz, "The Great Wall of China," in Kafka, *Complete Stories*, pp. 235–247.
Kafka, Franz, "The Judgment," in Kafka, *Complete Stories*, pp. 77–88.
Kafka, Franz, "The Metamorphosis," in Kafka, *Complete Stories*, pp. 89–139.
Kafka, Franz, *The Trial*, trans. Breon Mitchell (New York: Schocken Books, 1998).
Kagan, Donald, *Outbreak of the Peloponnesian War* (Ithaca, NY: Cornell University Press, 1969).
Kahneman, Daniel, Paul Slovic, and Amos Tversky, eds., *Judgment under Uncertainty: Heuristics and Biases* (Cambridge: Cambridge University Press, 1982).
Kalberg, Stephen, "Max Weber's Types of Rationality: Cornerstones for the Analysis of Rationalization Processes in History," *American Journal of Sociology* 85, no. 5 (1980), pp. 1145–1179.
Kallet, Lisa, "The Pentecontaetia," in Balot, Forsdyke, and Foster, *Oxford Handbook of Thucydides*, pp. 63–80.
Kant, Immanuel, *Anthropology from a Pragmatic Point of View*, ed. Robert Louden (Cambridge: Cambridge University Press, 2006).
Kant, Immanuel, *Critique of Pure Reason. Critique of Pure Reason*, ed. Paul Guyer and Allen W. Wood (Cambridge: Cambridge University Press, 1996).
Kant, Immanuel, *Kant's Political Writings*, 2nd ed., ed. Hans Reiss, trans. H. B. Nisbet (Cambridge: Cambridge University Press, 1991).
Kant, Immanuel, "Perpetual Peace," in Reiss, *Kant: Political Writings*, pp. 41–53.

Katzenstein, Peter J. and Lucia Seybert, *Protean Power: Exploring the Uncertain and Unexpected in World Politics* (Cambridge: Cambridge University Press, 2018).
Kearns, Emily, "The Gods in Homeric Epics," in Fowler, *Cambridge Companion to Homer*, pp. 59–73.
Kelsen, Hans, *Pure Theory of Law* (Berkeley: University of California Press, 1967).
Kerferd, George B., *The Sophistic Movement* (Cambridge: Cambridge University Press, 1981).
Kern, Stephen, *A Cultural History of Causality: Science, Murder Novels, and Systems of Thought* (Princeton: Princeton University Press, 2012).
Kestner, Joseph, *Protest and Reform* (London: Methuen, 1985).
Knies, Karl, *Die Statistik als selbständige Wissenschaft* (Kassel: J. Luckhardt, 1850).
Knight, Frank, *Risk, Uncertainty, and Profit* (New York: Houghton Mifflin, 1921).
Knox, Bernard, *The Heroic Temper: Studies in Sophoclean Tragedy* (Berkeley and Los Angeles: University of California Press, 1964).
Knox, Bernard, "Introduction" to Homer, *The Iliad*, trans. Robert Fagles (New York: Viking Penguin, 1990), pp. 3–64.
Knox, Bernard, *Oedipus at Thebes: Sophocles' Tragic Hero and His Time* (New Haven, CT: Yale University Press, 1998 [1957]).
Koelb, Clayton, *Kafka: A Guide for the Perplexed* (Chippenham: Continuum International, 2010).
Konstan, David, *The Emotions of the Ancient Greeks: Studies in Aristotle and Classical Literature* (Toronto: University of Toronto Press, 2006).
Konstan, David, *Friendship in the Classical World* (Cambridge: Cambridge University Press, 1997).
Konstan, David, "*Philia* in Euripides' *Electra*," *Philologos* 129 (1985), pp. 176–185.
Konstan, David, *Pity Transformed* (London: Duckworth, 2004).
Konstan, David and N. Keith Rutter, *Envy, Spite and Jealousy: The Rivalrous Emotions in Ancient Greece* (Edinburg: Edinburgh University Press, 2003).
Kratochwil, Friedrich V., "Evidence, Inference, and Truth as Problems of Theory Building in the Social Sciences," in Richard Ned Lebow and Marc Irving Lichbach, eds., *Theory and Evidence in Comparative Politics and International* (New York: Palgrave Macmillan, 2007), pp. 25–54.
Kratochwil, Friedrich V., *International Order and Foreign Policy: A Theoretical Sketch of Post-War International Politics* (Boulder, CO: Westview, 1978).
Kronenbitter, Günther, *Krieg im Frieden: die Führung der k.u.k. Armee und die Grossmachtpolitik Österreich-Ungarns 1906–1914* (Munich: Oldenbourg, 2003).
Kuhn, Thomas S., *The Structure of Scientific Revolutions* (Chicago: University of Chicago Press, 1962).
Langbein, John, *Origins of Adversary Criminal Trial* (Oxford: Oxford University Press, 2003).
Lansbury, Coral, *The Reasonable Man: Trollope's Legal Fiction* (Princeton: Princeton University Press, 2014).
Lassman, Peter and Ronald Speirs, *Weber: Political Writings* (Cambridge: Cambridge University Press, 1994).
Leavis, F. R., *The Great Tradition: George Eliot, Henry James, Joseph Conrad* (London: Faber, 2008 [1948]).

Lebow, Richard Ned, *Avoiding War, Making Peace* (London: Palgrave Macmillan 2017).
Lebow, Richard Ned, *Between Peace and War: The Nature of International Crisis* (Baltimore, MD: Johns Hopkins University Press, 1981).
Lebow, Richard Ned, "Beyond Parsimony: Rethinking Theories of Coercive Bargaining," *European Journal of International Relations* 4, no. 1 (1998), pp. 31–66.
Lebow, Richard Ned, *Constructing Cause in International Relations* (Cambridge: Cambridge University Press, 2014).
Lebow, Richard Ned, "Contingency, Catalysts and International System Change," *Political Science Quarterly* 115 (2000–2001), pp. 591–616.
Lebow, Richard Ned, *A Cultural Theory of International Relations* (Cambridge: Cambridge University Press, 2008).
Lebow, Richard Ned, "A Data Set Named Desire: A Reply to William P. Thompson," *International Studies Quarterly* 47, no. 3 (2003), pp. 475–458.
Lebow, Richard Ned, "Evolution, Adaption, and Imitation in International Relations," in William P. Thompson, ed., *Encyclopaedia of Empirical International Relations Theory* (Oxford: Oxford University Press, 2018), vol. 1, pp. 799–819.
Lebow, Richard Ned, *Forbidden Fruit: Counterfactuals and International Relations* (Princeton: Princeton University Press, 2010).
Lebow, Richard Ned, "Greeks, Neuroscience and International Relations," in Daniel Jacobi and Annette Freyberg-Inan, eds., *Human Beings in International Relations* (Cambridge: Cambridge University Press, 2015), pp. 132–155.
Lebow, Richard Ned, ed., *Max Weber and International Relations* (Cambridge: Cambridge University Press, 2017).
Lebow, Richard Ned, "Miscalculation in the South Atlantic: British and Argentine Intelligence Failures in the Falkland Crisis," in Jervis, Lebow, and Stein, *Psychology and Deterrence*, pp. 89–124.
Lebow, Richard Ned, *National Identifications and International Relations* (Cambridge: Cambridge University Press, 2017).
Lebow, Richard Ned, "Nuclear Luck," in Benoit Pelopidas, *Nuclear Luck*, forthcoming.
Lebow, Richard Ned, *The Politics and Ethics of Identity: In Search of Ourselves* (Cambridge: Cambridge University Press, 2012).
Lebow, Richard Ned, *The Rise and Fall of Political Orders* (Cambridge: Cambridge University Press, 2018).
Lebow, Richard Ned, "Texts, Paradigms and Political Change," in Toni Erskine and Michael Williams, eds., *Reconsidering Realism: The Legacy of Hans J. Morgenthau in International Relations* (Oxford: Oxford University Press, 2007), pp. 241–268.
Lebow, Richard Ned, *The Tragic Vision of Politics: Ethics, Interests, and Orders* (Cambridge: Cambridge University Press, 2003).
Lebow, Richard Ned, "Thucydides the Constructivist," *American Political Science Review* 95, no. 3 (2001), pp. 547–560.
Lebow, Richard Ned, "Weber's Search for Knowledge," in Lebow, *Max Weber and International Relations*, pp. 40–78.
Lebow, Richard Ned and Thomas Risse-Kappen, *International Relations Theory and the End of the Cold War* (New York: Palgrave Macmillan, 1994).

Lebow, Richard Ned and Janice Gross Stein, *We All Lost the Cold War* (Princeton: Princeton University Press, 1994).
Lerner, Melvin J., and D. T. Miller, "Just World Research and the Attribution Process: Looking Back and Ahead," *Psychological Bulletin*, 85, no. 5 (1978), pp. 1030–1051.
Lévi-Strauss, Claude, *Savage Mind* (Chicago: University of Chicago Press, 1966).
Lewes, George Henry, *Problems of Life and Mind*, 2 vols. (Cambridge: Cambridge University Press, 1875).
Linton, Ralph, *The Study of Man: An Introduction* (New York: Appleton-Century-Crofts, 1936).
Lloyd, G. E. R., ed., *Hippocratic Writings* (London: Penguin, 1978).
Locke, John, *An Essay Concerning Human Understanding*, ed. Roger Woolhouse (London: Penguin, 1988).
Loeb, Jacques, *The Mechanistic Conception of Life* (Chicago: University of Chicago Press, 1912).
Longinus, Cassius, *On the Sublime*, trans. W. Rhys Roberts (Cambridge: Cambridge University Press, 1899).
Loraux, Nicole, *Tragic Ways of Killing a Woman*, trans. Anthony Foster, 2nd ed. (Cambridge: Harvard University Press, 1987).
Lord, Albert Bates, *The Singer of Tales* (Cambridge: Harvard University Press, 2000).
Low, Polly, "Thucydides on the Athenian Empire and Interstate Relations (431–404)," in Balot, Forsdyke, and Foster, *Oxford Handbook of Thucydides*, pp. 99–114.
Lynch, Dierdre S., *Economy of Character: Novels, Market Culture, and the Business of Inner Meaning* (Chicago: University of Chicago Press, 1998).
MacDowell, Douglas M., *The Law in Classical Athens* (Ithaca, NY: Cornell University Press, 1978).
Machiavelli, Niccolò, *Discourses on Livy*, trans. Julia C. Bondanella and Peter Bondanella (Oxford: Oxford University Press, 1997).
MacIntyre, Alasdair, *Against the Self-Images of the Age: Essays on Ideology and Philosophy* (South Bend, IN: Notre Dame University Press, 1978), pp. 60–69.
Mackie, J. L., *The Cement of the Universe: A Study of Causation* (Oxford: Oxford University Press, 1974).
Macleod, Colin, "Thucydides and Tragedy," in Oliver Taplin, ed., *Collected Essays* (Oxford: Oxford University Press, 1983), pp. 157–158.
MacMillan, Margaret, *The War That Ended Peace: How Europe Abandoned Peace for the First World War* (London: Profile, 2013).
Mahler, Margaret S., "Human Symbiosis and the Vicissitudes of Individuation," *Journal of the American Psychoanalytic Association* 15, no. 4 (1967), pp. 740–763.
Mahler, Margaret S., with Manuel Furer. *On Human Symbiosis and the Vicissitudes of Individuation, Vol. 1: Infantile Psychosis* (New York: International Universities Press, 1968).
Maine, Henry S., *Ancient Law: Its Connection with the Early History of Society and Its Relation to Modern Laws* (New York: Dorset Press, 1896).

Malebranche, Nicolas, *Search after Truth*, trans. T. M. Lenon and P. J. Olscamp (Columbus: Ohio State University Press, 1980).

Mann, Thomas, *The Magic Mountain* (New York: Random House, 1927).

Mann, Thomas, "The Making of Magic Mountain," in Mann, *Magic Mountain*, pp. 717–729, originally appeared in *Atlantic*, July 1953.

Mann, Thomas, *Reflections of a Nonpolitical Man*, trans. Walter D. Orr (New York: F. Unger, 1983).

Marquardt, Franka and Yahya Elsaghe, "Naphta and His Ilk: Jewish Characters in Mann's *The Magic Mountain*," in Vaget, *Thomas Mann's Magic Mountain*, pp. 171–200.

Martin, Richard P., *The Language of Heroes: Speech and Performance in the Iliad* (Cambridge: Harvard Center for Hellenic Studies, 1989).

Martin, Thomas R., *Pericles: A Biography in Context* (New York: Cambridge University Press, 2016).

May, Henry, *The End of American Innocence: A Study of the First Years of Our Own Time, 1912–1917* (Chicago: Quadrangle, 1964).

McAdam, Doug, Sidney Tarrow, and Charles Tilly, *Dynamics of Contention* (Cambridge: Cambridge University Press, 2001).

McArthur, Neil, "Hume's Political Philosophy," in Russell, *Oxford Handbook of Hume*, pp. 489–504.

McIntyre, Jane L., "Hume and the Problem of Personal Identity," in Norton and Taylor, *Cambridge Companion to Hume*, pp. 177–208.

McMaster, Rowland D., ed., *Trollope and the Law* (Basingstoke: Macmillan, 1986).

Mearsheimer, John, *The Tragedy of Great Power Politics* (New York: Norton, 2001).

Meiggs, Russell, *The Athenian Empire* (Oxford: Oxford University Press, 1972).

Michie, Elsie B., "The Odd Couple: Anthony Trollope and William James," *Henry James Review* 27, no. 1 (2006), pp. 10–23.

Mill, John Stuart, "Bentham," in John Stuart Mill and Jeremy Bentham, eds., *Utilitarianism and Other Essays* (London: Penguin, 1987), pp. 132–176.

Mill, John Stuart, *England and Ireland* (London : Longmans, Green, Reader, and Dyer, 1868).

Mill, John Stuart, "The Spirit of the Age," in *The Spirit of the Age* (Indianapolis: Liberty Fund, 2013), http://oll.libertyfund.org/titles/2572 (accessed August 7, 2018).

Millender, Ellen G., "Sparta and the Crisis of the Peloponnesian League in Thucydides; History," in Balot, Forsdyke, and Foster, *Oxford Handbook of Thucydides*, pp. 81–99.

Miller, D. A., *The Novel and the Police* (Berkeley and Los Angeles: University of California Press, 1988).

Miller, J. Hillis, *The Form of Victorian Fiction* (South Bend, IN: Notre Dame University Press, 1968).

Miller, J. Hillis, "Introduction," in Charles Dickens, *Bleak House* (Harmondsworth: Penguin, 1971), pp. 11–34.

Moe, Terry M., "On the Scientific Status of Rational Models," *American Journal of Political Science* 23 (February 1979), pp. 215–243.

Molloy, Seán, "'Cautious Politics': Morgenthau and Hume's Critiques of the Balance of Power," *International Politics* 50, no. 6 (2013), pp. 768–783.

Molloy, Seán, *Kant's International Relations: The Political Theology of Perpetual Peace* (Ann Arbor: University of Michigan Press, 2017).

Mombauer, Annika, *Helmuth von Moltke and the Origins of the First World War* (Cambridge: Cambridge University Press, 2001).

Mombauer, Annika, "Of War Plans and War Guilt: The Debacle Surrounding the Schlieffen Plan," *Journal of Strategic Studies* 28, no. 5 (2005), pp. 857–885.

Mommsen, Wolfgang J., "Ideal and Pure Type: Two Variants of Max Weber's Ideal-Type Method," in Wolfgang J. Mommsen, eds., *Political and Social Theory of Max Weber* (Chicago: University of Chicago Press, 1989), pp. 121–132.

Mommsen, Wolfgang J., *Max Weber and German Politics, 1890–1920*, 2nd ed., trans. Michael S. Steinberg (Chicago: University of Chicago Press, 1984 [1974]).

Mommsen, Wolfgang J., and Jürgen Osterhammel, eds., *Max Weber and His Contemporaries* (London: Allen & Unwin, 1987).

Montaigne, Michel de, "In Defense of Seneca and Plutarch," in *Complete Essays of Michel de Montaigne*, trans. Donald M. Frame (Palo Alto: Stanford University Press, 1958), pp. 544–549.

Montesquieu, Charles-Louis de, *The Spirit of the Laws*, trans. Anne M. Cohler, Bbaisa Carolyn Miller, and Harold Samuel Stone (Cambridge: Cambridge University Press, 1989).

Morgenstern, Oskar, "Perfect Foresight in Economic Equilibrium," in Andrew Schotter, ed., *Selected Writings of Oskar Morgenstern* (New York: New York University Press, 1976), pp. 169–183.

Morgenstern, Oskar, "The Time Moment in Value Theory," in Schotter, *Selected Writings of Oskar Morgenstern*, pp. 151–167.

Morrison, J. V., "Interaction of Speech and Narrative in Thucydides," in Antonios Rengakos and Anthonis Tsakmakis, eds., *Brill's Companion to Thucydides* (Leiden: Brill, 2006), pp. 251–277.

Morrison, Margaret, "Capacities, Tendencies and the Problem of Singular Causes," *Philosophy and Phenomenological Research* 55 (1995), pp. 163–168.

Morrow, James D., *Game Theory for Political Scientists* (Princeton: Princeton University Press, 1994).

Mulligan, William, *The Origins of the First World War* (Cambridge: Cambridge University Press, 2010).

Mumford, Stephen, "Causal Powers and Capacities," in Beebee, Hitchcock, and Menzies, *Oxford Handbook of Causation*, pp. 265–278.

Nagy, Gregory, *Poetry as Performance: Homer and Beyond* (Cambridge: Cambridge University Press, 1996).

Nayder, Lilian, "Collins and Empire," in Taylor, *Cambridge Companion to Wilkie Collins*, pp. 139–152.

Neisser, Ulric, "John Dean's Memory: A Case Study," *Cognition*, 9 (1981), pp. 1–22.

Neisser, Ulric, ed., *The Perceived Self: Ecological and Interpersonal Sources of Self-Knowledge* (Cambridge: Cambridge University Press, 1993).

Neisser, Ulric and Robyn Fivush, *The Remembering Self: Construction and Accuracy in the Self Narrative* (Cambridge: Cambridge University Press, 1994).

Bibliography

Nelson, Katherine, *Language in Cognitive Development: Emergence of the Mediated Mind* (New York: Cambridge University Press, 1996).

Nemorov, Howard, "The Questor Hero: Myth as a Universal Symbol in the Works of Thomas Mann," PhD dissertation, Harvard University, 1940.

Nenno, Nancy P., "Projections on Blank Space: Landscape, Nationality, and Identity in *Der Zauberberg*," in Vaget, *Thomas Mann's Magic Mountain*, pp. 95–122.

Nesselrath, Heinz-Günther, *Ungeschehenes Geschehen: Beinahe-Episoden in griechischen und Römischen Epos von Homer bis zur Spätantike* (Stuttgart: Teubner, 1992).

Neumann, John von and Oskar Morgenstern, *Theory of Games and Economic Behavior*, 2nd ed. (Princeton: Princeton University Press, 1947 [1944]).

Nietzsche, Friedrich, *The Birth of Tragedy*, in *Basic Writings of Nietzsche*, ed. and trans. Walter Kaufmann (New York: Modern Library, 1962), sections 1 and 3.

Nietzsche, Friedrich V., *Daybreak: Thoughts on the Prejudices of Morality* (Cambridge: Cambridge University Press, 1982).

Nietzsche, Friedrich, *The Gay Science*, ed. Bernard Williams, trans. Josefine Nauckhoff and Adrian del Caro (Cambridge: Cambridge University Press, 2001).

Nietzsche, Friedrich, *On the Genealogy of Morals*, trans. Walter Kaufmann and R. J. Hollindale (New York: Random House, 1967).

Noble, David W., *The Paradox of Progressive Thought* (Minneapolis: University of Minnesota Press, 1958).

Noble, David W., *The Progressive Mind, 1890–1917* (Chicago: Rand McNally, 1970).

Norton, David Fate, "Editor's Introduction," in Hume, *Treatise of Human Nature*, pp. 19–105.

Norton, David Fate, "The Foundations of Morality in Hume's *Treatise*," in Norton and Taylor, *Cambridge Companion to Hume*, pp. 270–311.

Norton, David and Jacqueline Taylor, eds., *Cambridge Companion to Hume* (Cambridge: Cambridge University Press, 2008).

Novak, Maximilian E., *Realism, Myth, and the History of Defoe's Fiction* (Lincoln: University of Nebraska Press, 1983).

Novick, Peter, *That Noble Dream: The "Objectivity Question" and the American Historical Profession* (Cambridge: Cambridge University Press, 1988).

Noyes, Dorothy, "'Incalculably Diffusive': Revisiting the Disciplinary Deficit (A Response to Elliott Oring)," *Journal of American Folklore* 132, no. 524 (2019), pp. 175–184.

Nye, Joseph S. Jr., "The Future of American Power," *Foreign Affairs* 89, no. 6 (2010), pp. 2–12.

Oakes, Guy, *Weber and Rickert: Concept Formation in the Cultural Sciences* (Cambridge, MA: MIT Press, 1988).

Organski, A. F. K. and Jacek Kugler, *The War Ledger* (Chicago: University of Chicago Press, 1980).

Ostwald, Martin, *Anangkê in Thucydides* (Oxford: Oxford University Press, 1988).

Otte, Thomas G., *July Crisis: The World's Descent into War, Summer 1914* (Cambridge: Cambridge University Press, 2014).

Owen, David, *Hume's Reason* (Oxford: Oxford University Press, 1999).
Parry, Adam, "The Language of Achilles," *Transactions and Proceedings of the American Philological Association* 87 (1956), pp. 1–7.
Parry, Milman, *The Making of Homeric Verse* (Oxford: Oxford University Press, 1971).
Parsons, Talcott, *The Structure of Social Action: A Study in Social Theory with Special Reference to a Group of European Writers* (New York: McGraw-Hill, 1937).
Pascal, Blaise, *Pensées*, trans. A. J. Krailsheimer (Harmondsworth: Penguin, 1966).
Patomäki, Heikki, *After International Relations: Critical Realism and the (Re)Construction of World Politics* (London: Routledge, 2001).
Pelz, Stephen E., *Race to Pearl Harbor* (Cambridge: Harvard University Press, 1974).
Penelhum, Terence, "Hume's Moral Psychology," in Norton and Taylor, *Cambridge Companion to Hume*, pp. 238–269.
Pentagon Papers: The Defense Department History of United States Decisionmaking in Vietnam, Senator Gravel Edition, 4 vols. (Boston: Beacon Press, 1971).
Philipps, Eustace D., *Greek Medicine* (London: Thames and Hudson, 1978).
Pindar, *Nemean Odes*, in Pindar, *The Complete Works*, trans. Anthony Verity (Oxford: Oxford University Press, 2008).
Plato, *The Republic*, in Edith Hamilton and Huntington Cairns, eds., *The Collected Dialogues* (Princeton: Princeton University Press, 1961).
Plato, *Symposium*, in Hamilton and Cairns, *Collected Dialogues*.
Plutarch, *Life of Pericles*, in Philip A. Stadter, ed., *Plutarch: Greek Lives* (Oxford: Oxford University Press, 2009).
Polkinghorne, D. E., "Narrative and Self-Concept," *Journal of Narrative and Life History*, 1 (1991), pp. 135–153.
Pomeranz, Kenneth, "Counterfactuals and Industrialization in Europe and China," in Tetlock, Parker, and Lebow, *Unmaking the West*, pp. 241–276.
Pomeranz, Kenneth, *The Great Divergence: Europe, China and the Making of the World Economy* (Princeton: Princeton University Press, 200).
Poovey, Mary, *A History of the Modern Fact: Problems of Knowledge in the Sciences of Wealth and Society* (Chicago: Chicago University Press, 1998).
Popper, Karl, *Die bieden Grundprobleme der Erkenntnistheorie*, ed. Troels Eggers Hansen (Tübingen: Mohr, 1976).
Popper, Karl, *Conjections and Refutations* (New York: Basic Books, 1963).
Popper, Karl, "Epistemology without a Knowing Subject," in Karl Popper, *Objective Knowledge* (New York: Oxford University Press, 1972), chap. 3.
Popper, Karl, *The Logic of Scientific Discovery*, 2nd ed. (London: Routledge, 2002 [1959]).
Popper, Karl, "The Logic of the Social Sciences," in Theodore Adorno, Hans Albert, Ralf Dahrendorf, Jürgen Habermas, Harald Pilot, and Karl Popper, eds., *The Positivist Dispute in German Sociology*, trans. Glyn Adey and David Frisby (London: Heineman, 1976), pp. 87–104.
Porter, Theodore, "Speaking Precision to Power: The Modern Political Role of Social Science," *Social Research* 73, no. 4 (2006), pp. 1273–1294.

Porter, Theodore, *Trust in Numbers: The Pursuit of Objectivity in Science and Public Life* (Princeton: Princeton University Press, 1996).

Press, Daryl G., *Calculating Credibility: How Leaders Assess Military Threats* (Ithaca, NY: Cornell University Press, 2007).

Psillos, Stathis, "Regularity Theories," in Beebee, Hitchcock, and Menzies, *Oxford Handbook of Causation*, pp. 131–157.

Pykett, Lyn, "Collins and the Sensation Novel," in Taylor, *Cambridge Companion to Wilkie Collins*, pp. 50–63.

Quandt, Jean B., *From the Small Town to the Great Community: The Social Thought of Progressive Intellectuals* (New Brunswick, NJ: Rutgers University Press, 1970).

Radbruch, Gustav, *Die Lehre von adäquaten Verursachung* [Theory of Adequate Causation] (Berlin: Abhandlungen des Kriminalistischen Seminars an der Universität Berlin, NF vol. 1, 1902).

Radkau, Joachim, *Max Weber: A Biography*, trans. Patrick Camiller (Cambridge: Polity, 2011).

Rapoport, Anatol, *Strategy and Conscience* (New York: Harper & Row, 1964).

Rawlings, Hunter R., *The Structure of Thucydides' History* (Princeton: Princeton University Press, 1981).

Rawlings, Hunter R., III, *A Semantic Study of Prophasis to 400 B.C. Hermes: Einzelschriften* 33 (Wiesbaden: Franz Steiner, 1975), pp. 92–95.

Rawlings, Hunter R., III, "Writing History Implicitly Through Refined Structuring," in Balot, Forsdyke, and Foster, *Oxford Handbook of Thucydides*, pp. 195–210.

Read, Rupert and Kenneth A. Richman, eds., *The New Hume Debate*, 2nd ed. (London: Routledge, 2007).

Reed, John R., "English Imperialism and the Unacknowledged Crime of the *Moonstone*," *Clio* 2 (1973), pp. 281–290.

Reed, T. J., *Thomas Mann: The Uses of Tradition*, 2nd ed. (Oxford: Oxford University Press, 1996).

Reich, Simon, and Richard Ned Lebow, *Good-Bye Hegemony! Power and Influence in the Global System* (Princeton: Princeton University Press, 2014).

Reisch, George, *How the Cold War Transformed Philosophy of Science: To the Icy Slopes of Logic* (Cambridge: Cambridge University Press, 2005).

Remak, Joachim, "1914 – The Third Balkan War: Origins, Reconsidered," *Journal of Modern History* 43, no. 3 (1971), pp. 353–366.

Rickert, Heinrich, *Die Grenzen der naturwissenschaftlichen Begriffsbildung* (Tübingen: J. C. B. Mohr, 1902). Abridged English version: The Limits of Concept Formation in Natural Science, ed. Guy Oakes (Cambridge: Cambridge University Press, 1986).

Ricks, Christopher, "The Novelist as Critic," in Rodensky, *Oxford Handbook of the Victorian Novel*, pp. 634–662.

Riesman, David, Reuel Denney, and Nathan Glazer, *Lonely Crowd: A Study of the Changing American Character* (New Haven, CT: Yale University Press, 1950).

Ringer, Fritz, *Max Weber: An Intellectual Biography* (Chicago: University of Chicago Press, 2004).

Ringer, Fritz, "Max Weber on Causal Analysis: Interpretation, and Comparison," *History and Theory* 41 (2002), pp. 163–178.
Robinson, Solveig C., "The Victorian Novel and the Reviews," in Rodensky, *Oxford Handbook of the Victorian Novel*, pp. 129–146.
Rodensky, Lisa, *The Crime in Mind: Criminal Responsibility and the Victorian Novel* (Oxford: Oxford University Press, 2003).
Rodensky, Lisa, ed., *The Oxford Handbook of the Victorian Novel* (Oxford: Oxford University Press, 2013).
Rood, Tim, *Thucydides: Narrative and Explanation* (Oxford: Oxford University Press, 1998).
Rosenmeyer, Thomas G., *The Art of Aeschylus* (Berkeley and Los Angeles: University of California Press, 1982).
Ross, Dorothy, *The Origins of American Social Science* (Cambridge: Cambridge University Press, 1991).
Ross, L., M. R. Lepper, F. Strack, and J. Steinmetz, "Social Explanation and Social Expectation: Effects of Real and Hypothetical Explanations on Subjective Likelihood," *Journal of Personality and Social Psychology* 35 (1977), pp. 817–829.
Ross, Lee, "The Intuitive Psychologist and His Shortcomings: Distortions in the Attribution Process," in Leonard Berkowitz, ed., *Advances in Experimental Social Psychology*, vol. 10 (New York: Academic Press, 1977), pp. 173–220.
Russell, Bertrand, "On the Notion of Cause," *Proceedings of the Aristotelian Society* 13 (1913), pp. 1–26.
Russell, Paul, ed., *The Oxford Handbook of Hume* (Oxford: Oxford University Press, 2016).
Rusten, Jeffrey, "Tree, Funnel, and Diptych," in Balot, Forsdyke, and Foster, *Oxford Handbook of Thucydides*, pp. 225–238.
Ruth, Jenifer, "The Victorian Novel and the Professions," in Rodensky, *Oxford Handbook of the Victorian Novel*, pp. 397–412.
Sahlins, Marshall, *Apologies to Thucydides: Understanding History as Culture and Vice Versa* (Chicago: University of Chicago Press, 2004).
Sani, Fabio, ed., *Self Continuity: Individual and Collective Perspectives* (New York: Psychology Press, 2008).
Saxonhouse, Arlene W., "Nature & Convention in Thucydides' History," *Polity* 10 (Summer 1978), pp. 461–487.
Scardino, Carlo, "Indirect Discourse in Herodotus and Thucydides," in Edith Foster and Donald Lateiner, eds., *Thucydides and Herodotus* (Oxford: Oxford University Press, 2012), pp. 67–96.
Schluchter, Wolfgang, "The Paradox of Rationalization: On the Relation of Ethics and World," in Guenther Roth and Wolfgang Schluchter, eds., *Max Weber's Vision of History: Ethics and Methods* (Berkeley: University of California Press, 1984 [1979]), pp. 11–64.
Schijndel, Teressa J. P. van, Kim Huijpen, Ingmar Visser, Maartje E. J. Raijmakers, "Investigating the Development of Causal Inference by Studying Variability in 2- to 5-Year-Olds' Behavior," *PLOS One*, https://journals.plos.org/plosone/article?id=10.1371/journal.pone.0195019 (accessed September 23, 2018).
Schneewind, J. B. "Good out of Evil: Kant and the Ideal of Unsocial Sociability," in Amelie Oksenberg Rorty and James Schmidt, eds., *Kant's Idea of Universal*

History with a Cosmopolitan Aim: A Critical Guide (Cambridge: Cambridge University Press, 2009), pp. 94–111.

Schneider, C., *Information und Absicht bei Thukydides: Untersuchung zur Motivation des Handelns* Hypomnemeta 41 (Göttingen, Vandenhoeck & Reprecht, 1974).

Schramm, Jan-Melissa, *Testimony and Advocacy in Victorian Law, Literature, and Theology* (Cambridge: Cambridge University Press, 2000).

Schramm, Jan-Melissa, "The Victorian Novel and the Law," in Rodensky, *Oxford Handbook of the Victorian Novel*, pp. 507–528.

Schütz, Alfred, "'The Problem of Rationality in the Social World': A Lecture Delivered at the Faculty Club of Harvard University on April 13, 1940," in Alfred Schütz, ed., *Collected Papers* (Dordrecht: Springer, 1996), p. 7.

Seaford, Richard, *Reciprocity and Ritual: Homer and Tragedy in the Developing City State* (Oxford: Oxford University Press, 1994).

Segal, Charles, "Introduction," in Burian and Shapiro, *Complete Plays of Sophocles*, vol. 1, pp. 5–37.

Segal, Charles, *Sophocles: Tragedy and Civilization. An Interpretation of Sophocles* (Cambridge, MA: Harvard University Press, 1981).

Seigel, Jerrold, *The Idea of the Self: Thought and Experience in Western Europe since the Seventeenth Century* (Cambridge: Cambridge University Press, 2005).

Shakespeare, William, *A Midsummer Night's Dream* (London: Palgrave Macmillan, 2008).

Siebert, Donald T., "Hume's History of England," in Russell, *Oxford Handbook of Hume*, pp. 546–568.

Simmel, Georg, *Über soziale Differenzierung: Sozialogische und psychologische Untersuchungen*, in Karl Kehrbach, ed., *Sämtliche Werke* (Leipzig: Duncker & Humbolt, 1890).

Singer, J. David, "The Level-of-Analysis Problem in International Relations," *World Politics* 14, no. 1 (1961), pp. 77–92.

Singer, J. David, Stuart Bremer, and John Stuckey, "Capability Distribution, Uncertainty and Major Power War, 1820–1965," in Bruce Russett, ed., *Peace, War and Numbers* (Beverly Hills, CA: Sage, 1972).

Skinner, Andrew S., "Hume's Principles of Political Economy," in Norton and Taylor, *Cambridge Companion to Hume*, pp. 381–413.

Skinner, Quentin, "Introduction: The Return of Grand Theory," *The Return of Grand Theory in the Human Sciences* (New York: Cambridge University Press, 1985), pp. 1–20.

Smith, Adam, *An Inquiry into the Nature and Causes of Wealth of Nations*, ed. Edwin Canaan (Chicago: University of Chicago Press, 1976).

Smith, Adam, *The Theory of Moral Sentiments*, ed. Knud Haakonssen (Cambridge: Cambridge University Press, 2002 [1759]).

Smith, Mark, *Social Science in the Crucible: The American Debate over Objectivity and Purpose* (Durham, NC: Duke University Press, 1994).

Snow, C. P., *The Two Cultures: A Second Look*, 2nd ed. (Cambridge: Cambridge University Press, 1964).

Snyder, Jack, *The Ideology of the Offensive: Military Decision Making and the Disasters of 1914* (Ithaca, NY: Cornell University Press, 1984).

Sobel, David M. and Cristine H. Legare, "Causal Learning in Children," *Cognitive Science* 5, no. 4 (2014), pp. 413–427.
Sondhaus, Lawrence, *Franz Conrad von Hötzendorf: Architect of the Apocalypse* (Boston: Humanities Press, 2000).
Sontag, Susan, *Illness as Metaphor* (New York: Farrar, Strauss & Giroux, 1978).
Sordi, Marta, "Scontro di Blocchi e Azione di Terze Forze nello Scoppio della Guerra del Peloponneso," in Richard Ned Lebow and Barry R. Strauss, eds., *Hegemonic Rivalry: From Thucydides to the Modern Age* (Boulder, CO: Westview, 1991), pp. 87–100.
Spence, D. P., *Narrative Truth and Historical Truth: Meaning and Interpretation in Psychoanalysis* (New York: Norton, 1982).
St. John Green, Nicholas, "Proximate and Remote Cause," *Boston Law Review* 4 (1870), pp. 201–216.
Stach, Reiner, *Kafka: The Decisive Years* (New York: Harcourt, 2005).
Stahl, Hans-Peter, *Thucydides: Man's Place in History* (Swansea: Classical Press of Wales, 2003).
Ste. Croix, G. E. M. de, *The Origins of the Peloponnesian War* (London: Duckworth, 1972),
Stein, Janice Gross, "Calculation, Miscalculation, and Conventional Deterrence I: The View from Cairo," in Jervis, Lebow, and Stein, *Psychology and Deterrence*, pp. 34–59.
Stein, Janice Gross, "Calculation, Miscalculation, and Conventional Deterrence II: The View from Jerusalem," in Jervis, Lebow, and Stein, *Psychology and Deterrence*, pp. 60–88.
Stein, Janice Gross, *The Cult of Efficiency* (Toronto: Anansi, 2001).
Stewart, Garrett, *Dear Reader: The Conscripted Audience in Nineteenth-Century British Fiction* (Baltimore, MD: Johns Hopkins University Press, 1996).
Strachan, Huw, *The First World War: To Arms* (Oxford: Oxford University Press, 2013).
Strauss, Barry, "Salamis without Themistocles, and the West without Greece," in Tetlock, Lebow, and Parker, *Unmaking the West*, pp. 90–118.
Strawson, Galen, *The Secret Connexion: Causation, Realism and David Hume* (Oxford: Oxford University Press, 1989).
Strong, Tracy B., "Entitlement and Legitimacy: Weber and Lenin on the Problems of Leadership," in Fred Eidlin, ed., *Constitutional Democracy: A Festschrift in Honour of Henry W. Erdmann* (Boulder, CO: Westview, 1983), pp. 153–180.
Strong, Tracy B., "Weber and Freud: Vocation and Self-Acknowledgment," in Mommsen and Osterhammel, *Max Weber and His Contemporaries*, pp. 468–482.
Summers, G. and N. S. Feldman, "Blaming the Victim versus Blaming the Perpetrator: An Attributional Analysis of Spouse Abuse," *Journal of Applied Social and Clinical Psychology* 2, no. 4 (1984), pp. 339–347.
Sutherland, John A., *Victorian Fiction: Writers, Publishers, Readers* (London: Macmillan, 1995).
Swales, Martin, *German Bildungsroman from Wieland to Hesse* (Princeton: Princeton University Press, 1978).

Tajfel, Henri, *Human Groups and Social Categories* (Cambridge: Cambridge University Press, 1981).
Tajfel, Henri, "Social Categorisation, Social Identity and Social Comparison," in H. Tajfel, ed., *Differentiation between Social Groups: Studies in the Psychology of Intergroup Relations* (London: Academic Press, 1978), pp. 61–76.
Tajfel, Henri and John Turner, "The Social Identity Theory of Intergroup Behavior," in Stephen Worchel and William Austin, eds., *Psychology of Intergroup Relations* (Chicago: Nelson-Hall, 1986), pp. 7–24.
Taplin, Oliver, *Homeric Soundings: The Shaping of the Iliad* (Oxford: Oxford University Press, 1992).
Tarrow, Sidney, "Expanding Paired Comparison: A Modest Proposal," *Comparative Politics Newsletter* 10, no. 2 (1999), pp. 9–12.
Taylor, Jacqueline, "Hume's Later Moral Philosophy," in Norton and Taylor, *Cambridge Companion to Hume*, pp. 311–340.
Taylor, Jenny Bourne, ed., *The Cambridge Companion to Wilkie Collins* (Cambridge: Cambridge University Press, 2006).
Taylor, Jenny Bourne, "Trollope and the Sensation Novel," in Dever and Niles, *Anthony Trollope*, pp. 85–98.
Tetlock, Philip E. and Aaron Belkin, "Counterfactual Thought Experiments in World Politics: Logical, Methodological, and Psychological Perspectives," in Tetlock and Belkin, *Counterfactual Thought Experiments in World Politics*, pp. 1–38.
Tetlock, Philip E. and Aaron Belkin, *Counterfactual Thought Experiments in World Politics: Logical, Methodological, and Psychological Perspectives* (Princeton: Princeton University Press, 1996).
Tetlock, Philip E. and Richard Ned Lebow "Poking Counterfactual Holes in Covering Laws: Cognitive Styles and Political Learning," *American Political Science Review* 95 (December 2001), pp. 829–843.
Tetlock, Philip E., Richard Ned Lebow, and Geoffrey Parker, eds., *Unmaking the West: "What-If" Scenarios That Rewrite World History* (Ann Arbor: University of Michigan Press, 2006).
Thomas, Ronald R., *Detective Fiction and the Rise of Forensic Science* (Cambridge: Cambridge University Press, 1999).
Thomas, Ronald R., "*The Moonstone*, Detective Fiction and Forensic Science," in Taylor, *Cambridge Companion to Wilkie Collins*, pp. 65–78.
Thompson, William R., "A Streetcar Named Sarajevo: Catalysts, Multiple Causation Chains, and Rivalry Structures," *International Studies Quarterly* 47, no. 3 (2003), pp. 453–474.
Thucydides, *The Peloponnesian War*, in Robert B. Strassler, ed., *The Landmark Thucydides: A Comprehensive Guide to the Peloponnesian War* (New York: Free Press, 1996).
Thucydides, *The Peloponnesian War*, The Crawley Translation, rev. and ed. T. E. Wick (New York: Modern Library, 1982).
Tin-bor Hui, Victoria, *War and State Formation in Ancient China and Early Modern Europe* (Cambridge: Cambridge University Press, 2005).
Todd, S. C., *The Shape of Athenian Law* (Oxford: Oxford University Press, 1993).
Tompkins, Daniel, "Aitia in Thucydides," unpublished manuscript.

Tompkins, Daniel, "Dialogue, Diplomacy, and the Crisis of Spartan Identity in Thucydides: 1.68–86," unpublished paper.
Tompkins, Daniel, "Stylistic Characteristics in Thucydides: Nicias and Alcibiades," in Adam Parry, ed., *Studies in Fifth Century Thought and Literature* (Cambridge: Cambridge University Press, 1972), pp. 181–214.
Travers, Martin, "Death, Knowledge, and the Formation of Self: *The Magic Mountain*," in Vaget, *Thomas Mann's* Magic Mountain, pp. 31–44.
Trollope, Anthony, *Autobiography* (Oxford: Oxford University Press, 2008).
Trollope, Anthony, *Can You Forgive Her?* (London: Penguin, 1975).
Trollope, Anthony, *The Duke's Children* (Oxford: Oxford University Press, 2011).
Trollope, Anthony, *Eustace Diamonds* (Oxford: Oxford University Press, 1998).
Trollope, Anthony, *Four Lectures*, ed. Morris L. Parrish (London: Constable, 1938).
Trollope, Anthony, *John Caldigate* (London: Create Space, 2017).
Trollope, Anthony, *John Caldigate*, vol. 2. (London: Nabu Press, 2012).
Trollope, Anthony, *The Last Chronicle of Barset* (London: Penguin, 1986).
Trollope, Anthony, *Orley Farm* (Oxford: Oxford University Press, 2000).
Trollope, Anthony, "On English Prose Fiction as a Rational Amusement," in Anthony Trollope, *An Autobiography and Other Writings*, ed. Nicholas Shrimpton (Oxford: Oxford University Press, 2016).
Trollope, Anthony, *Phineas Finn* (Oxford: Oxford University Press, 1999).
Trollope, Anthony, *Phineas Redux* (Oxford: Oxford University Press, 2000).
Trollope, Anthony, *Prime Minister* (Oxford: Oxford University Press, 1996).
Trollope, Anthony, *The Warden* (London: Penguin, 1986).
Tsakmakis, Anthonis, "Speeches," in Balot, Forsdyke, and Foster, *Oxford Handbook of Thucydides*, pp. 267–282.
Turner, Stephen, *The Social Theory of Practices* (Chicago: University of Chicago Press, 1994).
Tversky, Amos and Daniel Kahneman, "Extensional versus Intuitive Reason: The Conjunction Fallacy as Probability Judgment," *Psychological Review*, 90, no. 2 (1983), pp. 292–315.
Untersteiner, Mario, *The Sophists*, trans. Kathleen Freeman (New York: Philosophical Library, 1954).
Updike, John, "Foreword," in Kafka, *Complete Stories*, pp. ix–xxi.
Vaget, Hans Rudolf, "Introduction," in Vaget, *Thomas Mann's* Magic Mountain, pp. 3–12.
Vaget, Hans Rudolf, "The Making of 'The Magic Mountain,'" in Vaget, *Thomas Mann's* The Magic Mountain, pp. 13–30.
Vaget, Hans Rudolf, "'Politically Suspect': Music on the Magic Mountain," in Vaget, *Thomas Mann's* The Magic Mountain, pp. 123–142.
Vaget, Hans Rudolf, *Seelenzauber: Thomas Mann und die Musik* (Leipzig: S. Fischer, 2006).
Vaget, Hans Rudolf, ed. *Thomas Mann's The Magic Mountain: A Casebook* (Oxford: Oxford University Press, 2008).
Van Wees, Hans, "Thucydides on Early Greek History," in Balot, Forsdyke, and Foster, *Oxford Handbook of Thucydides*, pp. 39–62.

Vellacott, Philip, *Sophocles and Oedipus* (Ann Arbor: University of Michigan Press, 1971).
Vernant, Jean-Pierre, "Ambiguity and Reversal: On the Enigmatic Structure of *Oedipus Rex*," in Jean-Pierre Vernant and Pierre Vidal-Nacquet, eds., *Myth and Tragedy in Ancient Greece* (London: Zone Books, 1990 [1972]).
Veyne, Paul, *Did the Greeks Believe in Their Myths?*, trans. P. Wissing (Chicago: University of Chicago Press, 1988).
Vincent, David, *Literacy and Popular Culture in England, 1750–1914* (Cambridge: Cambridge University Press, 1989).
Vitz, Rico, "The Nature and Functions of Sympathy in Hume's Philosophy," in Russell, *Oxford Handbook of Hume*, pp. 312–332.
Walster, Elaine, "Assignment of Responsibility for an Accident," *Journal of Personality and Social Psychology* 3, no. 2 (1996), pp. 73–79.
Waltz, Kenneth W., "The Stability of a Bipolar World," *Dædalus* 93, no. 3 (1964), pp. 881–909.
Waltz, Kenneth W., *Theory of International Politics* (Boston: McGraw-Hill, 1979).
Ward, Ian, *Law and Literature: Possibilities and Perspectives* (Cambridge: Cambridge University Press, 1995).
Watson, John B., "Psychology as the Behaviorist Views It," *Psychological Review* 20 (1913), pp. 158–177.
Watt, Ian, *The Rise of the Novel* (London: Chatto & Wuindus, 1957).
Wawro, Geoffrey, *A Mad Catastrophe: The Outbreak of World War I and the Collapse of the Habsburg Empire* (New York: Basic Books, 2014).
Weber, Marianne, *Max Weber: A Biography*, trans. Harry Zohn (New Brunswick, NJ: Transaction, 1988).
Weber, Max, "Between Two Laws" [*Zwischen zwei Gesetzen*], in Lassman and Speirs, *Weber*, pp. 75–79.
Weber, Max, "Conceptual Exposition," in *Economy and Society*, ed. Roth and Wittich, pp. 9–21.
Weber, Max, "Deutschland unter den Europäischen Weltmachten" [Germany and the European World Powers], speech in Munich, October 22, 1916, in *Gesammelte Aufsätze zur Wissenschaftslehre*, p. 30.
Weber, Max, *Economy and Society*, ed. Guenther Roth and Claus Wittich (Berkeley: University of California Press, 1978).
Weber, Max, "A Final Rebuttal to a Critic of Capitalism," in *Protestant Ethic and the Spirit of Capitalism*, pp. 256–271.
Weber, Max, *Gesammelte Aufsätze zur Wissenschaftslehre* [Collected Essays on Epistemology] ed. Johannes Winckelmann, 3rd ed. (Tübingen: J. C. B. Mohr (Paul Siebeck), 1968).
Weber, Max, "Kritische Studien auf dem Gebiet der kulturwissenschaftlichen Logik" [Critical Studies in the Logic of the Cultural Sciences], in *Gesammelte Aufsätze zur Wissenschaftslehre*, pp. 215–290.
Weber, Max, "Die Objektivitätsozialwissenschaftlicher und sozialpolitischer Erkenntnis," in Weber, *Gesammelte Aufsätze zur Wissenschaftslehre*, pp. 146–214.
Weber, Max, "On the Situation of Constitutional Democracy in Russia," in Lassman and Speirs, *Weber*, pp. 29–74.

Weber, Max, "The Nation State and Economic Policy," in Lassman and Speirs, *Weber*, pp. 1–28.
Weber, Max, "Parliament and Government in Germany under a New Political Order," in Lassman and Speirs, *Weber*, pp. 130–271.
Weber, Max, "The Profession and Vocation of Politics," in Peter Lassman and Ronald Speirs, eds., *Political Writings* (Cambridge: Cambridge University Press, 2000), pp. 309–369.
Weber, Max, *The Protestant Ethic and the Spirit of Capitalism*, trans. Steven Kalberg (Oxford: Oxford University Press, 2011).
Weber, Max, "Roscher und Knies und die logischen Probleme der historischen Nationaleökonomie" [Roscher and Knies and Logical Problems of Historical National Economy], in *Gesammelte Aufsätze zur Wissenschaftslehre*, pp. 1–145.
Weber, Max, *The Russian Revolutions*, trans. Gordon C. Wells and Peter Baehr (Ithaca, NY: Cornell University Press, 1995).
Weber, Max, *Science as Vocation*, ed. David Owen and Tracy Strong, trans. Rodney Livingstone (Illinois: Hackett Books, 2004).
Weber, Max, *The Sociology of Religion* (Boston: Beacon Press, 1993).
Weber, Max, "Über einige Kategorien der verstehenden Soziologie" [On Some Categories of Interpretative Sociology], in *Gesammelte Aufsätze zur Wissenschaftslehre*, pp. 403–450.
Weber, Max, "Der verschärfte U-Boot Krieg" [Unrestricted Submarine Warfare], in *Gesammelte Politische Schriften* (Tübingen: J. C. B. Mohr, 1958), pp. 115–125.
Weber, Max, "Zur Lage der bürgerlichen Demokratie in Russland" [On the Situation of Constitutional Democracy in Russia], in Lassman and Speirs, *Weber*, pp. 29–74.
Weisberg, Richard, *The Failure of the Word: The Protagonist as Lawyer in Modern Fiction* (New Haven, CT: Yale University Press, 1984).
Weisberg, Richard, *Poethics: And Other Strategies of Law and Literature* (New York: Columbia University Press, 1992).
White, Hayden V., *The Content of the Form: Narrative Discourse and Historical Representation* (Baltimore, MD: Johns Hopkins University Press, 1987).
White, James Boyd, *Acts of Hope: Creating Authority in Literature, Law, and Politics* (Chicago: University of Chicago Press, 1994).
White, James Boyd, *The Legal Imagination: Studies in the Nature of Legal Thought and Expression* (Boston: Little, Brown, 1973).
White, Morton, *Social Thought in America: The Revolt Against Formalism* (Oxford: Oxford University Press, 1976).
White, R. T., "Recall of Autobiographical Events," *Applied Cognitive Psychology*, 18 (1989), pp. 127–135.
Wiebe, Robert H., *The Search for Order, 1877–1920* (New York: Hill & Wang, 1967).
Wiener, Martin, *Reconstructing the Criminal: Culture, Law, and the Policy of England, 1830–1914* (Cambridge: Cambridge University Press, 1990).
Wight, Colin, "They Shoot Dead Horses Don't They? Locating Agency in the Agent-Structure Problematique," *European Journal of International Relations* 5, no. 1 (1999), pp. 109–142.

Williams, Bernard, *Shame and Necessity* (Berkeley and Los Angeles: University of California Press, 2008).
Windelband, Wilhelm, "Geschichte und Naturwissenschaft," in *Präludien*, 3rd ed. (Tübingen: J. C. B. Mohr, 1907), pp. 355–379.
Winkler, Kenneth P., "The New Hume," in Read and Richman, *New Hume Debate*, pp. 52–87.
Wise, M. Norton, *Growing Explanations: Historical Perspectives on Recent Science* (Durham, NC: Duke University, 2004).
Wise, M. Norton, "Introduction: Dynamics All the Way Up," in Wise, *Growing Explanations*, pp. 1–22.
Wittgenstein, *Tractatus Logico-Philosophicus*, trans. Frank P. Ramsey and Charles Kay Ogden (London: Kegan Paul, 1922).
Wohl, Victoria, "Thucydides on the Political Passions," in Balot, Forsdyke, and Foster, *Oxford Handbook of Thucydides*, pp. 443–458.
Wong, R. Bin, *China Transformed: Historical Change and the Limits of the European Experience* (Ithaca, NY: Cornell University Press, 1997).
Woodman, A. J., *Rhetoric in Classical Historiography* (Portland: Aeropagitica, 1996).
Woodward, James F., *Making Things Happen* (Oxford: Oxford University Press, 2003).
Woodward, James F. and C. Hitchcock, "Explanatory Generalizations, Part 1: A Counterfactual Account," *Noûs* 37, no. 1 (2003), pp. 1–24.
Wooton, David, "David Hume: 'The Historian'," in Norton and Taylor, *Cambridge Companion to Hume*, pp. 447–449.
Wright, John P., "Hume's Skeptical Realism," in Russell, *Oxford Handbook to Hume*, pp. 60–81.
Wright, John P., *The Skeptical Realism of David Hume* (Manchester: Manchester University Press, 1983).
Xenophon, *Memorabilia and Oeconomicus*, Loeb Classical Library (Cambridge, MA: Harvard University Press, 1989).
Zanker, G. "Enargeia in the Ancient Criticism of Poetry," *Rheinisches Museum* 124 (1981), pp. 297–311.
Zhang, Feng and Richard Ned Lebow, *Rethinking Sino-American Relations* (Oxford: Oxford University Press, 2020).

Index

Aeschylus, 5, 20, 38, 39, 41, 58, 60, 115, 117, 273, 274, 313, 337
agency, 4, 5, 20, 21, 22, 23, 30, 31, 34, 38, 40, 41, 44, 45, 46, 48, 49, 50, 52, 53, 54, 57, 58, 65, 70, 71, 73, 77, 85, 143, 193, 194, 201, 202, 203, 205, 217, 237, 273, 274, 275, 296, 298, 301, 343
agent-based models, 306, 307
aggregation, 9, 13, 70, 165, 186, 214, 216, 276, 282, 284, 285, 290, 294, 306, 311
anger, 26, 27, 28, 32, 38, 40, 43, 46, 52, 55, 56, 60, 73, 74, 79, 85, 100, 105, 108, 109, 129, 164, 186, 271, 279, 318
anti-Semitism, 198, 251, 253
anxiety, 3, 108, 159, 201, 219, 245, 272, 298, 307, 308, 309
appetite, 2, 22, 32, 55, 90, 99, 109, 119, 120, 125, 130
Aquinas, Thomas, 223
Archidamian War, *see also* Peloponnesian War, 12, 20, 22, 69, 71, 72, 73, 75, 76, 94, 95, 99, 100, 102, 103, 104, 107, 110, 113, 114, 274, 275, 300, 312, 320
Archiv für Sozialwissenschaft und Sozialpolitik, 196
aristeia, 24, 25, 26, 271
Aristotle, 2, 5, 7, 14, 18, 19, 21, 22, 23, 24, 27, 28, 43, 55, 63, 64, 65, 66, 74, 75, 94, 113, 116, 124, 125, 132, 145, 150, 183, 263, 264, 267, 274, 284, 311, 314, 318, 329
art nouveau, 309
arts, 18, 142, 143, 312
Athens, 5, 6, 22, 27, 33, 44, 50, 51, 53, 57, 61, 62, 67, 68, 70, 71, 72, 75, 76, 77, 78, 79, 80, 81, 82, 83, 84, 86, 87, 88, 89, 90, 91, 92, 93, 94, 95, 96, 97, 98, 99, 100, 102, 103, 106, 108, 109, 110, 113, 262, 272, 273, 274, 275, 293, 294, 297, 331
Augustine of Hippo, 3, 18, 318, 325
Austen, Jane, 2, 8, 9, 156, 169, 294, 318

Austria-Hungary, 72
autonomy, 6, 298, 301, 310

Bauhaus, 309
Bayesian updating, 251, 304
Bernstein, Richard, 308
Bhaskar, Roy, 300
Bildungsroman, 249, 266, 292, 315, 340
Bismarck, Otto von, 196
Bloch, Ernst, 198
Bolshevik Russia, 197
Boswell, James, 160, 170, 294
Brest-Litovsk, Treaty of, 197
Britain, 8, 84, 142, 143, 145, 149, 156, 158, 160, 168, 215, 270, 296
bureaucracy, 197, 199, 233, 234, 253, 254, 258, 259, 261, 295, 312

capitalism, 17, 38, 200, 204, 207, 209, 212, 214, 215, 217, 219, 236, 277, 286, 287, 295
Carducci, Giosuè, 240
Cartwright, Nancy, 300
chance, 56, 58, 62, 98, 104, 109, 111, 144, 184, 205, 210, 257, 258, 271, 276, 287
China, 200, 206, 209, 215, 222, 230, 261, 328, 335, 340, 344
civil society, 8, 156, 160, 190, 193, 280, 294
Clausewitz, Carl von, 12
cognitive psychology, 121, 124, 278
Cold War, 4, 14, 114, 153, 217, 222, 230, 231, 311, 317, 320, 326, 330, 336
Collins, Wilkie, 7, 8, 9, 16, 156, 157, 158, 160, 178, 179, 180, 181, 182, 184, 185, 187, 188, 189, 190, 192, 270, 280, 284, 285, 286, 295, 305, 312, 318, 321, 328, 333, 336, 340
Comte, Auguste, 298
confluence, 57, 73, 103, 104, 183, 184, 284
constant conjunction, 7, 125, 134, 136, 137, 187, 194, 277, 279, 280, 285, 303

345

Constructing Cause in International Relations, ix, x, 12, 13, 218, 227, 229, 231, 315, 330
constructivism, 17, 106, 146, 147, 213, 290
contiguity, 9, 133, 134, 137, 156, 161, 164, 172, 182, 187, 279, 281, 282, 283, 285, 301
contingency, 57, 72, 73, 77, 98, 104, 105, 138, 144, 216
Copernicus, Nicolaus, 296
counterfactuals, 10, 99, 106, 122, 124, 150, 195, 204, 211, 212, 215, 216, 217, 223, 231, 286, 288, 289, 307, 311, 314, 320, 323, 325, 340, 344
Croesus, 272
cult of efficiency, 17
Czech, 9, 250, 252

Darwin, Charles, 296
deductive-nomological approach, 302, 310
deterrence, 4, 153, 173, 222
deviance, 8, 157, 161, 179, 258, 281
Dickens, Charles, 7, 8, 9, 16, 154, 156, 157, 158, 159, 160, 161, 162, 163, 164, 165, 167, 168, 169, 170, 172, 178, 179, 180, 181, 185, 186, 188, 189, 190, 191, 270, 280, 281, 282, 283, 284, 285, 286, 295, 305, 312, 322, 332
Dilthey, Wilhelm, 10, 195, 204, 219, 221, 247, 249, 292
Dostoevsky, Fyodor, 23, 63, 250, 323
Durkheim, Émile, 28, 148, 157, 189, 200, 201, 202, 295, 315, 322

economics, 9, 17, 127, 168, 193, 194, 196, 202, 204, 214, 224, 269, 296, 297, 299, 301, 302, 307, 314
economists, 4, 122, 225, 277, 291, 308
Egypt, 209, 259, 295
Einstein, Albert, 1
Eisner, Kurt, 197
emergent properties, 286
emotions, 4, 7, 8, 9, 11, 17, 20, 21, 24, 27, 28, 31, 32, 33, 34, 37, 38, 47, 52, 55, 63, 68, 69, 70, 73, 74, 75, 82, 93, 105, 106, 113, 123, 126, 127, 128, 129, 141, 142, 144, 145, 149, 160, 167, 168, 171, 176, 181, 182, 183, 184, 207, 209, 218, 233, 236, 240, 247, 248, 271, 272, 273, 278, 279, 284, 286, 287, 291, 292, 329
empathy, 11, 34, 52, 61, 126, 184, 204, 219, 224, 247, 248, 284, 287, 292, 293
emplotment, 75

England, 122, 129, 141, 142, 143, 144, 149, 153, 154, 173, 186, 189, 190, 198, 230, 277, 286, 295, 314, 321, 322, 323, 325, 327, 328, 332, 338, 342, 343, *see* Britain
epistēmē, 189, 263, 264, 286, 293, 300, 310, 312, 313,
ethics, 13, 22, 146, 197, 206, 226, 313
Euripides, 5, 20, 58, 272, 274, 329

Fachmensch (occupational specialist), 259
fate, 23, 34, 48, 54, 121, 327, 334
Flaubert, Gustave, 250
France, 198
Franco-Prussian War, 198
Frankfurter Zeitung, 197, 198
Freud, Sigmund, 3, 23, 38, 46, 63, 65, 226, 232, 234, 235, 244, 245, 265, 296, 309, 316, 323, 339
Friedman, Milton J., 304, 323

Galileo Galilei, 296
game theory, 297, 304
Geertz, Clifford, 226
Germany, 14, 84, 102, 122, 197, 198, 200, 227, 228, 247, 259, 309, 326, 342, 343
Goethe, Johann Wolfgang von, 21, 250, 265, 313, 317, 324
Gogol, Nikolai, 250
Grillparzer, Franz, 250

habit, 10, 17, 69, 125, 126, 127, 131, 134
Hacking, Ian, 17, 19, 138, 152, 231, 325
Harré, Rom, 300
Haskell, Thomas, 6, 62, 67, 201, 203, 228, 294, 295, 315, 325
Heidelberg, 196, 197, 198, 199
Hempel, Carl, 302
Heraclitus, 54, 66
Herder, Johann Gottfried, 199
Herodotus, 22, 69, 74, 91, 114, 115, 117, 272, 274, 314, 325, 326, 337
hierarchy, 8, 36, 37, 52, 110, 157, 160, 194, 245, 271, 294, 296, 301
Hitler, Adolf, 199
Homer, 4, 5, 7, 12, 20, 21, 23, 24, 25, 26, 29, 30, 31, 32, 33, 35, 36, 37, 38, 40, 42, 43, 46, 55, 57, 58, 59, 60, 61, 63, 64, 66, 70, 74, 85, 98, 104, 109, 111, 112, 138, 256, 270, 271, 273, 275, 308, 312, 313, 323, 329, 333, 334, 338
hubris, 28, 48, 61, 94, 109, 274, 276, 300
human nature, 7, 12, 37, 70, 109, 112, 118, 119, 120, 121, 122, 123, 140, 141, 143, 173, 255, 278, 293

Index

Humboldt, Wilhelm von, 198
Hume, David, ix, 3, 4, 7, 8, 15, 18, 19, 22, 24, 56, 59, 63, 75, 113, 118, 119, 120, 121, 122, 123, 124, 125, 126, 127, 128, 129, 130, 131, 132, 133, 134, 135, 136, 137, 138, 139, 140, 141, 142, 143, 144, 145, 146, 147, 148, 149, 150, 151, 152, 153, 154, 156, 160, 161, 164, 167, 172, 177, 185, 187, 191, 194, 195, 207, 233, 265, 270, 272, 276, 277, 278, 279, 280, 281, 282, 285, 286, 289, 291, 294, 307, 312, 314, 315, 319, 322, 324, 325, 326, 327, 328, 332, 333, 334, 335, 336, 337, 338, 339, 340, 342, 344,
hypocrisy, 26, 60, 63, 71, 128, 162, 176, 281

ideal types, ix, 2, 10, 13, 185, 195, 204, 208, 209, 210, 212, 218, 220, 221, 226, 227, 236, 248, 258, 286, 287, 288, 289, 290, 293, 299, 300, 303, 306
identity, 21, 40, 46, 52, 71, 76, 77, 86, 91, 99, 133, 146, 179, 180, 190, 215, 227, 246, 279, 282, 296, 312
induction, 124, 139, 140, 210, 281, 287
industrialization, 10, 154, 168, 193, 294
inefficient causation, ix, 13
instrumental reason, 73, 177, 269, 275, 276
interdependence, 6, 62, 203, 269, 281, 294, 295, 297, 310
Ireland, 175, 176, 230, 277, 314, 321, 332
irrationality, 27, 70, 210

Jaffé, Edgar, 196
Janoch, Gustav, 259
Japan, 222, 231, 327
Jugendstil, 309
justice, 26, 30, 32, 34, 35, 43, 54, 56, 58, 110, 121, 129, 130, 131, 146, 151, 155, 161, 165, 170, 174, 181, 198, 256, 257, 259, 260, 272, 273, 278, 281, 293, 294, 295
just-world phenomenon, 49

Kafka, Franz, 10, 11, 12, 16, 233, 234, 250, 254, 255, 256, 258, 259, 261, 262, 263, 264, 266, 267, 291, 293, 312, 328, 341
Kant, Immanuel, 1, 15, 18, 25, 63, 64, 119, 122, 123, 132, 148, 204, 277, 328, 333, 337
Kelsen, Hans, 309
Kern, Stephen, 16, 19, 329

Kleist, Heinrich von, 250
Klemperer, Otto, 74
kleos (fame), 24, 25
Knies, Karl, 211, 224
Knox, Bernard, 57
Kulturmensch (man of culture), 259

language, 14, 22, 25, 27, 56, 63, 71, 110, 123, 126, 128, 133, 140, 141, 144, 154, 172, 235, 246, 269
law courts, 9, 71, 111, 166, 170, 273, 295
levels of analysis, 11, 233, 262, 273
liberalism, 226
literacy, 193, 294
Longinus, 29, 64, 331
Lukács, Georg, 241
Lutheranism, 196

Machiavelli, Niccolò, 34, 73, 243, 265, 331
Mackie, J. L., 269, 303
Mahler, Gustav, 15
Mann, Thomas, 9, 10, 11, 12, 16, 114, 117, 230, 233, 234, 235, 236, 237, 238, 239, 240, 241, 242, 243, 244, 245, 247, 248, 249, 250, 262, 263, 264, 265, 266, 291, 292, 293, 299, 314, 315, 321, 325, 325, 327, 332, 334, 336, 341,
Marathon, battle of, 61, 92, 212
Mart, C. B., 300
Marx, Groucho, 38, 62, 64, 107, 117, 193, 200, 201, 225, 227, 295, 298, 301
Marx, Karl, 62, 64
Max Weber and International Relations, ix, xi, 2, 3, 9, 10, 13, 14, 17, 75, 185, 196, 203, 224, 227, 228, 229, 231, 233, 258, 264, 266, 268, 286, 293, 299, 302, 314, 320, 321, 323, 324, 325, 327, 328, 330, 333, 336, 337, 339, 342
mechanisms, 1, 34, 68, 111, 112, 125, 131, 134, 136, 202, 214, 215, 216, 217, 218, 264, 273, 276, 277, 279, 301, 307
Melian Dialogue, 69, 90, 107, 111
Merriam, Charles, 309
Michels, Robert, 198
Mill, John Stuart, 9, 148, 154, 156, 167, 189, 198, 202, 229, 277, 286, 294, 332
Miltiades, 61, 92
Mitchell, Wesley, 309
modernism, 233, 250
modernity, 3, 13, 38, 119, 148, 149, 206, 224, 232, 233, 258, 259, 269, 301, 312
Montaigne, Michel de, 1, 333
Morgenstern, Karl, 249, 304, 315, 333
Morgenstern, Oskar, 296, 333, 334
Morgenthau, Hans, 12

motives, 9, 11, 12, 16, 46, 60, 62, 70, 71, 75, 90, 92, 128, 144, 162, 167, 175, 177, 182, 183, 184, 185, 186, 187, 188, 207, 209, 210, 211, 213, 218, 219, 220, 222, 223, 226, 239, 240, 251, 252, 255, 263, 271, 273, 283, 284, 285, 286, 287, 290, 291, 293, 296, 297, 298, 300, 304
Munich, 198

narratives
nationalism, 198, 199
Neumann, John von, 304
Nietzsche, Friedrich, 21, 53, 62, 66, 120, 146, 148, 153, 200, 228, 233, 235, 259, 264, 266, 313, 314, 317, 334,
Nobel Institute, 307
nomos, 5, 6, 32, 35, 36, 39, 41, 58, 111, 112, 262, 263, 273
norms, 8, 22, 27, 34, 35, 43, 45, 54, 56, 68, 71, 73, 109, 130, 157, 201, 202, 206, 209, 218, 225, 272, 275, 287, 295

Oedipus, 5, 21, 22, 23, 38, 39, 40, 41, 42, 43, 44, 45, 46, 47, 48, 49, 50, 51, 52, 53, 54, 55, 56, 57, 58, 59, 60, 61, 65, 66, 67, 68, 69, 73, 94, 98, 103, 107, 108, 109, 111, 116, 117, 261, 262, 273, 274, 275, 314, 329, 341, 342
oikos, 5, 38, 58, 60, 71, 73, 110, 111, 275, 294
ontological gerrymandering, 20
Oppenheim, Paul, 302

Pacific rim, 294
Parry, Adam, 25, 341
passions, *see also* emotions, 3, 23, 31, 32, 35, 36, 48, 49, 84, 120, 122, 123, 125, 126, 127, 128, 129, 131, 135, 144, 146, 147, 164, 177, 238, 244, 246, 259, 279, 280, 281
Peloponnesian War, *see also* Archidamian War, 64, 71, 74, 81, 84, 87, 89, 90, 92, 94, 104, 110, 113, 114, 115, 117, 149, 153, 265, 300, 312, 314, 324, 326, 339, 340
Pericles, 57, 69, 74, 80, 81, 82, 83, 84, 85, 87, 93, 95, 96, 97, 98, 100, 102, 103, 105, 106, 107, 108, 112, 114, 115, 116, 149, 246, 275, 322, 332, 335
peripeteia, 43, 44, 94, 261
phrōnesis, 189, 263, 286, 300, 310, 312, 313
Plato, 2, 7, 18, 20, 22, 23, 28, 62, 63, 64, 75, 109, 117, 125, 126, 129, 246, 263, 264, 267, 312, 335

polis, 5, 6, 22, 23, 38, 39, 50, 52, 53, 58, 60, 61, 62, 67, 68, 71, 73, 77, 81, 86, 89, 102, 106, 109, 110, 111, 112, 270, 273, 275, 294
Polish, 198, 199
Popper, Karl, 3, 4, 19, 140, 335
positivism, 277, 310
postmodernism, 8
prediction, ix, 33, 101, 135, 143, 144, 194, 203, 263, 272, 294, 298, 299, 303, 307, 309
prophecy, 39, 40, 45, 47, 50, 51, 52, 53, 54, 56, 65, 77, 272, 274
Protestantism, 17, 209, 214, 215, 236, 287
proto-Enlightenment, 272
psychology, *see* cognitive and motivational psychology

racism, 198
rational choice, 2, 3, 127, 299
rationality, 2, 9, 10, 13, 17, 185, 188, 204, 209, 210, 211, 212, 218, 219, 220, 221, 223, 224, 234, 258, 269, 283, 284, 286, 287, 288, 289, 290, 293, 300, 303, 304, 306
realism, 69, 73, 137, 277, 278, 300, 301
regularity theories, 9, 10, 13, 138, 154, 194, 202, 277, 302, 303, 310
Renaissance, 13
rhetoric, 5, 60, 71, 73, 87, 93, 242, 263, 276
risk acceptance, 72
Romanticism, 176, 233, 250, 295
Rousseau, Jean-Jacques, 126, 131, 147, 148, 175, 277, 298
Russell, Bertrand, 1, 154, 303
Russian, 198
Russian Revolution, 197, 199

Salamis, battle of, 113, 61, 230, 325, 339
scientific realism, 300, 301
Scottish Enlightenment, 118, 276
self-interest, 60, 61, 73, 85, 98, 118, 127, 128, 144, 163, 255, 294
Shakespeare, William, 21, 24, 312, 338
Sicilian debate, 105, 106
Sicilian expedition, 12, 68, 72, 94, 95, 97, 99, 100, 102, 103, 104, 107, 110, 300
Simmel, Georg, 198
Simpson, O. J., 173, 282
Smith, Adam, 70, 118, 122, 141, 214, 276, 277, 294
Snow, C. P., 312
Socrates, *see* Plato
solidarity, 59, 166, 167, 246, 295
Sombart, Werner, 196

Index

sophia (wisdom), 263, 264, 300, 312, 313
sophism, 33, 69, 71, 93, 115, 325, 341
Sophocles, 5, 6, 12, 20, 21, 23, 24, 34, 38, 39, 40, 42, 43, 44, 45, 46, 49, 50, 51, 52, 53, 54, 55, 56, 57, 58, 59, 60, 61, 62, 67, 68, 69, 70, 73, 74, 77, 98, 103, 104, 107, 108, 109, 110, 111, 112, 117, 138, 261, 262, 263, 264, 270, 272, 273, 274, 275, 276, 281, 293, 294, 299, 300, 305, 308, 312, 313, 319, 320, 322, 324, 329, 338, 341
Soviet Union, 217, 259, 311
Sparta, 36, 70, 71, 72, 74, 76, 77, 78, 79, 80, 81, 82, 83, 84, 85, 86, 87, 88, 89, 90, 91, 92, 93, 94, 95, 97, 98, 99, 100, 102, 103, 104, 106, 108, 109, 110, 111, 113, 115, 323, 332
Spencer, Herbert, 193, 298, 301
state building, 193, 294
Stein, Janice Gross, 17, 328, 330
Strawson, Galen, 137, 278
stress, 8, 11, 49, 108, 129, 203, 247, 268, 292
Strong, Tracy, 226, 227

technē (technical knowledge), 263
telos, 3, 18
Thebes, 22, 39, 41, 43, 44, 45, 47, 48, 50, 56, 57, 61, 62, 66, 67, 88, 89, 111, 117, 314, 329
Thucydides, 5, 6, 12, 20, 22, 23, 33, 63, 64, 68, 69, 70, 71, 72, 73, 74, 75, 76, 77, 78, 80, 81, 82, 84, 85, 87, 88, 89, 90, 91, 92, 93, 94, 95, 96, 98, 99, 103, 104, 106, 107, 108, 109, 110, 111, 112, 113, 114, 115, 116, 117, 148, 149, 153, 246, 262, 265, 272, 274, 275, 276, 277, 281, 285, 294, 298, 300, 311, 312, 313, 314, 318, 319, 321, 322, 323, 324, 326, 328, 330, 331, 332, 333, 336, 337, 339, 340, 341, 344
thumos (spirit), 55, 99, 100, 109
Toller, Ernst, 198
Toscanini, Arturo, 74
tragedy, 5, 6, 15, 20, 21, 22, 24, 34, 40, 42, 43, 44, 47, 49, 50, 52, 55, 57, 58, 61, 68, 72, 75, 91, 94, 108, 109, 112, 116, 117, 150, 262, 263, 264, 270, 273, 274, 293, 299, 300, 305, 311, 312, 313, 314, 325, 328, 329, 331, 334, 338, 342
Tragic Vision of Politics, 12, 20, 77, 112, 113, 115, 153, 317
Treaty of Versailles, 197
Trollope, Anthony, 7, 8, 9, 16, 155, 156, 157, 158, 159, 160, 168, 169, 170, 171, 172, 173, 174, 175, 176, 177, 178, 179, 180, 181, 182, 185, 186, 187, 188, 189, 190, 191, 192, 270, 280, 282, 283, 284, 285, 286, 295, 305, 312, 319, 321, 322, 325, 332, 340, 341,
tuberculosis, 11, 242, 243, 246, 247, 250
Turner, Stephen, 138, 307
twelve-tone technique, 309

United States, 6, 8, 14, 90, 115, 122, 156, 193, 197, 201, 202, 213, 222, 234, 294, 309, 316, 326, 335
University of Freiburg, 196
University of Vienna, 197
urbanization, 193, 294

values, 2, 7, 11, 13, 17, 20, 25, 27, 28, 32, 35, 36, 38, 41, 57, 59, 60, 62, 68, 85, 86, 91, 98, 126, 141, 155, 157, 158, 176, 178, 187, 193, 195, 200, 201, 202, 205, 206, 208, 209, 210, 221, 224, 225, 226, 236, 241, 247, 249, 255, 259, 260, 262, 268, 269, 271, 273, 287, 291, 292, 295, 301, 304, 309, 313, 314
Vienna Circle, 225, 309
violence, 26, 41, 42, 271
vividness, 124, 278

Wagner, Richard, 235
Waltz, Kenneth, 311
Weber, Marianne Schnitger, 2, 3, 10, 11, 13, 15, 16, 17, 18, 19, 113, 132, 148, 176, 185, 189, 193, 194, 195, 196, 197, 198, 199, 200, 201, 202, 203, 204, 205, 206, 207, 208, 209, 210, 211, 212, 213, 214, 215, 216, 217, 218, 219, 220, 221, 222, 223, 224, 225, 226, 227, 228, 229, 230, 231, 232, 233, 234, 236, 237, 248, 254, 255, 258, 259, 262, 264, 266, 268, 269, 277, 286, 287, 288, 289, 290, 291, 293, 294, 295, 298, 299, 300, 302, 303, 306, 307, 311, 312, 313, 314, 315, 317, 321, 323, 325, 329, 330, 333, 339, 342, 343,
Weber, Max, 268
Weltanschauungen, 268
World War I, 11, 12, 18, 26, 72, 93, 102, 104, 198, 228, 235, 236, 245, 246, 247, 249, 250, 262, 263, 291, 292, 309, 310, 318, 342

xenia (guest-friendship), 26, 28, 35, 36, 41, 53, 64, 271

Yiddish, 250